COLIN
CHAPMAN
The Man and his Cars

COLIN CHAPMAN

The Man and his Cars

GERARD ('Jabby') CROMBAC

Patrick Stephens, Wellingborough

Frontispiece *A. C. B. Chapman, CBE, RDI, Hon Dr (RCA), BSc Eng, FRSA*

First published October 1986

British Library Cataloguing in Publication Data

Crombac, Gerard

Colin Chapman : the man and his cars
1. Chapman, Colin, 1928-1982   2. Automobile racing — Great Britain — Biography
I. Title   II. Stephens, Patrick J.
629.2'31'0924   GV1032.C4/

ISBN 0-85059-733-1

Patrick Stephens Limited is part of the Thorsons Publishing Group

Printed and bound in Great Britain

10 9 8 7 6 5 4

Contents

Ho conosciuto Colin Chapman a Monza, durante le prove del Gran Premio d'Italia 1960. Ci fu una riunione con John Cooper e Huscke von Hanstein alla vigilia dell'entrata in vigore della formula 1500 cc. La stampa si sbizzarri' a qualificare quell'incontro tra Lotus, Ferrari, Cooper e Porsche come il "summit" della Formula 1

Dieci anni dopo, ancora a Monza, in un Gran Premio particolarmente amaro per lui, lo ricordo perseguitato e soffrii il suo stato d'animo ben sapendo, per avere vissuto la stessa situazione, come in quei momenti le amicizie e le solidarieta' si rendano evanescenti.

Ci incontravamo alle riunioni della FOCA, quelle che si tenevano a Modena. Nelle discussioni mostrava chiarezza, determinazione. L'ultima volta fu nel gennaio 1981, quando varammo il famoso accordo "Concorde" con la regolamentazione della attuale Formula 1.

L'ho sempre ammirato e lo ricordo acuto precursore, sagace interprete dei regolamenti tecnici, geniale nelle sue intuizioni d'avanguardia.

Nessuno avrebbe potuto curare una biografia di Colin Chapman meglio di Gerard Crombac, che dell'intelligente innovatore inglese e' stato fin dagli inizi e per tanti anni amico sincero, convinto assertore, fedele collaboratore.
Nell'avvincente racconto del giovanotto appassionato di automobile, che muove i primi passi e poi affacciandosi alla vita svela le sue ambizioni e lotta per realizzarle, la figura di Chapman e' magistralmente delineata. Ancor piu' interessante risulta l'esposizione delle sue costruzioni, attenta e documentata, che diventa storia dell'automobilismo da competizione.

marzo 85

Enzo Ferrari

Foreword

I first came to know Colin Chapman during practice for the 1960 Italian Grand Prix. This was at a meeting with John Cooper and Huscke von Hanstein on the day before the 1,500 cc Formula came into being. The Press indulged itself by describing that meeting between Lotus, Ferrari, Cooper and Porsche as the Formula 1 'Summit'.

Ten years later, again at Monza, during a Grand Prix which was particularly trying for him, I remember him being harassed but I put up with his mood, knowing only too well how friendship and support at such times are all important, because I too had been in the same situation.

We met up again at the FOCA meetings which took place here at Modena. In the discussions he displayed clarity of thought and great determination. Our last meeting was in January 1981 when we launched the famous 'Concorde' agreement for the regularization of Formula 1.

I have always admired him and remember him as a subtle visionary, a wise interpreter of technical regulations, and so talented because of his ability to produce ideas ahead of their time.

No one could have written a biography of Colin Chapman better than Gerard Crombac who, from the start, has for many years been a sincere friend, a staunch defender and a faithful colleague of this intelligent English innovator.

In this enthralling account of the man, passionately fond of cars, getting himself started, openly declaring his ambitions and then struggling to achieve them, the figure of Chapman is described in a masterly manner. Still more interesting is the detailed and well documented account of his designs which becomes a story of competition motor racing.

March 1986   *Enzo Ferrari*

Acknowledgements

Besides using many of his own photographs, the author would like to acknowledge with grateful thanks the not inconsiderable help of many others whose photographs are reproduced in this book.

A large number were provided by Mrs Hazel Chapman from her own private family collection, and also by Mr Donovan McLauchlan of Lotus Cars Ltd and Mr Andrew Ferguson of Team Lotus International Ltd. Other photographs came from David Phipps, Geoffrey Goddard, Jutta Fausel, Gerry Stream, Franco Lini, Lynton Money, JPS, Ford Motor Company, 'Flight International', LAT, Keith Hamshere, Guardian Newspapers, Francis Costin, Esso Petroleum, Jesse Alexander, Hugh Wooton, 'Motor Sport', 'Motoring News', Franco Villani, 'Evening News' Norwich, Richard Spellberg, C. A. Bowles, P. Dreux, R. D. Rew, M. Toscas, Editora Abril, C. Briscoe-Knight, Michael Cooper, Nigel Snowdon, Sound Stills, John Wright Photography and OAMTC.

Publisher's Preface

Colin Chapman, like so many gifted, dedicated and hard-working men, had many acquaintances but very few close friends, and so there was only ever likely to be one person fully equipped to write the story of his life – Colin himself.

That was why I asked him – I think it was early in 1975 – if he would allow me to publish his autobiography whenever he felt ready to take on the task. I remember, as we sat together in his lovely office at Ketteringham Hall, his reply was typical. 'I promise you that you can publish it when I am ready,' he said, 'but that will not be until I have given up motor racing.' Then, with that special twinkle in his eyes, he added as an afterthought, 'The way things are going at the moment that could be at the end of next season, especially if our sponsors decide not to renew their contract!'

Since Colin Chapman was accomplished in virtually everything he ever tackled, his untimely death from a heart attack in December 1982 has robbed us all of the chance to read what would almost certainly have been not only a most fascinating autobiography but probably one of the most important motor racing books of all time.

If there were to be no autobiography then there could at least be a biography, but who would be able to undertake such an onerous yet rewarding task?

Gérard Crombac, always 'Jabby' to his many friends all over the world, was clearly a good candidate, for not only did he know Colin Chapman better than most but also he had spent a great deal of time working and helping in the Team Lotus pits over a period of almost thirty years.

Apart from a short time as a racing mechanic when a very young man, 'Jabby' Crombac – a Swiss living and working in Paris – has been a motor racing journalist all his life. He first became known to British enthusiasts in 1950 when he was appointed Continental Correspondent to the then new motor sporting magazine *Autosport*. A few years later he founded the French magazine *Sport-Auto*, of which he is still Editor. He first met Chapman in the early '50s and found he had a special *rapport* with him, when he bought Colin's own 1,172 cc Ford Ten-engined Mark VI Lotus. Since those early days 'Jabby' has become known and highly regarded by Lotus Cars, Team Lotus International and, above all, by Colin's family – his widow Hazel and his three children Jane, Sarah and Clive. 'Jabby' Crombac was, without doubt, the best choice.

However, this book is not just about Colin Chapman's life and personality. It also concerns itself with his Lotus company and especially with his Lotus racing cars and his racing drivers, their successes and their failures, simply because they were his life and are quite inseparable from the story of it.

June 1986 *Patrick Stephens*

Author's Introduction

Many years ago I remember joking with Colin Chapman about what we would do when we retired. I cannot recall which of us actually suggested it, but we both agreed that eventually we should together write Colin's memoirs. I was very much looking forward to it: we would have worked on it at his villa in Ibiza and I am sure we would have had great fun doing it.

Shortly before Colin's untimely death, when I was with him in his office at Ketteringham Hall, working on a little book I was writing about the history of Lotus, he suddenly said to me: 'I have just come across a drawing of a car which we never built!' 'Great,' I said. 'Can I have it for my book?' 'No,' he replied, 'it's for OUR book.' A week later he was no longer with us.

I was not then aware of Colin's earlier promise made to publisher Patrick Stephens, one of his helpers in the early days of Lotus, but I was delighted when Pat asked me if I would like to write this biography of Colin Chapman. He had already obtained the approval of Colin's widow Hazel, and his old friend and business colleague Fred Bushell, plus their promise of full support for me. It is a task which has involved a great deal of hard work but one which I have thoroughly enjoyed.

During the course of several trips to Norwich, I was able to record what has probably amounted to over thirty hours of conversation with many people. To this has to be added recordings and notes of my interviews and talks with Colin Chapman himself which, very fortunately, I had kept.

My deepest thanks go to Hazel and her family, Jane, Sarah and Clive, and to Fred Bushell, all of whom have contributed so much to the book.

Colin Chapman lived in the future, never in the past, so he kept very few mementoes. Unfortunately, therefore, a considerable amount of fascinating archive material has long since been lost or destroyed. Indeed, it was only on the insistence of his family that about fifteen years ago he started to build up a collection of examples of early Lotus cars.

Finding one of his childhood friends did not prove easy either, but eventually I was able to have a long talk with Alan Richardson who was at school with Colin, and to whom I am very grateful for the time and help he gave me.

Needless to say, a great many people have helped me in trying to describe 'the real Colin Chapman'. At Team Lotus I have had fantastic support from Peter Warr, Andrew Ferguson and Bob Dance. At Lotus Cars I was able to draw upon the memories of people who contributed tremendously to Colin Chapman's career, especially Mike Kimberley and Tony Rudd. Donovan McLauchlan kindly helped to co-ordinate my efforts and was another member of my team of 'proof readers'.

Geoffrey Kent, now Chairman of Imperial Group, was kind enough to recount for me how he first steered John Player into motor racing, while Walter Hayes, Vice-President of Ford, who played a tremendously important part in Lotus's story, recalled for me his association with Colin.

Keith Duckworth and Mike Costin, of famous engine manufacturers Cosworth Engineering, very kindly spent a great deal of time with me and also arranged for me to talk with Dick Scammell, an ex-Lotus mechanic who now works with them. I am grateful to all three for their help.

I also spoke with engineers Maurice Phillippe and Peter Wright; with racing drivers Stirling Moss, Jackie Stewart, Innes Ireland, Jackie Oliver, John Miles and Elio de Angelis; with team owners and managers Ken Tyrrell, Rob Walker, Gérard Larrousse and Bernie Ecclestone, all of whom could not have been more helpful.

Colin Gething provided me with considerable background detail about Colin's foray into the design and manufacture of powered boats, whilst pilots Mike Hamlin and Brian Kaye provided valuable information on his activities in the air. I am also indebted to Mike Tagg at the RAF Museum, Hendon, for his search of their archives for the background to the 'Mike's Mug' award.

At a very early stage in this book's gestation, several magazines and newspapers, including *Lotus World*, published at Patrick Stephens' request a note to say we would welcome any titbits of information about Colin Chapman's life. Several names from the past responded. Unfortunately, it has not been possible to quote them all but we could not resist the wonderful piece from Dave Kelsey, who welded up Lotus chassis frames in the early days. Also that from Roy Badcock, one of Colin's most faithful and longest-serving employees. My friend and famous colleague Denis Jenkinson was also very helpful in recalling his first meeting with Colin when he was completely unknown.

I have freely quoted from some wonderful books devoted to Lotus, written by Ian Smith, Doug Nye, Dennis Ortenburger and Leo Levine, to all of whom I am most grateful. I would also like to thank Peter Jowitt for the report on his investigation of the car in which Jimmy Clark lost his life.

I am also greatly indebted to Pat Stephens himself. Rarely does the Chairman of a publishing company edit one of his own author's books. However, I know that, as an old friend of Colin Chapman's, this was a task dear to his heart. He has made my text read as though I can actually speak plain English. Colin would have been amused, for he often used to talk about my 'Crombac-English!'

I should also like to include a special thank you to Peter Dyke and Imperial Tobacco Limited for their very valuable help to myself and the publishers in the launching of the book.

Finally, there is the matter of the Foreword. When, at Ketteringham Hall early in 1984, we first talked together about the book, we said, 'who should we ask to write a foreword?' Hazel Chapman answered immediately: 'There is only one man who Colin would have wanted to write the foreword and that is Enzo Ferrari.' I know she joins me in thanking Enzo Ferrari for providing his contribution to a book devoted to the man who had been his greatest rival in motor racing.

My deepest thanks to everyone, including those I am sure I must have mistakenly omitted.

D'Huison-Longueville   *Gérard Crombac*
France
January 1986

Chapter 1

Early Days in North London

There was no white sports coat, no pink carnation: there was little opportunity for luxuries in war-torn London. The Blitz was over but the 'doodlebugs' would soon start falling, and rationing was tight. In the crowded dance hall, however, such problems seemed far away for a moment. The blond sixteen-year-old with a shadow of a moustache, in baggy sports coat and even baggier 1940s trousers was dancing at Hornsey Town Hall with a slim, dark-haired girl in casual sweater, slacks and tiger-striped shoes. Anthony Colin Bruce Chapman and Hazel Patricia Williams had just met for the first time and neither could possibly have foreseen the triumphs and tragedies that their next 38 years together would bring.

One of the greatest racing car designers and engineers of all time, and an influential figure in the post-war motor industry, Colin had yet to make his mark on the world. That Saturday evening in March 1944 he made his way home inconspicuously by bicycle, and yet the signs were already there – the bicycle was painted gold.

Colin Chapman always attended the Hornsey dances, for the very good reason that he could get in free, since his father was in charge of the catering! The only son of Stanley and Mary Chapman, Colin had been born on 19 May 1928 in Richmond, Surrey, on the outskirts of south-west London, where his father owned the Orange Tree public house. Later, his parents moved to the Railway Hotel in Tottenham Lane, Hornsey, and Colin became a pupil at the nearby Stationers' Company's School. On the outbreak of war he had been evacuated to Wisbech, in Norfolk, but now he was back with his parents and hoping to gain entrance to London University.

Hazel Williams came from Muswell Hill, where she was studying at secretarial college. One of her first memories of her future husband was that he had gorgeous eyes. 'I was terribly shy,' she recalls, 'but so was Colin. What attracted me to him was that he seemed so capable in the way he did just everyday things. Even at that age he could always get things done and I remember thinking to myself after our first meeting, "Here is someone a bit different. This chap will go places."'

Colin and Hazel both came from very ordinary family backgrounds, and there was nothing at this first encounter between them to suggest what the future might hold in store. Colin's father, Stanley, was the son of a London butcher

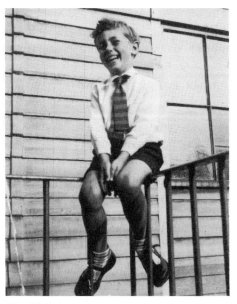

Colin Chapman at one year old.

The Chapman grin was very evident, even at eight years old.

Below Colin, second from the right in the front row, aged seven.

with three sisters and an ex-RAF Bomber Command 'pathfinder' brother. Always impeccably turned out, with distinguished-looking white hair and a neat moustache which his son was trying to emulate, he had acquired the catering concession at several regular Saturday night dances in the neighbourhood of the Railway Hotel, and was considered something of a success story by his family. He, too, can hardly have suspected the international reputation his son would gain in the not-too-distant future. The same applied to Hazel's parents, Vic and Annie. Her mother had a knitting shop in Muswell Hill, so the family never went short of clothing, while her father kept chickens, and even in the middle of wartime restrictions they could always barter some eggs for butter and sugar.

After the dance, Colin and Hazel agreed to meet the following day. Hazel recalls that 'we cycled over to the municipal course at Friern Barnet to play golf, with clubs which Colin had borrowed from his father.'

'At the beginning of the war Colin was living at the Railway Hotel in Hornsey, where they used to be bombed from time to time as it was quite near some large railway sidings. Stanley Chapman ran the pub himself at first but later he took on a manager and bought a house in Beech Drive, Muswell Hill. I remember he hated being referred to as a publican. He wasn't in the Forces during the war because he was a little too old, but he was very much involved

This was probably the last photograph ever taken of Colin without his moustache.

With Hazel at the Hornsey Town Hall dance.

in civil defence. He was in charge of transport, like fire engines and so forth, in the Islington area and so was always very friendly with the local mayors, the fire chief and others like that. He always had the ability to mix with the right people and had become quite an important person in the community.

'I remember, in late 1944 when the Germans were bombing London with their 'doodlebugs' (the V1 rocket planes), Colin and his father designed a device which spotted whether a particular 'doodlebug' was going to fall anywhere near the hotel. It was on the roof, and by lining this thing up on the 'doodlebug' they could tell whether it was going to drop anywhere near. They would then know whether everybody should take shelter or not!

'When I first met Colin he had this "gold" bicycle but it was not long before he bought a 350 cc Panther motor bike which, of course, he always rode with tremendous verve and enthusiasm. My mother hated it because she knew I used to ride pillion. When Colin came to our house to call for me he would leave the bike at the end of the road and walk the last few yards to collect me. We then walked back to the bike so that my mother wouldn't know we were actually going out on it. However, within six months Colin had an accident on the way to University, crashing through a London taxi with two very surprised old ladies in the back, and our biking days were over.

'In his usual impetuous way, Colin later discharged himself from the casualty department and I came home to find him sitting in his parents' dining room looking somewhat dejected! My mother suggested he buy a three-wheeler to replace the bike, which he in fact did, only to re-sell it a couple of days later to a friend for a small profit!

'Colin was keen on the Boy Scouts and had become very friendly with his Scout leader, a man called Archie, who really had quite a lot of influence over him. He had also become fond of hiking and camping and taking part in survival courses and things like that. However, by the time I met Colin he had left the Scouts, but he always kept in touch with Archie, although I only met him once or twice. In fact, Colin had been a King's Scout and throughout his life he was always keen on the movement as he felt that it had taught him so much. He would often go back to his Scout Troop and once, I remember, he went along to give them a talk.'

Alan Richardson was at school with Colin Chapman. Although being a couple of years older and therefore not in the same class, he remained a friend of Colin's throughout his life. Alan remembers those early days with much affection.

'We were both at the Stationers' Company's School in Hornsey and were both evacuated from London to Wisbech in Cambridgeshire on the day the war broke out. I stayed there for eighteen months but I can't remember whether

Right *Even at the early age of ten – judging by this school report – Colin Chapman was already showing promise. Despite earning a 'Merit' holiday he still seemed to be awarded a higher-than-average number of detentions due to his impulsiveness!*

The Stationers' Company's School

REPORT *for the* TERM *ending* 22nd July, 1938

Preparatory α Form, containing ___12___ Boys.

NAME ___Chapman, AcB___

Age ___10·2___   *Average Age of Form* ___10·0___

Examination Position ___1___

Detained ___11___ Times.   "Stars" Gained ___12___

Subjects	% Gained	Average % of form	Remarks (if any)
Latin ..			
French ..			
German ..			
English ..	63	69	V. Good. Spelling doubtful. JHo.
Geography	93	66	Excellent work: outstanding throughout year. DmT.
History ..	86	60.	Excellent. JHo.
Arithmetic	98	65	Excellent & much improved conduct.
Algebra ..			
Geometry ..			
Mechanics..			
Mag. & Elec.			
Chemistry..			
Physics ..			
~~Biology~~ Nature Study	76	85	Good.
Drawing ..	85	58	Shows great keenness, & should
Handwork..			do very well, judging by his present ability
Writing ..	80	60	Good.

Late ___2___ times   Absent ___2___ half-days

He is very willing & helpful, & shows considerable efficiency in his work. His impulsiveness leads to far too many detentions. *Horrod. B.Sc. ARCS.* Form Master

S.C.N_____ MA Head Master

Any Boy whose Report is marked "M" has earned a "Merit" holiday. M

The next Term will begin on 19th September at 10.30 a.m.

Colin might have returned to London sooner than me. The earliest recollection I have of him was that we used to cycle to school together. In the mornings we went to Wisbech Grammar School and in the afternoons we were all pushed off to another school. This was because there were three schools using only two premises.

'In those days Raleigh made quite a good quality bicycle for about £6 11s 0d (now £6.55) and my father had bought me a 'standard' black one. Colin, I remember, had the 'de luxe' model which was painted gold. I was all agog at it when he first showed it off to everyone. I suppose that was probably the very first time I had heard of Colin Chapman.

'It wasn't until some time later that I became close friends with Colin but I am quite sure I was with him at the Town Hall dance on the night he first met Hazel. As his father was running the bar, Colin didn't have to pay but we would only get one free drink out of him!

'Some time earlier I had pinched one of his girl friends, so for a time he wasn't too friendly. We formed a sort of clan of local lads and we would meet at this girl's house, where the door always seemed to be open to all of us. Even after Colin had split up with this girl, he would still appear at her house. I remember there was George Berisford, Timmy Taylor and a chap called Evershead.

'Later we would often go to Colin's house in Beech Drive and one thing I can remember very clearly is how possessive he was with Hazel. He wouldn't let anyone else go near her, and if they did he would quickly clamp down on her! We could never understand how she could tolerate him behaving like this.

'Stanley Chapman, his father, could be rather pompous and was always very fussy about the house in Beech Drive. One night Colin managed to get a trio from the big dance band – the one that usually performed at the Town Hall – over to his house, which had one very nice large room with parquet flooring that was wonderful for dancing. The chap who played the double bass was extra keen and in between slapping it he would spin it round and then lift it up before dropping it on the floor again – boom, boom, boom! When the party finally broke up we looked at the floor and it appeared just as though it had been blasted with a shot gun! We tried to hide it with a chair, I remember, but when Stan found out about it he was furious and that was the last party they had at Beech Drive for a long time.

'I remember the old Austin Seven he used to tinker with. One thing I will never forget is seeing him running along by the side of it, holding the hand throttle fully open, because if he had jumped in it would have ground to a halt!

'My father's furniture shop was in Highgate and next to it was a little shop which in those days was owned by a father and son named Merrick. They dealt in spare parts for Austin Sevens which they kept in three lock-up garages in their backyard. Colin regularly dropped into Merricks for parts and I would often see him then.

'Once he convinced me that we should buy a new French car called a Panhard, with a flat-twin cylinder engine. We both put down a £20 deposit but it was a washout and we both lost our deposit.

'At this time Colin's manners could be quite rude and I remember my father objecting strongly when he came into the shop one day and said, "Good morning Mr Rich!" He didn't like that sort of cheekiness at all. Mind you, when Lotus really got off the ground there was no better friend, for my father much admired him then.'

Colin entered University College in October 1945 to study engineering. He was extremely quick at learning and long sessions of study were not for him. 'He used to bomb off to his lectures on his motor cycle,' says Hazel, 'but when he returned he never spoke about it and you never saw him get his books out. Two or three days before the exams he might do a little bit of study – go through his notes.'

Thus he was left with a considerable amount of spare time and with a fellow student, Colin Dare, he became interested in second-hand cars. The centre of the used car trade in London was – and still is to some extent – Warren Street, just off the top end of Tottenham Court Road and only a stone's throw from University College. So it was not long before the two Colins had pooled their resources, bought an old banger and sold it for a quick profit.

Only two years after the war, and despite continued fuel rationing, cars were in great demand. British manufacturers had not long resumed normal activities and most of their production was being exported. Even then the cars that were being produced consisted mainly of barely modified pre-war small car designs such as Morris and Ford eight and ten horsepower models. Older second-hand versions of such cars were still reasonably up to date and buyers were easy to find for them, especially if a little time and ingenuity could be devoted to 'dressing them up'. A small business therefore rapidly developed and before very long the two Colins were buying and selling cars at the rate of one a week.

Stanley Chapman was not very keen on this type of activity. To him it was not very 'pukka', and he would not allow Colin to park his jalopies in the driveway of their house in full view of the neighbours. Fortunately, Hazel's father had three lock-up garages behind the house and Colin managed to rent one from him for ten bob (50p) a week, 'which he never paid!', recalls Hazel. Vic Williams also sometimes loaned Colin money for his deals which, in Stanley's opinion, just made matters worse.

With all Colin's financial resources being devoted to his little industry, he was always very hard up and the only form of entertainment in which Hazel and he could indulge – apart from the free Saturday evening dances they still regularly attended – was going occasionally to the cinema. Even then they'd sneak in through the 'exit' door to avoid paying!

After the motor bike and three-wheeler episodes, Colin's parents finally lashed out and bought him a maroon Morris Tourer. This proved much too mundane for Colin and, as he wanted to drive something rather more original, a Fiat 500 was acquired from an uncle. It was a left-hand drive model and therefore very cheap. Needless to say, this was duly converted to right-hand drive and resold some time later at a profit!

Unfortunately, Colin Dare failed his exams at the end of the first year so the youthful Chapman carried on, more or less on his own, for the next year when, in October 1947, another crisis arose – the basic petrol ration was withdrawn! At that time Colin had quite a large stock of cars – worth something like £900 – for which suddenly there were no takers. This meant selling them at well under cost and so losing in the process the odd £500 or so profit which the venture had made him so far. Back to square one.

With the engineering knowledge he was gathering he became wise to the failings of the somewhat antiquated machinery with which he had been dealing, and as he had been left with a particularly decrepit 1930 fabric-bodied Austin Seven saloon, for which he was quite unable to find a home, the idea came to him that he should modify it extensively.

At this time competition had not yet entered his head. He told me himself later: 'I was not really an enthusiast. In fact I never went to a race meeting until I actually raced myself. I was enthusiastic for building a thing which moved and so while at university I decided to build my own "special". This [the Mk I] was going to be a touring car and I had been working on it for almost a year when I came across a car trial which was taking place at Aldershot. I was quite fascinated by this and rushed back to the partly finished "special", scrapped the half-enveloping body and turned it into a trials car. Anyway, it was originally designed using ideas too advanced for what I was capable of doing.'

By this time Colin had taken up the opportunity offered to students to enlist and learn to fly in the University Air Squadron, and flying quickly became an essential part of his activities. As he was to do all his life, he was reading everything he could lay his hands on about his favourite subjects, and even

though this was not what he was then studying at university he became very engrossed with the principles of aircraft design and construction. In fact, throughout his career he was to apply these principles to the design of his cars and it is interesting to see that he started this practice right from the very beginning with this trials car by making use of alloy-bonded plywood to provide fully stressed bodywork in order to improve the appalling lack of rigidity for which the Austin Seven chassis was notorious.

The car was housed and worked on in one of the lock-ups belonging to Hazel's father, but the equipment with which to build it was spartan indeed, the only powered tool being an electrical hand drill 'borrowed' from Stanley. Thus, much of the work had to be sub-contracted to local specialists. There were no facilities for panel beating, nor had Colin any experience of the coach-building craft so the final product had a somewhat angular appearance to say the least. Nevertheless it worked, although it was only built by dint of much midnight oil burning: apart from polishing and painting chores, Hazel had to keep the plot going by brewing a continuous supply of tea.

Early in 1948 the car was completed and registered by the local licensing authority. The original registration number of PK 3493 became OX 9292 and, as Colin wanted to call it something different from just another 'Austin Special', it was decided that it should be called a Lotus Mk I.

Alan Richardson remembers the 'trials days', when he would often go along to support Colin and Hazel, sometimes travelling as far afield as Cheshire. Before that, though, they were big fans of speedway racing and Alan, Colin, and his father, sometimes with Hazel too, regularly went to Wembley in Stan Chapman's car.

Chapter 2

The Seed Germinates . . .

In 1948, Colin Chapman duly graduated as a civil engineer, having specialized in structural engineering. Although there is little relationship between this and automobile engineering, there is no doubt that Colin felt he could and should make full use of his particular knowledge of stress calculations in the design of cars. Indeed a trait of all future Lotus cars was to be that they would employ just the right amount of material – and no more – to achieve the desired degree of rigidity. This he had demonstrated, albeit in a rudimentary way, with his very first attempt at motor vehicle design.

By this time Colin was even more heavily engrossed in his flying. Through the University Air Squadron he had completed the required 35 hours' tuition, flown solo and obtained his Private Pilot's Licence. So, after graduation, he decided to take up the opportunity then offered to him of joining the RAF. This did not go down at all well with his father, probably because Colin's Uncle Reg, the Pathfinder pilot, had sadly failed to return from a bombing mission later in the war.

It is doubtful if Colin ever seriously considered making a career in the RAF. It is more likely that it was simply a good way of getting in plenty of flying at someone else's expense! It was the flying he really loved, so he accepted a short-term Commission and was duly posted to the RAF Station at Tern Hill, in Shropshire.

However, by no stretch of the imagination did he give up his other hobby. He was doing reasonably well in trials with the Mk I Lotus, ably 'passengered' by Hazel, and above all it gave him the opportunity of grasping the rather unique art of trials driving.

Eventually, he decided he would build a second car, which was to be – as we would call it today – the state of the art. To be able to achieve this he knew he would have to acquire the maximum amount of car design knowledge. So he spent hours and hours reading all sorts of technical papers in the Institute of Mechanical Engineers' library and technical articles in the motoring press.

Soon his attention was drawn to the 750 Motor Club which had been started just before the war by a few enthusiastic special builders, mostly those keen on cars based on the Austin Seven. He soon found out that the members had amassed an enormous amount of specialized knowledge on car design and, needless to say, he joined.

Denis Jenkinson – 'Jenks', the well-known motor racing writer and journalist, who was amongst the club's keenest stalwarts – recalls the visit Colin once paid to see him and Holland Birkett, then the club's president: 'I was living with Holland Birkett at Fleet, in Hampshire. He was the arch-priest of Austin Seven specials and I was his regular passenger in trials. One day he announced that a chap from the 750 Club was coming to talk Austin Sevens; that evening there was a knock on the door and there stood this young RAF 'erk' with curly hair and a little tooth-brush moustache. We lived pretty rough in those days and this spruce young man from the RAF did not seem to be our scene at all. However, we spent the whole evening in front of a large wood fire – there was no central heating in those days! – during which this chap asked all manner of intelligent questions about trials cars, trials driving, Austin 7s, special building and so on. It was a case of '. . . can I put a 1932 so-and-so into a 1927 thingumajig . . .' and '. . . will a 1934 such-and-such mate up with a 1925 thingumabob?' He needed to know all these things in order to achieve the ultimate in Austin Seven specials but, while his main interest was in a trials special, he was also asking about engine tuning and things to do with racing.

'After he had left, around midnight it must have been, Holly Birkett looked across to me and said, "That young man knows an awful lot, he should go far". Although the club member who had advised Colin to contact Holly Birkett had

Colin being presented with his RAF 'wings'.
It was a big day in his early life.

told us he was coming to see us, the name meant nothing and by the time he arrived we had forgotten it. We pondered over this visit and asked ourselves who he was. Later, someone said it was a chap called Colin Chapman, but it really meant nothing to us at the time. What had impressed us was the amount of "homework" he had done before his visit. He knew that the 1928 part had ten holes, while the 1934 part did the same job with only six holes! He knew that the diameter of that particular pin was 11/16th of an inch, while this one was only 9/16th and did the same job. We were very impressed by this young RAF chap, whoever he was.'

Obviously, with Colin being posted away in the RAF throughout 1949, the completion of the Mark II Lotus was a relatively slow job. However, all his leaves and 48-hour passes were devoted to working on it, and the moment he had to return to his base he would hand over to Hazel a long job list of things to attend to and items to be obtained before his next visit.

The Mark II was to have independent front suspension using a Ford Eight or Ten front axle cut in half, fitted with bushes and suspended from the front of the Austin Seven 'A' frame. As far as the rear axle was concerned, to conform to the regulations of the 750 Motor Club this had to be of Austin Seven origin using normally available half shafts and crown wheel and pinion. Now Colin felt that the standard axle ratios were not high enough for what he felt was required. The way he overcame this is typical of the man and is recalled by Ian Smith, co-founder and Chairman of the original Club Lotus, in his excellent book published in 1958.*

'. . . There were two types of crown wheels and pinions available for the Austin Seven – a 42-tooth crown wheel and 8-tooth pinion giving a final drive ratio of 5.25 to 1, or a 44-tooth crown wheel and 9-tooth pinion which gave a 4.9 to 1 ratio. Colin built up the axle of his car with the 9-tooth pinion and the 42-tooth crown wheel and then, instead of oil, filled the differential housing with neat Bluebell metal polish. The car was run in this condition for about fifty miles and then the back axle was inspected – the bearings were ruined but the crown wheel and pinion now meshed perfectly. New bearings were popped in and the 4.55 to 1 filled with its correct lubricant.'†

Crude but effective and a perfect demonstration of Colin's ingenious approach towards overcoming a problem. Another example, quoted from the same source, is the way in which he acquired a Ford Ten engine to replace the Ford Eight unit he had been forced to use by his chronic lack of funds, and which had proved too under-powered.

'. . . Most of Colin's spare time at Tern Hill was taken up in browsing round garages, peering over hedges and searching breakers' yards in the Market Drayton area. On one of these trips he found a burnt-out Ford Ten saloon in a garage. The car was virtually a 'write-off' and enquiries established that the

---

* 'Lotus: The First Ten Years' (Motor Racing Publications, London).

† The mathematicians will quickly work out that the ratio of 9 to 42 is, strictly speaking, 4.66 to 1.

insurance company involved was planning to sell it at auction. A brief inspection showed the engine to be unharmed by the conflagration. Hiding his real interest, Colin managed to locate the owner and casually asked him some questions. Imagine his surprise when he learned that the engine was a brand-new unit, only fitted about 1,000 miles before the fire! The snag now was how to raise the £35 which the insurance company hoped to get at the auction.

'At this time a certain dealer in the Midlands was buying up second-hand Ford Eight and Ten parts – particularly if the parts included a log book! Colin therefore offered them 'his' car for £40, with log book but less engine and gearbox. They jumped at the opportunity and were eager to collect the bargain. Now the tricky part of the deal was arranged – Colin found a 'breaker' who was keen to make an easy fiver. The middle-man bought the wreck for £35, Colin removed the engine and gearbox, then the remains were collected and the £40 handed over. Colin returned to his camp with a free, as-new, Ford Ten engine complete with gearbox.

'The old engine was removed at once and this, together with the unwanted Ford gearbox, was sold to his friend the breaker for £5 clear profit!'

In September 1949, Colin qualified for his 'wings' and was offered a permanent Commission but, in this somewhat lean period, a career in the RAF did not really appeal to him and he decided to resign. Stanley Chapman was very pleased to see that his son seemed ready to tackle a proper career, so he arranged with a friend – the owner of Cousins, a construction firm – for Colin to be given a job with them. Unfortunately, he did not enjoy this at all. He found that he had to be on the sites at 7 am, which meant getting up at 5 am, yet he was up most evenings until fairly late fiddling with the Mk II.

After a short period with Cousins he left and found himself another job, this time with a large firm, The British Aluminium Company. Here he was employed to visit potential customers in order to convince them that if they were planning to build a new factory or warehouse they should use aluminium in the structure of the roof. He seemed happy enough, but Stanley Chapman did not approve of his son resigning from the job that he had helped him obtain and their relationship became quite strained for a time.

The year 1950 was going to be a very busy season for the Mk II Lotus – and a very successful one, too. Clearly Colin had been doing all his sums right, because not only did his car become one of the best in its class in trials but it was quick enough to indulge in a bit of circuit racing, too.

As we saw earlier on, Colin had never watched a motor race until he came to take part in one and this turned out to be the 'Eight Clubs' Meeting held on the Club Circuit at Silverstone on 3 June. After qualifying in one of the half-hour Speed Trial events, he went on to what *Motor Sport* described in this way: 'A five lap scratch race came next and this featured a really furious duel between Chapman's Lotus and Gahagan's GP Bugatti, the latter cornering wider at Stowe and duly losing ground so that they finished in that order . . .'

This event had a deep influence on Colin, who from then on was to become more and more interested in circuit racing and less and less in trials. This change

Colin's first taste of circuit racing was in the Mk II Lotus (right) at the '8 Club's' Silverstone race meeting on 3 June 1950. He enjoyed himself so much that he gave up car trials completely.

of direction was rather disappointing to Hazel because in trials she was able to participate as the passenger, while in circuit racing she could only hope to be given the opportunity of an occasional drive. It also became clear that for circuit racing it would not make sense to use such a versatile vehicle as the Mk II and so Colin decided to make his next car a pure circuit racer.

Since he was still basically an 'impecunious enthusiast' – as they were known in those days – but with his new-found knowledge of the 750 Motor Club, he decided that he would build a car to compete in the Club's 750 Formula championship. This set out to be the least expensive form of motor racing, and to keep the costs to a minimum the regulations made it mandatory to use many Austin Seven parts, such as the chassis frame, the rear axle, the engine and gearbox and the prop-shaft. What is more, the resulting cars had to be roadworthy and capable of being driven to and from the circuit. So Colin set plans for a return to the Austin Seven engine and in the September issue of *Motor Sport's* (un)classified advertisement section was a panel showing a picture of the Mk II with the following text:

LOTUS

Ford Ten-engined all-round competition car and everyday transport. Weight 8 cwts; ifs; four-speed gearbox; Girling brakes. Gained 21 awards already this year in trials (8), circuit racing (3), sprints (4), driving tests (4) and rallies (2). Sprayed any colour if required. Just been stripped and checked ready for trials season. £325 (44 Beech Drive, London N2. tel TUDor 7123).

A 'customer' soon appeared. He was Mike Lawson, a trials driver who ran a garage business called Moss and Lawson Ltd, in Thornton Heath, near Croydon. (The 'Moss' part of the name turned out to be Stirling Moss's father Alfred, a non-active partner in the business.) Mike Lawson collected the car just in time to compete in the Wrotham Cup Trial and duly won it!

Colin and Hazel had entered the faithful Mk I in the same event and they also won their class, whereupon another advert appeared in *Motor Sport*, this time in the November issue. The text read:

> Austin Seven Special. Four-seater sports-cum-trials car. Much modified suspension and power unit; ifs; four-speed gearbox. Gained numerous awards latest being class win in 1950 Wrotham Cup Trial. Ideal mount for introduction to trials driving.

The address was the same but the price was considerably lower than that asked for the more competitive Mk II – only £135.

The Mk I was quickly sold, too, and so Colin now had sufficient funds to finance the building of the Lotus Mk III. The basis for this was to be an Austin Seven saloon, for which the princely sum of £15 was paid.

Hardly had Colin started work on the new car – as usual in Vic Williams's lock-up – than he met the Allen brothers, two young aspiring dentists who were neighbours of Hazel. Here, the big attraction for Colin was an exceedingly well-equipped garage at their home in Muswell Hill. In a very short time Colin had convinced the Allen boys that the thing they wanted to do most was to make themselves a Mk III Lotus, each being built up together at the same time as

The two semi-display advertisements (left and centre) which appeared in Motor Sport *in 1950, were Colin Chapman's first. The Mk II Lotus (centre) was offered for sale in the September issue and the very-Austin Seven-based Mk I was not advertised until November. The Mk III Lotus (right) was sold at the beginning of the 1952 season, when all Colin's attention was centred on the prototype Mk VI. This advertisement appeared in the May 1952 issue of* Motor Sport.

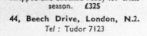

Colin's . . . in their garage! This scheme appealed to them and so all was agreed. The Williams's lock-up was suddenly deserted and from then on it was not Mrs Williams who had extra mouths to feed but the mother of Michael and Nigel Allen. Denis Jenkinson recalls one of his visits to this early Lotus workshop: 'After inspecting the car, Colin took me into the house for a bite to eat. I gathered that the lady who served us was Mrs Allen. Clearly, Colin already had the family well organized . . .'

The Mk III chassis was to be a considerable improvement over the Mk I. This time, although it would still have a stressed body shell, the strengthening would not be achieved by using flat alloy-bonded plywood, as with the Mk I. Instead, the chassis would be braced with the aid of a structure of tubes welded together in the form of a triangulated 'cage', designed to stiffen the notoriously 'whippy' Austin Seven A-frame chassis which, of course, had to be used to conform to the 750 Formula regulations of the time. The 'cage', which was attached to the A-frame by high-tensile bolts, was arranged around the engine so that, when it proved necessary for this to be removed from the car, the 'cage' first had to be dismantled. This was a small price to pay because, as it turned out, this car was streets ahead of those of any other competitors in the 1951 750 Formula championship. The 'top-hat' section of the Austin A-frame itself was also boxed-in to make everything even stiffer. Needless to say, all this welding was only achieved with the help of the Allen brothers' equipment.

Unlike the Mks I and II, the Lotus Mk III was designed as a circuit racing car complying with the 750 Formula. It was propelled by the famous 'de-siamezed ports' Austin Seven engine which made it virtually unbeatable in its class – and sometimes out of its class as well!

The very first Lotus space frame! To stiffen up its notoriously flexible Austin Seven A-frame chassis, the Mk III Lotus was fitted with this triangulated bracing structure made from simple welded steel tubing. As can be seen clearly, the cylinder head or engine could be removed quite easily once three nuts had been undone and the top of the framework removed.

Again, a split Ford Eight axle beam with a flattened semi-elliptic spring was used to provide the independent swing-axle front suspension. Of course, a great deal of care was given to making sure that the overall weight was as low as possible: in fact, the complete car weighed only 815 lb (370 kg).

Even though the chassis and body of this Austin Seven-based Mk III Lotus was at the time so far ahead of any of its competitors, the real secret behind its performance lay with the engine. With three years' competition experience already behind him, Colin Chapman realized that the race really started with the interpretation of the regulations. Those covering the 750 Formula prescribed the use of a standard Austin Seven side-valve cylinder block which, as was the case with many of the early low-priced small car engines, was designed with what were known as 'siamesed' inlet ports. That is to say, although the engine had four cylinders and four inlet valves, the cylinder block was equipped with only two inlet ports, each serving two cylinders. Technically this was a serious drawback when it came to obtaining higher performance from the engine because, due to the 1-3-4-2 firing order, the two adjacent cylinders firing immediately after their neighbour's would rob each other of their correct share of the incoming mixture.

Whilst everybody else competing under the formula seemed to accept this situation as a fact of life – not so Colin Chapman. He devised a relatively simple way of what he called 'de-siamesing' the inlet ports. First he enlarged the openings in the cylinder block by grinding away as much surplus metal as possible. He then built up a special inlet manifold with welded sheet steel, into which he inserted separating divisions to each of the two rectangular-sectioned pipes. These dividing pieces, which were also welded into place, were extended beyond the flange so that when the manifold was bolted on to the cylinder block they fitted into the two enlarged ports. The butt joints were sealed by asbestos strips fixed to the ends of the port dividers to provide a gas-tight seal and effectively split each port into two quite separate ports.

The specially made inlet manifold, equipped with four separate pipes instead of the normal two, was then fitted with an enormous twin-choke Stromberg carburettor – from a Ford V8 engine! – each choke of which was then supplying mixture in the sequence 1-4 and 2-3. Simple! The result, although no power output was ever documented for the simple reason that neither Colin nor any of his friends enjoyed the luxury of a test bed – or even the use of one – was simply devastating. The Mk III Lotus just walked away from the opposition, thanks mainly to its top speed of something in the region of 90 mph or more, all this from a crude 749 cc side-valve engine originally designed in 1922!

In most of the 750 Formula races in that 1951 season the Mk III Lotus ran away with everything, finishing the average five- or ten-lap race at least half a lap ahead. Most of the other competitors found it very disheartening, and the

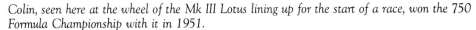

Colin, seen here at the wheel of the Mk III Lotus lining up for the start of a race, won the 750 Formula Championship with it in 1951.

end result was typical of what was to become one of Chapman's eternal problems: after he had dominated the club's 750 Formula in such a way, the regulations were changed for the following year and 'de-siamesed' ports were banned in order to restore the competitiveness to a class of racing which had very nearly been destroyed by his supremacy.

(Even though Colin Chapman was good at conceiving and designing, apparently he was often not entirely happy with his own practical handiwork. Fifteen years after the Mk III's success, when Lotus was a well-known established company at Hethel, the then Sales Manager, Graham Arnold, had by chance come upon the car and the directors had decided to present it to Colin. He took one look at it, saw what to him then looked like poor welding and said: 'Take it away, I never want to see it again!' Fortunately, it was not destroyed and it is now in the Nigel Moores Collection under the custody of ex-Team Elite driver Bill Allen.)

As the 1951 season had progressed it became apparent to the Allen brothers that there was going to be very little chance of their ever completing their own Mk IIIs, let alone actually racing them, for as soon as any progress was made on their cars it was always found necessary to cannibalize them for parts of one sort or another simply to keep Colin's car raceworthy. To be fair to everyone, therefore, it was decided that Colin should be the driver for each of the 750 Formula Championship races, whilst Michael and Nigel – and occasionally Hazel – should take turns at the wheel in the various non-championship scratch, handicap and team events for which the car was eligible. (On more than one occasion it was even entered in what was then called a Formule Libre race. The cycle-type front mudguards were removed for these free-for-all events!)

By the end of the season it became pretty obvious that the 'arrangement' was not going to last. Nigel Allen had decided that, although he would continue to help and drive occasionally, a career in dentistry was more important to him than motor racing. Michael, however, was still very keen to carry on in some form of partnership with Colin. At around the same time Colin began to realize that there might well be a good future in making cars. The spark for this idea came from Mike Lawson who, after enjoying a highly successful season in trials in the Mk II Lotus – which was, however, becoming somewhat outclassed – was very keen for Colin to build him a new car.

Other enthusiasts were also beginning to beat a path to his door wanting him to make up special components for their own 750 Formula cars. There was even one prepared to buy a 'replica' of the fantastically successful Mk III, so it was fairly obvious that the Allen brothers' garage – and Mr Williams' lock-up – would prove quite inadequate for manufacturing on any commercial scale and other more suitable premises would have to be found.

Although by then Stanley Chapman's catering business had expanded, his property still included the Railway Hotel in Tottenham Lane, Hornsey. (It was necessary to own a public house in order to be in possession of a catering and drinks licence.) Behind the pub was what at one time might have been a stable, the front part of which was used for storing empty bottles awaiting return to the suppliers. Although still very small, it was probably at least three or four times larger than any lock-up garage. There was even a small partitioned office area. The remainder of the 'stable' and the yard at the back was rented by a firm of local builders. (These premises, although slightly modernized since, can still be seen clearly by anyone taking the train to or from Kings Cross on the main East Coast railway line, which runs a few yards behind the Railway Hotel.) Stanley Chapman agreed that Colin should lease these premises for a small rental.

The official date on which business started for Lotus Engineering Co was 1 January 1952. The new arrangement was that Michael Allen should work full time but that Colin should carry on with his job at the British Aluminium Company during the day, so that he had something to live on, and work at Tottenham Lane every evening and at weekends. From then on life became very hectic for Colin. After rushing back from his office in BAC's building in St James's Square, just behind Piccadilly, he would usually have dinner with Hazel at his parents' home and then they would both dash off to Tottenham Lane where Hazel would deal with paperwork or the packing of components, while Colin would be working on the fabricating job of the moment. Both would stay there all evening, often into the small hours. Then Colin would be up again early, putting in another hour or so until having to hurry off to his office, where fortunately he was not required to start work until 9.30 am. And so it went on – but he thrived on it, of course.

One of the first big jobs was to complete the 'replica' Mk III which had been ordered by Adam Currie. The basis for this car was one of the chassis frames originally intended for the Allens. It was to be fitted with a Ford Ten 1,172 cc side-valve engine and designated a Lotus Mk IIIB. (Later, this car was to be bought and raced by Anthony Marsh, now a well-known Formula One race commentator.)

The Mk IV was the other car to be built that winter and, although construction was slower than originally planned and delivery delayed beyond the promised date, the car proved to be very successful for several seasons. This was built for Mike Lawson as a Ford Ten-engined trials special using the faithful Austin Seven chassis frame. The bodywork resembled that of the Mk III but was, however, a little roomier as the owner had specified a dual-purpose car which could also be used comfortably on the road. It boasted a special front suspension based on those often seen on agricultural tractors, providing extreme travel for very rough conditions. When the car was to be used on more normal surfaces, the system – nicknamed the 'jelly-joint' – was locked.

During this time the business fought hard to prosper, mainly by manufacturing small parts and conversions, springs, shock absorbers, modified cylinder heads, carburettors and so on, more often than not for 750 or 1,172 Formula constructors and competitors. Prices had to be kept to the minimum because most of the customers and potential customers were in the 'impecunious enthusiast' class. Life was not easy but a great deal of fun was had by all, including the many visitors to Tottenham Lane, many of whom were press-ganged into lending a hand – unpaid naturally!

That winter Colin had also been giving a lot of thought to his next design, which would be designated the Mk VI and would employ the first proper all-Lotus chassis frame design. (It should be pointed out here that there was no Mk V Lotus because Colin had reserved that number for what was, in his mind, to be the ultimate 750 Special, with a top speed of over 100 mph, which he always thought would be easily attainable. In fact, it was the car which he never found the time to build and eventually it was forgotten.)

Using all the knowledge he had gained through his work in structural engineering, the Mk VI chassis was to be a multi-tubular fully stressed space frame with the main body panels actually riveted to the frame's small-diameter tubes, of both round and square sections, thus providing extreme rigidity and strength yet keeping the total weight to the absolute minimum. It is of interest to note that around the same time Mercedes-Benz were just about to introduce their 300SL sports coupé, also designed around a tubular space frame, which was to win outright the 1952 Le Mans 24-Hours Race.

It was also round about this time that Patrick Stephens, the publisher of this book, first met Colin Chapman and in a more recently published reminiscence, which appeared in *Recent History* – the magazine of the Historic Sports Car Club – he recalls their early friendship:

'I first met Colin Chapman in 1951 at one of the club's [750 Motor Club] monthly meetings, at that time held in a pub called "The Red Cow" in Hammersmith Road, on the left-hand side just past Olympia [the famous exhibition hall]. It's still there. I remember he was flashing around a highly professional-looking drawing of a super-looking sports car, which eventually turned out to be the Mk VI Ford Consul-engined Lotus . . .

'For my part, at that time I was the manager of a bookshop in New Bridge Street in London, between Blackfriars Bridge and Ludgate Circus. The shop's speciality was books and magazines on cars and motor racing – I can't think why! – and at the weekends I was taking a mobile version of this shop, converted from a Rolls-Royce Phantom I hearse, to club race meetings. I was also pretty desperate to get into motor racing myself and this was a jolly good way of moving around in the right circles and not having to pay.

'It wasn't long before Colin, who was then working in St James's Square, SW1, for The British Aluminium Company as a young yet qualified structural engineer, discovered that in my shop's stock of car books and magazines was an unrivalled source of good technical information, all free of charge of course, because there was no need for money to be spent on buying such items when you had a memory like his.

'. . . It was during 1952 that Colin Chapman proved particularly helpful to me, when I finally managed to build a 750 'special' myself . . . Colin had by then started Lotus Engineering Co in Hornsey next to the pub owned by his father but, as he was still working for The British Aluminium Company, he didn't have a great deal of time for running the business and building cars in the evening.

'Now I wanted my 750 to be one of the quickest around, so I arranged with Colin that if he would shape the combustion chambers – of a blank cylinder head casting which I had acquired – in the same way as he had done on his own Lotus Mk III 750 Formula car, I would both lay out his monthly advertisement in *Motor Sport*, where he was advertising spares and service for 750 Austin and 1,172 Ford engines and cars, and design and have printed his first business letter heading . . .'

The first advertisement duly appeared, and thereafter usually every month. It said:

LOTUS ENGINEERING CO

At your service for:

Crankshaft balancing, rebores, remetalling, enlarged valves, surface grinding, double valve springs for Ford and Austin, ifs conversions, 7-inch Lockheed brake sets, lightweight wheels and springs etc.

In fact – A COMPLETE SERVICE FOR THE SPECIAL BUILDER – Call, write or telephone: 7 Tottenham Lane, Hornsey, N8. MOUntview 8353

This advertisement, and Colin's reputation, which was by then beginning to spread, kept the pot boiling for a while but it was fairly obvious to visitors that, in view of the paucity of machining equipment in the workshop, Lotus Engineering Co was selling knowledge just as much as their craftsmanship and they had to rely on sub-contractors for most of the advertised services such as rebores, remetalling and surface grinding.

Nevertheless, it did the trick and enabled Colin to proceed with the job of building the very first Mk VI, which turned out to be rather a hybrid and completely different from any of the many examples which would subsequently be built. Although it was based on the new space frame, the car was required by its owner Sinclair Sweeney for trials use and was equipped with a solid beam front axle. It was also rather ugly due to the extreme ground clearance. In fact, although very little was known generally about this car, like most of those earlier Lotuses it was quite successful in its own field.

In the meantime Colin was, as always, bristling with ideas and Denis Jenkinson remembers another meeting he had with him during that period: '. . . As is well known, Colin swept into the trials world with his Austin Seven special and we soon got to know him in the 750 club racing world. The 750 Club used to hold meetings at the Abbey Hotel* on the North Circular Road and after one of them we all adjourned to an all-night café a half mile or so down the road. (Actually, the later somewhat infamous Ace Café.) Colin was in the group and talk was of special building and racing cars and he told us about a project he had been offered by a man called Clairmonte who had been racing a 2 litre 6-cylinder Riley. This chap wanted a single-seater Formula 2 car and had asked Colin to design it for him. He told us his ideas for this front-engined Formula 2 car which sounded very ambitious for a 750 Club member who had only ever built Austin Seven specials.

'We could not enthuse over his project as we felt the whole basis of designing it around a 1936 Riley engine was wrong. We reckoned the engine would not be powerful enough to be competitive and was too heavy for its power output anyway. Colin was unimpressed. The engine was not his worry. He was concerned only with the chassis and suspension and the steering. I think that project was still-born as I do not ever recall seeing the car, but it was clear that C. Chapman had his sights set on

---

* The 750 Motor Club moved to this new venue from The Red Cow in Hammersmith in the winter of 1951-52.

bigger things than 750 Club specials.' (In fact, this car did eventually appear, although not under the name Lotus.)

That great Lotus enthusiast from America, Dennis Ortenburger, has provided more details about this very much one-off car. In his book 'The Legend of the Lotus Seven'* he says: 'The Original Lotus Seven – In early 1953 [1952?] just as development was beginning on the Six [VI], Chapman received an enquiry from two brothers by name of Clairmonte. Impressed with the trials and circuit racers built by Lotus Engineering Company, they wondered if Chapman could design a Formula 2 [car] for them. The proposal was for Lotus to design the body, chassis and suspension for which they would provide an ERA engine and suitable gearbox. (The ERA engine was a racing development of the Riley.) Chapman agreed because he figured the project might be a ticket into big time racing. If successful, there would obviously be a market for replicas. The Clairmontes didn't care what the car was named – all they wanted was a Colin Chapman design – but to suit Chapman's plan it had to be called a Lotus. Since the next model designation was seven, the Hornsey drawing boards were coded Lotus Mk VII Formula 2 Car.

'Apparently the project soured shortly after construction began on the prototype. Perhaps the Clairmontes didn't have sufficient financial backing or their organization was not up to standards. Or maybe Chapman felt the car was too much too soon. What is known is that a rolling chassis was completed and delivered. When Chapman learned that the ERA engine had blown up before installation, he used the occasion to withdraw from the project and take his name and his mark number with him. The number 'seven' was then set aside for the successor to the VI.

'The Clairmontes completed the car but with a significant alteration to the chassis and a body of their own design. The 'Clairmonte Special' was run as a sports car with a Lea-Francis engine. With a Chapman space frame, double wishbone front suspension and a de Dion axle at the rear, the car would make for some interesting comparisons today. (Wonder if the Special still exists?) . . .'

Now, just to show how difficult it can be to recall history, I must go back to an interview I had with Colin some years ago in which he told me that the 'Clairmonte Special' was to be fitted with an Alta engine!

Throughout 1952 Colin was kept very busy with the Mark VI, which can certainly be considered to be the first real Lotus because, even though many proprietary components were used in the interest of keeping costs to a minimum, it nevertheless had a chassis which was completely Lotus designed and built.

The front suspension was again, as in all the earlier cars, by swing axle using the Ford Ten beam axle split in half but, for the first time, employing suspension units consisting of coil springs surrounding telescopic dampers. These units were very light and convenient since they required only two common mounting points. The arrangement was really quite a trend-setting move and such a layout, similar in principle, is still used in most racing cars today. The rear axle and drive was again Ford Ten but with the torque tube and drive shaft somewhat shortened to suit the wheelbase of the car. The rear suspension employed coil spring and damper units

---

* Osprey Publishing Co, 1981.

similar to those at the front. Brakes and steering also used proprietary Ford parts.

Without realizing it at the time, Colin was designing a car which, in the form of its direct derivative the Lotus Seven, was destined to become a cult and is still being manufactured over thirty years later. Colin himself once described this car: '. . . it was the simplest, most basic high performance car you could come up with for two people. It was a student's car. When I first started myself it was the car I dreamt about. The Mk III was very nice but it was questionable for two people to sit side by side. It was a four-wheel motor bike . . .'

Right from the start it had been decided that the Mk VI should be capable of accepting any one of the several types of engine and for the prototype a Ford Consul – just newly introduced – was selected. Unfortunately, it was so new that none was available through the normal trade channels. Even letters to Ford's Chairman were to no avail. As usual, though, Colin found a way over the problem by simply touring around all the Ford dealers in the London area, buying up bit by bit all the spare parts

The first Mk VI Lotus at a Silverstone club event in the summer of 1952. This was the first 'real' Lotus inasmuch as it boasted a chassis entirely designed and built by Lotus and their sub-contractors, while the earlier cars had used modified Austin Seven chassis. Here Nigel Allen is talking to Dave Kelsey of Progress Chassis Co (in chequered shirt) who, with his partner John Teychenne, built most Lotus space frame chassis. Colin appears to have a problem with the rear axle.

The prototype Mk VI was powered by a Ford Consul engine reduced in capacity to just under 1,500 cc. Colin is seen here at the wheel during a Silverstone club meeting in 1952.

necessary to make up a complete engine.

Because the cubic capacity of the Consul engine was actually 1,508 cc, to enable it to compete within the 1,500 cc class of racing the capacity was reduced by the simple means of grinding the crankshaft big-end journals eccentrically and fitting oversize bearing shells. This Consul-engined Mk VI Lotus first raced at the MG Car Club's meeting at Silverstone on 5 July 1952, where it created quite a stir although, in fact, it only finished second in both the races for which it had been entered.

After another club meeting at Silverstone later that month, where it managed to perform very encouragingly despite a few mechanical problems with the engine, it was decided to enter the car for the quite prestigious 100-mile sports car event at the International *Daily Mail* race meeting at Boreham Airfield in Essex, to be held on August Bank Holiday Monday. Unfortunately, in practice Nigel Allen became rather over-confident and managed to spin it four times, collecting several marker drums in the process. So it was back to Hornsey for repairs to the body and panelling.

It seemed, however, that the car was destined not to race at this meeting. On the way back to the circuit the following morning, whilst Nigel Allen was again driving, a milk float came out of a side turning without warning and the Lotus ran slap into the side of it. Although, happily, Nigel was unhurt the car was a complete write-off. Fortunately, it was comprehensively insured, and if it had not been it is possible that the Lotus Engineering Co might well have foundered there and then simply through lack of cash. Fortunately, the advertisements in *Motor Sport* were still pulling in some conversion work and orders for special spares, which just about kept the little company going until the insurance money was finally paid later that autumn.

By then the time had come for a complete reappraisal of the situation. Michael Allen, who had not been seeing eye to eye with Colin, decided he would leave the company, taking with him – by agreement – the wreck of the Mk VI.

So Colin was now on his own. For some time it had been quite clear to him that he had found what he wanted to do in life and that the time had come when he must apply all his talent, skills and energy to make a success of it. He had tasted motor racing and what he wanted more than anything else was to drive faster and better racing cars. In order to be able to afford to do so he was prepared to set himself an incredibly strenuous schedule for the next two years. Even so, it is doubtful if, at the time, he ever thought for a second that Lotus would ultimately become a fully-fledged automobile manufacturer. Indeed, even if that did enter his mind, it is questionable whether that was ever what he really wanted.

Chapter 3

. . . and Blossoms in Hornsey

The first thing Chapman then did was to borrow £25 from Hazel which he spent on the formation of a new limited company. The second was to change the yellow and green stationery to read:

LOTUS ENGINEERING CO LTD,

Automobile and component manufacturers. Racing and competition car design and development

Directors: A. C. B. Chapman (BSc Eng), H. P. Williams
Manufacturers of the Lotus chassis frame.
7 Tottenham Lane, Hornsey, London, N8. Telephone MOUntview 8353.

They were in business!

Colin had for some time been nurturing the idea that the car (the Mk VI) should be offered for sale as a kit of parts, to which the buyer would add further components from a production car which would also be modified by Lotus for an extra charge. The great advantage of such an idea was that it would avoid the necessity of charging the customer Purchase Tax (the predecessor of Value Added Tax) simply because, while complete motor vehicles were taxable, spare parts were not! Since the rate of tax then was 25 per cent on top of the retail price this – added to the saving in the cost of labour compared to the cars being assembled by Lotus – represented a considerable reduction.

However, the first problem was that, in order to attract customers, it was first necessary to have a 'works demonstrator' available to take part in competitions and thus spread the word. Unfortunately the company's financial position made this impossible – a most frustrating situation for Colin who, after all, was only in this business to get free drives! He just had to find a way of building up the first batch of cars in order to generate enough cash to build one for himself.

Building cars meant acquiring people and Colin was indeed fortunate in meeting – through Adam Currie, the owner and builder of the Mk IIIB – two designer/draughtsmen from the de Havilland aircraft factory at Hatfield, Peter Ross and 'Mac' McIntosh. Their enthusiasm for cars stemmed from having helped Adam Currie to put his car together and it was not long before they were turning up in the evenings at Hornsey, either to help Colin with drawing and stress calculations, or generally lending a hand. All this was just for the fun of it because there was no way that Colin could afford to pay any wages.

One day Peter Ross explained the situation to another young colleague at de Havilland, Mike Costin, and it was not long before he paid a visit to 7 Tottenham Lane.

'I saw Colin one evening in the pub,' he recalls, 'and he offered me a part-time association deal to start in January. The idea was that we would together build the first seven Mk VI cars which would finance the construction of the eighth, of which we would share the driving!' Now Mike was really a glider enthusiast who knew nothing about cars and was not, at the time, especially attracted to them either. Why on earth did he pledge all his leisure time for the next few months with the sole reward of some race driving, of which he knew nothing? 'I am an idiot!' chuckles Costin. 'But Colin had that most fantastic ability to motivate people.' In January 1953, Mike Costin started working part-time for Lotus . . .

The 'plan' was that the manufacture of the Mk VI frame would be sub-contracted to two other enthusiasts, Dave Kelsey and 'Johnny' Teychenne, who had formed a small business which they called The Progress Chassis Company. Finished and painted frames were then to be delivered to the Lotus 'works' at Hornsey, where Charlie Williams and his partner Len Pritchard would fabricate and fit the riveted stressed panelling and make up the remainder of the bodywork, wings, engine compartment cover, instrument panel, radiator shell, 'egg-box' grille and so on. This would all be done during the day, and in the evening, when Charlie and Len had gone home, Colin and Mike would arrive from their day jobs at British Aluminium and de Havilland, to put the whole thing together so that the customer would have a partly assembled car. All they would then have to do to complete it would be to fit the axles, engine, gearbox and transmission and upholstery. Through all this activity Hazel was usually on the scene, taking care of the secretarial work, the letters and invoices that required typing – and producing endless cups of tea.

(Eventually, Williams and Pritchard moved into the other end of the Tottenham Lane 'stable block' – the end which up to then was rented by the builders – thus alleviating the rather critical problem of lack of working space. Later still they were to move into a small factory in First Avenue, Edmonton, London N18, where the neighbouring unit was occupied by Dave Kelsey's and John Teychenne's Progress Chassis Company. A perfect example of how companies can benefit from the success of others.)

Dave Kelsey recently recalled those early days in Hornsey: '. . . I built all the Mk VIs from No 2 onwards – there were about eighty – and all the other subsequent marks up to about Chassis No 500, when I moved on to other things. I had become interested in racing in 1950, through my friendship with John Teychenne, a school friend of Colin's, and spent most weekends helping John build a special based on an Austin Seven A-frame he had acquired from Colin.

Right *In 1952 advertisements for Lotus Engineering Co began to appear regularly in the motor sporting press. This selection, copywritten and laid out by Colin's friend and publisher of this book, Patrick Stephens, appeared in* Motor Sport *during the year. By December Lotus had become a limited company.*

'One Sunday morning John arrived at my house in Hornsey with Nigel Allen in the brand-new Lotus VI, on its first road outing. I remember that my first impression of this car, unlike most specials of the day, was that the engine compartment appeared to be almost empty – no unnecessary bits, neat and tidy wiring and an engine that looked far too small for the car. This engine – a Ford Consul – was, I believe, the one that Colin and Michael Allen built up from spare parts acquired piecemeal from Ford dealers from miles around, since no-one would supply a complete engine at the time. Not long afterwards, on the way to a race, Nigel stuck the car into a milk float, effectively writing it off, and also damaging the knees of Pauline Gooch, his passenger and later his wife. I seem to remember that the insurance payout was £600 [it was actually £800], and this money was used to found Lotus Engineering Co Ltd in a shed at the Railway Hotel in Tottenham Lane, Hornsey, where Colin's father was the landlord.

'Johnny Teychenne and I were by now engaged in building the Clairmonte Special, a Leaf-[Lea-Francis]engined car that Colin had designed for Clive Clairmonte, but never finished. The car had inboard springs and cantilever wishbones that later featured on other Chapman designs. Colin asked us if we would like to build another Mk VI for Nigel, and having nothing better in mind we agreed.

'This was the foundation of the Progress Chassis Co in John's father's garden shed in Ribblesdale Road, Hornsey. At this time John was working as a draughtsman for Poplar Council, and I was a statistics clerk in a City timber brokers. We didn't dare give up our day jobs.

'The first Mk VI took us about six weeks to make. We had a rudimentary drawing, but much of the design was on the basis of "bung that bit in here, and weld some tubes to hold it"! The drawing was gradually consumed by careless welding torches, and by the time we finished the car what was left – being badly fixed photographic paper – had faded away.

'We got £30 for the chassis and suspension parts, including brush painting with Valspar battleship grey, and delivered it on foot to Colin's shed two hundred yards away. On this occasion I believe we were paid but there were other times when we would pick up the chassis and march it back again until the money was forthcoming!

'We were very surprised to be asked to build another one. We began to fantasize about maybe building five or six, by which time we knew the market would be saturated. By the time we finished the second car, in about a month, the drawing had completely vanished, and all the subsequent VIs were built entirely from my memory of the dimensions of the eighty tubes, brackets, suspension parts, engine mountings and so on. Fortunately, at the age of 22, I had total recall of numbers, and we made no mistakes. The current crop of car builders, working in super new factories with million-pound sponsorships, would not believe the conditions under which the finest racing cars of the day were built. Our workshops of about 300 sq ft were heated by one small coal stove, on which we kept a bucket of water for the occasional wash. The whole building was ramshackle, and in bad winter weather there was almost as much snow inside as out.

'Our plant and machinery consisted of two old hacksaws, two ancient vices, a couple of 14-in bastard files, a heavy hammer or two, a hand-turned 'gut-buster' drill and – the pride of the works – a Wolf ¼-in electric drill. Our precision measuring kit was composed of one Stanley tape and a wooden yardstick, rather charred. The chassis jig was an old iron bedstead to which we clamped the chassis tubes with G-clamps, and corrected distortions with 4-ft sash clamps. Since the jig was a good deal flimsier than the chassis, we became expert at welding in sequence to avoid distortion, and tacking in temporary braces to support panels which would later be covered with aluminium.

'John and I worked every night after our day jobs until at least 1 am and all day and evening on Saturdays, Sundays and Bank Holidays. The sole exception to this rule was Thursdays, when I worked alone while John went to play poker to raise the bread for the next batch of materials.

'The tubing we used was brand-new welded furniture tube, but the brackets and other sheet metal parts were cut from whatever we could find – old filing cabinets, bread tins, bits of pranged cars, scrap of all kinds. This was recycling at its best, and long before the Friends of the Earth.

'Wheel arches and body frame tubes were bent – usually by me, in a hole in an old railway sleeper, inch by inch, matching to a full-size drawing on brown paper. Colin would appear from time to time to badger us, or even lend a hand, but it was really the blind leading the blind in engineering terms. You could reasonably say that the first few hundred Lotuses were genuinely hand-built to a much greater extent than any other car before or since.

'During this period, I was asked on two occasions by Connaught to join them as manager of their sports car factory, and I went with Nigel Allen to talk to them and to look at the operation. I simply could not believe the opulence of their factory . . . actual milling machines, lathes, power drills, presses, hundreds of tools, 45 staff (of whom 23 were in the offices, as I remember) and an amazing array of benches, drawing boards, chassis jigs and part-built cars.

'At the time I was building single-handedly one Lotus chassis a week and we were getting about £50 for it. Connaught told me their streamliner single-seater, which they proudly unveiled for me, cost £10,000 and took nine months to build. I felt sure one of us must be doing it wrong. Connaught asked me to name my price for joining them but, as I have never been greatly motivated by money, I decided to stick with our crude, but highly successful outfit in the back streets of Hornsey.'

Meanwhile, for Hazel, things were becoming rather more difficult. Probably in a bid to distract her daughter's attention from this young man and his racing cars, Mrs Williams had moved out to Cuffley, in Hertfordshire. When Hazel had settled in Colin repaid her original loan by buying her, for £25, an Austin Seven 'Chummy' (what else!) and she started commuting regularly in it to Muswell Hill, where she was now running her mother's woolshop. In fact, this 'Chummy' proved a good investment as it was destined to become the 'tender car' to the racing team. Much later, after putting many more miles on the clock, it was sold to a mechanic at Lotus. His name was Graham Hill.

Of course, word was getting round about the goings-on behind the Railway Hotel in Tottenham Lane, what with strange people turning up in odd-looking cars, the noise they made, and the disturbance from sports cars being driven around the 'test

When Hazel's mother moved to Cuffley, in an effort to separate her daughter from 'this young man and his cars' Colin bought her an Austin Seven 'Chummy' so that she could continue to travel to and from Hornsey without difficulty. Later Hazel sold it to Graham Hill, then a mechanic at Lotus, on condition that he would lend it back to her each year so that she could take part in the annual Wrotham Cup car trial. She is seen here driving it during the 1954 event with Graham sitting next to her, while Colin seems to be enjoying the ride.

track' of local suburban roads. This aroused considerable curiosity from neighbours and passing strangers alike, and people were often dropping in just to see what was going on.

One evening in the summer of 1953 a local enthusiast who called by picked up a spanner and asked if he could help. Although this in itself was not an infrequent occurrence, he was not the usual run-of-the-mill visitor. His name was 'Nobby' Clarke, and he became so keen on helping that eventually he left his brother's small electrical firm to become the first full-time Lotus employee. Later, 'Nobby' became Works Manager but sadly he died nine years after, at a very early age.

Another encounter with an ordinary member of the public, and one which was to have a considerable bearing on the Company's progress, was Colin's meeting with Fred Bushell. Fred was an accountant with the leading City firm of Peat Marwick Mitchell & Co. He lived in Hornsey and on nice evenings he would often walk home from the tube station. He recalls his first meeting with Colin Chapman.

'. . . I had passed the Tottenham Lane workshop many times late at night and seen the lights on in the building. It so happened that there was a gents toilet close by, primarily there for the use of the patrons of the pub next door, where I would sometimes have to make a call. On this particular occasion Colin was in there, in his cap and overalls and, as men do, we got talking and he invited me to have a look in the workshop.

'They were working on a small racing car, and he explained to me in his usual enthusiastic way what he and his colleagues were doing. Then he asked me what I did. Upon hearing that I was an accountant he took me to a tiny cubicle, where there was a trestle table propped up on beer crates, on which were piles of papers. Principally these amounted to a series of open envelopes on which there were columns of figures and which he explained was his accounting system and would I like to sort it out for him?

'We made an appointment to meet a week later and on this occasion it seemed to me to be a very friendly operation where everyone had a lot of fun and, while I had no mechanical knowledge or inclination, I was looking for things I could do in my own right, so I said I would have a go. I reorganized his accounting systems and turned what had appeared to me to be more like a club into a business . . .'

The first Mk VI cars were bought by customers who were to fit their own engines, most of which were to be the then very popular Ford Ten 1,172 cc unit. With this they were able to compete in the 750 Club's other low-cost racing class – the 1,172 Formula. The attraction of this over the 750 Formula was that whilst the regulations were based on the principle of using a standard production engine, gearbox and back-axle, competitors were free to put them into whatever chassis they pleased.

Eventually, in 1953, Colin and Mike Costin were able to find the time to build their own 'works' car. This was chassis no 9 (registration no 1611 H) and it was decided that the company would benefit most if it, too, were fitted with an 1,172 engine linered down to under 1,100 cc so that it would also be able to enter that class of race.

Once again Colin gave a great deal of thought to finding ways and means of circumventing the regulations so as to have the fastest 1,172 Formula car on the circuits. The loophole he was looking for seemed to be the camshaft because, although the regulations quite clearly stated that the standard – and very tame – camshaft had to be used, there was nothing to say that the standard *timing* had to be used, too! So Colin designed special cam followers of concave shape which completely changed the timing, as if an entirely different camshaft were in use.

The construction of these cam followers was entrusted to Mike Costin and, in the event, the job proved to be a real nightmare. Although he was able to have some special tools made up by friends at the de Havilland factory, most of the work had to be done by hand over a period of many, many hours. However, in the end it was all well worth it for the result was fantastic and – as with the Mk III – the new car was quite uncatchable in its class. Strategically, it was decided then that Mike would do the driving in the 1,172 Formula races while Colin would tackle the 'big league' sports car classes. Hazel, too, was able to drive – and with considerable success – in some events. Even Stan Chapman had a go on the odd occasion!

Ian Smith, in his book 'Lotus: The First Ten Years', recalls one amusing incident when the Lotus 'team' turned up at the Tarrant Rushton Speed Trials too late for practice. They were, however, allowed to motor round the course in Hazel's 'Chummy':

'. . . from a straight start the road curved right, there was a short straight then a long bend to the right, dropping away as it finished. Colin whisked the little saloon round and said to Hazel, "piece of cake, flat-out through the gears, keep your foot flat through the second bend and then up to the finish". Hazel did exactly as she was bid and easily won the 1,172 Formula class – Colin and Mike were seen to wince at the revs reached on the finishing line! It was then Colin's turn in the up-to-1,300 cc class. All went as he had planned until the second bend when he found that he was travelling so fast he had to lift off. Result: slower than Hazel! Imagine his surprise when he questioned her about this bend and she replied that of course she had kept her foot down hard – "You said I should!". Colin tried it on his second run, scared himself considerably, and just beat Hazel's best time. He won the class and Mike drove the car into second place.'

Up to now the name Lotus was only really familiar to those enthusiasts attending club events. However, this was to change with an important international race meeting, held at the new Crystal Palace circuit in South London on 19 September 1953, when Colin entered the Mk VI in the 1,500 cc Anerley Trophy event against the cream of the class, including the American Bob Said in a 1,500 cc twin-cam OSCA. The public was treated to the fantastic sight of this little 1,100 cc three-speed side-valve car holding its own in such distinguished company.

In its 23 September report of the event, *The Motor* said: '. . . Chapman having the time of his life with the preposterously fast Lotus.'

In the 2 October issue of the weekly motor sporting magazine *Autosport*, John Bolster road-tested that same car. His comments, which were to prove a great help to the company in selling more Mk VI cars, were enthusiastic to say the least.

With a weight of only 8½ cwt (952 lb/432 kg) the car could accelerate from 0-60 mph in 12.6 sec and Bolster was able to reach a maximum speed of 88 mph (141.6 kph). He estimated that the engine was probably producing at least 40 bhp at 6,000 rpm. He explained the 'kit car' system in some detail, showing that it was possible for customers to build a car with all-new components for as little as £425. The only extras would be the special engine tuning and a set of close-ratio gears.

Forecasting that some people might buy the car, not for racing at all but for the sheer enjoyment of such a means of transport – and he was quite right, of course – Bolster commented in his inimitable style: '. . . the weather protection, with hood and side flaps in position, was much better than one would expect even though a slight defect in the body allowed some water to enter my right shoe during heavy rain. As Mr Chapman has no intention at present of invading the Roll-Royce and Bristol market, he has given a little less attention than those two manufacturers to sound deadening and exhaust silencing . . .'

In conclusion, Bolster said: 'I feel the Lotus is the best yet attempt to provide the enthusiast with a competition car at a price he can afford to pay. In essentials it is just as sound an engineering job as the most expensive sports cars and the economy is only brought about by the clever adaptation of mass-produced components.'

I was one of those avid young enthusiasts who read this story at just about the time I was planning to go motor racing in partnership with my British friend Alf Hitchings. I decided there and then that this was the car for me. I had always been a keen follower of motor racing and, as I lived in Paris, I had successfully landed myself the position of Continental Correspondent for *Autosport* when it was first launched back

Right By 1954 Lotus advertisements had become more sophisticated and the enormous number of competition successes for the company's cars were being highlighted in time-honoured fashion. These two advertisements appeared in the October and December 1954 issues of Motor Racing, of which Patrick Stephens was by then Advertisement Manager.

Overleaf The first Lotus sales brochure, and the separate (even in those days) price list which was given out with it. This was produced in the Winter of 1953/54 and makes most interesting reading in itself (even if you do need a magnifying glass to do so as reproduced here), especially the prices!

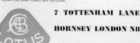

PRICE LIST

SPECIALISED LOTUS COMPONENTS

	£. s. d.
CHASSIS FRAME	110. 0. 0.

Including all mounting brackets for I.F.S., engine and gearbox, suspension units, steering column, pedals and brake gear, radiator, wing stays, Pannard rod, etc., and fitted with all stressed aluminium panels, i.e. under-tray, body panels, toe board, scuttle and wheel arches

CONVERSION TO INDEPENDENT FRONT SUSPENSION — 15.10. 0.

For this we require customer's axle beam, radius arms, track rod assembly and drag link only. These to be in a clean and tidy condition and all parts must be from a post 1938 Ford 8/10 (i.e. with spring in front of the axle)

MODIFICATIONS TO BRAKE LINKAGE — 2. 1. 6.

New nearside transverse cable, cable guide and special compensator arm adaptor

SHORTENING FORD 8/10 TORQUE TUBE — 3.10. 0.

SHORTENING FORD 8/10 PROP SHAFT — 2.10. 0.

It is essential that this is of the tubular type and not a solid shaft

PANNARD ROD with special mounting bolts — 1. 5. 0.

SUSPENSION UNITS

Special LOTUS coil spring and telescopic shock absorber unit   4 required @ £5 each — 20. 0. 0.

REAR SUSPENSION UNIT ADAPTORS for rear axle only, 2 @ £1 each — 2. 0. 0.

STEERING COLUMN — 7.17. 6.

Special LOTUS column with light alloy box with mounting strap

HANDBRAKE ASSEMBLY — 4. 7. 6.

Comprising modified lever, ratchet quadrant, cable inner and outer, and cable end stop

FOOTBRAKE ASSEMBLY — 5.15. 6.

Comprising footpedal, adjustable for reach, cable inner and outer, and cable support bridge

OPTIONAL EQUIPMENT

LIGHT ALLOY PETROL TANK — 10. 0. 0.

Designed and constructed for this chassis. Weight approx. 7 lbs. Capacity 6 galls.

RADIATOR — 13. 0. 0.

New Morris Minor radiator modified to the requirements of the chassis and power unit, i.e. -
LOTUS type "A" for Consul & M.G.
LOTUS type "B" for Ford 8/10

-1-

Optional Equipment CONTD.

	£. s. d.
UPHOLSTERY KIT	22. 0. 0.

This comprises a 4" Dunlopillo one piece seat squab, two 4" Dunlopillo seat cushions, all covered in good quality real hide; 2 padded and beaded matching side panels covered in vynide. Complete with fixing screws

LIGHT ALLOY WINDSCREEN — 11.10. 0.

Full width quickly detachable rigid windscreen with attachment points for hood with highly polished finish

EXTENSION BACK — 10. 5. 0.

This is a removable back to replace the boot door when absolute economy of weight is not required but additional luggage room, spare wheel mounting and hood frame mounting is considered necessary. Weight approx. 10 lbs.

HOOD & FRAME — 13.15. 0.

Designed to fit extension back and LOTUS windscreen, complete with frame fabricated from light alloy tubing

The following components apply specifically to the Ford 10 installation:-

CLUTCH PEDAL ASSEMBLY FOR FORD 10 — 3. 0. 0.

Comprising pedal, adjustable for reach, adaptor arm for gearbox cross-shaft and connecting link

REMOTE CONTROL — 4.13. 0.

For this conversion we require the customer's standard Ford gear lever

BATTERY CRADLE — 2.10. 0.

THROTTLE LINKAGE — 2. 0. 0.

WATER OFFTAKE — 1.15. 0.

RACING COMPONENTS

LOTUS small light weight silencers — 1. 7. 6.

Special light competition wheels to take Dunlop range of racing tyres
Front 4.50 X 15 — 3.16. 0.each
Rear 5.25 X 15 — 4. 3. 0. "

High ratio crown wheels & pinions to fit in Ford axle
For Ford 10 engines 4.7:1 — 7.18. 6.pair
For 1½ litre engines 4.125:1 — 17. 0. 0. "

Close ratio gears for Ford 8/10 gearboxes — 10.15. 0.

For builders of LOTUS Replicas only

Engine modifications and specialised tuning can be undertaken and quotations will gladly be given.

DELIVERY

This is subject to variations in market conditions but at the present is as follows:-

Chassis & Body	-	2 months
Modifications to customer's components	-	1 month from receipt
Other LOTUS parts	-	ex-stock or to order

N.B.:
OUR TERMS OF SALE ARE STRICTLY NETT: £50 DEPOSIT WITH ORDER & BALANCE ON DELIVERY

-2-

in August 1950. Colin, of course, had read my name in the magazine so, when the *Autosport* secretary phoned on my behalf to fix an appointment, he thought I must be a 'Very Important Person' indeed and all car building activities were halted so that all hands could set to tidying up the factory, to make a good impression on the first visit of this influential foreign journalist.

As I was a year younger than Colin, and fairly youthful looking for my age, he told me many years later that his first thought on seeing me was that the great journalist had been called away at the last moment (an urgent visit to Enzo Ferrari perhaps?) and had sent his assistant instead! Nevertheless, we immediately became quite friendly and a deal was struck. I was to buy the 'works' car 1611 H for – in view of its extremely successful record and the highly tuned engine – the very reasonable sum of £450. Not a word was said about the special cam followers, then still very much a top secret, and it was not until the following year – when a British Mk VI owner, Dick Hardy, came over to partner me in the Bol d'Or 24-Hours Race, the first long-distance event in which a Lotus competed – that I found out about them. Dick had heard about them on the 'grapevine' and was keen on getting the full details. When Colin found out he was furious and raised hell with me, saying that I should never have let Hardy see them.

It was also at this time that I discovered 'my' car had been panelled with lighter gauge sheet alloy. So, even in those very early Hornsey days, Colin Chapman was well aware of the significance of an 'unfair advantage'. As for those special cam followers – you've guessed it – the 750 Club banned them at the end of that season!

Chapter 4

Aerodynamics and Serious Racing

On the strength of the great successes during the 1953 season – their first full one really – and with the backing of a continually full order book for Mk VI cars, many inspired by John Bolster's road test, Colin decided that the next car should be built to a much more ambitious design. What he was after was a more powerful engine, four-speed transmission, a more advanced form of rear suspension, hydraulic brakes and, last but not least, a fully streamlined body. To offset the extra weight of this larger fully-enclosed body shell, the frame would have to be very light indeed and what eventually evolved – becoming the Mark VIII prototype – was designed entirely on first principles and was arguably the purest space frame ever applied to a racing car.

Chapman then sketched a suitable design for the all-enveloping body, which was not unlike John Tojeiro's famous Bristol-engined car raced so successfully by F. C. (Cliff) Davis. However, when Mike Costin saw it he was not enthusiastic and suggested that since aerodynamics was a science they had better ask the opinion of an expert. Now it so happened that Mike's brother, Frank, was just such an expert[*] and Colin readily agreed that he should be shown the model which chassis builder Dave Kelsey had already produced.

Of this quite historic meeting, Dave Kelsey recalls: '. . . I remember the first Mark VIII with some affection. Colin came to my house one evening, clutching an eighth-scale drawing of a car that looked rather like a small C-type Jaguar, and asked me if I would build a model of it for Frank Costin to test in a wind tunnel. I quoted him £4 for the work and spent the next ten nights of spare time building a balsa model, with leather upholstered seats, turned brass steering wheel, aluminium gear lever and dummy instruments. Colin found this all too much and danced up and down in frustration while I finished the model to my satisfaction. At the first chance, he grabbed it and rushed off to Frank with it.

'Frank then attacked it with various brutal instruments, and stuck Plasticine all over it. When it finally came back to me it had grown tail fins, a tonneau cover and a brand-new front end. Meanwhile, Colin and his friends at de Havilland had designed a new chassis frame, based on large triangles, to be made in 80-ton tensile strength tubing, with 20-gauge sheet metal engine and suspension mountings, all brazed together with sifbronze.

---

[*] See Dennis Ortenburger's fine book, 'Flying On Four Wheels: Frank Costin and his car designs', published by Patrick Stephens.

'We built two of these frames and for a while our small workshop was continually full of aircraft boffins, while Colin and I applied sash cramps to various parts of the chassis to test the stiffness. I had grave misgivings about the whole thing, compounded by the fact that one of the chaps had designed the Comet engine mountings, and Comets were regularly falling out of the sky at the time.

'Colin had attracted a motley crew of part-time workers – all unpaid, but rewarded with the chance to drive the car on running-in sessions before a race. This became somewhat of a nightmare to me, especially with the VIII. No sooner had I crawled into bed at 1 or 2 am after seeing off a new car, than Colin would be on the phone – "Sorry laddo, the idiot's graunched it – can you come and fix it?" Theoretically I got four shillings an hour for this work, but I never actually claimed the money. I eventually learned to weld vulnerable parts like suspension mountings very lightly, with very little penetration, so that when the inevitable prang occurred the parts would tear along the dotted line without wrenching great holes in the chassis tubes.

'There were two major problems with the VIII. One was the extreme stiffness of the chassis, which meant that it could not yield to distorting forces, but would break. The other was the use of high-tensile tube and brazed joints which, under stress, would break just outside the weld, even with ordinary road-going loads. The general

The first streamlined Lotus, the Mk VIII, seen here in the paddock at Goodwood, was built for the 1954 season. The chassis was a far advanced space frame of such ultimate design that the MG 1,500 cc engine had to be dismantled each time it was installed or removed, the cylinder head then being reassembled in situ. This was the first Lotus with a four-speed gearbox, hydraulic brakes and a de Dion rear suspension. Frank Costin designed the body and the car was extremely successful, enabling Colin to beat Hans Herrmann's works 550 Porsche in the sports car race that was the curtain-raiser to the 1954 British Grand Prix.

Colin Chapman with two of his most successful private customers, Mike Anthony and Peter Gammon (right), both of whom drove highly tuned Mk VIs. Although Anthony remained faithful to Lotus, and later bought a Bristol-engined Mk X, Gammon went on successfully to campaign one of the first Lola Mk I sports cars.

concept was good and the chassis weighed only 35 lb (16 kg), but the high failure rate and my consequent lack of sleep necessitated a rethink. The answer was to return to the Mk VI chassis frame with body hoops added to the Mk VIII shape. . .'

With the licence number SAR 5 the Mk VIII made a tremendous impression when it was unveiled. It boasted a de Dion rear suspension with inboard brakes while at the front there was still the tried and trusted swing-axle layout. The car was equipped with an MG 1,250 cc engine bored-out to 1,498 cc with a special alloy cylinder head which enabled it to develop 85 bhp, and as the entire car weighed only 10¼ cwt (1,148 lb/521 kg), it became – with the help of its very 'slippery' shape – the most potent 1,500 cc sports car in England, if not the world.

Its greatest success was, without doubt, the curtain-raiser race to the 1954 British Grand Prix at Silverstone on 17 July, when Colin won handsomely, beating the 'works' Porsche 550 of Hans Herrmann. Apart from anything else, this result proved two things: the Mk VIII was an extremely good car and Colin Chapman was rapidly becoming a most competent racing driver.

In order to race the works car without the costs bearing on the more commercial car-building side of the organization, Fred Bushell advised the setting up of an independent company, which in effect was the beginning of Team Lotus Ltd. Although the basic workforce remained the eleven enthusiastic amateurs, two of them later became permanent employees. Colin Bennett, who was appointed Team Manager and John Standen who, although initially taken on as a storeman, was to become Chief Buyer and then, for several years, a Director.

The Mk VIII, however, was not without its problems, the most serious being that the very advanced spaceframe was so devoid of compromises that it was virtually impossible to install or remove the engine in one piece. Because of the constrictions placed by the arrangement of the tubes, it was first necessary to dismantle the engine, install the crankcase and then re-assemble the cylinder head and accessories with the engine *in situ*. This was a quite unsatisfactory time-consuming state of affairs and one which made life extremely difficult for the Lotus mechanics.

Nevertheless, the Mk VIII was soon in great demand from other competitors and therefore, to make life easier for them, as Dave Kelsey has explained, a return was made to the Mk VI basic frame with the addition of more supporting tubes for the all-enveloping body shell. In all, eight Mk VIII Lotuses were built, for well-known drivers of the day such as John Coombs, Brian Naylor, Dan Margulies and 'Tip' Cunane. Most of these cars were fitted with MG engines, similar to that in Colin's 'works' car, although Coombs's had a Connaught engine.

Meanwhile, Colin continued to race his Mk VIII in an almost impossible schedule of events, demonstrating once again his enormous determination to achieve success as often as possible and at almost any cost. Towards the middle of the season, when he and Mike Costin began to take the car abroad to compete in foreign events, life became particularly hectic. Because he would have to be at his office until late on Friday afternoons, and back there again by Monday morning, they would have to drive the car – yes, on the road! – to the overnight cross-Channel ferry, practice on the Saturday, probably rebuild the engine during that night, race on the Sunday, drive back to the ferry that evening and Colin would have to be back sitting at his desk, at 9 am the following day!

One particular Bank Holiday weekend was even more feverish than usual. After competing at the Nürburgring in Germany on the Sunday, on Monday Colin managed to take in a sports car race at Brands Hatch, after which he *drove* SAR 5 to

On 16 October 1954 Colin Chapman married Hazel Williams at Northaw Church, in Hertfordshire. On the left of this wedding group is Hazel's father Vic with Colin's mother, and on the right is Stan Chapman with Hazel's mother. The Best Man was Colin's cousin Laurence Boxhall.

Above *At Colin and Hazel's wedding, the venerable Team Lotus transporter – an old single-decker bus – was pressed into service to convey Tottenham Lane guests to the church and reception. Besides the bride and groom sitting on the bonnet, and Hazel's father Vic Williams standing beside them, on the cab roof can be seen (clockwise) John Standen (in bowler hat), 'Nobby' Clark, Mike Costin and Fred Bushell. The destination board read 'The Last Lap'!*

Left *Colin talking with Frank Costin and Hazel in the garden of Gothic Cottage, their first home, while young daughter Jane concentrates on learning to drive.*

the Crystal Palace circuit, about twenty miles away, raced there until the engine blew up after a couple of laps, then returned to Brands where he borrowed another Lotus to compete in his fourth event at three different race meetings – one of which was several hundred miles away – in two days!

When John Bolster road-tested the Mk VIII for *Autosport* at the end of that season he found it had a top speed of 121.5 mph (195.5 kph) – a remarkable achievement from only 85 bhp – while it accelerated over a standing quarter-mile in 15.5 sec.

On 16 October 1954 Colin and Hazel somehow found time to be married at Northaw Church, near Cuffley, afterwards spending their honeymoon in Majorca. Colin had bought a new Ford Anglia to go away in after the reception only to find that the Lotus mechanics had plastered it with whitewash, toilet rolls, tin cans and such like. Colin gave five pounds to a car park attendant at Heathrow to clean it up for their return, but it was never quite the same again. Even on honeymoon they found there was no getting away from motor racing – racing driver Reg Bicknell was staying in the same hotel!

Then, towards the end of the year, Colin finally decided that, with the business really beginning to thrive and a very full order book for 1955, the time had come for him to give up his job at The British Aluminium Company and devote all his time to Lotus Engineering Company. His father was very upset when he heard of his son's decision. 'Stan had visions of Colin building bridges, railways and fantastic monuments and Colin wanted instead to build little cars,' recollects Hazel. 'There was a lot of friction between them because of it.' There is no doubt that he had been steadily encouraged in going this way by Fred Bushell, who had finally succeeded – as we have heard – in 'turning the club into a business'.

Mike Costin took the plunge, too, and left de Havilland and on 1 January 1955 he and Colin both started working full-time at Tottenham Lane. By then Colin and Hazel had bought a house, a small converted stable called Gothic Cottage in a very secluded position at Monken Hadley, near Barnet. Here he found the peace and quiet he needed to set up his drawing board and work late into the night on new designs.

Demand for the 'standard' Mk VI frame and 'kit' of parts was as high as ever and some people were wanting Mk VIIIs with larger engines while others felt that a streamlined car with a smaller engine would be just the thing. First then came the Mk IX, inspired by the original Mk VIII but with the simpler Mk VI type of space frame 'tidied-up' somewhat by using lighter gauge tubing in places, thus effecting some useful saving in overall weight.

The streamlined bodywork and tail fins were retained, both being similar to those of the Mk VIII except that the fins were taller and somewhat thicker although not so long. Mainly because of this the overall length of the Mk IX was also shorter. Whatever the official reasons stated at the time, Mike Costin remains adamant that it was simply to enable the car to fit into the available space in the 'transporter' – an old short-wheelbase double-decker bus – they had by then acquired!

The Mk IX made its debut in March 1955 and it was not long before several had been delivered to customers. Team Lotus – as they now called themselves – had plans to field two Mk IXs. One was to be fitted with the 1,500 cc MG unit out of the old Mk

VIII, which had by then been sold, while the second car was to be fitted with one of the new 1,100 cc FWA Coventry Climax engines. Basically, this was a development of a lightweight portable fire-pump engine originally commissioned from the Coventry Climax company by the Home Office. As far as its 'career' in motor racing is concerned, it had originally appeared in a Kieft competing in the 1954 Le Mans 24-Hours Race, where it did extremely well until the car broke its rear axle. It was not long before it was noticed by other small sports car manufacturers, such as Cooper and Lotus, so that Coventry Climax were eventually persuaded to develop the engine further by increasing its capacity to just under 1,100 cc, and to put in hand the production of a batch of 100 engines which were made available at a price of £250 each.

The FWA was really quite a remarkable engine. It was especially suited to racing as it was so light, simply because, in its original role, it had to be able to be carried by no more than two men. It also had an extraordinarily high power output because as a fire-pump engine it had to be capable of delivering 350 gallons of water every minute! The high performance was partly due to its single overhead camshaft, a somewhat unusual feature at the time.

In the late 1950s and '60s, under the Chairmanship of Leonard Lee – a great British patriot – and ably assisted by Wally Hassan, their Chief Engineer (and designer of the Jaguar XK engine) and Harry Mundy, another well-known engineer in the Midlands, Coventry Climax were to become one of the world's largest racing engine manufacturers.

To return to the two 'works' Mk IXs; the MG-engined car was to have lighter bodywork using magnesium alloy to help offset the weight of the cast-iron block. Colin was to drive this car while Peter Jopp – an ex-500 cc racing car driver – would, in exchange for some financial support, be entrusted with the 1,100 cc Climax-engined car.

In order to meet the increasing number of orders, Chapman just had to do something about the critical lack of space at Tottenham Lane. The problem was settled by Stan Chapman and Fred Bushell being persuaded to buy a piece of land adjacent to the existing property. This was then loaned to the company and an extension built on to the workshop which more than trebled the total working area.

At around the same time another separate company was formed. Called Racing Engines Ltd, its main purpose was to handle engine and gearbox development work under Mike Costin's guidance, but its great attraction to Fred Bushell was that it would make it possible to invoice parts sold to customers from two different sources, a most useful way of avoiding any problems with Purchase Tax!

With only one job to do now, Colin was at last able to relax a little and he was even able to employ a part-time draughtsman, Ivor Jones, who would work during the day at Gothic Cottage on the detail drawings from the sketches Colin had prepared for him the night before. Even though Colin was still the number one 'works' driver, this very necessary new tempo of life represented quite a change for him. Mike Costin, however, recalls this period in the company's growth as a sheer nightmare: 'It really was a case of survival. We lived on pills: the blue one to get going and the yellow one to go to sleep. I remember one night I was driving the transporter with Peter Jopp and in the dark I took the wrong pill.

'My wife never knew when I was coming home or when I was going to work. There was the famous occasion when she woke up one morning, saw me standing by the bed, half dressed and asked: "Are you coming or going?" This really was a 9 to 5 job – 9 am to 5 am!'

Hazel also remembers those busy days when they were first married and living at Gothic Cottage – working all hours during the week and racing virtually every weekend: 'When Colin was racing he had a favourite chequered shirt which he liked to wear. It was a dark green tartan thing which he called his "lucky" shirt. Every Monday I was allowed the morning off to do the washing, and I would rinse this shirt in some special fire-resistant stuff – Borax I think it was.'

In view of the publicity that always seemed to be generated by the Le Mans 24-Hours Race, Chapman decided it was time for a Lotus to put in an appearance there. He therefore sent off an entry – which was duly accepted – for an 1,100 cc Climax-engined Mk IX which was to be fitted with disc brakes. As co-driver he invited Ron Flockhart, the Scotsman who was destined to be the winner of the race in the two following years.

Unfortunately success eluded them. They started confidently enough and led the class initially, but were slowed later by clutch trouble. Then, during the night – and precisely where Don Beauman was digging out his D-type Jaguar – Colin spun off into the sandbank at Arnage. He was able to reverse out and rejoin the track but unhappily the marshal there reported the incident in such a way that the stewards disqualified him for 'having failed to wait for the marshal's permission to rejoin the track'. This was a bit ridiculous really but it should be remembered that this was 1955, the year of the dreadful accident in which Pierre Levegh's Mercedes plunged into the crowd in front of the grandstand, killing over 100 people. The race marshal was, quite understandably, probably over-excited but it was certainly not a good start to Chapman's relationship with the Automobile Club de l'Ouest, although Le Mans would soon prove to be the scene of the first international success of any magnitude for Lotus.

At the end of the season John Bolster was invited to road test the Mk IX and his report was even more interesting than usual to *Autosport* readers, because Colin lent him *both* 'works' cars so that it was possible to compare the differences between the two varieties of engine. The 1,500 cc gave the car a maximum speed of 128.6 mph (206.9 kph), 7.1 mph (11.4 kph) quicker than the Mk VIII, and covered the standing quarter mile in 15.4 sec, against 15.5 sec. The engine power was, more or less, the same but apart from the improved shape the car was considerably lighter. At 9 cwt (1,008 lb/458 kg) it weighed about 120 lb (54 kg) less than the Mk VIII.

Amazingly, the 1,100 cc-engined car had nearly the same power output – 81 bhp at 6,700 rpm – but a great deal less torque. As it was lighter by 60 lb (27 kg) it managed to achieve almost the same figures: 127.7 mph (205.5 kph) and 15.8 sec.

Bolster also gave high praise to the Girling disc brakes on this car. His only real criticism (and this was probably due to the very high-geared steering) was that the car tended to wander a bit at low speed until the driver became more familiar with the handling.

Left *Colin in his lucky check shirt.*

Below *Colin Chapman's first attempt at the Le Mans 24 Hours race was in 1955 in a Coventry Climax-engined Mk IX, fitted for this race with Girling disc brakes and co-driven by Ron Flockhart. They were disqualified when Colin went off into the sandbank at Arnage and then reversed out 'without asking permission from the marshals'. The officials were especially nervous that year because of the dreadful, tragic accident which had already cost the life of one driver and more than a hundred spectators.*

Right *In 1955 Colin had left his job at The British Aluminium Company to work full-time at Lotus. He was also the team's number one driver. John Standen is seen here attending to the tyre pressure of the Mk IX before practice for the Goodwood Nine Hours Race, while Colin is talking to John Eason-Gibson, who was acting as Team Manager. The Lotus led the 1,500 cc class at the seven-hour mark when the engine blew. On the right is another of the works drivers Ron Flockhart.*

During the season Chapman came up with a further modification to the original Mk VIII design in order to satisfy those customers who wanted to use larger engines. This became the Mk X, of which three examples were made – for Mike Anthony, Cliff Davis and Peter Scott-Russell – with a somewhat larger and modified engine compartment to accommodate the Bristol 2 litre engine which these drivers had chosen. Lotus lost an overseas Mk X customer when film star James Dean was killed in a road accident in the USA while driving his new Porsche Spyder. Dean had recently taken delivery of one, into which he was fitting an Offenhauser engine.

During the course of 1955, Lotus built 23 Mk IXs and four Mk Xs, whilst according to 'official' records the total number of Mk VIs had risen to 110. (This raises a question as to whether or not this is an accurate figure, since Dave Kelsey reported earlier that his company built about eighty Mk VI chassis.) It was also the year when Lotus first exhibited at the Motor Show, then always held at Earls Court, in London. However, because the company was not a full member of the Society of Motor Manufacturers and Traders (which is another story to come later) their display – a Mk IX in the form of a very highly polished chassis – was located among the accessory manufacturers. Fortunately the site of the stand was on the ground floor, not too far from the main entrance and fairly close to other, much larger, manufacturers, so their first Earls Court Motor Show proved an extremely successful venture.

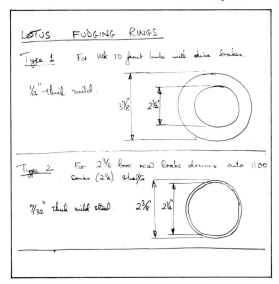

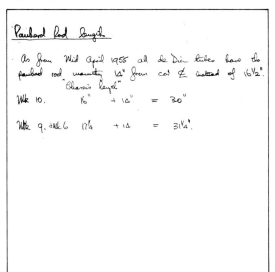

Four pages of notes and sketches applying to the Mk X Lotus and taken at random from an old notebook which Hazel Chapman recently discovered while this book was being researched.

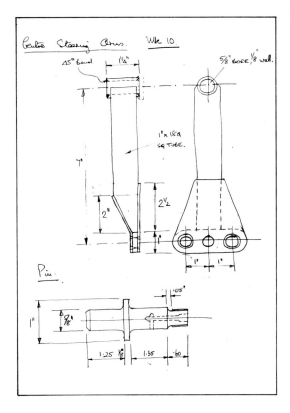

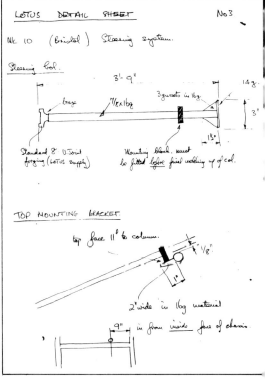

Chapter 5

The Eleven's Hour

By the end of the 1955 season Chapman had decided that he would not build any more Mk VIs, IXs or Xs but would concentrate all his still-modest resources on a new car. The Lotus Eleven was introduced to the sports car racing world in February 1956, and it set that world on fire! The frame of the 'Eleven' was a further development of Chapman's original fully triangulated space frame but its rigidity was greatly increased by the introduction of a fully stressed transmission tunnel. It retained the split-beam swing axle with coil spring and damper suspension but the steering was by rack and pinion.

The body, again the work of aerodynamicist Frank Costin, was highly streamlined but the fins over the rear wheels were much less pronounced than those on the three earlier models. High speed stability was therefore imparted by a large, beautifully shaped driver's headrest which really set the car apart from the others and this blended beautifully into the rear bodywork. Together with a wrap-around windscreen on the cockpit and flush-fitting headlamps set into the long front wings of the all-enveloping engine cover, the car simply looked terrific (and still does thirty years later!).

The standard engine was to be the FWA 1,100 cc Coventry Climax unit mated to a slightly modified Austin A30 four-speed gearbox, although some enthusiasts plumped for the larger FWB 1,500 cc engine which then, because of the greater torque, required a more robust gearbox of MG origin.

It would perhaps be as well to explain here why this car was always referred to as the Lotus 'Eleven', with the mark number spelt out. Up to this particular car, Lotus mark or type numbers had been designated in Roman numerals. Chapman felt that a change had to be made to Arabic figures because people would soon cease to understand the Roman characters as they grew longer! However, if the Arabic figure '11' was used to designate this next model, it was possible that some would confuse this with the Roman figure 'II'. Hence Lotus Eleven. At the same time "Mk" became "Type".

There were, in fact, three versions of this car: the 'Le Mans' model which had de Dion rear suspension and disc brakes all round, the 'Sports' with drum brakes and a live rear axle, and the 'Club' which was to the same specification as the 'Sports' except that it was fitted with the 1,172 cc Ford Ten side-valve engine, and was mainly intended for use in club and 1,172 Formula racing, or on the road.

Prices ranged from £872 for the 'Club', through £1,083 for the 'Sports' to £1,337 for the 'Le Mans'. Of course, these prices were free of the dreaded Purchase Tax because, at least for the home market, the cars were still sold in kit form. In fact, some consternation arose that year when the Government threatened to extend Purchase Tax to spare parts and kit cars in their forthcoming Budget that March. Happily, the threat was not carried through, principally due to the uproar from the motoring press, led by John Bolster of *Autosport*. If the Government had gone through with this proposal there is little doubt that it would have had a disastrous effect on the, by then, quite substantial British 'kit car' industry, amongst which Lotus was probably the most prominent company involved. One of the main factors for the Government's second thoughts was that export figures could have been seriously affected if the companies had been forced out of business due to a dwindling home market.

With the availability of the 1,100 cc Climax engine, the 1,100 sports car class was becoming tremendously popular in Britain – and abroad, too – and several other manufacturers were now eyeing this quite lucrative market. For the time being, though, Lotus's only serious rival was going to be Cooper with their central-seat rear-engined car.

I had decided to change my Mk VI for one of the new Eleven 'Sports' and Colin very kindly allowed me to build it at the Tottenham Lane workshop, under the guiding hand of one of the mechanics – Graham Hill. The thing I remember most about that week in the winter of 1956 was the extreme cold: it was said that it had not been so cold for a hundred years! Some of the Lotus mechanics had their cars parked nearby – mostly decrepit Austin Sevens, of course – and when it was time for them to go home it was usually so cold that they could be seen thawing out the brakes with the aid of a welding torch and with the Austins tilted over on to one side!

Every day we would all adjourn for lunch to a miserable little café close by the railway station. Wednesday was the BIG day because that was when *Autosport* was on sale and everyone would share the cost of one copy which was then passed around. The only talk – apart from motor racing – was about the nurses from the nearby hospital. In spite of the fact that everyone was very short of money, there was still tremendous enthusiasm and when I came to drive my newly completed car off into the night towards Dover, and back to my well-paid job in my nice warm office in Paris, I couldn't help but envy those lucky guys getting up every morning to do, unlike me, something they really loved.

Roy Badcock, who had joined Lotus full-time the year before, and who remained a faithful employee until after Colin's death 27 years later, still remembers the completion of the first Lotus Eleven:

'We finished building the prototype Series One Eleven during a wet Friday, early in 1956. After a test run around our local circuit, which incorporated Alexandra Park, Muswell Hill, a section of the North Circular Road and back to Tottenham Lane, Colin announced that he and Hazel were driving the new car to Brighton for the weekend. Thoughts of all the potential problems, even failures, went through my mind but, with a typical show of Chapman's complete confidence, they drove off into the rain and the night. The rain never let up during the entire weekend and it was with some relief that we saw Colin drive into the yard on the Monday morning. When asked what it was like, he grinned and said, "It gets a bit choppy round the ankles".'

Right and middle right *In 1955 Stan Chapman and Fred Bushell acquired a piece of land which was loaned to Lotus to build an extension to the original workshop in Tottenham Lane, Hornsey, thus trebling the floor area. These are two shots of the 'new' shop where Lotus Elevens are coming out 'on stream'.*

Right *Lotus Elevens under construction in the factory extension at Hornsey.*

Above In the paddock at Oulton Park in 1956. Colin is surrounded by (left to right) Mike Costin, who played such an important part in Lotus's story until he left in 1962, Cliff Allison and Reg Bicknell. Although the latter only enjoyed a year of works drives, Allison scored the first World Championship points for a Team Lotus driver two years later.

Below The three Lotus Elevens entered for the 1956 Le Mans 24 Hours, posing in front of the transporter before leaving for the Sarthe circuit. Left to right: the Chapman-Frazer 1,500 cc destined to blow its engine, the 1,100 cc of Bicknell-Jopp which finished seventh overall and first in the class, and the 1,100 cc of Allison-Hall which was forced to retire after hitting a large dog when travelling at high speed.

Colin was, of course, going to drive the works car again but this season his team partner was going to be Reg Bicknell, another ex-500 cc racing car driver turning to sports cars, who came from Southampton where he had a garage business. The Eleven became such a huge success that 200 of them were built and sold that year, the customers including some very famous drivers like Mike Hawthorn. In the rival small sports car 'camp' at Coopers were two others, Stirling Moss and Roy Salvadori, and the battles in some of the races were tremendous, with Colin often ending up the victor.

A three-car entry was sent in for that year's Le Mans 24-Hour Race and Colin asked me to make contact with the officials of the Automobile Club de l'Ouest to see if I could help smooth out any repercussions from the previous year's disqualification. I did the best I could and, in fact, the team put up a much better performance with Peter Jopp and Reg Bicknell sharing the 1,100 cc class-winning Climax-engined Eleven. Colin drove a 1,500 cc car with an American driver, Herbert Mackay ('Mac') Frazer, but they retired after twenty hours when a big-end bolt gave way. The third car, driven by Cliff Allison and Keith Hall, was forced to retire after nine hours' racing when Cliff hit a large dog while travelling at full speed down the Mulsanne Straight.

In September, Stirling Moss went to Monza with a specially prepared Lotus Eleven fitted with a bubble-top over the cockpit. He succeeded in breaking the International Class G speed records for 50 km and 50 miles, at 135.5 mph (218 kph) and 132.7 mph (214 kph), respectively. The attempt to go for further records had to be called off when the rear sub-frame fractured. Early the following month the car was again taken to Monza and this time, driven by 'Mac' Fraser, six new records were created, amongst which was once more the 50 km record which was pushed up to 138 mph (222 kph). The fastest lap was an incredible 143 mph (230 kph) – not bad for a car with an engine of only 1,100 cc! But 1956 was important for various other reasons, firstly the birth of Hazel and Colin's first daughter, Jane, and secondly the success of the new Vanwall Formula 1 racing car which raced in Grands Prix during the season and owed much to Colin Chapman's genius.

The late David Yorke, then the Vanwall Team Manager, told me in an interview many years later, and only a few months before he died at a relatively early age: 'In 1955, the chassis then in use in the Vanwall was derived from the Cooper. It was what one called a "ladder" chassis, and it had not been very successful. Colin was into space frame chassis and at Vanwall we had no engineer with the slightest clue about this. However, it so happened that our truck driver, a man named Derek Wooton, was an old friend of Colin's from the early Austin Seven days and he introduced him to Tony Vandervell.

'Colin came to our racing shop in Acton and he literally scribbled a rough sketch for our engineers and explained to them the principles of the space frame. For the rear suspension he advised us on a Watts linkage location for the de Dion axle.'

While he was at it, Colin also suggested to Vandervell that he knew just the chap who would design a beautifully streamlined body for the car. This just happened, of course, to be Frank Costin! 'It was a friendly deal,' said Yorke, 'and he certainly put us on the road to success. We would have been struggling if we hadn't had this introduction to space frames and modern suspension.' So from then on the Vanwall

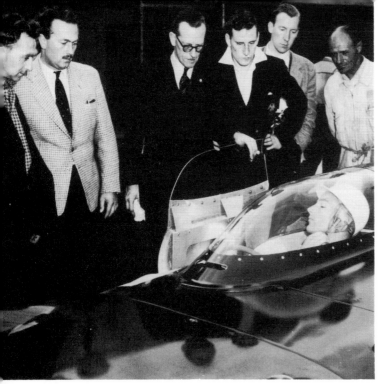

Left Colin is here seen talking to chief mechanic Willie Griffith while Stirling Moss makes himself comfortable in the streamlined 1,100 cc car in which he successfully attempted international records at Monza in September 1956. The car managed 135.5 mph (218 kph) before the rear sub-frame fractured. Later the same year 'Mac' Frazer pushed this figure up to 138 mph (222 kph) in the same car.

Middle left and left The skid marks on the road at Thillois, and the damaged signpost, after the brakes had locked on the Vanwall in which Chapman was practising at Rheims for the 1956 French Grand Prix. Unfortunately it could not be repaired in time so Colin never actually drove in a Grand Prix race.

was raced with a Chapman-inspired chassis and a Costin-designed body.

Although, almost certainly, some money did change hands in return for the Vandervell work, the deal was mainly of interest to Colin because he could see it as a ticket into Formula 1 racing, which had now become one of his burning ambitions. Indeed, his new-found friendship with Vandervell went one stage further when he was presented with the opportunity of actually driving a Vanwall in a race, and an important one at that.

The Vanwall drivers for 1956 were Harry Schell and Maurice Trintignant, but for the French Grand Prix to be held at Rheims on 1 July Trintignant was committed to drive the new rear-engined Bugatti. As Vandervell wanted to enter three cars – the other driver being Mike Hawthorn – he was on the lookout for a substitute driver. Stirling Moss, who was very friendly with Tony Vandervell, suggested he should approach either 'Taffy' von Trips or Colin Chapman, whose skill Moss had witnessed at first hand whilst racing against him in the Cooper. Vandervell – another great patriot – declined to employ a German driver, so Colin was invited to try the car at Goodwood, after which he was nominated as the third driver.

Unfortunately, while practising for the race at Rheims, a brake locked up and he ran into the back of another car . . . that of his team-mate Mike Hawthorn! Both cars were extensively damaged and there was only sufficient time to repair one car for the race which had to be Hawthorn's, as he was the senior driver. In the event itself, Harry Schell's car was retired on the sixth lap so he took over Hawthorn's car, but after a brilliant performance, holding fourth place for many laps while in pursuit of Fangio, this car also succumbed on the 56th lap. However, there was little doubt that, from then on, the 'Chapman-Costin Vanwall' was going to be a force to be reckoned with in Grand Prix racing.

If this unfortunate situation had not arisen, Colin would almost certainly have made his Grand Prix debut. No further opportunity ever presented itself, and when he went into Formula 1 racing with his own cars he had long since given up competing seriously.

Another notable milestone for Colin Chapman in 1956 was when he made the decision to design and build his first out-and-out single-seater racing car – of 1,500 cc capacity in order to qualify for the new Formula 2 which was to be introduced the following year. One factor which influenced this decision so much was that he had for some time been very critical of the international rules which governed sports car racing and of the constant changes which were being made every year. This, in his view, seriously marred the sports class and, ultimately, nearly destroyed it.

I have a letter from Colin, dated 22 November 1955, in which he writes: '. . . I am absolutely mortified at the Le Mans regulations insisting on a 50 cm width for the seat. This strikes me as absolutely ridiculous as I have measured my armchairs at home and these are only 18 in instead of the required 20 in!' He really envied the apparent stability of the various single-seater racing formulae, and was therefore only too pleased to snatch this opportunity to build a suitable car.

There was, however, one other – and for him most interesting – design job he tackled that year. Duly impressed by the improvements which Colin had effected to the Vanwall the previous winter, BRM asked him if he could do a similar job for

Colin Chapman was first awarded the Ferodo Gold Trophy in 1956, for his '. . . contribution towards the advancement of the design of a British Grand Prix racing car' – the Vanwall – that year. On the left is John Eason-Gibson, then Secretary of the British Racing Drivers Club, who presented the trophy. In the centre is the Managing Director of Ferodo Limited, who have always been great supporters of motor racing.

them, and it was not long before he had evolved a new rear suspension and put the car on coil spring and damper units all round. By way of payment he was very happy to accept a Raymond Mays-converted Ford Zephyr, which added even more zest and gusto to his already fairly frantic style of road driving! Besides being Team Manager of BRM, Raymond Mays – who was a very well-known former racing and hill-climb driver – also ran a production car engine conversion and tuning business, and the 2½ litre Ford Zephyr of the day was one of his 'specialities'. It is perhaps worth noting that Chapman was then in the position of having played some part in the design of two of the three existing British Formula 1 racing cars!

Chapman wanted to reveal the new Formula 2 car as part of a much expanded display at the London Motor Show in October but, before he could do so, it was necessary for Lotus to be accepted as full members of the Society of Motor Manufacturers and Traders. This meant they had to prove to the Society that they were fully-fledged car manufacturers, otherwise they would again have been allocated a much smaller space amongst the accessory companies. Colin wanted a proper stand alongside all the big car manufacturers, and was virtually prepared to stop at nothing to get it, as Dave Kelsey recalls: '. . . Colin had been trying for some time to get into the Motor Show (as a manufacturer) and eventually the SMM&T agreed to inspect his factory as a prelude to letting him in. Colin had no factory, so we (Progress Chassis Co, at the other end of the building) were nominated to be part of Lotus for the day! I have often wondered what the powers-that-were in the motor trade thought as they compared our shed with Jaguar. We must have made some impression because Lotus did get into the show and we built a super Eleven for the occasion, finished in grey stove enamel with chromed bits everywhere. I think King Hussein bought the Show car . . .'

In fact, besides that rather special and beautifully upholstered 'road' car, and the Formula 2 car – which was actually fitted with a dummy engine and gearbox! – the display also included another sports-racing Eleven. It was quite a show for the little company. The new single-seater was called the 12 and what a tiny machine it turned out to be. Shaped like a cigar, it was really rather an ugly duckling but, as was only to be expected, it was bristling with innovations.

Contrary to the rival Formula 2 Cooper, the engine was still in front of the driver, as with the sports cars. It was the entirely new 1,500 cc four-cylinder Coventry Climax FPF, for Leonard Lee – the Chairman of Coventry Climax – had agreed to carry on playing Godfather to British racing car manufacturers. When the new Formula 2 rules had been announced, he authorized Chief Engineer Hassan to come up with something good. In fact Wally did not have to look very far. He had already been commissioned by Lee to design a 2,500 cc V8 engine suitable for use in a Grand Prix car, and although this engine, designated the 'FPE', developed 264 bhp – as competitive a figure as any of the Formula 1 cars of the day – the project was shelved. However, it was to have its uses eventually, for Wally Hassan decided that the easiest and cheapest way to produce a 1,500 cc 'four' would obviously be to use one of the banks from the V8 engine. This is precisely what he did, but with some modifications to dimensions and cylinder measurements in order to produce the necessary swept volume. This engine, which became known as the 'FPF', immediately gave 141 bhp.

It was mated with a five-speed trans-axle gearbox unit, specially designed by Richard Ansdale, which enabled the prop-shaft to be set low down in the frame and to pass under the driver's seat.

One rather unsatisfactory feature of the unit was that, with the changing of gears being effected through a lever operating in a quadrant, the driver would, for instance, be unable to change straight down from fourth to second gear on braking. The system was similar, in effect, to changing gear on a motor cycle.

Obviously, the chassis of the new car was again a space frame but at the front was a brand-new design of double-wishbone suspension. A typical Chapman weight-saving detail was that the roll-bar also acted as a locating link to the top wishbone! At the rear was a de Dion axle and two disc brakes fitted inboard up against the final drive axle casing. Another novel – and at the time unique – feature was the specially made light alloy wheels, the centres of which had a curiously 'wobbly' pattern: yet another example of the clever Chapman approach to obtaining maximum rigidity with minimum weight. Contrary to the then-current single-seater practice, these wheels were not secured with the usual large-eared single knock-on locking nut but with six normal studs and small wheel nuts. These, of course, were very much lighter and again helped to keep unsprung weight to an absolute minimum, and Chapman reasoned that wheels would never require changing in the middle of a short F2 race. The overall weight of this little car was an amazing 660 lb (299 kg) and with the 140+ bhp expected from the engine – giving a power-to-weight ratio of over 450 bhp per ton – it would surely produce an extremely impressive performance.

Unfortunately, this first pure Lotus racing car never performed well. Very soon after the prototype had been tested, Chapman decided to replace the de Dion rear axle and suspension with what became known as the 'Chapman Strut' system. Continuing his role as an innovator, Colin came up with a suspension design which, in simple terms, consisted of three basic elements: a single forward-facing radius rod, a long coil spring and telescopic damper unit and the half-shaft itself which, besides transmitting the drive, also provided the lateral location of the rear wheel. With the consequent reduction in both overall and unsprung weight and the better roadholding due to the much improved rear wheel geometry, the system proved most satisfactory.

A total of eight of these Lotus 12s was built, but during 1957 not one scored a single victory. The car's major weakness was that special gearbox which continually gave trouble and which the wags at Lotus quickly dubbed the 'queerbox'. Facing up to the problem, Colin decided that he must find an engineer capable of taking over the responsibility of looking after gearbox development. The engineer would be given a special part of the factory in which to carry out his work and it would be called 'the Fine Limits Engineering Shop'. In fact, it turned out to be a wooden shed in the Tottenham Lane yard!

The engineer Colin selected for this new and important post was a young and enthusiastic Mk VI owner, another part-time helper who had been working at Lotus during his holidays from Imperial College, London, where he was an engineering student. He started full-time work – in the shed – immediately after his graduation in 1957. His name was Keith Duckworth.

Although the 12 was not proving successful, on the sports car front matters were much better. The Eleven had been updated and, while under normal circumstances it should have qualified for an entirely new type number, Colin – who could be somewhat superstitious at times – decided it should be called the Lotus Eleven Series 2. The most important modification over the earlier model was the introduction of the wishbone front suspension, first evolved for the Type 12 single-seater. Many examples of the new model were being raced in England and, in their classes, they were proving virtually unbeatable.

Altogether, seventy of these Series 2 cars were built, making a total of 270 of both types. This quantity was sufficient to enable me, at Colin's request and through my contacts with members of the Commission Sportive Internationale (the motor sporting division of the Fédération Internationale de l'Automobile, the governing body based in Paris) to apply for the Lotus Eleven to be homologated in the Grand Touring class for international sports car racing. This class was much more popular on the Continent at the time and the acceptance of the car enabled Lotus to sell several more examples to owners in France, where they were soon trouncing the opposition, most of which came from the drivers of Alfa Romeo Giuliettas who were absolutely furious. In fact, they were so incensed that they succeeded in having the Team Lotus entries excluded from the 12-Hours of Rheims race by lodging a protest saying that they had arrived for the evening start half-an-hour after the time prescribed in the regulations.

The reason for the Team being late, as I recall, was that one of the drivers, Cliff Allison, had suffered a minor accident in his road car in the town of Rheims and had been promptly put in jail! Not only that, but another of the drivers, the American Jay Chamberlain, had been quite badly injured in a practice accident. Colin, having to rush about between police station and hospital, had quite understandably overlooked the time. In my position as 'trouble-shooter' for Team Lotus when they were in France, I should really have been there to sort things out on the spot. Unfortunately, this was not possible because at that time I was still managing my family's department stores in Paris and, since Saturday was always a very busy day, I could not leave until after closing time. When I eventually arrived at the circuit with the race well under way I was very surprised to find that there were no Team Lotus cars running.

In fact, the entire weekend was a disaster for Lotus because on the Sunday morning, as a curtain-raiser to the Grand Prix, a Formula 2 race was held in which another American Lotus driver, 'Mac' Frazer, tragically lost his life at the wheel of the 1,500 cc twin-cam Climax-engined Eleven. It had been decided to enter this car instead of the single-seater because its all-enveloping streamlined bodywork made it so suitable for the ultra-high speed circuit at Rheims.

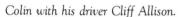

Colin with his driver Cliff Allison.

Colin apparently in deep discussion with the Le Mans scrutineers – or perhaps treating them to some of the persuasive Chapman 'flannel'!

The Eleven Series 2 fitted with a 750 cc FWC Climax engine was the first Lotus to score an important international win, the Index of Performance classification at the 1957 Le Mans 24 Hours. The car was driven by Cliff Allison and Keith Hall.

Success in the 1957 Le Mans race was completed with the class win scored by the Eleven Series 2 driven by the Americans 'Mac' Frazer and Jay Chamberlain. They were originally entered in a 1,500 cc twin-cam FPF-engined Eleven, but Colin blew up its engine in practice – in which, incidentally, he had proved quicker than his professional drivers! Jay and 'Mac' took over the Ashdown-Stacey 1,100 cc car.

'Mac' about to jump into the cockpit of the class winner.

Everything is shipshape in the Le Mans pits, waiting for refuelling time. Colin is standing on the left of the timekeeper's team led by Ian Smith, ex-Lotus driver, founder of the original Club Lotus and author of the first book to be published about Lotus.

Victory lane at Le Mans. Cliff Allison answers a question from a journalist in the foreground while Keith Hall talks to Colin. Behind Cliff are the brothers Costin – Mike in overalls and Frank in glasses.

Colin's Ford Consul and the team outside the Auberge Saint Nicholas, in Mayet, where Team Lotus stayed for the Le Mans race from 1955 until 1962. Colin and Hazel are standing with Monsieur Mica, the owner, and his family. Ian Smith is next to him and then Peter Ashdown, Jay Chamberlain, Alfred Woolf (who was doing some PR work for Lotus), Cliff Allison, John Lawry (a member of the signalling team, who later won the Auto-sport Championship in a Lotus), Alan Stacey and Keith Hall.

The Index-winning car was built with light gauge material and therefore it was no surprise that its panelling was rather crumpled at the end of the day! (There are some well-known faces amongst the hordes of people surrounding the car. Note Graham Hill – in cap – on the far right, for instance.)

Lotus headquarters during the week of the 24 Hours, the bar of the Auberge Saint Nicholas. Left to right, Alan Stacey, Peter Ashdown, Ian Lawry, Colin, Jay Chamberlain and Hazel celebrate their success with champagne.

After the race, while organizing poor 'Mac's' funeral, I remember there were some rather heated exchanges between Colin and the famous and somewhat volatile 'Toto' Roche, the organizer and Clerk of the Course at Rheims. Having already had the task of pacifying the Le Mans organizers after Colin's incident in 1955, it was very obvious I would have to exercise considerable diplomacy in the future to get Roche back on Lotus's side! It was an especially sad time, and a severe shock for Colin, because 'Mac' was the first driver to be killed in a 'works' Lotus. However, I do recall one bright moment which did much to cheer him up when, on the drive back to Paris in Colin's Ford after the funeral, we suddenly came across an enthusiastically driven small silver sports car on British registration plates: amazingly, it was the original Mk III Austin Seven-engined 750 Formula car.

On the other hand, at Le Mans one week earlier things had gone much better. In an effort to win the much-coveted and highly rewarding 'Index of Performance' prize, Colin wanted to enter an FWA-engined Eleven, the capacity of which had been reduced to a mere 745 cc. As most French sports cars of the period were either Panhards or DBs propelled by the 750 cc twin-cylinder Panhard engine, the formula used to calculate the Index of Performance very much favoured these small cars, so there was at least always the strong prospect of one success in the race that would please the French public. Therefore it was not going to be very easy for me to persuade the organizers to accept an entry from a foreign 750 cc car specially produced simply to carry off their 'own' prize!

Using considerable diplomacy, I eventually succeeded in obtaining an entry by simply offering a drive in one of the 'works' 1,100 cc cars to two local French drivers, Héchard and Masson. As a matter of interest, as Colin put the management of this car into my hands, I nominated Graham Hill as reserve driver, thus enabling him to drive 'their' car in practice when he lapped much faster than either of the two Frenchmen. During the race, though, these two put up a very respectable performance by finishing in 16th place overall. In fact, Roger Masson quite excelled himself, his picture appearing on the front page of every French daily newspaper when, having run out of fuel at Mulsanne, he pushed the car the three miles or more back to the pits, not surprisingly collapsing from exhaustion on arrival and suffering from severely blistered feet!

In the event, the 750 cc Lotus driven by Cliff Allison and Keith Hall romped home in 14th place overall and walked away with the Index of Performance, a victory which ensured a tremendous amount of publicity everywhere since Le Mans was then, even more so than it is now, probably the most important motoring event in the world. In fact, it is perhaps interesting to note that this 750 cc car was really only suitable for Le Mans and was only entered in one other motor race, at Rouen the following week-end, which it won. Coventry Climax produced the engine – known as the FWC – at the special request of Chapman. To save the time and trouble they simply shortened the stroke of the basic 1,100cc engine so that the cylinders were very much over-square. The cylinder head was a perfectly standard one with the normal port size, which was really much too large for the engine's displacement. Although it was finally coaxed into giving 59bhp at 8,000rpm, there was virtually no power below 6,000rpm. However, it was very fast, the organizers timing it on the Mulsanne Straight at 114mph (183kph),

Left *The transporter with the class-winning 1,100 cc car on the trailer in front of the Auberge on the Monday morning after the 1957 Le Mans race.*

Below left *A shot of the winning drivers taken at the castle where the prize-giving took place. Left to right, Keith Hall, 'Mac' Frazer, Cliff Allison and Jay Chamberlain, plus 'attendants'.*

comparing very favourably with the 128 mph (206 kph) achieved by the 1,100 cc car.

Colin had been much less busy at the wheel this season and at Le Mans had confined himself to the role of Team Manager. However, always being one to expect the unexpected, he did take his crash helmet along and it was perhaps very fortunate for 'Mac' Fraser and Jay Chamberlain that it was Colin at the wheel of the 1,500 cc (a twin-cam Formula 2 engine) Eleven when it dropped a valve in practice after lapping quicker than his two drivers! This car was therefore a non-starter, but luckily 'Mac' and Jay were able to take over the wheel of another 1,100 in which they won the class easily, covering over 209 miles (336 km) more than yet another 1,100-engined Lotus Eleven driven by Walshaw and Dalton. They ran a total distance of 2,378 miles (3,827 km) in the 24 hours at an average speed of 99.1 mph (159 kph).

The celebrations lasted several days and on the following Tuesday the entire team adjourned to the famous 'Crazy Horse Saloon' in Paris's Avenue George V, where one of the mechanics just finally had to give in, falling asleep during the show and finishing up on the floor! Meanwhile, Colin had the comforting thought of the large pile of bank notes, tucked safely away under the mattress back at my flat!

Chapter 6

Birth of the Elite

Lotus returned to Monza for another record attempt at the end of the 1957 season. This time the streamliner was equipped with supercharged versions of the 1,100 cc FWA engine for Cliff Allison and the very same ex-Le Mans 750 cc engine, when I was to drive it. The thinking behind this move was that the existing 750 cc one-hour class record was held by a Frenchman, Pierre Chancel, driving a Panhard and it was thought that our sponsors, Esso, might be a little more generous if the record was taken by another Frenchman, since this would provide more potential for advertising in France. As it turned out, the 750 cc FWC engine blew up on me due to a carburation defect, so that was the end of my one and only 'works' drive! As for Cliff Allison, he also had mechanical problems, so this particular attempt ended in failure. In fact, he returned to Monza in December when he succeeded in taking 'Mac's' 50 km (31 miles) record at 141.9 mph (228.4 kph) with a fastest lap of 145.5 mph (234.2 kph).

Colin Chapman did not go to Monza. He was far too busy preparing for the London Motor Show at Earls Court, where he was planning to introduce two entirely new models – the Type 14 and a replacement for the 'old' Mk VI at the bottom of the market which was to be called the Lotus Seven. The Type 14 was the legendary Lotus Elite, the introduction of which proved to be a milestone in the company's history, since it was the first time that Lotus marketed a road car aimed at their more affluent potential customers.

Colin had great hopes for the new car. His dream was to build a fast Grand Tourer which could be used quite normally on the roads, but which would also be capable of winning its class in both the Le Mans 24-Hours race and the Monte Carlo Rally. It is perhaps surprising that, considering the success he was then enjoying with the pure racing cars, he was still prepared to become involved with all the inherent problems

Above right *In 1957 another record-breaker was produced, which could be fitted with alternative supercharged Coventry Climax engines. The author (seen here) drove the 750cc version which blew its engine, while Cliff Allison drove the car fitted with the 1,100 cc engine.*

Right *The engine of the record-breaker showing the supercharger driven by three belts from the end of the crankshaft.*

Far right *The peculiar gearchange of the 1957 Monza record-breaking car. It used the Formula 1 5-speed gearbox in order to give greater freedom of gear ratio choice with the two engines of different capacities which were employed in the attempt.*

In the wake of success, Colin aspired to drive a prestige saloon car on the road as the Lotus Elite was really too small for his family. He managed to acquire a Mk II 3.8 Jaguar, the keys to which are here being handed over by 'Lofty' England, Jaguar's Managing Director and also Team Manager. Colin had by then stopped driving his own cars in racing but occasionally he piloted a tuned Jaguar with great zest in British saloon car events.

that were likely to be created by manufacturing and marketing a road car, such as arranging dealership networks, spare parts supply, warranties and so on. However, the sale of competition cars is generally a seasonal activity and Fred Bushell, who by then was assuming more and more of the responsibility for running the company, suggested that if Colin wanted to build up a sound established business, and yet continue to design and race motor cars, then some variation from pure racing cars would have to be offered to a more general market.

Did Colin aspire to become an established car manufacturer? 'No,' says Fred Bushell, 'he just wanted to go racing. With anything I ever suggested, if it was a way in which a full-time business could afford to have a racing side, then that was all right. Colin never changed his views about this; the selling of racing cars or road cars had to provide the foundations upon which he could achieve his own racing ambitions.'

It was clear that the size of the production run planned for the Elite would never warrant the high costs of tooling-up for a pressed-steel chassis and body construction. On the other hand, the then-current Lotus technique of alloy panels riveted to steel tubes would not only be expensive but also extremely impractical for a road car. Chapman had therefore investigated the possibilities of using a glass-fibre reinforced resin-bonded structure. This technique was then being applied mostly only to boats, although some car manufacturers – notably Fiat and DB Panhard – had already tried it.

Colin had hated chemistry while at school but he tackled the science of plastics in his usual thorough fashion, learning rapidly by reading all the books, magazines and technical papers he could get his hands on, and by attending lectures and seminars on the subject. He soon decided that he would design and build the Elite almost entirely in plastic with only the few vital steel elements, such as body hoops and sub-frames, encased in the glass-fibre to serve as mounting points for the engine, transmission and suspension. This was where his knowledge and experience of structural engineering proved of real value to him.

Having settled that, the next thorny problem was choosing the most suitable power unit. This was not easy because there was no mass-produced engine available which could provide him with the kind of power-to-weight ratio that he was seeking. Finally, he succeeded in persuading Leonard Lee to build a specially enlarged version of the FWA Coventry Climax engine which had proved so successful in the Lotus Eleven. It used the cylinder block and bore of the FWB engine but the shorter stroke of the FWA, so that the resulting displacement was 1,216 cc. This engine became known as the FWE. Unfortunately, the power output of 75 bhp was somewhat limited by the small displacement and yet the price of this all-alloy engine was high by production car standards. Thus the Elite, despite its many other qualities, was somewhat down on performance considering its relatively high price.

A further problem which arose was excessive interior noise. Because Chapman had virtually no experience of building road cars, where major manufacturers spend years developing prototypes especially to avoid the dreaded 'NVH' (Noise, Vibrations, Harshness), he never gave those matters a thought and the construction process he had chosen generated an extremely high interior noise level. There was nothing to absorb vibrations, and road noises were 'telephoned' through the plastic where they were amplified so that the body resonated like the sound box of a violin! However, the Lotus Elite did have two things going for it. The first was its race-bred suspension which used the coil springs and wishbones at the front and the 'Chapman Strut' at the rear that had originally been developed for the Type 12 single-seater. As a result of this and the splendid rigidity of the body shell, coupled with the almost perfect weight distribution, the car handled beautifully, and driving it was the nearest thing to driving a racing car. It was indeed 'a racing car for the road'.

The second thing that the Elite had going for it, and which was more readily visible, was its breath-taking shape, which was years ahead of its time. In the design of the body Colin had worked very closely with Peter Kirwan-Taylor – later to become a director of the company – who, although a financier by profession, had become deeply interested in sports car design when, as a student, he had bought a Mk VI Lotus to which he had fitted a fully-enveloping body of his own design. Colin had been very impressed by its lines and, having become friendly with Kirwan-Taylor, the two worked closely together on the Elite. Frank Costin was also brought in to look at the aerodynamics and the somewhat chopped-off tail was due primarily to his influence. The resulting shape was not only extremely handsome but, with a Cd (drag co-efficient) of only 0.29, was also very efficient.

In order to build the prototype Elite with some measure of secrecy, as well as to help the acute shortage of space at Hornsey, Colin had rented a small workshop in nearby Edmonton, and on one occasion when I was in England he took me along

In 1957 a 'showroom' was incorporated in an extension at the front of the Hornsey premises. The Elite on display here is the Earls Court show model which, in fact, was a mock-up. After a few months the windows were papered over and the area became an extra office.

there to have a look at the mock-up. I remember that the car was being worked on by three men he had 'pirated' from Ford: John Frayling, Ron Hickman* and Peter Campbell. I remember, too, that in typical Lotus fashion this excursion into the future, so to speak, was brought to a conclusion by us all adjourning to the nearby café for the traditional meal of fish and chips – and a deep discussion about cars!

Colin's original – and somewhat ambitious – plans for this car had called for it to be ready in time to run at the 1957 24-Hours Le Mans race, for which I had secured an entry, but many delays made that quite impossible. It was only by the burning of much midnight oil by a small team of workers, led by Graham Hill, that the prototype 14 was ready to make its appearance at the Earls Court Motor Show. Needless to say, it made a tremendous impression with press and public alike, and the publicity value of this launch to Lotus was enormous.

Tentative orders for the new car were so good, both at home and in the States, where Jay Chamberlain was the main distributor, that it was quite obvious that a new factory would have to be found or built before the Elite could be manufactured in any quantity, and a search began for a suitable site or premises in the area. Meanwhile a small brick office block had been built on to the 'stable' at 7 Tottenham Lane, on the ground floor of which was a small showroom just large enough to accommodate one car on display. Into this went the prototype Elite straight after the show, but it was not long before the front windows were papered over and the car removed in bits so that the showroom could be used as an extra office. Space really was at a premium by then.

Earls Court 1957 had, however, brought another surprise: the return of the Mk VI

---

* Ron Hickman later became famous, and made a fortune, as the inventor and designer of the Black & Decker 'Workmate' portable bench.

in the shape of the new Seven, looking very much like its forerunner although, in the interests of standardization, fitted with the same front suspension as the Elite. The frame was, in effect, a simplified version of that used in the Eleven and the rear axle was now a proprietary unit from the Standard 10 production saloon of that time.

Since the demise of the Mk VI in the year before, Chapman had been besieged with a stream of requests for a similar replacement car, much cheaper than the Eleven and perhaps more adapted towards club racing, where the Eleven's all-enveloping bodywork design was more susceptible to minor damage which was expensive to repair. This was one of the contributing factors towards the rear wings, nose cone and later the front wings being made from glass-fibre instead of the aluminium cycle-type mudguards at first fitted, to provide better weather protection for touring purposes.

The very first Lotus Seven originally had the stalwart Ford 1,172 cc engine and the basic car was offered at a price of £587 in kit form, which was considered at that time to be extremely good value for money. However, as always, some customers felt they wanted to fit more powerful engines, so before long the FWA Climax-engined Super Seven was introduced. Eventually Super Sevens appeared with all manner of engines, and even some with de Dion rear axles, so that there became both a 'Series 2' and a 'Series 3' model, and then, in 1970, even a 'Series 4'! By that time, the Lotus Seven was being manufactured and marketed by a separate subsidiary company called Lotus Components Ltd but eventually, in 1973 when Colin decided to wind up that company, the manufacturing rights to the car were sold to Graham Nearn, a Lotus dealer in Caterham, Surrey.

Initially Nearn marketed the 'Series 4' version but he was soon to find out that it was the 'Series 3' with the original look which the enthusiasts really wanted. Believe it or not, the car is still being produced today under the name 'Caterham Super Seven' and, thanks to Graham Nearn's efforts, the total number of Sevens built is pushing 5,000! Indeed, it is conceivable that this model, having now been in existence for 29 years, could happily continue in production – regulations permitting – for several more decades. The continuing demand is such that delivery still takes several months, thus encouraging imitators, but of course the 'real' Seven only comes from Caterham. In fact, it was the Lotus Seven, in its first few years of production, which was the key element in Chapman and Lotus staying in business.

This was especially true in 1958, which proved to be a somewhat unsuccessful year, during which Colin introduced the Lotus 15, a sports-racing car designed to accommodate the larger engines that were becoming available. Initially, the car was designed with its Coventry Climax FPF twin-cam engine canted over to the right in the chassis at an angle of 62 degrees in order to reduce the frontal area. This proved somewhat unsatisfactory as the engine failed to produce its full power and so they had to revert to a more upright position by reducing the angle to about 17 degrees. On top of this the 15 was equipped with the same 'queerbox' as the single-seater and, although improvements had been made since it was first introduced, it was still not man enough for the job and proved difficult to maintain, especially for private owners. Although the 15 did quite well in the shorter 'sprint' races so popular in Britain, it was never a force to be reckoned with in international long-distance events. Nevertheless some thirty examples were built.

Above *'You're pulling my leg!' Porsche's Team Manager, Huschke von Hanstein, with two of his drivers at Le Mans – Jean Behra (left) and Richard von Frankenberg (right). The latter, who became a journalist, was later involved in a controversy over the capacity of the Team Lotus Formula Junior engines and lost a £1,000 bet with Colin.*

Left *Colin with Aston Martin's Team Manager, Reg Parnell, at Le Mans. On the right is Jay Chamberlain, Team Lotus driver and also one-time Lotus Cars distributor in the United States.*

Above right *Colin Chapman about to embark on a tuning session at the wheel of the author's Eleven Series 2 which was entered for the 1958 Le Mans 24 Hours with a 750 cc FWMA engine, forerunner of the Hillman Imp unit. On the left is Peter Windsor-Smith of Coventry Climax, next to Willie Griffith and the author.*

Two 15s were entered for the 1958 Le Mans 24-Hour race: a 2-litre for Graham Hill (by then promoted to a team driver) and Cliff Allison, and a 1,500 cc version for Jay Chamberlain and another American, Pete Lovely. Team Lotus also entered an 1,100 cc Eleven for Innes Ireland and Mike Taylor, and a fourth car, fitted with a brand-new FWMA 750 cc single-cam Coventry Climax unit, for Alan Stacey and Tom Dickson. This used an entirely different block, smaller and lighter than the basic FWA, derived from a project for a four-stroke outboard boat engine.

Colin was extremely keen to develop a car for this class of racing, so popular on the Continent, and for some months he had kept me busy running round trying to find in France a suitable cheap five-speed trans-axle and gearbox unit, but to no avail. This 750 cc Eleven was also supposed to have a strut-type suspension – or so said the entry form I sent in to the Automobile Club de l'Ouest! Hindsight proved that Colin was already working on the design for a car to replace the Eleven and which ultimately became the Lotus 17. I was particularly interested in this car from a personal point of view because I had bought one myself, also fitted with the 750 cc FWMA engine. (I remember I paid £1,264 10s 0d – £1,264.50 – less engine of course, that was lent by Coventry Climax, but minus a twenty per cent 'friendly' discount!) It was entered for Héchard and Masson to drive, our French team from the previous year. There was also a fifth car, an 1,100 cc Eleven for private entrants Bob Hicks and Bill Frost.

All the Le Mans entries were fitted with bodywork best described as having a 'high tail' configuration intended to improve the streamlining. They also sported a tonneau cover which was, in effect, an inflated cushion, the object of which was to prevent the cover flapping and drumming in the air stream. I remember it attracted a great deal of attention in the paddock as again it was an ingenious loophole around

Colin at his drawing board in Gothic Cottage, with Hazel and their youngest daughter Sarah.

the rule which forbade covering the passenger space, for aerodynamic purposes, with a rigid fairing which would prevent the driver from ducking down inside the cockpit in the event of the car turning over.

In practice, the performance of the FWMA engines was disappointing with both of them blowing up, so that for the race the works reverted to the 'old' FWC engine (the one I had blown up at Monza) while we had to soldier on with the French-entered car since there was no alternative. Peter Windsor-Smith from Climax worked on it with us throughout the night before the race, and although we did succeed in strengthening the centre main bearing – one of the weak points – it was all to no avail as the cylinder block proved to be porous, necessitating frequent pit stops for water. However, after three hours, Héchard crashed at White House, writing off the car, so we were put out of our misery. Climax were very disappointed with this but the engine eventually came good by powering, in an enlarged form, the little rear-engined Hillman Imp, the project engineer for which was Mike Parkes, who had stood in as 'works' reserve driver at Le Mans that year.

Although in practice Graham Hill shook everyone by putting up the fifth fastest lap in 4 min 12.7 sec, a speed of 119.15 mph (191.75 kph), in the race neither 15 performed at all well. The 2 litre car blew up after only three laps, and the 1½ litre crashed after seven hours' racing, although the engine had been misfiring for most of that time. Bob Hicks also retired after an accident and, although it kept going for twenty hours, the Ireland/Taylor works entry retired when the distributor failed. The only car to complete the race was the works 750 which ended up last amongst the finishers in 20th place, having been delayed by an excursion into a sandbank by Tom Dickson.

Although not a good Le Mans showing this time round, the 15 had shown an astonishing turn of speed in practice, when it proved quicker than the 3 litre Ferrari. And at scrutineering my 750 – a hybrid with disc brakes at the front, but with a live axle and drum brakes at the rear – actually broke a record when it proved to be the lightest car in the race at just on 400 kg (882 lb). The normal weight of an Eleven was 960 lb (435 kg) while the 2 litre 15 scaled 1,090 lb (494 kg).

No, 1958 was certainly not one of the vintage years for Lotus. The Elite was not yet bringing in any revenue at all, despite the volume of orders, because not only was it a long way from being ready for production but there was nowhere to build it either!

So it was the Lotus Seven which proved to be the money-spinner and which kept Lotus going through these difficult times. 'It was the Seven and the sports cars that really started Lotus,' said Colin, in a later interview. 'We squandered the profit from that part of the business in trying to build road cars, and spent five years on that before we made a penny profit out of it. If it had not been for that business subsidizing road cars, they would never have got off the ground. That is fundamentally how Lotus managed to survive in the first place.'

For the single-seater, 1958 was no better so to try to improve the potential of the car Colin planned a complete redesign, the main feature of which was to be a new aerodynamic body. This was designed by Lotus bodybuilders Williams and Pritchard and not by Frank Costin, as previously believed – probably because it looked very like Costin's Formula 1 Vanwall single-seater design. It was quickly dubbed the 'Mini Vanwall'. Keith Duckworth, as gearbox development engineer, had carried out extensive work on the gearbox, which had certainly improved the reliability, but he was still very dubious about it: '. . . the gearbox was going to be built in a new form but using the same gears. The insufficient length of the gear locking dogs meant a useful life of about two hours. We needed longer dogs. I told Colin my views about this and he asked if I was prepared to tackle a brand-new design. But I felt that at that time I did not have sufficient experience to do so. Colin then took the decision to press on and so I left, because I was not prepared to go on wasting my time.' His job was taken over by Steve Sanville.

Fred Bushell was not particularly happy about this drive unit. He reckoned: 'This transmission was very cost-absorbing and it proved a considerable drain on our resources, at a time when we needed money badly to build our new factory . . .'

Keith Duckworth had struck up a strong friendship over the years with Mike Costin, who was also rather disillusioned at the time because he felt he had too much work on his plate with very little reward. So the two decided to go into partnership together and form a company of their own, the name of which was made up from their own family names. Thus was formed Cosworth Engineering Ltd. When Colin came to hear about it, he made Mike one of those 'offers he could not refuse'! Unlike Duckworth, who was still a batchelor, Mike had a family to feed and clothe, and he rightly felt that in the early days of a new company he might have to go through similar hard times to those he had already lived through at Lotus. So he accepted

Above *The first appearance of a Lotus in a Grand Prix was at Monaco in 1958, when Cliff Allison (above) and Graham Hill were entered in Formula 2 Lotus 12s propelled by 2 litre engines. Cliff finished in sixth place but Graham was forced to retire on the 70th lap through engine trouble.*

Left *Tony Brooks, the great British driver, was a member of the Vanwall Grand Prix team that used a chassis designed with the help and advice of Colin Chapman.*

Colin's offer to return and it was not until a few years later that Mike Costin finally left Lotus to join Cosworth Engineering.

It was originally intended that the engine of the new 16 would be positioned on its side, as had been planned for the 15 sports car, but when this idea proved unsuccessful the design for the car needed extensive modification. This meant a long delay, so the 16 was not ready for its first race until the French Grand Prix meeting at Rheims in July.

However, Team Lotus actually made its debut in Grand Prix racing some two months before, when Cliff Allison and Graham Hill were both entered in the 'old' 12s for the Monaco race on 18 May. Allison finished sixth and Hill retired after 70 laps when lying in sixth place. They were also entered for the Dutch Grand Prix at Zandvoort on 26 May when Hill again retired, this time on the 41st lap and Allison once more finished sixth. With the new 16 still not ready, the 12s were entered for the Belgian Grand Prix at Spa on 15 June. Cliff Allison excelled himself by finishing fourth, the only one on the same lap as the winner, Tony Brooks in a Vanwall. Graham Hill's engine expired on the sixth lap.

In point of fact, Chapman had not been at all enthusiastic about becoming involved in Grand Prix racing, as he explained to Doug Nye, during research for his book on Team Lotus*: 'I was only interested in Formula 2, sports cars and the Elite. I didn't want to get involved in Formula 1 – we weren't ready for it – but the drivers were all fired up and Climax were making bigger engines, so away we went!' The larger engines which Colin referred to were actually the 2 litre versions of the FPF 1,500 cc unit which were developing 176 bhp.

In the French Grand Prix at Rheims both the new 16s retired for one reason or another, and at the British Grand Prix, where three were entered – the additional car being driven by Alan Stacey – all three drivers retired. Both Hill and Allison managed to finish, ninth and tenth respectively, in the German Grand Prix but, in fact, during the entire season Graham Hill failed to score any points towards the World Championship of Drivers. Mike Costin spent most of his time looking for cracks in the chassis and suspension, mainly caused through material too light. It was clear that Chapman, who had so far only worked on cars with a relatively low power-to-weight ratio, was having great difficulty in adapting his ideas to single-seater racing cars, especially because of his conviction that saving weight was of such paramount importance. The only outright victory by one of these single-seaters was at Crystal Palace, in London, where private owner Ivor Bueb won a Formula 2 race in his 1,500 cc Type 12.

One of the reasons behind these many failures was that Colin had really bitten off rather more than he could chew. Although he was no longer racing himself, the company was very heavily involved in building and selling so many different types of car: there were Sevens, Elevens, 15s and 12s for customers, Team Lotus was racing 16s and the sports-racing cars, and at the same time he was busy developing the new Elite, two prototypes of which were racing very successfully in the hands of Ian

---

* Theme Lotus: 21 Years of Grand Prix and Indianapolis Cars, by Doug Nye. Motor Racing Publications, 1978.

Graham Hill testing the Lotus 16. Although Frank Costin did not design this very attractive 'Vanwall-style' body, as popularly believed, the small strands of wool fixed to the body panels to indicate the air flow over the surface were attached to the car by Frank who, in fact, actually took this photograph during the test.

Walker and John Lawry. As if all that were not enough, there was the new factory to be built so that the Elite could go into full-scale production!

Fred Bushell was also kept very busy over this period and decided to join the company on a full-time basis so he could devote himself fully to the job. Fred recalls: 'From 1956 to the beginning of 1958 Colin and I spent a lot of time viewing various factory sites. One, near Hornsey, was roughly the size required but was on sloping ground. Colin thought this might have some advantage so, over the weekend, he came up with a scheme for a production line operating by gravity feed! This illustrated his philosophy that you could do anything if you wanted to but the idea was discarded.

'Stanley Chapman eventually came up with a parcel of land in Cheshunt which was twice the size we initially required and it was he who played a big part in acquiring the land and paying the substantial deposit. Fortunately, it was possible to sell off half the land at a considerable profit immediately afterwards.

'Stan was obviously very proud of all that Colin was doing and was now extremely supportive of him. Colin respected his father immensely for his general worldly business knowledge, but he did find difficulty in communicating with him and they had very different concepts of the speed at which things should be done. Perhaps, in current terms, this would be called the 'generation gap'. Colin, at that time, did not respect the niceties which Stan expected, such as when Colin parked his decrepit vehicles outside Stan's rather prestigious home. Stanley didn't actually invest any money in Lotus but, by simply being there, and by his general standing in the community, Colin was attributed with greater financial standing than he actually merited.

'Once I had decided to join Lotus full-time, I first had to give three months' undivided attention to finalizing my affairs and during that time I was not in touch with Colin very often. On the day I turned up to start my full-time employment, he presented me with a contract which he had just signed to build the new factory. I told him that the contracted price was fifty per cent more than I thought I could finance, so my first assignment was to meet with the building contractor.

'He was by no means a small man and when he visited the Hornsey premises his bulk almost filled the 6 ft by 8 ft office! When I told him that the contract would have to be cancelled or amended, he became very pugnacious and came near to threatening violence. But at the end of the interview, with Colin's support, I explained to him the facts of life and we worked out a revised specification which brought the cost within the budget. Although I did much of the spadework in financing the new factory, as always with Lotus, because of the risks attached, there were great difficulties in convincing financiers of the tremendous opportunities they were being offered! Eventually, Peter Kirwan-Taylor (the Elite body designer, who had established a position for himself in the City) was able to play a major part in persuading the Eagle Star insurance company to provide the mortgage to go ahead with the building.

'As always, this was a very demanding period although it was manageable, otherwise I wouldn't have joined the company at the time. Most of us, having seen the car [the Elite] at the '57 Show, were left with the feeling that this was a complete motor car. In my naïvety I certainly didn't realize that it would have to go through such a long development period. This was also probably due to misreading Colin's enthusiasm, at that time not having developed my own "Chapman-meter"!

'The programme was dependent on Maximar Mouldings at Pulborough developing, with Lotus Cars, the Elite body and producing the production mould. During this period Ron Hickman and Albert Adams worked full-time down at Pulborough. From the time I joined in August 1958, when the programme was running late, Colin and I would visit Pulborough almost every week, to monitor Maximar and endeavour to speed things up. Colin was checking the technical side and I was taken along to bring commercial pressure. We used to go by car and Colin never ever allowed sufficient time for the journey, so each trip seemed to me like hell on wheels, as I was a very bad passenger and most of the time I was travel sick!

'Usually Colin would respect my malaise, but as conversation became more and more fraught, his driving would become faster and more disconcerting.

' Maximar was always promising progress but gave the appearance that, tucked away in the beautiful Sussex countryside, they were going to work at their pace, irrespective of what we wanted. Eventually they did produce the mould in time to coincide with the opening of the new factory, but we had lost confidence in their ability to perform on what was really a very critical item. We then contacted the Bristol Aircraft people who took over the construction of the body shells themselves.'

Chapter 7

First of the Rear-engined Racers

Lotus moved into the new factory at Delamare Road, Cheshunt, in June 1959 although it did not become fully operational until September. The factory itself consisted of two main buildings, in the first of which was Lotus Cars Ltd – the new name given to Lotus Engineering Co Ltd – where Fred Bushell was made General Manager. The second building accommodated Team Lotus (the racing division), and a new company to be known as Lotus Components Ltd, formed to look after the manufacture and sales of the Seven and the racing cars bought by private customers. 'Nobby' Clarke was put in charge here. Fortunately, most of the employees from Hornsey agreed to make the move to Cheshunt and an extra workforce was recruited locally without too much difficulty. The shareholders were now Colin, of course, who held the large majority, Peter Kirwan-Taylor, Fred Bushell, 'Nobby' Clarke and John Standen, the last three being allowed to buy some shares by taking a reduction in salary!

Colin and Hazel had meanwhile decided to move a little closer to Cheshunt and had bought a larger house at Hadley Wood from Lotus customer and driver Ian Walker. The extra space had become necessary because of the birth in January 1958 of their second child, another girl, who was christened Sarah. Colin was very happy about this, although perhaps a trifle worried that he still had no heir.

The 1959 racing season was at its busiest during the time of the move and it was not turning out to be any more successful than the previous year. Cliff Allison had been head-hunted by Ferrari, so Colin replaced him with Innes Ireland. It was an extremely disappointing season of Grand Prix races, despite the appearance of the new 2½ litre Coventry Climax engines in the Type 16 single-seaters, and the works cars finished in only three out of the eight grand épreuves. Graham Hill's best and only results were seventh place in the Dutch GP and ninth in the British. He was so sickened by his string of retirements that he left the team in disgust after the Italian GP and joined BRM. His departure was not at all amicable as Colin took him to court for breach of contract and lost the case.

In sports car racing, the 15 had also been revamped, mainly by redesigning the cooling system but also by fitting an Austin-Healey gearbox, which proved much easier for customers to service themselves. The new model was called the 15 Mk II. The new 17 was also introduced as a contender in the 1,100 cc class but unfortunately it was proving no match for the new Lolas of Eric Broadley, which were winning most of the short-circuit races. 'It was supposed to be the big breakthrough,'

The Cheshunt factory was opened in 1959 by the Mayor of Cheshunt, here seen talking to Works Manager Nobby Clarke, on the left of whom stands Michael Allen, one of Colin Chapman's original partners.

There were many well-known drivers and personalities at the opening ceremony. Here Cliff Allison (left) is talking with Innes Ireland (centre) and Alan Stacey.

Another important guest was Leonard Lee of Coventry Climax, here with Colin Chapman. On the left is Climax engine designer Wally Hassan.

Above *Lotus cleverly introduced the Seven – the successor to the Mk VI – at the same time as the Elite. This car caught the imagination of the small sports car enthusiast and went from strength to strength, becoming a cult car. Sales of the Seven kept Lotus solvent while Colin was busy sorting out his new Elite and building the Cheshunt factory. Here Nobby Clarke can be seen examining a dash panel on a line of cars in the course of construction.*

Below *'High Point', at Hadley Wood in Hertfordshire, was Colin's and Hazel's home from 1960 to 1966.*

Right *The prototype Lotus Elite – the very first of many – raced very successfully by Ian Walker.*

Peter Warr explained to me recently. 'It was the smallest, the lightest and the most compact Lotus sports-racing car ever and Lotus's reputation had always been in sports car racing. It didn't work at all well and by that time the Lola driven by Peter Ashdown was coming into its own and starting to win everything.'

Peter Warr, who first joined Lotus in August 1958, was to play a major role in the company in two successive stints. Invalided out of the Army after an accident, he had decided to pay Lotus a casual visit when they were still at Hornsey. He had become interested in them because, with his home being close to Brands Hatch, he had watched their cars perform on the many occasions when he went there as a spectator. 'I went along to Hornsey and asked if I could have a look round, and was told "yes". I had been standing and gazing in wonder at the cars I had seen racing, when after half an hour Roy Badcock – who was the foreman in the production shop – said: "Don't just stand there, give us a hand". Later he took me to Colin Bennett, who was the Sales Manager, and he offered me a job. I started the next day as his assistant for the princely sum of £500 per year!'

One of the problems with the 17 was that it was fitted with the strut-type suspension units at both front and rear and, because it was probably rather too early for the technology then available, the struts tended to seize up under load when in the middle of a corner. 'It nearly killed me and several other drivers too!', remembers Mike Costin. On the other hand, this little car, designed by Len Terry, was probably one of the prettiest Lotuses ever.

By the end of the year, the retail price of the Elite had risen to £1,949 and while only a handful had been delivered, mostly for racing purposes, they were proving extremely successful. One of the first had been ordered by a Scottish farmer, Ian Scott-Watson, for a protégé of his named Jimmy Clark, and at the 1958 Brands Hatch Boxing Day meeting this young man had nearly beaten both Colin Chapman and

Mike Costin driving similar Elites. Colin only just managed to pass him by surprise on the last lap, but it had been touch and go all through the race and Jimmy made a big impression on Colin. In actual fact, Clark was originally going to have a Formula 2 car and had gone down to Brands Hatch for a test session. Unfortunately, after Jimmy had put up some very fast laps in this, his first outing in a single-seater, Graham Hill took the car out and promptly lost a wheel, a fairly common occurrence in these cars but enough to put off both Clark and his backers, so they took an Elite instead.

At the 1959 Le Mans race, not one of the three sports-racing cars entered – one 2 litre 15 and two 742 cc 17s – managed to finish, but out of the three Elites which started two finished and Peter Lumsden and Peter Riley won the 1,500 cc class, finishing eighth. The Jim Clark car, which he shared with John Whitmore, finished tenth, despite being delayed by starter motor trouble. The third Elite, my own entry for the French drivers Malle and Vidilles, caught fire on the straight and was burnt out.

Clearly, it was time for Colin to devote more attention to the racing cars if he was ever to get back on top again because there was no doubt that the past two seasons, competing in Grand Prix racing with what were little more than 'stretched' Formula 2 cars, had tainted the name of Lotus. It took many years of success to restore this reputation to its former glory.

As I have made clear, 1959 had been a very difficult year for Colin. Although he had worked his way into Formula 1, the very pinnacle of the sport, he had only done so by paying the price. Had it not been for the exquisite design and sheer brilliance of the Lotus 16, as distinct from its unreliability, he would have been dismissed as a joke, with his cars leaving a trail of lost wheels, broken chassis, blown engines, stripped gears and wrecked clutches behind them. Nevertheless, there was an explanation for it. Even Colin Chapman, with his quite incredible working schedule, could not possibly pursue successfully two such major goals at the same time: establishing himself as a major Formula 1 racing car designer, manufacturer and entrant, as well as turning the little workshop business in Hornsey into an orthodox automobile manufacturing plant, where he was building cars which, for all their defects, were as highly esteemed as they were controversial. Although the Elite was an unprofitable product, it would be quite unfair to dismiss it, for it certainly put Lotus on the map and kept a whole generation of enthusiasts drooling over its fantastic looks and incredible road manners. Now, of course, it has become a classic for collectors, and values are soaring for what is more often than not considered to be the best looking Grand Touring car ever built.

So, now was the time for Chapman to come up trumps with a new racing car. For one thing, apart from the ever-popular Lotus Seven, they were still the only way to generate sufficient cash to subsidize the development and manufacture of the Elite. It had to be faced that the Lotus 12 and 16 single-seaters were no match for the rival Coopers, especially as far as roadholding was concerned. These rear-engined cars were now running rings round the Lotuses, and Jack Brabham had even humiliated the once all-conquering front-engined Ferraris by winning the 1959 World Championship of Drivers. What is more, he had done it with the very same type of 2½ litre Coventry Climax engine with which Lotus had put up such depressing

It took the inexperienced people at Lotus a long time to really get the Elite into production. Launched at the Motor Show in October 1957, it only came on stream when the Cheshunt factory was operational. Here is one week's production proudly parked in front of the Cheshunt building in August 1959.

results. Clearly a deep rethink on Colin's part was long overdue and fortunately the need for this came at a time when he was at last free from most of the worries and torments of introducing the Elite. Now the car was finally a workable proposition and he could concentrate on his racing cars.

After considerable thought Colin realized that the time had come when he must put the engine behind the driver. Many years later, when I interviewed him for an article to appear in 'Automobile Year', I asked him to explain the advantages that the rear-engined car had over a car with the engine in front of the driver. He explained: 'It is a much more elegant structural proposition, you are able to react the loads between the transmission and the engine directly in one package. You have reduced heat problems for the driver in the cockpit, and you can put the fuel much nearer the centre of gravity. You see, the old front-engined cars really did everything wrong: you had the weight of the mass of the engine in the front, the driver in the middle, and the fuel in the back. As the fuel load changed, it produced tremendous variations in the weight distribution which made it virtually impossible to balance the car for full as well as empty tanks. And so the distribution of the weight masses was superior in the rear-engined car and at the same time it was a much happier structural proposition.'

So, the new generation of Lotus racing cars was to have engines at the back but in addition to that it was also the beginning of Chapman introducing something that, up until then, was entirely new to motor racing. The idea developed gradually as he began to realize the significance of toe-in bump steering from the rear-axle, and through this he designed a fully adjustable suspension system with anti-roll bars front and rear which eventually gave him complete mastery over what was to become known as 'chassis tuning'.

Later he was to import from the Indianapolis race the procedure of taking sequential temperature readings across the tread of racing tyres, simply to find out if they were in full contact with the track and therefore doing their job properly. That, in its turn, was to put more emphasis on the control of wheel camber angles, although the full significance of that did not come until later still. One of Chapman's great strengths in those years to come was the way in which he always made the best use of tyres and their contact with the track surface. As Keith Duckworth once put it: 'Racing is all about the utilization of rubber'.

Thanks to the brilliance of the Coventry Climax engine in 1957, the introduction of the new Formula 2 had given Lotus the opportunity to build their first single-seater. In 1958 the change to the mandatory use of pump fuel and the reduction in the length of Grands Prix made it possible to turn a Formula 2 car into a Grand Prix winner, as Cooper had demonstrated so successfully. Another great opportunity came in 1960 – Formula Junior.

Introduced originally in Italy, where it had quickly become a popular national formula, it initially had very little appeal to British manufacturers. This was probably because they were so deeply involved with the ever-popular 1,100 cc class of sports car racing, and an international formula at the lower end of the market may have posed too much of a threat. But after the Italian Stanguellini car had totally dominated the first Formula Junior season, most of the British companies realized that maybe there was something in it after all and, somewhat reluctantly, under pressure from their customers they took the plunge.

At first, the new Lotus rear-engined single-seater – type number 18 – had been designed specifically for Formula 1 and 2, but Lotus received so many requests at the 1959 Motor Show that a somewhat simplified Formula Junior version was quickly added to the range. With the 18 Chapman had, in his usual way, again gone back to first principles and, since he was tackling what was, for him anyway, an entirely new concept, he decided that above all this must be a simple car, and that is exactly what it was. It had a relatively simple space frame, with a minimum frontal area, fitted with the very latest in suspension design. In appearance, it was by no means a beautiful looking car and one or two unkind critics likened it to a biscuit tin on wheels although, in the end, it turned out to be a very effective biscuit tin!

The front suspension was the same as that used for the later versions of the 16, when Colin had realized that what was good enough for the Lotus Seven was not necessarily suitable for a Formula 1 car. So it now had two wishbones and a separate anti-roll bar. He also gave up the use of the 'Chapman Strut' at the rear which, although it was doing yeoman work on the Elite, was no longer suitable for a single-seater. Also, as had been the case with the later examples of the 16, the half-shafts were partly relieved of their wheel-locating task by the addition of an extra lower wishbone. In order to suit the rear wheel geometry the wheel uprights had to be of such a length that the bottom end came so close to the ground that, if a tyre punctured, the upright would scrape the track surface before the wheel rim!

The 18, in F1 and F2 form, was still using the 'queerbox' but it was now a Mk III version, developed for the 15 works car, in which the gear cluster had been moved to the back of the rear axle, making the changing of ratios a much simpler job. The Formula Junior version, however, was designed to take a Renault gearbox: a four-speed version for customers but one with five speeds for the works cars. I was busy shipping those from 'Station 102' in Paris at a cost of 1289.00 frs (approximately £100). As a matter of interest, the owner of 'Station 102' was Jean Redelé, the builder of the Alpine-Renault cars.

Paradoxically, the first of the three types of Lotus 18 to be ready for racing was the Formula Junior car, but unfortunately it made a somewhat inauspicious debut at the Brands Hatch Boxing Day meeting. Not only was it rather ugly, but its temporary unpainted alloy bodywork gave it a somewhat unfinished look. (The production bodies were going to be in glass-fibre.) Not only that, but the performance was not all that good either. Peter Warr recalled those early days of the Lotus 18: 'At the 1959 Boxing Day meeting the first Lotus 18 appeared with Alan Stacey at the wheel and it finished a very poor fourth. After Boxing Day we used to go straight from Brands Hatch to the Racing Car Show, which was held in the Old Horticultural Hall. I stood there for ten days trying to sell that rather unprepossessing car that had finished fourth at Brands behind three Elvas – and everyone rushed off and bought Elvas! But, in March or April, when the season opened, the works team of Jimmy Clark, Peter Arundell and Mike McKee just swept everything before them. Coopers didn't do badly but it was obvious that the car to have was the Lotus, mainly because it had the Cosworth-Ford engine which was more than a match for the A-series BMC engines which, for contractual reasons, Coopers had to use. It wasn't very good, whilst the Ford was of the new generation of engines. They started winning absolutely everything and in no time at all we had a tremendous order book on the Lotus 18. They replaced the volume of business on racing cars that had been done with the Eleven. It was a complete switch from sports cars to single-seaters and that year (1960) we sold 125 Formula Junior cars! The problem was that, with only about 60 people, we had no more than four months to build them before the season finished.'

Now, as Peter has explained, one of the reasons for the success of the Lotus 18 Formula Junior car was the Ford-Cosworth engine and for that Lotus had mainly to thank Mike Costin. Although part of the deal he had made with Colin to stay on at Lotus was that he would resign from Cosworth Engineering Ltd, he nevertheless kept close and friendly ties with Keith Duckworth. He knew only too well the progress that Keith had made with the development of this small 997 cc Ford engine, and its showing on the test bed, and it was Mike's persuasion that convinced Colin to fit these engines.

Left *Colin Chapman with Jimmy Clark and Trevor Taylor in the paddock at Oulton Park during their all-conquering Formula Junior championship-winning season of 1960.*

Below *Colin circulating on the back of Trevor Taylor's Formula Junior Lotus 18 after it won a race at Snetterton in September 1960, giving them the Formula Junior championship.*

At this point we should look at the way in which Jim Clark came to drive for Lotus. Through one of his Scottish backers, Jimmy had been invited to test the new Formula 1 Aston Martin which it was intended should contest the World Championship that coming season. While he was at Goodwood testing the prototype, Team Lotus just happened to be there, too, with the 18. He recalled that day in his book*: 'Mike Costin of Lotus was down there with the Junior car doing some testing, and he asked Reg [Reg Parnell, the Aston Martin Team Manager] if he would let me try out the Lotus Junior to see what I thought of it. So, after testing the Grand Prix Aston, I leapt into the Junior and, oh, my goodness, the Lotus in comparison was simply fantastic. I wouldn't have believed that any car could hold the road the way this Lotus did. I could go through St Mary's – the adverse-cambered left-hander with the deep dip in the middle – so quickly that I didn't think it was possible. The car seemed to be glued to the road.'

Actually, the presence of the Lotus on that day at Goodwood was not merely a coincidence because Jimmy had previously told Mike Costin that he would be there testing with Aston Martin! Although Jim Clark was, at the time, under contract to drive the Aston in the Formula 1 races, he would be quite free to drive for Lotus in Formula 2 or Junior events, and it was because of this that he was so keen to try the car. Needless to say, Jimmy was sufficiently impressed with the 18 – as were Lotus with him – that he signed up with them for the season and, since Aston Martin were to withdraw from Formula 1 after a most disappointing début, Jimmy soon found his way into the Lotus Formula 1 works team. Even so, he became the 'King of Formula Junior' that year.

Meanwhile, the Formula 1 Lotus made its first appearance in the 1960 Argentine GP at Buenos Aires in the hands of Innes Ireland, and its performance proved most promising. Despite the fact that, in typical Lotus fashion, it was only finished a few hours before it had to be flown to Argentina, it was second fastest to Moss's Cooper in practice, and led the race at the start, although Ireland had the misfortune to spin it on the second lap. Eventually he finished sixth, despite a mechanical defect in the gearbox.

Back in Europe, Innes scored the first victory for the Lotus 18 in a Formula 2 event at Oulton Park, quickly followed by his day of glory when he trounced Stirling Moss's Cooper in both the F2 and non-Championship F1 events at the popular Goodwood Easter Monday meeting. Moss was terribly impressed by the new Lotus and he asked his entrant Rob Walker to buy one. This was delivered just in time for Stirling to drive it at Monaco, where he notched up Lotus's first-ever GP victory.

Unfortunately, the strength of the 18 was not yet fully up to the task and tragedy later struck during the Belgian Grand Prix at Spa. First, in practice, both Stirling Moss and Michael Taylor crashed their privately entered cars quite badly due, in both cases, to mechanical failure. Stirling was very seriously hurt, with two badly fractured legs, due to the cracking of a defective rear hub – caused, it was thought, because the draughtsman designing the part had failed to radius the flange on the outboard shaft. In fact, new modified parts were flown out for the other cars in time for the race itself.

---

*   'Jim Clark: At the Wheel' (Arthur Barker).

The first Grand Prix victory by a Lotus GP car (although not a Team Lotus entry) was Stirling Moss's win in Rob Walker's Lotus 18 at Monaco in 1960.

In the case of Taylor's car, the steering column was found to have fractured. In addition, Alan Stacey's car also suffered from a fractured bolt in the steering gear. Although Taylor subsequently sued Lotus for negligence, and obtained a settlement, Colin told me afterwards that he was convinced that the steering column had sheared because it had been tampered with by a mechanic who had then failed to weld it properly.

Even though Jim Clark, in his second Formula 1 Grand Prix drive for Lotus, finished sixth, race day was even worse, but not because of a mechanical defect. Alan Stacey suffered the misfortune of being struck in the face by a bird. He lost control and was killed instantly. This was the second fatal crash of a Lotus works driver, and Stacey's loss was deeply felt by everyone in the team. In his early youth, Alan had lost his right leg below the knee, but coped very well with an artificial leg. His mechanic, Bill Basson, one of the best in the business, had also lost a hand, and the two of them had always enjoyed a special relationship. They were tremendously popular with everyone because, despite their particular handicaps, they had each risen to the top of their branch of the sport.

Despite his serious injuries, Moss was back on his feet in time to drive in the Portuguese GP in August, and he managed to repeat his Monaco victory by winning the last Grand Prix of the season at Riverside in the USA.

Ex-motor cycle World Champion John Surtees had now joined the team to replace Alan Stacey and he and Innes Ireland finished second and third in the British GP at Silverstone. Other good results for the Lotus 18 that season were Ireland's second place in the Dutch GP and Jim Clark's third place in the Portuguese GP.

Back at the new factory in Cheshunt, apart from turning out another large batch of the ever-successful Sevens, Lotus Components had mercifully dropped the 17 and were concentrating on turning out the new 19, basically a two-seater version of the 18 and therefore the first rear-engined Lotus sports-racing car. In Europe, the UDT-Laystall racing team were running three of these cars with considerable success, especially since Stirling Moss was one of their drivers. However, the chronic shortage of 2½ litre FPF Climax engines restricted the production to sixteen cars, the bulk of which went to the States where they were tremendously successful. Some cars later acquired the more powerful 2.7 litre version of the FPF engine, which Climax had developed specially so that Cooper could run at Indianapolis in 1961.

Dan Gurney, the famous American entrant and driver, also ordered a rather special Lotus 19 to which an American V8 engine could be fitted. This car became known as a Lotus 19B. Roy Badcock still remembers the negotiations which went on over this car between Dan and Colin: 'I was present at the final meeting in Colin's office at the Cheshunt factory, where not only were the technical details thrashed out but also the financial side of the deal. After about one-and-a-half hours Dan shook Colin's hand to seal the agreement and said: "Well, that is the first car I have ever bought where the clutch was an optional extra!"'

With the Elite now fully established in GT racing, six were entered for the 1960 Le Mans race. Although only four cars started and only two of them finished, the marque succeeded in covering itself with glory. Officially, all six cars were entered by customers, although one – fitted with the 2 litre FPF engine and driven by Formula 1 works drivers Innes Ireland and Alan Stacey – was very obviously factory prepared and boasted special front suspension straight off the 18 single-seater. With the unfortunate death of Alan Stacey at Spa only a week earlier, his place was filled by the car's owner, Jonathan Sieff, heir to the Marks and Spencer stores business and, although a very keen motor racing enthusiast, a driver with somewhat limited experience.

Sieff had entered another standard Elite which he had originally planned to drive himself, and to become better acquainted with the 8.4-mile circuit he started practising with this car. A mechanic had mistakenly fitted an ordinary inner tube into one of the rear tyres, instead of using a racing tube where the valve is secured by a lock-nut. While accelerating out of the Tertre Rouge corner at the beginning of the long Mulsanne straight, a bout of acute wheelspin caused the tyre and tube to slip on the rim, so that the valve itself was torn out of the tube. A mile further down the straight, when the car had virtually reached maximum speed, the tyre deflated completely and Sieff suffered a monumental crash. He was found lying badly injured in the garden of a house, having been thrown clear over the wall. His intention had been to take out the 2-litre car for practice after completing a few warm-up laps in the smaller-engined Elite, but now, as a result of this serious accident, both cars had to be withdrawn from the race. No-one was more relieved about this than Innes Ireland who said he had frightened himself silly with the 2 litre, mainly because of an apparent shortage of brakes.

This left four 1,216 cc Elites in the race itself – the two Team Elite entries of

Buxton and Allen and Wagstaff and Marsh, a third car driven by Mike Parkes and Sir Gawaine Baillie, and a French entry I was managing for Masson, this time partnered by Laurent. The quickest driver of the eight was undoubtedly Parkes, who told me at the time: 'I can take White House absolutely flat out but it's touch and go if anybody sitting on the roadside sneezes!' Unfortunately, in the race Parkes retired with transmission trouble, as did the Buxton and Allen car, leaving the one remaining Team Elite entry and our French car still in the race. Despite a burnt-out valve, our car managed to win the class, averaging nearly 91 mph (146 kph), but the other, which had averaged only 89.5 mph (144 kph), was announced to be the winner of the Index of Thermal Efficiency award, for which there was a large cash first prize. We could not understand this at all because, by our calculations, we should have won it.

A week later, Masson was able to take a look at the organizers' calculations and it was found that, on the winning car, the pit marshals had not taken into account one of the fuel stops. Therefore, it had indeed used more fuel than our car and we had really won the Index of Thermal Efficiency after all. The final result of all this was that the Automobile Club de l'Ouest had to pay out another substantial amount of cash for a second first prize! The performance of the Elite had been quite staggering: an average speed of 90.95 mph (146.37 kph) for a fuel consumption of only 22.57 mpg (12.5 l/100 km) and top speed, officially measured, of 129.27 mph (208.04 kph).

It was just as well that Team Lotus and the new company, Lotus Components Ltd, were doing well because commercially the Elite was not proving the success it should have been, and the simple reason lay with the American market. Originally, in the days of the Mk VI, Lotus had some financial problems with their distributor, who at that time was a company known as Autextra. Because of this, Fred Bushell had insisted that export shipments could only be made against irrevocable letters of credit.

In 1956 Colin first met Jay Chamberlain at Sebring, where he was driving an American-owned Mk IX, and the two quickly struck up a friendship. Not only was Jay invited to drive at Le Mans in 1957 (where he won his class), and at Rheims (where he had the misfortune to suffer a serious accident), but Colin also gave him the franchise to sell Lotus cars in the United States. He did extremely well at it, too, selling a total of 64 Elevens. So, when the Elite was first introduced at the end of 1957, Jay placed a very large potential order, which was one of the reasons why a new factory was so important. Unfortunately, when the time came to sell the cars – in 1959 and 1960 – it was another story: sales were extremely disappointing, and unsold cars began to pile up in the USA. It is fair to say that this was not entirely the fault of Jay Chamberlain. The early Elites certainly possessed a number of defects in manufacture, one of the most serious being the location of the rear axle, which was apt to part company with the bodyshell. Steps therefore had to be taken to rectify these problems, which were not conducive to good business anywhere – especially so in the States, where the sheer size of the country and the sparsity of the dealer network put special emphasis on reliability.

'The default of Chamberlain was a drama of the first order,' recollects Fred Bushell. 'There were some hundred cars in the States, unsold, but for which Lotus had been paid. They had been financed by Jay Chamberlain through his "Guardian

Angel". I went to California in an endeavour to sort out the situation. Chamberlain complained that there had been heavy warranty problems on the cars, both mechanical and particularly paintwork and, to support his allegations, he produced a large number of warranty payment documents, which appeared even to me to be excessive. Colin hired me a Minox camera and, with great patience, showed me how to operate it and I photographed various samples of these warranty documents. This was before the time of photocopying. I then visited the paint shops from where they had originated and compared them with their copies, which showed that Jay Chamberlain had altered the documents very substantially, by adding a hundred or more dollars to each of the bills.

'I attempted to involve the local police on what I considered to be a fraud and, much to my surprise, they took the view that this was normal commercial practice in America and there was nothing they could do. I then confronted Jay with the evidence. Chamberlain was much bigger than me, to say nothing of his "minder" (a Mexican "toughie") who was with him, and he was also very dramatic. We had a big shouting match and, when Jay was out of the room, his friend even produced a knife and chased me round the office! This only stopped when Jay came back, much to my relief. I then went to see Chamberlain's "Angel", a man called Dr Jack Briggs, who was a medical specialist, and also a member of the very wealthy Briggs family – of Briggs and Stratton engine fame. I explained to him about the fraud which had been perpetrated and pointed out that he owned a hundred Lotus Elites. Dr Briggs (a rather non-commercial gentleman) was very perturbed that his friend Jay Chamberlain should have got into this situation. As Chamberlain had no way of continuing the business, I advised Briggs to take action in order to protect his interest and arranged for him to see a leading Californian attorney who eventually persuaded him that Chamberlain should be removed from the corporation. Dr Briggs, in conjunction with the attorney, then appointed a new general manager for the operation, Peter Hessler, who continued running the business for several months on what were certainly more correct lines, although without any great financial success. He did, however, reduce the stock of cars considerably.

'I then had cause to go back to America to negotiate with Hessler, accompanied by the Lotus Sales Manager, Robin Read. We tried to establish why the business was not doing as well as it should and discovered that Peter Hessler's business management was beginning to deteriorate. He was padding expenses, and generally not behaving in a faithful manner to Dr Briggs. Hessler realized that we were close to making an adverse recommendation to Dr Briggs and he became rather emotionally unstable. I believe that it was partly because of this pressure that he took a car on to a local race track where he met with a fatal accident. This terminated Dr Briggs' desire to be involved and we were, for a time, without any US representation.

'We were finally approached by a concern called Ecurie Shirlee which was owned by Bob Challman. I spent a long time negotiating with them and, much to my surprise, they found the finance to come up with a reasonable programme of purchases and complied with the letter of credit requirements. In a limited way, they represented the company fairly ably for a time.

'Obviously, through this period, the American intake of the Elite was much below the originally planned volume and we had to find a way to increase sales in the UK.

'By this time Bristol Aircraft were on stream and were producing a higher volume of bodies than we could absorb, so an accumulation of about a hundred built up at Cheshunt. During this period of low Elite sales, Lotus were fortunate that the sales of the Formula Junior car were going very well and this provided salvation for the cash flow. With the help of Peter Kirwan-Taylor, we were able to re-negotiate deferred terms with Bristol and eventually our commitment to them was fully discharged. To activate the UK market, which had always been supplied with fully-built Elites, we decided to offer them in component form as with the racing car market. The big reduction in the price of the Elite, as offered in kit form, gave a tremendous boost to the market and, for a while, sales picked up and all stocks were disposed of.'

It was at the 1961 Earls Court Motor Show that the Elite was first introduced in kit form, with the price of the standard model reduced to £1,299, a tremendous saving of £819! There was also an S/E (special equipment) model on show which was equipped with an all-synchromesh four-speed ZF gearbox, twin SU carburettors and a special exhaust system boosting the power output to 83 bhp. Even more important, since the introduction of bodies manufactured by the Bristol Aeroplane Company the rear suspension had been revised to reduce the effect of toe-in steer. These cars were designated as Series 2 models, which became standard for cars with either stage of engine tune.

In kit form the car was fairly easy to put together, with full assembly taking only about 25 man-hours, since the body came already trimmed, wired and plumbed, and all one had to do was to drop in the engine, gearbox and back axle and bolt the suspension units into place. The customers attracted to this type of car did not seem to object too much to having to carry out this work, especially bearing in mind the cash saving they were making. It also gave them useful first-hand knowledge of a car, the maintenance of which could prove difficult. Any problems in this direction were compounded by the fact that these kit cars were sold direct from the factory without the backing of a dealer network.

The Lotus entry at the 1961 24-Hours race at Le Mans was again an all-Elite affair, one reason being that the catalogue no longer included any sports-racing cars as the factory was too busy turning out Formula Juniors. But there was another good reason, too. Since the previous season, open sports car racing had been severely handicapped by the introduction of new international regulations which imposed such requirements as minimum cockpit measurements, luggage accommodation space and full-height windscreens, the latter tending to act as an air brake, and Colin was just not interested in building cars to conform to such restrictive rules. Only in the UK and the States did sports car racing continue under the old rules.

Five Elites were thus entered and again one of these was a rather special vehicle from UDT-Laystall, the private team that was racing Lotus 19s in England. (They were also by now running two 18s in Grand Prix races.) This car was fitted with a 750cc Climax engine, but it was not the FWMA type which had been fitted in my car three years earlier. The new engine was an FWMC fitted with a twin-overhead camshaft cylinder head as a development study for the new V8 engine which Coventry Climax were preparing for the new 1,500 cc Formula 1 introduced that year. Technically, this was a very much more effective engine and it produced an amazing 83 bhp. It was thus comparable with the 83 bhp of the S/E Elite, which had over 50 per cent more engine capacity. This 750 cc car was aimed directly at winning the coveted Index of Performance, so often the property of the small French cars.

Amongst the 1216 cc Elites, I was looking after one which belonged to Jean-François Malle, the brother of a famous film director, who was to be partnered by Robin Carnegie, later to become Lord Rosehill. I was especially keen on us winning the Index of Thermal Efficiency – officially this time, of course! – and as Malle had given me what was virtually an unlimited budget I was able to enlist the services of Frank Costin. Frank came over to Le Mans for the April Test Day and busied himself with pounds of Plasticine and tufts of wool. For the race, the car had been permanently modified, both in the nose and in the windscreen areas. The performance, although not documented, was certainly much improved. Unfortunately, at the time Lotus were offering special structural fuel tanks which formed part of the body moulding and, in the interests of saving as much weight as possible, we fitted

The birth of 'DADIO'! The author commissioned Frank Costin to improve the aerodynamics of the Elite he was preparing for Jean-Francois Malle in a special effort to try and win the Index of Energetic Output at Le Mans in 1961. Costin is here seen putting Plasticine on the front end of the car during April test day. He later sold this successful modification to Les Leston, who was racing his own Elite (registration number 'DAD 10') with much success. On the right is Malle's co-driver Robin Carnegie (now Lord Rosehill).

one of these tanks, but after eight hours' racing it sprang a leak and we ran out of fuel on the circuit. The Costin body 'mods' were later supplied by him to many of the successful racing Elites of the time, including Les Leston's famous DAD 10.

The 750 cc Elite, driven by Cliff Allison and Mike McKee, was most impressive during the early part of the race, leading on Index of Performance for a time until the oil pump drive broke after ten hours' racing. The final results were not as good for Lotus as they had been the previous year because, although the Team Elite entry of Trevor Taylor and Bill Allen won its class, it finished nowhere on Index of Performance. Second in the class, and on Index of Thermal Efficiency, was the French Lotus importer's entry of Kosselek and Massenez.

During the 1961 season, Lotus's Formula 1 results had been somewhat less successful than in the previous year, although this was really nothing to do with the design of the cars, but more because the formula itself had been changed from 2½ litre to 1½ litre engines. This alteration had been made at the suggestion of the then President of the CSI, Augustin Perouse, most probably at the instigation of French 'experts' on the subject! The British manufacturers were not at all impressed and, at first, decided they would not build any cars to the new formula. For a time, efforts were made to introduce a new 3 litre 'Inter-continental' Formula, but eventually this was hit on the head by Coventry Climax announcing that they were not prepared to build a 3 litre engine. So British constructors really had no other choice but to go out and race in the 1,500 cc formula, for which the only suitable engine currently available was the old faithful FPF four-cylinder Climax.

Meanwhile, Ferrari had foreseen all this and, as usual, he was ready with a new, much more powerful 1½ litre engine before any of his main rivals, Coventry Climax and BRM, who had wasted time in the belief that the new Formula 1 would not prove to be a success. Right from the beginning of the season, Ferrari fielded his new cars with the V6 156 engine, initially with the two banks of cylinders at an angle of 65 degrees to each other, although quite early in the season a new version appeared with the cylinders at 120 degrees. Either way, this engine looked hard to beat – and so it proved.

After the success of the 18, Chapman developed and perfected the concept with a revised chassis in which the centre of gravity was lowered, simply by doing away with the 'saddle' fuel tank over the driver's legs and replacing it with two pannier-type tanks arranged along the sides of the chassis frame. The rear suspension was also modified, principally because Dunlop had just introduced a new tyre size, and the half-shafts were now completely relieved of any wheel locating duty by the fitting of top and bottom wishbones. Colin also decided to use rubber 'doughnut' half-shaft couplings instead of the more usual cv (constant velocity) joints. The rear brakes were moved outboard in the interests of improved cooling and, finally, the Lotus gearbox gave way to one specially made for them by ZF.

Right *Colin at the wheel of the Lotus 18 which turned the tables in his favour in 1960. It was the first mid-engined Lotus and soon proved to be the best Formula 1 chassis, besides scoring heavily in both Formula 2 and Formula Junior.*

Above all, Chapman made a great effort to improve air penetration and the new car – to be called the Lotus 21 – was given a very slim cigar-shaped body in which the driver was positioned almost lying down, the frontal area being very much reduced because of this. With the same aim Colin also introduced new front suspension on the rocker-arm principle acting on inboard springs, a system which, as Dave Kelsey explained earlier, had already figured on the Chapman-designed 'Clairmonte Special' back in 1953.

Although Colin had by now given up any serious thoughts of race driving, occasionally he did get the opportunity to keep his hand in with short bouts of test driving when new models were being developed. Dick Scammell, who was one of the Team Lotus mechanics at the time when the Lotus 21 Formula 1 car was being tested, remembers an amusing incident at Silverstone, which proved that Colin's driving had certainly not lost its edge: 'Innes Ireland had been complaining about the car and so Colin got into it for a few laps. He just rolled up his sleeves and put on a crash helmet, and by the end of his second lap he wasn't far off the time. On his third lap he was on the time and on the fourth lap he was quicker. When he came in, Innes asked: "What is it like when you really get on the brakes?", to which Colin replied: "I didn't really get on the brakes, because I'm not a racing driver, am I?"'

In February 1961 Andrew Ferguson joined Lotus as Competitions Manager. He had previously worked for Cooper where he had produced a small publicity booklet, sponsored by Esso and entitled 'The Golden Year'. Andrew had been introduced to Colin at a trade function by Ken Tyrrell, and when Colin learnt that he had written and produced this book, he told him: 'You are just the bloke I want. I need someone to write a book about Lotus.' At the time Andrew had left Cooper and was working for the American Camoradi team, where he had been in charge of their single-seater racing programme (David Yorke, ex-Vanwall, was running the sports cars) and a few days after this first meeting Ferguson had to go to the Lotus factory to collect a chassis. While he was there he went to see Stanley Chapman, who said: 'Come and see Mr Colin'. It transpired that Stanley was thinking of retiring to Devonshire and here was the ideal replacement. So Ferguson was duly taken on to the staff where his main responsibilities lay, as they had for Stanley, with organizing and maintaining the logistics of Team Lotus – no mean feat at the best of times!

One of the first problems Andrew had to face arose after the Pau Grand Prix, a non-Championship event held in this very attractive town in south-west France. This incident, which I can remember very vividly as I was there myself to support the team, is another illustration of a less well-known side to Colin Chapman's character. After the prize giving, to which we had all driven – mechanics included – in Colin's rental car, we got back to our hotel and he went straight to bed. Unknown to either Colin or me, two of the mechanics had kept the key to the car and had gone out again. While I was having a quiet night-cap in the bar, the telephone rang. It was the local police saying that the car had been in a serious accident outside the town.

I had the job of waking Colin, which was no easy task as he was taking sleeping pills and they had already begun to take effect. Eventually he appeared, although in somewhat of a stupor, and we both drove off with Colin's school chum, Alan Richardson, who had joined Team Lotus for this trip, to the hospital to find that one of the mechanics had been very seriously injured and was suffering from a fractured skull. We even had to help the doctor by holding the poor chap down while he was given a thorough examination. Finally he was sedated and, because Colin had then realized that he had left his briefcase in the back of the hire car, we drove off to the scene of the accident. In the briefcase, apart from other important documents, was Colin's little black book containing all his notes on the chassis and suspension settings, and it would be a serious loss if we failed to find it. Eventually, after what seemed hours of searching in the dark with a torch, we were much relieved to find the briefcase lying in a ditch.

When Colin arrived back at Cheshunt, he called Andrew, who recalls the incident well: ' "You know what you have to do, don't you?" he told me. "Yes," I answered, "I'll fire him," because that's what we would have done at Coopers. "No, no," said Colin, "he's in a terribly bad way, so make arrangements to fly his mother over to him." ' Eventually the lad recuperated and returned to a job, although he was not fit enough to remain a racing mechanic.

The Lotus 21 Formula 1 car was ready in time for the first race of the 1961 Grand Prix season, the Monaco Grand Prix, and the works cars were to be driven by Ireland and Clark. Both were fitted with a new version of the old four-cylinder engine which was called the Mk II, and which was giving 152 bhp. This was no match for the 65-degree V6 Ferrari, or the new 120-degree engine giving 190 bhp. Unfortunately, Innes Ireland's car was eliminated by a crash in the tunnel during practice, when he missed a gear change, hit the barrier and fractured a knee. Clark had been third fastest in practice but managed to finish only tenth and last in the race, which was brilliantly won by Stirling Moss in Rob Walker's privately owned 1960 Lotus 18. Many say this was Stirling's greatest victory because, even though his car also had the new Mk II Climax engine, he was up against the entire might of three even more powerful Ferraris.

In the meantime, Wally Hassan and Peter Windsor-Smith (Harry Mundy having left Climax to become a journalist) were beavering away with the new 1,500 cc V8 engine, based on the little 750 cc FWMC four-cylinder unit that was first raced in the UDT Le Mans car that year. Although the prototype eventually made its debut at the German Grand Prix in Jack Brabham's Cooper, it was plagued with overheating problems right up to the end of the season.

While Moss in Rob Walker's Lotus was the only driver and car combination which seemed to be able to beat the red Ferraris, Rob was having a problem in obtaining one of the new Lotus 21s for Stirling to drive that season. This was because Moss was sponsored by the BP oil company whereas the Lotus factory had always been strongly supported by Esso. Reg Tanner – the Esso Competitions Manager – was not at all happy about Moss's two 1960 Grand Prix victories in the Walker Lotus and had forbidden Chapman to sell Rob a new 21! Eventually, after the first couple of races, the 18 was modified as closely as possible to the 21's specification by Rob Walker's mechanic, the famous Alf Francis.

I asked Stirling Moss quite recently about his experiences with these early rear-engined Lotus Formula 1 cars. 'I think Colin Chapman was a brilliant designer,' he said, 'but in my view he did not give sufficient consideration to the problems which could arise if the car was driven very hard. If you drove a Lotus very hard, as was often necessary, then a wheel would fall off and this happened with me several times. In fact, unbeknown to me, Rob Walker was fitting new drive-shafts for every race because they were simply not strong enough. I liked Colin but he didn't have much of a sense of humour. I remember after I had won the US Grand Prix in Rob's Lotus, they bought me a cake with the shape of the car modelled in the icing. The first piece I cut off was a wheel, so I said, "Please pass this to Mr Chapman." He didn't think it was at all funny! Although I won both the 1960 and 1961 Monaco GPs in Rob Walker's Lotus, Chapman never sold us his latest model because, you must understand, I was driving against the factory team. However, to my mind, the Lotus was the best car although not the easiest or the most fun to drive. You had to be very precise in the way you drove it. You could not throw it around like you could a Cooper, which was really a bit of a blacksmith's job.'

Although the Ferraris walked away with almost all the other GP races that year – except the US, which they did not enter – Moss also managed to win the German GP at the Nurburgring. Thus he had achieved both his victories on the two most demanding circuits, proving beyond doubt his mastery as a racing driver. However, it was in the German race that he demonstrated just how cunning he could be, too. It had rained for the morning practice session so everyone had used their wet-weather tyres. However, for the race the track had virtually dried, so Dunlop – the sole supplier of F1 tyres at that time – specified a return to dry tyres. Moss decided otherwise, though, and by dint of his tremendous ability, the perfect balance of his car and because it started to rain again three laps from the end he managed to make his soft tyres last throughout the race and so beat the Ferraris. This was the fourth GP victory by a Lotus car, but so far not one had been captured by a works entry.

Innes Ireland's crash at Monte Carlo had sidelined him for a little while and his place in the F1 team was taken by the young Trevor Taylor who had been doing well in the Lotus Formula Junior team. Innes recovered in time for the Belgian race at Spa, where the Ferraris trounced everyone by taking the first four places!

At Monza, Moss had been planning to use one of the new V8 Climax engines in his Lotus 18/21 but there were continuing problems with it so, as Moss still had a fleeting chance of winning the World Championship, Colin decided that Innes should swop cars with him. In the race neither driver finished and the event was clouded in tragedy when Jimmy Clark's Lotus collided with the Ferrari of Wolfgang 'Taffy' von Trips. The popular German's car careered through the wire fence at the Parabolica Curve and plunged into the crowd, killing the driver instantly and also fourteen spectators, with many more injured. Jimmy's car was immediately impounded by the police and it was years before the wreck was returned to Lotus. Jimmy himself was unscathed by the accident but was naturally shattered by the experience, so Colin, who by then had acquired a Piper Comanche aircraft, flew him back home immediately. This aggravated the police who had not been given the opportunity of questioning Clark, and it was not until two years later that he was entirely cleared by the court of any blame.

The last GP of the season was at Watkins Glen in the USA, and because their driver Phil Hill was already assured of the World Championship – and probably also

After his joint ownership of a veteran Miles Messenger aircraft with Mike Costin, Colin's first 'proper' plane was this Piper Commanche G-ARIN which he used to attend most race meetings. He eventually sold it to Jimmy Clark when he acquired his twin Comanche.

out of respect for von Trips – Ferrari did not enter. This was the chance that Lotus had been looking for. Apart from the somewhat uncompetitive Porsche flat-eight engine, and Jack Brabham's Cooper, still persevering with the prototype V8 Climax, all the runners were using four-cylinder engines. The race saw many a turn of events but, finally, Innes Ireland went on to win, much to Colin's unbounding delight, and he ran out on to the track throwing his cap high into the air – an action which was to become a familiar sight in the years to come. It was the first GP victory by one of his own works Lotuses and the marque's total score had also gone up to five. Apart from this win, the team's record for the season in Grand Prix races consisted of three third places for Jim Clark and two fourth places, one each for Clark and Ireland. The Lotus had certainly established itself as the best Climax-engined car of the season, as Cooper seemed to be losing their grasp somewhat and many customers were now turning to Lotus.

By way of a celebration after this very first Team Lotus GP win, Colin hired a small aeroplane for the flight back to New York City. John Cooper sat up front with Colin, while Jimmy Clark sat in the back with Colin's old school chum, Alan Richardson, who had accompanied him to Watkins Glen and who remembers the occasion very well. The engine suddenly cut out when they were flying directly over the Empire State Building and Colin had to fiddle with the fuel switch between the front seats before the engine quickly restarted!

Innes Ireland was also highly elated by his American victory and was bubbling over with enthusiasm for the next season, when the team should have their Climax V8 engines. But it was not to be, for Innes was told at the Motor Show in October that he

The first Team Lotus Grand Prix win came when Innes Ireland took the US Grand Prix at Watkins Glen in October 1961. Standing behind Colin is Jim Endruweit, who went from Chief Mechanic to Engineering Director during his many years with Team Lotus.

would not be part of the Team Lotus plans for 1962. Recently I asked Innes if he had any idea as to why Colin replaced him. 'No,' he replied, 'I never knew then and I still don't know to this day why I was dropped. Obviously one can make various conjectures. I think one of the factors was that Colin never wanted to pay the full "works" to two people, and I had gone all the way through the business of the first 25 per cent of the starting money, then thirty-three-and-a-third, and by 1961 I was on a full 50 per cent. I had always been faithful to Colin. I always gave him my best and I won a great many races for him.

'The way my sacking came about was that the day after I returned to England having been driving an Aston in the 1,000 km of Montlhéry, I went to the Motor Show at Earls Court where one of the first people I saw was Geoff Murdoch, the Competitions Manager of Esso. I was on top of the world having just won my first Grand Prix, and also the first for Team Lotus. The first thing I said to Geoff was, "What's the form for next year then Geoff?" "Haven't you seen Colin?" he replied. "No," I said, "I haven't seen him yet." Looking a bit long-faced, Geoff then said, "Well, you'd better go and see him then." So I went and searched out Colin on the Lotus stand and said, "Geoff Murdoch tells me that I ought to be seeing you about something." Whereupon Colin shuffled about from one foot to another, and said, looking down at the floor, "I won't be requiring your services next year." Then he turned round and walked off, and that was the end of that. He never explained anything or ever gave me any reason.

'I had tremendous faith in Colin and in his design ability. I felt that if he was not a genius then he was bloody close to being one. I never really raced for myself, it was all for Lotus. In those early days there was not one journalist writing kind words about Lotus. Chapman was very much the underdog and to me the challenge was, "By God, between Colin and I, we will make Lotus the top dog," and by 1961 we were just beginning to see the light through the trees.

'At the end of 1959, I was asked to go with Graham Hill to BRM but I didn't. Everybody was saying to me, "Boy, you want to get out of Lotus, you'll kill yourself." You'll remember, I ran out of brakes four times in 1959 and once, at Rouen, I finished up 150 feet down a ravine! But still I felt, "If I leave Colin he is not going to have anybody," and I still had this burning desire that, by God, we had to get it right. As an engineer myself I knew he had terrific design ability and so my dismissal came as a very great blow to me and undermined many of the things in life in which, up to then, I had always believed. You can imagine, it was the deepest upset I have ever had – much more traumatic than my two divorces!'

There was no doubt that sacking Ireland was rather a controversial decision because, at the time, Innes was still a little faster than his less-experienced team mate Jim Clark. But Colin had always been tremendously impressed with Jimmy's driving, ever since they had fought it out together in Elites in that Boxing Day race at Brands Hatch three years earlier. There was something else about him, too. Out of the car Jimmy still remained a 'tiger' in whatever activity he was taking part. For instance, you could play table tennis with him and perhaps beat him at first, but he would insist on continuing to play until, eventually, he would beat you. He lived a 'clean' life too; he hated smoking and drank very little, whereas Innes was quite the opposite and all for going to parties where he could pay homage to the product of his native Scotland. He could then become very difficult, picking fights and even threatening to burn the place down! Colin just could not put up with such behaviour, not because he did not like a bit of fun himself – Team Lotus post-race parties were usually hilarious affairs and Colin was often the first to start the bun fight – but he knew when to stop. Innes apparently did not. Of course, Grand Prix racing then was a completely different scene from what it is now. The financial rewards were much lower and most people were in it simply because they enjoyed it. The atmosphere was also much more friendly – more like a club or even a family, and Jimmy revelled in it. He was also a tremendous admirer of Colin: in fact, he never drove any other make of Grand Prix car in his entire eight-year career.

However, Jimmy and Innes, although both of Scottish birth, did not hit it off together particularly well. It was really nothing to do with racing. It was more the fact that Jimmy perhaps seemed somewhat of a prude, by showing that he was put off by Innes's antics off the track, while the latter could also see that Jimmy's performance was getting closer and closer to his own, so that maybe there was a trace of jealousy.

On the other hand, Trevor Taylor enjoyed a very good relationship with Jimmy and they knew each other well because of their partnership in the Formula Junior team the previous year. Also Trevor had already driven a Formula 1 Lotus in the Dutch Grand Prix, while Innes had been out of action following his Monaco accident, and everyone had enjoyed his company on that occasion. So Colin took a big gamble. He knew Trevor would not be as quick as Innes Ireland but he decided that he should stake everything on Jimmy for the time being, and make sure that the atmosphere in the team was just right for him to enjoy himself and, at the same time, give of his best. With hindsight, we know that Colin's decision was the right one, for it was only the beginning of the famous Chapman/Clark partnership which so dominated the years that were to follow. Innes, unfortunately, took it all rather badly, as was probably only to be expected, and it was many years before he finally forgave Colin.

With the old Formula 2 having effectively become the new Formula 1, it was to be some time before the introduction of a new Formula 2, although the CSI was planning to bring in a new 1,000 cc formula for 1964. So, for the time being, the only other international class of single-seater racing was Formula Junior which had now become hugely successful, and for which the Lotus 18 had been replaced by the new Lotus 20. This car was basically an FJ version of the 18, upgraded in much the same way as the 18 F1 car had become the new Lotus 21.

The FJ Lotus 20s were extremely successful, having started the season well when Peter Arundell won the prestigious annual curtain-raiser event held on the day before the Monaco Grand Prix. The price of the Lotus 20 was £1,450 and Lotus Components Ltd built 118 examples.

Chapter 8

The Halcyon Days Begin

Although the introduction of the new 1,500 cc V8 Coventry Climax had been delayed in 1961 because of politics, which had seriously weakened Britain's chances that year, it was at last fully tested and developed by the beginning of the 1962 season, and Lotus could now expect to be more on a par with the engine power of the Ferraris. Also, with it being very obvious that the Lotus chassis was far superior, the prospects for the future were extremely encouraging. Indeed, the next four years undoubtedly proved to be Colin's most successful ever – and probably his happiest as well. During the four racing seasons of 1962 to 1965, out of the 39 Grands Prix which took place, Jimmy Clark in a Lotus won no fewer than 19 of them. He was World Champion Driver twice – in 1963 and 1965 – and on the other two occasions lost the title only in the last race of the season through trivial mechanical defects, whilst actually in the lead.

At no time in the history of motor racing has one man, or one make of car, dominated Grand Prix racing in such a manner. There was also no doubt whatsoever that Colin Chapman, having learnt the lessons of the previous fifteen years, had successfully mastered the task in full measure. He further proved the point by introducing the rear-engined 'funny cars' – as the Americans at first called them – to the unique Indianapolis 500-mile race, and then, in 1965, winning that, too, at only his third attempt, having deserved to do so on the first two occasions in the eyes of many observers.

It all began really with the introduction of the Lotus 25 and it was on a day, towards the end of 1961, when Colin was having lunch with Mike Costin, John Standen and one or two others, that he first had the inspiration, and there and then sketched out on a napkin a design for the first racing car to be built on the principle of the monocoque. 'I can remember quite clearly when I thought about it,' Colin told me. 'It came to me one day over lunch. I was discussing the problems of aluminium fuel tanks fitted to space frame cars. They were pannier tanks fitted along each side because that was where the weight needed to be. Of course, they needed to be made to fit as closely as possible to the driver, and so they had to fit round and through between the tubes of the structure. This made them very complicated, very difficult to make and, above all, very unreliable. They were always leaking because of welds coming apart and it occurred to me that the thing to do was to try and get rid of the structure which was in the way, and I suddenly thought, "Why the devil don't we just take two fuel tanks and bolt the front suspension on to one end and the engine on to the other?" I remember drawing it out on a paper napkin. I rushed back home and started drawing it that night and within a week we had a working scheme out for it and we started building right away.' On that day in that restaurant at Waltham Cross, near Cheshunt, the destiny of Formula 1, and motor racing in general, was being reshaped, because from then on every racing car built was to be of monocoque construction.

As a back-up while the 25 was being built, and as a means of insurance just in case it proved to be unsuccessful, Colin also produced early in 1962 the conventionally designed Lotus 24. Although at first glance this simply appeared to be a Lotus 21 adapted to take the new V8 engine, in fact none of the main components was interchangeable. And, incidentally, the 24 was the first Lotus frame not to be made by Dave Kelsey's Progress Chassis Company. The job went to a firm called Arch Motors who took over chassis frame construction for the next ten years or so, concentrating mainly on Lotus Sevens once all the racing cars had gone over to monocoque construction.

In fact, there were plenty of orders for the Lotus 24 and in all about a dozen were built, the first appearing at the non-Championship F1 event in Brussels when Jimmy Clark led from pole position only to experience valve gear failure. This was the first time the brand-new V8 Coventry Climax engine was raced in a Team Lotus car. Called the FWMV, it turned out about 186 bhp and it is perhaps of some interest to note that one of the problems Climax had met with concerned the design and construction of the rather complicated exhaust system. Finally they came up with a rather curious 'snake-pit' arrangement, where the four pipes from each bank of cylinders joined together into two main outlet pipes at the rear of the car. This enabled the pulsations in the inlet and exhaust ports to be harmonized by linking the exhaust system of the right bank of cylinders with that of the left. In a way this is somewhat reminiscent of the 'de-siamesed' ports on the Austin Seven engine in the Mk III Lotus of 1951! The FWMV engine was sold to the car manufacturers for £3,000, not a great deal more than the much simpler FPF four-cylinder engine which had been priced at £2,250.

Jim Clark won the next race for the 24, a minor F1 event at Snetterton in England, and when easily leading the non-Championship Pau Grand Prix he was side-lined by a broken gear linkage and the Frenchman Maurice Trintignant won in Rob Walker's Lotus 18/21. Rob had entered Maurice in the French race because the starting money he had been offered was so good and, at the same time, he made a deal with the UDT-Laystall team to borrow their Lotus 18/21 which his main driver, Stirling Moss, drove in UDT colours at Goodwood on the same day. Unfortunately, for a reason which will always remain one of those unsolved mysteries of motor racing, Stirling crashed heavily, fracturing his skull very badly and effectively putting an end to his motor racing career. There is no possible doubt whatsoever that Stirling Moss was the world's best driver at the time, and it was a tragedy that he never succeeded in winning the World Championship title which everyone felt he so richly deserved.

The new monocoque Lotus 25 was duly entered for the Dutch Grand Prix to be held at Zandvoort on 20 May, and what a sensation it created when it turned out for the first practice session on 18 May! Photographers had difficulty in getting anywhere

Above *A short-staffed Team Lotus took the new Type 24 to Pau in 1962. Colin had to don his overalls to help prepare Jimmy's and Trevor Taylor's cars.*

Below *Colin preparing his flight plan prior to taking off from Pau airport in his faithful Piper Comanche G-ARIN.*

near because of the crowds around it, all revelling in the sleek lines and incredible simplicity. Instead of the usual network of chassis tubes there were two nacelles, each containing a rubberized fuel bag, linked by an undertray and fabricated bulkheads. In those days engines were not yet fully stressed so the power unit had to be carried on tubular extensions from the monocoque 'tub', which Colin always referred to as 'the trouser legs'! The suspension was virtually identical to that of the Lotus 24, as was the ZF gearbox. The driver's seating position was even lower in the cockpit and, because the opening at the top was somewhat narrower, a smaller-diameter steering wheel was necessary.

The car went as well as it looked and, with a frame about four times more rigid than that of the Lotus 24 and slimmer lines, it is not surprising. The only disappointed people were the customers who had bought 24s earlier in the season. Innes Ireland was one of the people affected by this, and he recalls the incident well. 'After my being fired by Colin, I agreed to drive for Ken Gregory's UDT-Laystall team for 1962, who had received an assurance from Chapman – and this took a bit of the sting out of my departure – that we would always have the same cars as Team Lotus. So to begin with, of course, we had a new Lotus 24 which we took to Zandvoort. When we got there, there was this monocoque Lotus 25, so I went breezing up to Colin, saying, "That really looks terrific". It really looked a fabulous car and I got quite excited about it. "When do we get ours?" I said. "Oh you won't be getting one of these," he replied, "They are our 1963 cars."' In fact, the Lotus 25 was actually built in the Team Lotus racing shop rather than by the racing car manufacturing arm of Lotus Components.

In the race John Surtees in a Lola, also with a Climax V8 engine, was in pole position on the grid, and Jimmy, with third fastest practice time, was on the outside of the front row with Graham Hill in a BRM between them. At the drop of the flag Jimmy was first away and led for eleven laps before arriving slowly in the pits with clutch trouble. The repair took quite a long time and Jimmy eventually finished in ninth place, ten laps in arrears. Meanwhile, Graham Hill had finally scored his first Grand Prix win for BRM and it became clear that the battle during the remainder of the season would be between Jimmy and Graham. And so it proved.

Trevor Taylor, the Team Lotus No 2 driver, finished second at Zandvoort in the space frame Lotus 24 but, through various misfortunes, he failed to score another point that season. Alan Richardson, Chapman's old school friend who, in his earlier Grand Prix racing days, often used to accompany him, well remembers another perfect example of Colin's utter determination to succeed against all odds, which was behind this very satisfactory placing of Trevor Taylor's.

'I remember at Zandvoort once,' recalls Alan, 'when Trevor Taylor's engine blew up in the final practice, Colin decided to take the engine back to Coventry Climax, get it repaired and then get it back to the circuit the following day. Having taken the engine out of the car, off we went to Schipol, Amsterdam's airport, where we got hold of a fork lift truck and hoisted the V8 unit into the passenger seat of his plane. I sat straddled across this damned engine and somehow we managed to get it to Coventry, despite flying through an abominable thunderstorm over the Channel when at one time I thought I'd had my lot! Eventually, we got the engine back to the factory from where we were taken to the house of one of the directors – a very posh place I remember – for a few hours' sleep. The engine was ready in four or five hours or so, and in the morning we flew back to Zandvoort where it was quickly refitted into the car. There was no time for any more practice but nevertheless Taylor finished second.'

Jimmy did not win at Monaco either. He was fastest in practice, led for most of the race, but again his clutch gave in and he had to retire only eight laps from the finish. Bruce McLaren went on to win in a Cooper.

The next race for the 25 was in the Belgian Grand Prix at Spa, a circuit which Jimmy really hated. One of his main reasons for this was that his first race on the Continent, in a D-type Jaguar, had taken place here in 1958 and had been marred by the fatal crash of the very popular British driver, Archie Scott-Brown. Also, in 1960, Jimmy had seen both Chris Bristow in a Cooper, and his own team-mate Alan Stacey killed there, and throughout his career he could never get over his dislike of Spa.

However, whether he liked it or not, Jimmy Clark was THE racing driver and, as it happened, the Spa-Francorchamps circuit suited his style and skill perfectly. Nobody could drift a Grand Prix car as well as he could on this super high-speed course. Clearly no-one else was in the same league. But practice did not start at all auspiciously because he missed a gear change and over-revved his engine. So, while a

Colin lends a hand to Jim Endruweit while he works on the engine of Jimmy Clark's Lotus 25 at Spa in 1962.

Jimmy Clark wins at Zandvoort in 1963.

new one was being rushed over, Colin set about designing some sort of interlocking system which would prevent such a thing happening in future. I will never forget the episode, as it was so typical of the man. He first sketched out the part on a small piece of paper – his drawings were always meticulously neat and clean – and a mechanic then cut out this small slotted plate from a piece of suitable metal. Colin then adjusted it into position very carefully and . . . it worked beautifully, of course!

With his poor practice time Jimmy was on the fourth row of the grid but, despite his vizor being carried away by the wind, he soon caught up the front runners. By the end of the fourth lap he was in fourth place and by the ninth lap he had overtaken both Willy Mairesse and team-mate Trevor Taylor to take the lead. These two had been having a tremendous battle for the lead and they continued to contest second place right up until lap 26, when they collided with each other. Mairesse's Ferrari overturned and caught fire, with the driver suffering minor cuts and burns, while Taylor was unhurt. Jimmy cruised on to win by the enormous margin of 45 secs. The celebration that evening, in the Val d'Ambleve Hotel in Stavelot, where I was sharing a room with both Jimmy and Trevor, was terrific!

At Rouen, for the French GP, Chapman had provided Jimmy Clark with a brand-new Lotus 25, which had probably been somewhat hastily put together, and Taylor took over Jimmy's original Lotus 25. Whilst Jimmy was fastest in practice, he was never happy with the handling and the race was over for him when a suspension ball-joint broke. Trevor Taylor then managed to write-off the first 25 when he collided with Rob Walker's Lotus 24, after being prevented from getting into the pits at the end of the race by over-enthusiastic French gendarmes. Fortunately for Jim Clark and Lotus, with their eyes firmly fixed on the World Championship, the race was won by the American Dan Gurney driving the Formula 1 Porsche to its one and only victory.

Clark came within two points of leading the Championship by winning the British Grand Prix at Aintree, near Liverpool, when despite persistent misfiring throughout the race due to carburation problems he led from start to finish.

Next came the German GP at the Nurburgring and, with hindsight, this was probably the turning point in that year's race for the Championship. Jimmy made a very bad start due to an uncharacteristic mistake which he later explained in his book: 'In this race I did a very silly thing. The start of the race had been delayed as there was a freak thunderstorm. After it had eased off, the organizers decided to allow each car to do one exploratory lap so that each driver could check the track for flooding. Finally, we took up positions on the start line, and having started the engine, I found that my goggles were steaming up as they had got excessively wet during the warming-up lap. I had switched off the fuel pumps, as had been my custom since a fouled plug had given me trouble on the first few laps at Monaco earlier in the season. In the last seconds before the start I was so concerned with those confounded goggles that I forgot to switch the petrol pumps back on. At precisely the moment the flag fell, the engine – which had been running on the petrol lying in the carburettors – expired. I felt so annoyed, sitting there in a silent car as the rest of the field roared away in a great cloud of spray!'

Not only did he lose twelve valuable seconds at the start but now he had to overtake all the backmarkers. Although by the end of the fifth lap he was in fifth place, he never did catch the leading bunch and finished fourth. Graham Hill drove a masterly race in the wet to win in his BRM and thus establish an even greater lead in the Championship.

The Italian GP at Monza turned into a shambles for Team Lotus, although Jimmy was again fastest in practice. On race morning, while the mechanics were warming up Clark's car, the gearbox seized. Colin thought this might have had something to do with a new oil additive they were testing but, whatever it was, the gearbox had to be changed even though the time of the start was fast approaching. With so much still to be done, there seemed to be a distinct shortage of mechanics, too, and it was not long before I was roped in to top up the fuel tanks whilst my fellow journalists crowded round wondering what all the kerfuffle was about! Eventually the car was ready in time for the start, but again the gearbox failed and Clark was forced to retire on the 13th lap, while Graham Hill went on to win his third Grand Prix of the season.

Jimmy managed to even the score at Watkins Glen for the US Grand Prix and so he and Graham had each won three races. However, Hill also had two second places, a fourth and a sixth, against which Jimmy only had his fourth place at the Nurburgring. (During that year the Championship was to be decided by totalling the points from the drivers' best five results.) This meant that, for Clark to become World Champion, he would have to win the last race – the South African GP at East London – because then his best five results would be four wins and one fourth place, against Hill's three wins and two seconds. In both cases the total number of points gained by each driver would be 39 but Jimmy would be Champion because of his greater number of wins.

There was tremendous 'needling' between the two teams before the race and BRM had somehow succeeded in encouraging the rumour that they had built a much lighter car for Hill. Tony Rudd, who was then BRM Team Manager, remembers that during scrutineering Colin went and stood close to the weighbridge while the BRM was on it and was absolutely furious when he saw that it weighed only 5 lb (2.27 kg) less than normal. Because of all the rumours, he had by then spent a large sum of money and a great deal of time in reducing the weight of the 25, for no real purpose!

It was a nail-biting race, with both aspiring Champions sharing the front row of the grid. Jimmy was in pole and immediately took the lead. By half distance in the 82-lap race he was thirty seconds ahead of Hill. Then, on the 60th lap, an ominous puff of smoke was seen as the car flashed past the pits. When Colin called him in next time round, it was to find that the engine was covered in oil from a leak caused when a small bolt in the distributor shaft housing had worked loose and fallen out, simply because it had not been provided with a lock washer! Such are the disappointments of motor racing, so Colin Chapman and Jim Clark failed to win their first World Championship. Nevertheless, Colin had proved a point over racing car design and gradually all the other manufacturers adopted the principles of the monocoque chassis. Without a doubt, this played a significant role in making motor racing so much safer for the drivers: Jimmy certainly felt it did, and he never again drove a space-framed single-seater in which, in a crash, bent and broken tubes can prove so damaging to the driver.

At the 1962 Racing Car Show in London in early January Lotus announced and showed two new cars to be built by Lotus Components for sale to retail customers. One was the new Lotus 22 Formula Junior, which was fitted with the 1,100 cc Ford-Cosworth Mk IV engine inclined in the chassis at an angle of 30 degrees. Priced at £1,550, the 22 soon proved to be another winner, with Team Lotus driver Peter Arundell scoring 18 victories out of 25 starts during the season, including that most prestigious event the Formula Junior curtain-raiser to the Monaco Grand Prix. However, Brabham was also becoming a racing car manufacturer to be reckoned with and, in view of all this competition in what was a fairly limited market, Lotus in fact only made a total of 77 examples of the Lotus 22.

During the season, another member of Team Lotus, Alan Rees, had the misfortune to crash his FJ 22 at the Nurburgring, suffering slight injuries which put him in hospital for a few days. Whilst there, he was visited by some German reporters and during the conversation with them Alan happened to mention that some competitors were using over-size engines in their FJ cars. Due to the language problems, they misunderstood him, thinking that he meant that his team-mate Peter Arundell was the culprit because he was winning so many races. Former racing driver-turned journalist, Richard von Frankenberg, then wrote a rather offensive story which was published in one of the German motor sporting magazines. This, of course, was eventually brought to Colin's notice, and when he showed it to his solicitors they recommended that he should sue the magazine for a large sum of money.

However, Colin had a more sporting idea: he wagered Frankenberg £1,000 that Peter Arundell would return to the Monza circuit – where he had won the Formula

In 1962 the German magazine Auto Motor und Sport *published a story written by former racing driver Richard von Frankenberg suggesting that Team Lotus were using an oversize engine in the Formula Junior car with which Peter Arundell was winning everything that season. Rather than sue him, Colin suggested a bet which necessitated Peter driving round the Monza circuit on a chilly November day. At first the track was actually frozen and a team of helpers, under Colin's direction, had to go to the Lesmo Curve to thaw it out!* **Below right** *Peter Arundell gets going in the morning mist at Monza under Colin's watchful eye.*

Arundell drove his Lotus 22 over the same distance as the Monza Lottery race, beating his own winning time by over a minute. After he had lapped faster than in the actual race, von Frankenberg apologized and handed over to Colin a cheque for £1,000. It would have been nice if the matter had ended there but unfortunately it did not. Von Frankenberg lost his job and from then on he led a savage battle against Lotus every time he could get his hands on a road test car!

Junior Lottery race – and would lap on his own until he had covered the same distance, at a speed equal to or greater than the speed he had achieved in the race. Afterwards, the cylinder head would be lifted by Italian scrutineers who would then measure the engine's displacement. Von Frankenberg really had no option but to take up the challenge, so the Italian magazine *Auto-Italiana* hired the track and took on the organization of the 'event' which, of course, made a big news splash, especially in German and Italian motor sporting circles.

The Monza circuit had been chosen because it was felt that there would be less risk of frost or snow in early December but, on the day, it was quite foggy and the track was indeed frozen at the Lesmo Curve, so buckets of salt had to be used to defrost it. Finally, at 1.40 pm, the 'trial' was under way and Peter Arundell soon proved to be well up to his task, beating his previous time by over a minute and posting a fastest lap of 117.169 mph (188.56 kph)! The scrutineers duly measured the cylinder capacity to be 1,092 cc; Richard von Frankenberg apologized and the Editor of the magazine handed over a cheque for £1,000. Needless to say, it was not very long before the Editor had him replaced. One other person who attended this event was Mike Costin who was there to look after the interests of the engine manufacturer, Cosworth Engineering. By then, he had finally left Lotus to take up the position which Keith Duckworth had originally offered him some years earlier.

The second new car which Lotus Components had announced at the Racing Car Show heralded their return to manufacturing small sports cars, the type aimed at club racing events and which had originally put Lotus on the map. This was the Lotus 23, a very pretty rear-engined car which shared the suspension and the power-train of the 22 single-seater. At 970 lb (440 kg) it was the same weight as the Eleven.

Since Colin was already working on the design of his next road car which was to have a new engine using a Ford 1,500 cc block with a special Lotus-designed twin-overhead camshaft cylinder head, he was most keen to race-test the engine. Giving 103 bhp at a very modest 6,000 rpm, it was duly fitted into the new 23 recently ordered by John Ogier's Essex Racing Team (not to be confused with David Thieme's Essex Petroleum, which was to sponsor Lotus in the '80s) and already entered for the 1,000 km of the Nürburgring. The plan was that the Ogier mechanics would look after the chassis while Lotus prepared the engine. Colin was also on hand for the race, especially since Team Lotus drivers Jim Clark and Trevor Taylor were to drive the car.

At the start it was drizzling but Clark immediately took the lead. At the 'Ring there was a very elaborate display board in front of the grandstand, giving the position of the cars and their times at different points around the circuit. It was really quite incredible: at the Karussel the Lotus was 17 sec ahead and by the time it was round to 'Start und Zeil' – the finishing line – it led Gurney's Porsche by 27 sec. We could not believe our eyes! After the second lap Jimmy's lead had increased to 47 sec and at the end of the third lap it was up to 1 min 13 sec, and all this against top-class opposition from V6, V8 and V12 Ferraris varying in capacity from two to four litres, besides several 2 litre Porsches! On the seventh lap Clark's lead was 1 min 47 sec and he had turned in a fastest lap of 9 min 46.3 sec but, unbeknown to him, although the engine was still in fine fettle, the exhaust system had worked loose and he was slowly

A happy team. Trevor Taylor and Jimmy Clark always got on very well together. Here they are with Derek Wilde, one of the Lotus mechanics.

becoming intoxicated by the fumes. 'This was incredible, but it could not last for much longer,' wrote Clark. 'The exhaust manifold started to leak. I didn't notice it at first, but then I began to feel drowsy. At the same time the brakes were not so good and a combination of all this led to my downfall. Coming into Kesselchen I changed down but the car jumped out of gear and went into a slide. My reactions were too slow and I just couldn't correct it and the car went off into the bushes.' Nevertheless, his quick lap times before the accident created quite a furore and also helped to build up considerable pre-race excitement for Le Mans a month later, where Colin had entered a similar combination of car and drivers.

Although, officially, Stan Chapman had retired from the job of Team Manager, he was still in charge of the Le Mans operation. He very much enjoyed his annual French trip. During all the years that the team was running at Le Mans, Stanley would come over to Paris in early March before the closing date for entries, when I would have arranged lunch for us with Jacques Finance, the Automobile Club de l'Ouest's Vice-President. Finance used to enjoy Three Nuns pipe tobacco, always difficult to buy in Paris, so it was a tradition that Stanley would arrive with a suitably large supply. After an enjoyable lunch, we would both drive down to Le Mans where Stanley would ceremoniously hand over the entry forms to Raymond Accat, the Club's Secretary.

We had successfully stuck to this routine for several years and I am quite sure that this had been a great help in making it possible for Lotus to enter, more or less, whatever cars they wanted, even down to the point that we could choose which of the private entries were to be 'favoured'! Between then and the race there was, of course, much correspondence for Stan to deal with, like sorting out the team's room reservations at Monsieur Mica's Hotel St Nicolas in Mayet, close to Le Mans, where Team Lotus had always stayed since 1955.

When the new car arrived for scrutineering, complete with high windscreen to comply with the then-current Le Mans regulations, it immediately attracted a great deal of attention and there was little doubt that it would start the race as the clear favourite to win the Index of Performance, especially since it was now equipped with a 1,000 cc version of the twin-cam Ford Lotus engine, for the smaller the displacement the better chance there was of winning the Index. Unfortunately, the car was so new that, to be quite frank, it was just not ready to race. The French scrutineers immediately rejected it, along with a second car entered by UDT-Laystall and fitted with the 750 cc FWMC Climax engine. They were ruled out on the grounds that the fuel tanks were oversize, the turning circle, restricted by the wheels touching the bodywork, was too great and there was insufficient ground clearance. But worst of all was that, while the rear wheels were held on by six studs and nuts, those at the front were retained by only four. The regulations stated, '. . . the method of fixation of the wheels must be the same at front and back'. Although the car did, in fact, comply with the letter of the law, ie, studs were used at front and rear, the Le Mans people felt it should comply with the spirit of the rules as well. There was, of course, a great deal of argument and discussion, as can be imagined, but eventually they turned the cars down flat.

At this time Colin was still back in England and Mike Costin was in charge of all technical matters. The Stewards then asked him, 'How long do you need to get the car prepared in accordance with the regulations?' and Mike replied, 'We can get the ground clearance, the turning circle and the fuel tank capacities modified for tomorrow's practice session (it was then Tuesday), and if you can give us another day for the hubs, and let us practise tomorrow with them in their current state, we will get them right in time for the second practice session on Thursday.' I think it was at about this point that some outside pressures were brought to bear on the Stewards, as they replied: 'Get it all right by tomorrow midday, at the close of scrutineering, or you won't race!'

Obviously they never thought it would be humanly possible to make such a deadline, but they had not reckoned with Colin Chapman. Mike quickly phoned him and he immediately set about designing the necessary parts to change the rear hubs over to four-stud fixing. When this was done he rushed over to the factory where the parts, sufficient for both cars, were machined overnight. In the morning they were delivered to a light aeroplane, hired by UDT-Laystall, and flown direct to Le Mans where they arrived with just sufficient time for them to be fitted to the 23s before scrutineering ended. However, despite this quite remarkable achievement, the Chief Scrutineer decided that Lotus had not done what he wanted: if six studs were originally fitted to the rear hubs, then that is what he wanted to see on the front

'You have until tomorrow midday to change your hubs if you want to race,' said the scrutineers at Le Mans in 1962. But, by burning much midnight oil, new parts were made and flown in on the Wednesday morning and fitted on both cars just before the end of scrutineering. It was to no avail. The officials found another reason to kick Lotus out.

ones! Mike Costin then carefully explained that the car was actually designed to accept the 2 litre BRM engine, and therefore the running gear was much stronger than was really necessary for the much less powerful 1,000 cc Ford engine. Mike even took the scrutineer by the arm and, waving his slide rule, told him: 'If you say my car is unsafe, it means you must be qualified to say so. Perhaps, therefore, we should together work out the stress calculations and I am sure you will then agree with me!' But it was all to no avail.

Colin was beside himself with fury and flew in to Le Mans the next day in his Piper Comanche, bringing along with him Dean Delamont, the Secretary of the Royal Automobile Club Motor Sport Division, because the Club's on-the-spot representative, Harold Parker – a charming but elderly gentleman with very little technical knowledge – was clearly out of his depth. But even Delamont failed to convince the Stewards and the 23s did not start.

However, there were still the two Team Elite cars in the race and Stan Chapman, as the official entrant, was – technically anyway – still in charge of these. Now, as we know, one of the Le Mans regulations was that cars had to conform to a minimum ground clearance, and it was a well-known dodge of most entrants that, in order to pass the scrutineers' inspections, they would – before their cars were to be scrutineered – raise the setting of the springs by whatever margin was necessary. Then they would drop them back to the normal ride level just before their cars went out on the circuit! Although the organizers would often turn a blind eye, in view of the amount of attention and publicity given to their attitude over the two Lotus 23 entries they now had to be seen to be equally strict with all competitors.

Now, amongst the darlings of the Le Mans crowds were the Rodriguez brothers, Ricardo and Pedro, who were entered in an experimental V6 rear-engined 2.4 litre Ferrari, and on race morning this car flunked the ground clearance test. We knew this because we had posted one of our mechanics in the scrutineering bay! Immediately Stan Chapman entered a protest and, with this in his hand, Vice-President Jacques Finance considered it for a minute, and then he approached Eugenio Dragoni, Ferrari's Team Manager, saying, 'You have half-an-hour to get the Rodriguez car in order.' To which Dragoni simply replied, 'You have five seconds to tell me that the Rodriguez car is in order or else I will withdraw the entire Ferrari team!' Naturally, the matter went no further and it was a somewhat sheepish Harold Parker who sought out Stan Chapman to hand back his protest deposit money and assure him 'all was in order now'!

The race results proved another overwhelming success for the Elites when both the cars entered finished first and second in Index of Thermal Efficiency, with David Hobbs and Frank Gardner in the winning car, averaging 99.623 mph (160.33 kph) and consuming fuel at the rate of a shade under 20 mpg (14.3 l/100 km). What is more, both cars had been timed down the straight at 141 mph (227 kph). However,

Chapman had not arrived at Le Mans when the scrutineering incident took place. He flew in later during the week with Dean Delamont, the Secretary of the Motor Sport Division of the RAC. They are here waiting in the Clerk of the Course's office with Major Parker (left), the RAC's representative on the spot.

not even this spectacular success could pacify Colin, who was still fuming over the rejection of the Lotus 23 entries. The press generally sided with Lotus and finally, after the race, the Club began to realize that they had perhaps misjudged matters and that, if Chapman stood by his threat never to enter for Le Mans again, it would be a severe loss to the race.

The Chairman of the Automobile Club de l'Ouest, Jean-Marie Lelièvre, who was also the Chairman of a large Paris-based insurance company, invited Colin to visit him in his office to discuss the matter. I was invited along to translate. Lelièvre told Colin, 'We feel we may have made a mistake and we would like to compensate you. How much did this business cost you and we shall refund you to that amount.' Colin thought carefully for a moment, added some figures together on the back of an envelope, and passed the total to Lelièvre who took one look at it and said, 'It is too much!'. 'In that case,' replied Colin, 'we shall never again race at Le Mans.' The meeting was over and Colin Chapman kept his word. No Team Lotus entry has appeared at Le Mans since 1962.

In the aftermath of the race, Bernard Consten – one of the best French drivers of the time – approached me to say that, with the help of BP, he was prepared to buy the UDT-Laystall car and race it in other French events during the season, provided Colin would lend him the 1,000 cc engine and the services of a mechanic to look after it. Consten's co-driver was to be José Rosinski who was already carrying out road tests for *Sport-Auto*, the magazine which I had started with Jean Lucas at the beginning of that year. Colin agreed to this proposal, but only on condition that the four-stud wheels were retained so that he could, once and for all, prove to the Le Mans officials that they were more than strong enough – and prove it he did! UDT-Laystall sold the car which duly won its class handsomely in both the races in which it was entered – the Clermont-Ferrand 6-hours and the 1,000 km of Montlhéry – both circuits much more gruelling to the cars than Le Mans. Colin Chapman had made his point.

It is important to realize here that the main reason for Chapman being so keen to race this 1,000 cc twin-cam engine was that he thought it could be developed very successfully for racing under the new 1,000 cc Formula 2, due to start in 1964.

The mechanic provided for those two events was Bob Dance who had started working for Lotus in 1960, soon after they had moved to Cheshunt. He had originally applied for a job with them when they were still at Hornsey, '... but unfortunately the money was hopeless, so I went back to a garage for a couple of years. Then they advertised some jobs at Cheshunt so I went to see them, and as the money was much more realistic, I joined them.' At first Bob started working on gearboxes – the 'queerbox' and then Hewlands and Colottis (he became a great specialist in this Italian 'box of tricks' which earned him his nickname of Boblotti!). But he was, at heart, a racing enthusiast and eventually he asked if he could be transferred to the racing department and here he worked under Steve Sanville, who was developing the twin-cam engine. Bob's first racing assignments were the Nürburgring 1,000 km race followed by Le Mans a month later. It was after that when he joined us in France. Incidentally, it was also around that time that Bob had a young engineering student from the Royal Aircraft Establishment at Farnborough learning under him. His name was Robin Herd, later to become the head of the very successful March team.

Chapter 9

First Championship Year

Meanwhile, Chapman had been making useful progress with the design for the Elite replacement. One of his parameters for this was that it should be an open car, primarily because the largest market for sports cars was undoubtedly California, where the generally better weather enabled owners to make more use of them. Originally, he had wanted the car to retain the principle of using a one-piece glass-fibre moulded chassis and body shell, as had been used in the case of the Elite. Unfortunately, designer Ron Hickman, who was put in charge of the project, was finding it extremely difficult to obtain sufficient rigidity without the bracing usually provided by the roof of a closed car.

Colin was very impatient to solve the problem, mainly because the power-train was all ready to be tested. So, in some measure of despair and almost as a makeshift solution, he came up with a design for a backbone type of chassis; a very simple, cheap and light affair, made from folded and pressed steel. It forked at the front end to accommodate the engine and gearbox, the transmission passed through the centre, and at the rear there was a T-piece to which the rear suspension units would be attached. This was in the form of a modified Chapman Strut with a wide-based lower wishbone. The half-shafts played no part in locating the rear axle, their angular movements being taken care of by two rubber doughnut-type flexible joints. The front suspension consisted of simple pressed steel wishbones with coil spring and damper units. Hickman then quickly adapted a proprietary Falcon glass-fibre sports car body shell to fit on to this 'jury-rigged' chassis so that testing could get under way. In fact, it all worked well and the idea proved so good that Colin decided he would retain the concept although, of course, using a Lotus-designed body. So a pre-production prototype was put in hand to be ready in time for the 1962 Motor Show. It was called the Lotus Elan.

It had seemed pretty obvious for some time, especially to Fred Bushell, that Lotus were steadily losing money on the Elite. In fact, it has been estimated that on every one of the 1,000 or so Elites sold during the seven years since it was first introduced, Lotus lost £100! Fred therefore wanted something more economical to manufacture and which could be sold at a lower price, but this time make a healthy profit. The crux of the matter was, of course, the engine, and bearing in mind the successes he had achieved in the early days, using what were basically mass-produced engines, Colin decided he should look to see what some of the big manufacturers were able to offer.

First he tried a Ford Consul engine fitted with a special 'Raymond Mays' cylinder

Three generations of the Chapman family stand by a Lotus Elan when it was first introduced at the Earls Court Motor Show in 1962. Left to right: Colin, his father Stanley and grandfather Frank.

head, but this was quickly discarded as unsuitable. Ford had also recently introduced a new short-stroke 1,000 cc engine which, on paper anyway, seemed attractive but was really not sufficiently powerful. So Colin took the decision to build a special twin-overhead camshaft cylinder head to fit the block of this engine, entrusting the actual design to Harry Mundy, late of Coventry Climax. At first the capacity was increased to 1,340 cc and then it was pushed up further to 1,477 cc, at which point Chapman discovered that Ford were about to introduce a brand-new 1,500 cc engine, with a crankshaft running in five main bearings and therefore very much stronger. It was just what he wanted and the new cylinder head was quickly adapted to suit it. This was the engine which then powered the Lotus 23s so successfully that year.

On a personal note, 1962 had been good to Colin for he now had an heir, with Hazel having given birth to a son, Clive.

It was also around this time that Walter Hayes began his somewhat meteoric rise in the hierarchy of Ford of Britain. Walter had first met Colin Chapman when he was Editor of the now defunct *Sunday Despatch* newspaper and recently, in a conversation with me, he recalled their first meeting: '... I wanted a motoring column which would be somewhat different from the others. I asked several people to suggest someone who might fit the bill and Colin Chapman's name was put forward. So I invited Colin and Hazel to dinner and had one of the most interesting evenings of my life!

'Unfortunately Colin was really too busy and rather than producing a regular column, we decided he should do it when he felt like writing. That income should have been a big help to him in building his little cars because he took a lot of money from us!'

Colin went to see Wally Hayes to talk about the twin-cam engine project, at just about the time he had been charged with the task of strengthening the image of the Ford range, especially with the object of attracting a younger market. The parent company, Ford of America, had been pursuing that policy and were just about to launch their world-wide 'Total Performance' programme, in which Lotus would soon play an important part.

When Wally Hayes heard about the twin-cam 1,500 cc engine project, he immediately conceived the idea of putting this into the Ford Cortina saloon car which was proving so successful in the family car market. He offered Chapman the heaven-sent opportunity to redesign the Cortina's rear suspension, dress the car up a bit, market it as the Lotus-Cortina and then assemble it at the Lotus factory in Cheshunt. Colin did not have to think twice, for it was an offer he could not possibly refuse.

The Lotus-Cortina (the Lotus Type 28) was announced in January 1963. The car itself was the standard two-door version but the body was painted cream with a 'Lotus Green' flash along the waistline, and a circular Lotus radiator badge was fixed to each of the rear side panels. It was an extremely smart looking car. Apart from the twin-cam cylinder head, the only other important difference between this and the standard Ford product was the new rear suspension, in which coil springs replaced the standard leaf springs. However, soon after its introduction Ford decided to

By the end of 1962 Colin Chapman had made his mark with the Ford Motor Company, as indicated in this telegram from the Chairman Sir Patrick Hennessy.

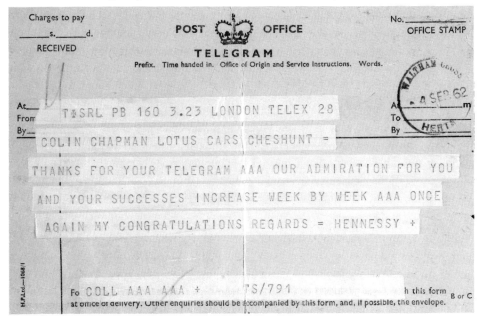

A deal which proved very successful for Lotus and Colin Chapman was their arrangement with Ford over the Lotus-Cortina (Type 28). Lotus fitted their own rear suspension and engine – a twin-cam cylinder head on a Ford block – into the standard two-door saloon. There was only one paint scheme available – white with 'Lotus green' waistline flutes, plus circular Lotus badges above the radiator air intake and on each rear panel.

increase the capacity of the engine to 1,600 cc for racing purposes and when Colin heard about this he decided it would make sense to adopt this size for the new Elan, by which time some of the early pre-production examples had already been sold. These few cars were therefore recalled to the factory for a free-of-charge engine exchange.

The Elan (the Lotus Type 26) had been a great success at the Motor Show and orders were pouring in. It was not by any means as pretty as the Elite but, even though it weighed approximately the same, it out-performed it, thanks to the increased power (105 bph) and improved flexibility. Above all, at £1,499 in completely assembled form, it was much less expensive than the Elite which had carried a £2,000 price tag. It was also a much simpler design and therefore easier to maintain. Finally, there was the attraction of it being an open car with a soft-top, although there was a hard-top available as an optional extra. Also, by then Jim Clark had virtually become a household name and, since he used an Elan for his own personal transport – often being photographed in it – there was considerable kudos to be gained by 'buying a car like Jimmy Clark's'.

The Elan remained in production in one form or another for many years, being modified regularly throughout its life. The 'Series 2' model with larger brakes appeared in 1964 and then, in 1965, came the 'Series 3' which was the first fixed-head coupé, to be followed later by a soft-top version which this time was watertight, a quality which the original Elan had lacked. Then came the 'Special Equipment' model with a much modified 115 bhp engine, to be followed soon afterwards by the

'Series 4' with wider wheels. Finally, in 1971, came the Elan 'Sprint' which was equipped with a very powerful 126 bhp engine, fitted with enlarged valves and developed by engineer Tony Rudd. Prior to that, though, a +2 version had been introduced in June 1967, aimed primarily at the sports car enthusiast with a young family, as Colin was himself. This was eventually superseded by the +2S, designed to suit a more sophisticated market and not offered in kit form – an alternative which had always been available to purchasers of the other models. The interior of the +2S was also much more luxurious and it was the introduction of this car which paved the way for the more 'up-market' image that Lotus was to present in later years. The +2S was also given the 'Sprint' engine, becoming known as the +2S/130, and the final example of the type was the +2S/130/5 with a five-speed Lotus-manufactured gearbox using an Austin gear cluster.

There is no doubt that the Elan was the car which really put Lotus on the road to financial success. Throughout its life it became more and more reliable and, naturally, its roadholding and general handling was beyond question. Although it was certainly not designed with racing in mind, as to a great extent was the Elite, customers soon wanted to start racing them, a proposition to which Colin initially objected most strongly. However, he soon realized that, since he could not really stop them, he had better make sure the cars were fully raceworthy and so he introduced a pure racing version, the 26R, which did quite well at club level and Team Lotus even raced a

Colin and Hazel Chapman with a Lotus Cortina and Jimmy Clark and girl friend Sally Stokes with his Elan, meet up at Heathrow Airport on their way back from the States after their 1965 Indy win.

'works' example for a time. One young driver of a 26R was Jackie Oliver who later became a member of the Lotus Formula 1 team.

Unlike the Elan, the Lotus-Cortinas emerging from the Cheshunt factory in the Spring of 1963 were, from the outset, designed to be raced, and as a result did not prove too successful as touring cars. Colin's advice at the time was, 'For Heaven's sake, don't spoil the roadholding by putting passengers on the back seat!' The Lotus-Cortina was introduced to the press at Monte Carlo and the prototype was to be driven there by a friend of mine, Jo Schlesser, the Ford-France racing driver. Unfortunately, the timing chain tensioner had broken by the time he reached Paris, and so as to avoid any embarrassment, Colin flew a mechanic over from England and he worked hidden away from prying eyes in the lock-up where I kept my touring car!

Although Lotus had just failed to win the World Championship in 1962, in 1963 Colin was on top of the world and it was fairly obvious to most people, but especially to him, that the Lotus 25 needed very little modification or improvement for it to realize his supreme ambition. As far as the chassis was concerned, no important changes were necessary, but Coventry Climax had now produced a short-stroke version of the FWMV engine which, fitted with Lucas fuel-injection, was developing 195 bhp and providing an extra 1,000 rpm. Actually, at the end of the previous season, Leonard Lee had felt that producing Formula 1 racing engines was costing the company too much money and, in fact, he went so far as to issue a press release to announce that Coventry Climax would be withdrawing from motor racing. However, the British racing car manufacturers got together and, with the help of those traditional sponsors – the fuel and oil companies – they offered to pay a more commercially acceptable sum for the services they were receiving from the Coventry firm. As a result of this agreement, the price of new complete engines was increased to £3,000 while existing engines could be updated to the new specification for £2,000.

The 1963 International Formula 1 Grand Prix season turned out to be a dream for Lotus with Jimmy Clark winning seven out of the ten qualifying events, with seven pole positions and six fastest laps! He won the World Championship with 54 points – from his best six results – with Graham Hill (BRM) and Richie Ginther (Ferrari) in joint second place with only 29 points each. What more can be said?

Well, it can and should be said that one reason for the total supremacy of the Lotus was that most of the rival teams, realizing that they had to avoid being left behind technically, were busy suffering the pangs of now having to develop their own monocoque cars. A small but not insignificant incident which occurred around that time concerned the designer, Len Terry. He had now returned to work at Lotus having left some years earlier to concentrate on his own Terrier sports car which he had been racing with Brian Hart, later to become a well-known engine manufacturer. One day Colin was flying down to see the fuel tank makers together with Len and upon arrival asked, 'Where is that drawing of the 25?' Whereupon Terry answered, 'I don't have it Colin, I thought you must have picked it up off my drawing board.' That drawing was never to be seen again and obviously someone, somewhere, was putting it to good use.

During the 1963 season two modifications were made to the Lotus 25. The first was the introduction of the Hewland gearbox – nowadays virtually standard

Above *From 1962 to 1965 – the end of the 1,500 cc GP formula – Lotus's hopes in Formula 1 rested upon the V8 FWMV Coventry Climax engine, which made its debut in Jack Brabham's Cooper during the middle of 1961. Lotus themselves only used it from 1962. Here, Leonard Lee, the Chairman of Coventry Climax (left) shows the engine to Jimmy Clark and Colin when they visited the factory. On the right is Wally Hassan, the Chief Engineer, who designed it.*

Right *During their visit Colin and Jimmy found time to test a fork-lift truck!*

equipment on all Formula 1 cars – which was tried out later in the season and which had originally been developed for the UDT-Laystall Lotus 21s. The second modification was the reversion of a conventional exhaust system on the V8 engine. In order to change the firing sequence of the cylinders, thus enabling the emission of the exhaust gases to be 'tuned' without having to mix the two banks of cylinders, it was necessary to design a flat-plane crankshaft. This change was originally made at the request of the Ferguson people who were planning to build a four-wheel drive F1 car using the FWMV engine positioned in front of the driver, it being almost impossible to alter the existing exhaust system layout to suit this new car. In the event, engineer Wally Hassan's fears of excessive vibration from this form of crankshaft proved unfounded.

By the time Clark had won the Italian GP at Monza he was confirmed as World Champion, having already won five Grands Prix. Unfortunately for Jimmy, the celebrations were spoilt because the moment he returned to the pits, having won the race, he was asked to go to race control to face questioning by the police over the von Trips accident which had taken place a full two years earlier. As Jimmy said later, 'This was a miserable end to what should have been the most memorable day of my life.'

While Lotus's Grand Prix activities were, in 1963, running as though on rails, Colin and Jimmy had also tackled a new and much more difficult project, which had

Jim Clark was awarded the Ferodo Gold Trophy in 1963 for his World Championship victory.

all started the previous year when Colin had unveiled the new Lotus 25 at Zandvoort. Dan Gurney, then driving for Porsche, was so impressed that he had told Colin, 'You should take a car like this to Indianapolis, you could win with it!' Later on Dan, who in 1962 was going to drive a new rear-engined car at Indy, designed by American Mickey Thompson, made a more formal approach to Colin and offered to pay his fare over to the States just so that he could watch the race and make up his own mind about the possibilities. I well remember after his return, when he described the old-fashioned front-engined 'roadsters' he had seen, he was laughing his head off!

In July 1962, Colin flew with Dan Gurney to the USA for a meeting at the Ford factory in Dearborn, Michigan. Ford, with whom Chapman was already working very closely in Europe, were now very keen to obtain a foothold at Indianapolis and they decided that for the 1963 race they would develop a special light-alloy version of their Fairlane V8 engine. They were encouraged in this because they had previously acquired an example of the four-cylinder 4.2 litre Offenhauser engine – used up to then by almost every competitor – and had been surprised to discover that it was giving only 407 bhp. After considerable development they had succeeded in coaxing 400 bhp out of the Fairlane engine and, what was even more interesting, it was capable of giving 365 bhp on normal gasoline, which would mean a saving of two pit stops over the cars using the methanol-burning Offy engines. Ford agreed to supply two of the engines and to foot the bill for the entire operation. In return for his introduction, Dan Gurney was to be Jimmy's team-mate in a second car.

Clark made his first acquaintance with the 2½-mile Indianapolis track after the 1962 US Grand Prix at Watkins Glen (which he had won), when the team took the winning Lotus 25 to the circuit to carry out some tests and to be observed by the officials prior to them accepting an entry for 1963. 'Indianapolis is big and impressive,' wrote Jimmy in his book, 'with quite the largest grandstand I have ever seen. Everything was laid on and everyone was interested in our ploy. After all, it was not every day that someone arrived with a puny little 1½ litre racing car producing only 175 bhp on their sacred track and, just to see that I was a good little boy, the officials had invited a number of drivers along to watch me go round and to see that I did the correct thing at the correct time. This was one thing which really annoyed me. They treated me like a kid who had never raced before.

'On this first occasion I took things easily and tried to get the hang of driving round left-hand corners all the time. Remember this car had come straight from Watkins Glen, so it was running on normal racing tyres and not set up for the left-hand turns or the banking. I did about 100 laps on that occasion and I remember thinking it was all a bit dull. My fastest lap of 143 mph average made most people sit up and take notice, but what made them even more interested was the speed at which I was taking the turns. The Indy cars rely on their acceleration between the bends to give them high lap times and the fastest time an Indy car had recorded on the turn was something like 138 mph. Our Lotus was doing over 140 mph on the corners so what we lost on the straights in sheer acceleration, we gained on the corners.'

Meanwhile, back in Cheshunt, Len Terry was busy designing the new car for Indianapolis. Although designated the Lotus 29, it was in fact a scaled-up 25 with a 5 in longer wheelbase in order to conform with the local minimum length regulations.

Jimmy Clark in the Lotus-Ford 29, a joint effort with Ford of America who provided the finance and the V8 'stock-block' engine with pushrod-actuated valves. It was Lotus's first attempt at the Indianapolis 500 miles race – and they very nearly won it.

Generally, however, the construction was beefed-up considerably which made things relatively easier for the designer because he was forced to conform to a much higher minimum weight requirement than Formula 1 regulations allowed. Provision also had to be made for an asymmetrical length to the suspension links, to allow for the fact that all four corners of the track were left-handed, which would even out the rate of wear of the tyres.

The prototype was ready in March and was flown to Ford's test track in Arizona after a short de-bugging session at the Snetterton circuit in England. At first the team met with a considerable number of engine problems but, by the time they had moved on to the 'brickyard', Ford finally managed to obtain some reliability from their production-based V8. Once out on the track during the protracted practice sessions, Jimmy's and Dan's performance was soon on a par with the best that the American 'roadsters' could achieve. Clark's qualifying speed was 149.750 mph (241 kph) with Gurney only fractionally slower at 149.019 mph (240 kph).

A furore was created amongst rival teams when it was seen that the Lotus cars were fitted with 15 in tyres specially made for them by Firestone and this was to have far-reaching effects on the future of motor racing. The traditional Indy teams were very concerned that Firestone had provided these smaller tyres for Lotus and, as if they felt they were the main reason for the Lotuses being so fast, they petitioned for them to be made available to everyone! When it became apparent that not everybody was going to be able to race on these tyres, some drivers – notably A. J. Foyt – phoned up the

Goodyear tyre people and said, 'Come to Indy, we are waiting for you!' This was to spark off Goodyear's entry into motor racing in a very big way over the years to come.

I attended Indy that year and I well remember that the atmosphere was really quite unique. The Americans had, of course, seen rear-engined cars before, the last time being in 1961 when Jack Brabham managed to finish in ninth place in his Cooper-Climax, but the Cooper attempt then was on a scale nowhere near approaching that of the Lotus undertaking in 1963, backed as it was by the full strength of the second largest car manufacturer in the United States. It was this which was really the 'fly in the ointment', since the Indy 'establishment' deeply resented seeing so many US dollars being pumped into a foreign team.

Although socially we were looked after very well indeed, with plenty of parties to keep us entertained, on the track it was a very different story and the Americans pulled no punches in their efforts to prevent a Lotus win. Moreover, the race officials were even openly against us, as we would find out on race day.

After three-quarters of the race had been run, the only two cars left in contention were Jimmy's Lotus and Parnelli Jones's Offy roadster owned by that arch-priest of Indy racing, 'Aggie' Agajanian. However, because numerous crashes and incidents had meant that the yellow warning lights had frequently been on, Jones had suffered less than had been expected from the two extra pit stops which he had been forced to make due to running on methanol. When there were only another 25 laps to go – out of a total of 200 – Jimmy started to put the pressure on and began to catch his rival. From being ten seconds behind he gradually reduced the gap to seven, six, five and then 4½ seconds, by which time all quarter-of-a-million spectators were on their feet, quite unable to believe that their own great champion might be defeated by this little green car from England in the hands of, to them, an unknown driver.

Colin in front of the Lotus garage in Indy's 'Gasoline Alley', in deep conversation with chief mechanic Dave Lazenby and designer Len Terry.

Above *David versus Goliaths! Jimmy in the tiny Lotus-Ford amongst the herd of dinosaurs at the start of the 1963 Indy race. Two years later, almost every car that qualified was built on the lines of the Lotus.*

Below *A pit stop for Clark. Colin Chapman, in white shirt and tie, is overseeing the operation.*

Colin Chapman talking with 'Aggie' Agajanian (right) and Parnelli Jones. 'Aggie' bought a Lotus for Parnelli and perhaps Colin is here selling it to him! But it was in the 1963 Indy race that he crossed swords with 'Aggie' – his Offy-engined roadster, driven by Parnelli, should have been black-flagged for leaking oil on the track.

Suddenly, the leading car began to lose oil and it was not Parnelli Jones who was slowing down, but Clark who was having to ease his pace simply because the track was becoming increasingly slippery from the oil dropped by the big American machine. The oil was leaking from a crack in the side of the external oil tank and was plainly visible to those on the trackside, so Colin Chapman naturally rushed up to the Clerk of the Course, Harlan Fengler, to protest: 'What are you waiting for man, his car is a danger to everyone?'. But Fengler, stalling for time, sent for a pair of binoculars under the pretext of wanting to examine the car as closely as possible. Meanwhile 'Aggie' Agajanian had also joined them, screaming every bit as loud as Colin that Jones should be left alone. However, while all the arguments were taking place, the level of the oil in the Offy's tank had fallen below the split, which of course meant that oil was no longer leaking. By then, though, the track was so slippery, with cars spinning everywhere, that the race had to be completed under the yellow warning lights and so that was that.

Although Jimmy Clark and Lotus had to be satisfied with second place, there is no doubt that under the circumstances, and since it was the Team's first attempt, it was their moral victory at least and the next day the American press were very critical of the Indy 'establishment'.

In point of fact, second place was still worth around 100,000 US dollars so, with expenses paid, the prize money and bonuses from Ford and other manufacturers, it was not such a bad deal for Lotus after all! Later in the season Jimmy proved the superiority of the Lotus 29 by annihilating all the opposition at the important Milwaukee race, and threatening to do the same at Trenton, New Jersey, until an oil line fractured. Chapman had certainly now made his mark in the USA and, in particular, at Indianapolis.

It was just as well that Lotus were all-successful in Formula 1 and at Indianapolis, because things were not going so well for them in the lesser formulae. For the last year of Formula Junior Colin had designed a monocoque car, the 27, which was to be the forerunner of a line of cars for the next year's two new formulae: Formula 2 and Formula 3. In order to keep the price down, the sides of the monocoque shell were made with glass-fibre, with the unfortunate result that the frame proved insufficiently rigid. Valuable time was therefore lost while the car was redesigned and manufactured with an all-alloy monocoque, at a price of £1,890. By then, all the prospective customers had already rushed off and bought the latest, and very successful, Formula Junior Brabhams!

To take the pressure off Team Lotus, the responsibility of running the works Formula Junior team was delegated to Ron Harris, with drivers Peter Arundell and Mike Spence, but it was not until later in the season that the Lotus 27 began to score victories and clearly 1963 was Brabham's year in Formula Junior.

A somewhat modified Lotus 23 sports car had also been introduced that year, the 23B adapted to take the 1,600 cc twin-cam engine also being used in the new Elan. In May, Peter Warr himself took one of these (fitted with a special push-rod engine) to the Suzuka circuit to win the first Japanese Grand Prix.

The Lotus-Cortina was already beginning to prove successful but, because of production delays, it was not possible for it to be homologated until September, thus curtailing its racing activities somewhat. Colin even did some of the test driving himself, occasionally ending up with the car facing the wrong way or even upside down! But things were certainly not going very well at the factory, where production of the Elan was also running well behind schedule – so much so that Fred Bushell had, to keep things going, ordered another batch of fifty Elite chassis-body units from the Bristol Aircraft Company. Then towards the end of its useful life the Elite range had, at the instigation of the new Sales Manager, David Buxton (formerly of Team Elite), been extended by the introduction of the 'Super 95', 'Super 100' and 'Super 105' models. Actually, some of these figures turned out to be rather misleading because the '105' for instance, complete with Stage III Climax FWE engine, with five-bearing camshafts and twin Weber carburettors, was only managing to produce about 100 bhp!

Fred Bushell well remembers these somewhat difficult times: 'The Elan was scheduled to be introduced about January '63 along with the Cortina and Colin assumed personal control of the introduction of these two new models. Several additional senior personnel were recruited for the programme and new premises had been constructed for the Cortina so that the two projects could start in tandem. Colin made one of his typical 'monumental decisions' which decreed that, to enable the company to concentrate on the new Elan, no more Elites were to be produced and this meant that the fifty bodies scheduled from Bristol were sidelined into an adjoining field and became, in Colin's terminology, "Fred's Folly".

'Despite Colin's personal handling, no cars were produced until May and the company's cash flow was in even bigger problems. Ford were unhappy at the delayed start for the Cortina and, with the cancellation of the Elite programme, the dealers, with no Elan either, were having severe problems. Colin's desire for perfection was one of the main causes for the hold-up in getting into full production but, with the mounting financial crisis, Colin finally came into my office in May and announced that he had had enough and was going to take himself off to Team Lotus, and if I wanted to salvage the production car side I had better become the Managing Director!

'Fortuitously or otherwise, my production team commenced deliveries of both the Elan and the Lotus-Cortina early in June, in sufficient volume to be able to pull back the situation. Things on the commercial front then began to look quite good again. The next major problem arose with the suppliers of the Elan bodies, Bourne Plastics, who, apart from having difficulty in producing the volume and the quality, were also having trouble with continually escalating costs. After a number of meetings Colin and I decided that we could no longer live with this situation and another monumental Chapman decision was made that we should undertake the manufacture of the bodies ourselves.

'We returned from the final meeting on the Friday and on the Saturday morning we noticed that there were some empty premises in Delamare Road, quite close to our factory. It turned out to be an old bedding spring factory and, by the end of the week we owned it! Within another three months we had initiated a production programme and had commenced moulding and painting. Space was relatively cramped but Colin personally laid out the production areas and, with the mould tools we took over from Bourne Plastics, production of cars commenced. While there were many problems to be overcome, at least they were on our doorstep and in the end we successfully surmounted them.

'This production unit remained operational most of the time we were in Cheshunt although, when the decision was made to move to Hethel in Norfolk, this department was the first to be transferred where it operated on the basis of a satellite factory before the main building was opened. We had actually applied for consent to erect a new purpose-built bodyshop next to the existing spring factory on land we owned in Delamare Road but, much to our surprise and even though permission was granted, we were advised that Lotus would not be allowed to build any more on the Cheshunt site even though further land was available. It was this Government decision which prompted Colin to move from the area completely and, in fact, the search for a new home for Lotus commenced at about that time. The new bodyshop was built although it was never occupied by Lotus.'

Although still small, Lotus was now a highly prestigious company, with considerable skills and experience in its specialized field, and so it was understandable that some of the bigger companies might be tempted to try and take it over. For instance, in late 1962, Ford of America attempted to buy out Ferrari, mainly because they felt this was the best way of putting the Ford name on the Le Mans 24-Hours race-winner. But finally their overtures were rejected so chief executive Lee Iacocca

The Cheshunt factory in full swing. The building on the left housed Team Lotus and Lotus Components, who built Sevens and racing cars for sale to customers. The close proximity of the housing estate can be clearly appreciated from this aerial photograph.

initiated what was called the 'High Performance Special Model Operation'. In June of that year a group of Ford executives comprising Roy Lunn, a former Aston Martin and Jowett engineer who had emigrated to the States some years earlier, Ray Geddes and Al Sperlich, the Production Manager, were sent to Europe. This was the time of the Le Mans race and during the following week they visited England with the express purpose of looking round for a firm that could be taken over and which could undertake a programme to produce what was to become the Ford GT40. Two of the firms they visited were Lola and Lotus and Fred Bushell recalls the meeting at Lotus which, of course, he attended:

'There had been a number of approaches made to Colin to buy the company and several of these came from the States, none of which got very far. The first serious one was from Ford of America who came after us when they had been turned down by Ferrari. The meeting resulted in a quick review of our business followed by a discussion about the GT40. In fact, the appointment had been made through a firm of steel wholesalers, who had been asked by Ford whether they thought we might like to be taken over. Colin's reaction was: "If they want to talk to me they can". The visit to Cheshunt had followed and although Colin was quite co-operative throughout he was never over-enthusiastic. However, somewhat typically of Ford, we never heard the reasons why they didn't want to proceed.'

In his book 'Ford, the Dust and the Glory' (published by Macmillan, USA) Leo Levine reports this meeting: 'At the start the most obvious choice was Chapman. Not only did the Ford Division and Ford of England both have contracts with him, but he was generally considered the finest chassis designer in the world. It should have been no contest, but there were things militating against Chapman. There was the question of how well he would take direction, whether or not he and Shelby would rub egos [Carroll Shelby, who was building the Ford-engined Cobras, was also part of the GT40 programme], whether the capacity of his plant was such that it could absorb the Ford GT along with the other things under development – and just how much publicity would Chapman seek . . .' The Ford party finally decided to do business with Lola, and Carroll Shelby only recently told me that, in his view, it was Roy Lunn who had influenced this decision because he felt that Colin would profit most from the operation through which he personally intended to boost his own image.

But there were other approaches made to Lotus, says Fred Bushell: 'That was followed by an approach from Sir William Lyons of Jaguar, who talked to Colin before he himself was taken over by British Leyland. This led to a series of discussions and we went quite a long way down the road, but the stumbling block came when Lyons said he wanted Colin to play an active role at Jaguar and Colin felt that volume production of cars was really not his scene. It boiled down to the fact that Lyons was trying to find a successor but Colin did not see that as the way he wanted to spend most of his life. These were very earnest meetings with Lyons being very charming to Colin with whom he seemed most keen to be associated.'

Colin Chapman receiving the 1963 World Constructors' Championship Cup from Maurice Baumgartner, President of the Fédération Internationale de l'Automobile.

Chapter 10

From Disappointment
to Double Victory

There is a saying amongst Formula 1 people that it is always more difficult to do well following a previous season of complete dominance, and that certainly proved to be true in 1964 as far as Lotus were concerned. The Lotus 25 was modified to take the latest lower and wider Dunlop 13 in tyres in place of the previous 15 in, and became the Lotus 33. The monocoque tub was simplified, the suspension geometry revised and the wheelbase lengthened by three-quarters of an inch. Coventry Climax also produced an engine with an even shorter stroke which punched out over 200 bhp at 9,500 rpm.

As far as the drivers were concerned, obviously Clark was to remain number one but, after so many crashes, Trevor Taylor had finally fallen out of favour with Colin and so his place in the team was taken by Peter Arundell. Colin explained to me once why he had chosen Peter as his number two man: 'Jimmy was so good that every other driver was mesmerized by him. But when I spoke to Arundell, he said, "Give me an equal car and I can beat him!" This is why I signed him up. I felt he had the correct mental approach.'

Unfortunately, Lotus did not succeed in sorting out the 33's roadholding quite as well as they did the previous year on the 25. On top of this, Jimmy crashed the new car in a non-Championship race at Aintree early in the season, when he was baulked by one of the back markers, and so he could not use it for the first two GPs. At Monte Carlo, the first race, both Team Lotus 25s arrived sporting a broad yellow stripe painted along the middle of the bodywork, very similar to that which appeared on the Lotus 29 at Indianapolis the previous year. This had been applied in order to liven up the appearance of the car while it was amongst all the garishly colourful American cars, where there was no rule obliging entrants to use their national racing colours and where even advertising was allowed on racing cars! An all-green Lotus would have been very dull indeed, apart from the fact that it was considered to be an unlucky colour in USAC races. The yellow stripe certainly improved the look of the cars.

Jimmy qualified on pole position again but it was not long before the rear anti-roll bar broke loose on one side and eventually a quick visit to the pits became necessary for the offending part to be wrenched off. Although he regained second place for a while, he lost all oil pressure only three laps from the finish and was forced to retire but was finally classified in fourth place because only the winner, Graham Hill, completed the full distance of 100 laps. Peter Arundell's season started quite favourably with third place, despite also suffering from falling oil pressure in the closing stages of the race.

At Zandvoort, however, Clark won the Dutch Grand Prix at record speed, still in the 25, smashing the lap record into the bargain. But the Belgian Grand Prix at Spa turned into quite an incredible race. In practice the new 33 was brought out but it was not handling at all well, probably because it had reverted to 15 in wheels and tyres in the interests of providing higher gearing to suit the circuit. Jimmy was in and out of the pits all the time but, just before the session was due to end he had still not put up a quick lap. Colin – who had been watching the Clerk of the Course getting his flag ready – suddenly shouted to me, 'Quick, go and ask him not to put the flag out until Jimmy has gone by!' So I rushed over to the man but, realizing that I could hardly ask such a favour, I chose instead to engage him in conversation, during which I managed to put my foot on the flag. Being a very polite gentleman, he did not push me away but instead kept gently tugging on the handle of the flag, hoping I would understand. It was only after the green and yellow Lotus had flashed past that I casually removed my foot so that the flag was then able to be displayed! In the meantime Jimmy did manage a somewhat faster lap, although he still had to settle for a position on the outside of the third row of the grid. Gamesmanship of this nature was then quite typical of Team Lotus, when the rules and regulations were nothing like as strict as they are today.

Still not happy with the new car, it was decided that Jimmy should drive the 'old' Lotus 25B in the race, during which many cars suffered from fuel starvation. This came about mainly because of a phenomenon peculiar to a circuit such as Spa. In a racing car, the fuel normally reaches the outlet pipe from the tank – and thus the fuel pump – simply by the movement of the car causing it to splash around in the tank. However, at Spa, with its long straight sections and only a few places where the cars have to decelerate rapidly, towards the end of the race when the quantity of fuel was getting low it was tending to accumulate at the rear of the tank and away from the outlet point, so that there was insufficient fuel available to feed the pump.

Dan Gurney in a Brabham, whilst well in the lead, was the first to suffer but when he called into his pit no more fuel was available. He was so incensed by this that he rejoined the race only to come to a stop by the roadside a couple of miles further on! Graham Hill's BRM took over the lead only to succumb to the same problem soon afterwards, leaving Bruce McLaren's Cooper in first spot but, just as he arrived at the last corner, his engine went dead, too. Fortunately, from there to the finish was downhill so he was able to coast towards the line but just as he was about to cross it Clark flashed past to win by just 3 sec! A minute or so later, while on his slowing-down lap, he also ran out of fuel and stopped at the same point as Gurney. Both men were commiserating together, Jimmy not realizing he had won because in all the excitement the chequered flag had been shown in error to Richie Ginther. It was thought that Graham Hill had won when, over the loudspeakers, came the announcement that Clark was the winner! In fact, Jimmy was told of his victory by his team-mate Peter Arundell who went out to collect him.

The French GP at Rouen was less successful because, when well in the lead, Jimmy's engine inhaled a small stone which broke a piston. But at the British Grand

Prix, held for the first time ever at Brands Hatch, he was again in pole position and led from start to finish, notching up his third successive victory in his home Grand Prix. Here the second Team Lotus car was driven by Mike Spence because Peter Arundell had been seriously injured in a Formula 2 race at Rheims.

So far during the season the battle for the Championship had been between Clark and Hill, but now Ferrari had developed a new V8 engine which was slowly getting into its stride and at the German GP John Surtees won with it, while Jimmy had to retire with valve trouble. At the next race, the first-ever Austrian Grand Prix held on a NATO air base at Zeltweg where the track had been badly affected by frost, all the cars took a tremendous hammering. Both Lotuses broke steering arms in practice, and in the race both retired with broken half-shafts after completing about 40 laps. At Monza they were no match for the BRMs or the Ferraris, particularly on the long straights, and Surtees won again while Jimmy broke a piston and Spence finished sixth. By then the order in the World Championship was Hill-Clark-Surtees but fuel feed problems eliminated both Clark and Spence in the US Grand Prix at Watkins Glen, so when the teams arrived in Mexico for the final Grand Prix of the 1964 season, Jimmy had to win if he was to retain the title.

For most of the race it looked very much as though this would be the case but suddenly he noticed a streak of oil on the track, so he changed his line to avoid it. On the next lap round he realized that the oil streak followed the line he had taken on his previous lap, so he knew then that the oil was coming from his own car. Sure enough,

After Peter Arundell was injured in a Formula 2 accident at Rheims in 1964 his place in the team went to Mike Spence, seen here between Colin and Jimmy Clark at the French GP in 1965. Mike was killed three years later in a practice crash at Indianapolis.

Colin Chapman with his friend and rival Jack Brabham and the latter's twin-engined aeroplane. During their racing days they shared many a flying escapade.

as Colin and the mechanics were preparing to greet their new Champion, one lap from the finish the Lotus coasted in with a dead engine covered in oil. A broken oil line had cost Clark his second World Championship and Surtees, who finished second to Dan Gurney in the race, took the honours from Graham Hill by only one point. In the constructors' championship Lotus were third to Ferrari and BRM.

Early on in 1964 the Japanese motor cycle manufacturers Honda had decided to launch into Formula 1 motor racing and they sent their Chief Engineer, Yoshio Nakamura, over to Europe to find a British team who might be prepared to use a Honda engine. They were also planning to bring out their own chassis, using a similar engine. At the time this was happening I was helping the Japanese Automobile Club with the organization of their own Grand Prix at the Suzuka circuit, and they asked me to set up meetings between Nakamura and the leading British racing car manufacturers. The proposed deal would, in fact, be somewhat 'double-barrelled' because Honda were also planning to manufacture a Formula 2 engine.

Jack Brabham was kind enough to fly over to Paris in his twin-engined Cessna aircraft to pick us up and after a visit to his factory we went on to see Cooper and then Lotus. We also paid a visit to Cosworth because Keith Duckworth was toying with the idea of building his own chassis, too. Although Nakamura kept his thoughts very much to himself after the visit, my feelings were that it was Brabham who had made the best impression. However, the morning after our return to Paris Colin telephoned me to say, 'Please arrange for me to have a meeting with Soichiro Honda. I am prepared to fly to Japan as soon as he can receive me.' The trip duly took place and Colin – who arrived in Japan before Mr Nakamura returned – had little difficulty in convincing the head of this large company that he should be given the use of their new Formula 1 engine for the 1965 season. Brabham, as a consolation perhaps, was given the use of the Formula 2 engine.

A short while later a mock-up of the transverse V12 Honda engine duly arrived at Cheshunt, but nothing more came of the proposed arrangement and it was clear that Chapman created the opportunity in order to put pressure on Coventry Climax by threatening to use the Honda if they would not further develop their own engine.

Team Lotus, under the management of Andrew Ferguson, was tremendously busy during the 1964 season because it was now competing in so many different forms of racing. Apart from the very full season of Grand Prix races, Lotus were again going to Indianapolis with a new car; they were also heavily involved in both Formula 2 and Formula 3, where Ron Harris was still carrying the flag; they were still in sports car racing with a brand-new Ford-engined car; and there was the Lotus-Cortina with a full programme of races both at home and in the States!

For Indianapolis, Ford had decided to develop their own twin-cam engine and, in rather typical fashion, they simply bought an Offenhauser engine and studied the design of the cylinder head to produce one that would fit their special V8 block. Unfortunately, the engineers failed to take into consideration the importance of the gas velocity in the inlet ports and these, shaped for a big four-cylinder engine, were really too large for the V8 of the same capacity. Nevertheless, it did develop a healthy 425 bhp and a batch was sold to some American entrants, although Lotus remained the official Ford factory team.

Again two cars were entered in the '500' for Jim Clark and Dan Gurney. These Lotus 34s were really a development of the previous year's 29, adapted to accept the new engine and with somewhat slimmer bodywork. The Hilborn fuel-injected engine, still running on pump fuel, was mated to a ZF gearbox, replacing the earlier Colotti box. But Colin, being Colin, had another trump card up his sleeve – or so he thought. Before the race he had asked Dunlop, who were way ahead of Firestone in road racing tyre technology, to design special tyres for him using much softer rubber. With these British-made tyres Clark duly qualified on pole, but in full-load tests carried out the following week it was discovered that the tyres on Dan Gurney's car were 'chunking' badly – they were too soft. Since it was against the rules to switch the type of tyres after qualifying, Dunlop hurriedly made a new batch of somewhat harder tyres over the Whitsun weekend. These were flown post-haste to Indy where Colin was maintaining his normal poise, having assured the Ford top brass that all would be okay for the race.

In the event, the race was halted after the second lap because of a fiery crash, which unfortunately claimed the lives of two drivers. After the restart, delayed for almost two hours while the charred debris was cleared and fire extinguishers refilled, Clark took an immediate lead but was soon passed by Bobby Marshman, a very fast new boy who was driving one of the previous year's Lotus 29s bought for him by Lindsey Hopkins. Whilst overtaking another car, Marshman got off line and rolled on to the grass infield slightly but enough to snap an oil line, forcing his retirement and leaving Clark firmly in the lead. Seven laps later, just in front of the grandstand, a rear tyre on the Lotus threw a tread and the resulting vibrations were so great that the rear suspension broke, leaving Clark up against the inside retaining wall in what was basically now a three-wheeler. After a quick consultation with Vic Barlow, the Dunlop field representative, Colin decided that he must now call Gurney in, since there was no guarantee that the same would not eventually happen to his tyres.

The next day Colin and Andrew Ferguson were summoned to Detroit for a most unpleasant meeting with Ford's top management. Ford's Lee Iacocca was furious because one of his Vice-Presidents, Charles Patterson, had reported that Colin had refused to allow A. J. Foyt to drive the team's spare car, just in case one of his own drivers had needed it, as had happened the previous year when Dan Gurney had crashed his car during the qualifying trials. Much to Foyt's annoyance he had to stick with his Offenhauser roadster but in the end he had the last laugh because he won the race in it and it was the rude gesture he made to Patterson as he drove into Victory Lane which had upset Iacocca so much!

When he originally made the decision to use the special Dunlop tyres, Colin found himself right out on his own with all the Ford racing personnel becoming conspicuous by their absence, and he therefore accepted full responsibility for making the choice. At first he even offered to sell all three cars to Ford because they were especially keen to enter them in the two other most important US Auto Club events at Trenton and Milwaukee. But as soon as the meeting was over, and when he had regained his composure, Colin pretended that he had misunderstood them and that he was keeping the cars to enter them himself in both events. He pleaded his case so well that finally he won them over and, in fact, Parnelli Jones, driving one of the Lotus 34s, actually won both the Trenton and Milwaukee races, so there was never any reason for Ford to regret having allowed Chapman to get away with anything!

The year 1964 also marked the first season for the new Formula 2, the main specification for which was the use of a production-based cylinder block with a capacity of no more than 1,000 cc. For this, Chapman had designed the new Lotus 32, a neat little monocoque based on the Mk 27 Formula Junior car of the previous season. Unfortunately, the twin-cam cylinder head used on the Elan engine proved unsuitable for Formula 2 and Coventry Climax also abandoned the idea of 'stretching' half their 1½ litre V8, so Colin decided to use the new Cosworth SCA engine. This was based on the 1,000 cc Ford cylinder block, for which Keith Duckworth had been able to design a single-overhead camshaft cylinder head with the valves in-line because, due to the very large bore, there was sufficient space available to accommodate extra-large inlet valves. Despite the small capacity, the engine developed 115 bhp. As fitted in the Lotus 32, the unit was canted over at an angle of 32 degrees and used a Hewland gearbox.

Ron Harris, who for some time had been the entrant for Team Lotus in Formula 3, now took over in Formula 2 as well and was given the use of both works drivers, Jim Clark and Peter Arundell, but since there were now four cars he also signed up Mike Spence and Peter Procter. The Lotus 32 was also made available to ordinary private customers, and in all twelve were built.

Although Jimmy did manage a win at Pau, in the first race of the French championship series, the Formula 2 season in 1964 belonged to Brabham. As already recorded, Lotus had some bad luck at Rheims when Peter Arundell was badly injured: while travelling at very high speed down the straight, he had briefly taken his eyes off the road to glance at his rev counter and inadvertently put a wheel on the grass. Immediately, the Lotus spun sideways and was rammed by the Lola of Richie Ginther and Peter was out of action for the remainder of the season.

It also proved a rather lean year for Colin and Lotus in Formula 3 racing, which took over from where Formula Junior had left off. This year's Formula 3 Lotus, the 31, was a development of the very successful Lotus 22. It, too, was available to private customers and in all about twelve of these were built. But, with Cosworth devoting most of their efforts to the F2 SCA engine, the BMC-engined Coopers entered by Ken Tyrrell's team virtually walked away with the season, ably assisted by another young Scotsman, Jackie Stewart, who made such a tremendous impression in Formula 3 that he very quickly found himself in Ron Harris's Formula 2 team. He even drove for Team Lotus in Formula 1 at the non-championship end-of-season race in South Africa, deputizing for his friend Jim Clark who had unfortunately slipped a disc while taking part in a snowball fight during a Ford public relations exercise at Cortina d'Ampezzo!

It was in 1964 that Lotus also introduced a new sports-racing car – the Lotus 30. This was a big, relatively inexpensive machine at £3,495 and was specially designed for the so-called 'return of power' which had become the fashion at the British circuits. It used the backbone chassis, similar to the Elan, but réversed to suit the rear-

Colin Chapman was rather angry that Ford, with whom he was already closely associated, had chosen Lola for their Le Mans project. This was particularly so, because at the same time he was introducing his Type 30 sports car and no doubt when he designed this coupé version of it (which was never built), he thought about a possible return to Le Mans to try and beat the Ford-Lola GT40 . . .

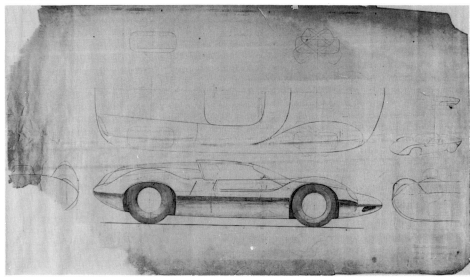

Jimmy Clark could always be relied upon to put up a terrific performance at the wheel of a 'works' Lotus-Cortina. Once he even rallied one . . . but it ended up on its roof! Graham Hill was pretty good too.

engined configuration. The engine was a 4.7 litre Ford V8 with four double-choke Weber carburettors giving all of 350 bhp. Basically, this engine was a legacy from the Ford-Indy contract and it was very probable that Colin, still somewhat annoyed with Ford for giving preference to Lola with the Le Mans project, was hoping to show them a thing or two! In fact, only recently, Andrew Ferguson found a drawing of a coupé, designed at the time to provide an alternative body for the Lotus 30, and which was intended to become a rival for the then so far unsuccessful Ford GT40.

Unfortunately, the Lotus 30 proved a big disaster. The basic faults were that the frame was too flexible, the engine overheated and the brakes were just not good enough. Jim Clark drove the works car both at home and in the States but its only victory was in a race at Mallory Park. In England, the official team was entered by long-term Lotus enthusiast Ian Walker, but even he gave up before the end of the season. Rather surprisingly, 21 Lotus 30s were built that year.

The salvation of the 1964 racing programme came from the Lotus-Cortinas which proved to be very successful, with Jimmy winning several saloon car races in England. It also did very well in the hands of private customers, many of whom had ordered their special racing versions at the 1964 Racing Car Show, where it was priced at £1,725. The twin-cam 1,600 cc engine delivered 140 bhp, and with modified suspension, a more direct steering-gear ratio and limited-slip differential, the car would achieve – with the highest available axle ratio – a very commendable 128 mph (206 kph).

Although the racing side had not been very successful, commercially Lotus Cars had a very prosperous year in 1964 and Lotus Components did well too, selling Lotus 30s, 31s and 32s as well as the ubiquitous Lotus Seven.

If 1964 had been a disappointment for Lotus as far as motor racing was concerned, the following year was one of absolute triumph. Jim Clark dominated Formula 1 just as he had done two years earlier and on top of this he succeeded in winning the Indianapolis '500' at his third attempt. He also won both the French Formula 2 Championship and the Tasman series in Australia and New Zealand! Coupled with the huge commercial success of the Lotus Elan, 1965 was probably the most fruitful year in Colin Chapman's entire career.

Before the Grand Prix season had even started Coventry Climax dropped a bombshell by introducing a brand-new F1 engine, Wally Hassan and his team having excelled themselves and outdone Honda by coming out with a flat-16 cylinder wonder. With this news came the official announcement that this was to be their last season in Formula 1. Although Leonard Lee had recently sold Coventry Climax to Sir William Lyons's Jaguar company, it was not Lyons's decision that they should retire from active participation in motor racing. It came about principally because 1965 was to be the last season of the current 1½ litre GP formula and a great deal of expense would be incurred in designing and building, from scratch, a completely new 3 litre engine to comply with the Formula 1 regulations. The building of the 16-cylinder engine for only one season's use (in point of fact it was never raced) simply proved just how keen Leonard Lee had been to succeed in motor racing. He really did want to remain at the top until the very end of the formula, and then he would feel that he had done his best for the sport and for his country. Apart from this, he was also upset with the complete disregard by the Commission Sportive Internationale (the CSI, and forerunner of today's FISA) for the manufacturers' enormous

At the 1964 Lord Mayor's Show, Lotus and Coventry Climax were honoured by being given a display float for the procession through the City of London.

investments, when they suddenly decided to change the rules at short notice, as was so often the case.

For Colin the situation was particularly difficult, for how was he going to find an engine for the next formula? He later recounted to Doug Nye just how he set about overcoming the problem: 'I asked Keith Duckworth if he could produce a Grand Prix engine and he thought he could, so I offered to find the money to finance it. He said he would need £100,000 and I shopped around in several places. On first contact with Ford they didn't want to know, so we then had meetings with David Brown of Aston Martin. He was very interested, but he wanted far more control over the project than Keith was prepared to give him; he virtually wanted to buy Cosworth. Then we tried McDonald of the British Sound Recording company, and there were several other interested parties, but we didn't really seem to be making much progress. We had virtually made up our minds to go back to Brown at Aston Martin when I was invited to dinner one night with Harley Copp (Ford's Vice-President in charge of engineering). I said, "Look, you're missing out on the best investment you have ever made . . . for £100,000 you can't go wrong." He thought that was nothing like enough to get initial work done, but I managed to convince him that it was and that Keith was really someone special. Harley went back to Walter Hayes (the Ford Director of Public Affairs) and within a few days it was all under way.'

Walter Hayes played a large part in these negotiations because Colin's meeting with Copp had actually been at his instigation and he was able to 'steam-roller' the project through so successfully that it was possible to announce it to the press at the end of 1965.

Meanwhile, Team Lotus had a job to do, and that was to recapture the World Championship for Jimmy and to win the constructors' cup. Since the Lotus 33 of the previous year had now been properly set up, there was no need for any modifications to be made to it. But, despite this, a new chassis – the Lotus 39 – was designed, with a wider engine bay ready to accept the new flat-16 engine. However, pending its completion, Climax had yet another trump card – a 32-valve version of the V8 engine! This came about because when Wally Hassan first introduced the extra-large bore engine, its main purpose was to try out a new four-valve cylinder head. At first this had given a very disappointing performance until Hassan decided to try advancing the ignition considerably more than normal, and suddenly the missing power increase was found.

Two such engines were therefore made, one to be loaned to Lotus for Jim Clark's car and the other for Jack Brabham. Each had slightly different sized valves, and the engine to be used by Lotus gave 212 bhp (against 203 bhp for the normal 16-valve engine) while Brabham's enjoyed slightly more power at the expense of some loss of torque. Although Clark's 32-valve unit proved very successful, despite some unreliability, Brabham somehow did not like the 'feel' of his engine, using it only once, and then unsuccessfully. With both the new 32-valve and the normal 16-valve engines proving adequate, and with the end of the current formula in sight, work on the flat-16 FWMW engine was stopped and, in fact, it was never even installed in a car.

The first Grand Prix of the 1965 season was held at East London in South Africa and resulted in a win for Jim Clark, the first of six such victories in succession. Because of the clash of dates and Jimmy's involvement in the all-important Indianapolis race, Team Lotus were not able to enter the Monaco Grand Prix, but Jimmy won both the Belgian and French GPs and then followed this up by winning his fourth consecutive British Grand Prix, although it proved to be a difficult race for him. With the high oil consumption of the 32-valve engine and fluctuating oil pressure towards the end, he only just managed to maintain a lead over Graham Hill whose BRM, somewhat fortuitously for Clark, was afflicted with failing brakes. With further victories in the Dutch and German GPs, Jimmy was assured of being World Champion for the second time. After the Nurburgring race the whole team enjoyed a much happier celebratory evening in the Christophorus Restaurant, under the grandstand, than they did after his Championship-clinching win at Monza in 1963, when he had received a summons. Unfortunately, the remaining three Grand Prix races each resulted in Clark's retirement with engine problems.

But it was the Dutch Grand Prix which was probably the most memorable of the year because of a small but unpleasant incident which later assumed quite large proportions. It was a very hot day for once and Colin was wearing a short-sleeved open-neck shirt, making it difficult for him to wear the official armband giving him access to the track. Consequently, this was attached to his belt – a quite normal alternative. As Colin was walking back to the pits, after bidding good luck to Jimmy on the start line, his arm was grabbed by an auxiliary policeman charged with the task of clearing the track. Seeing no armband, he was trying to force him over to the other side of the guardrail. Colin was not going to put up with treatment like that, and he promptly floored the man with a solid left hook! He thought no more about it and the race ended in another triumph for Jimmy Clark, but as soon as it was over a large contingent of Dutch police descended on the Lotus pit and tried to arrest Chapman on the spot.

Lotus mechanic Dick Scammell later explained to Doug Nye just what happened: 'He was sitting on the pit counter and the police were in the back of the pit ordering him to go along. When he refused they grabbed him and there was the old man roaring "come on lads". We had his feet while the coppers had his head and arms and we were all tugging away. Hazel Chapman had hold of one of the policemen by the hair . . .' They finally managed to get hold of him and he was smartly marched off to the race control tower where Louis Stanley of BRM duly came to the rescue and, with the help of the race organizers, he was able to suggest and agree a compromise. The Clerk of the Course was to act as bail to guarantee that Colin would appear at the police station after having returned to his hotel for a shower and a change of clothes. An hour or so later, 'Big Lou', in his impressive limousine, delivered Colin to the police station where he was to spend the night.

In the meantime, because Jimmy had to leave immediately after the race, I had been instructed to deputize for both Colin and Jimmy at the prize-giving party to be held in the nearby hotel. I was to accept the trophies on their behalf and deliver a powerful speech based on guidelines provided by Colin! On arrival in the ballroom where the function was to take place, I warned the organizers of my intentions. They

Colin signals yet another 1965 Grand Prix victory for Jim Clark, the French at Clermont-Ferrand and his third out of a total of six for the season. (Note the gloves which Colin always tried to wear in Summer to keep his hands permanently clean, in an effort to curb his hay fever.)

The famous Zandvoort incident of 1965. Colin Chapman returns to the pits prior to the start, nursing a bruise to his right elbow. A policeman, failing to see his pass (plainly visible, however, on his belt in this picture), had tried to force him to leave the track. Colin responded with a punch to the man's face!

Colin greeting Jimmy after his fifth victory of the season. He doesn't yet know that he was to finish up in jail that evening!

were, of course, horrified that Colin had been put in jail and they decided that the best thing they could do was to cancel the prize-giving altogether.

Later that evening, a large party of Team Lotus people, friends and supporters, gathered under the windows of the police station and sang rude English songs to cheer up the inmate who, meanwhile, was using the time to good effect by working on an initial design for his next Formula 3 car, using the back of the writ with which he had just been served!

The following day, the British Embassy helped in obtaining the services of a lawyer to prepare a defence for the court case which was to be held on the Tuesday. It was just as well for Anglo-Dutch relations that the outcome of the case was successful for Colin, because by then a large contingent from the British press had descended on the court and, had he lost the case, there would have been a great deal of adverse criticism of Dutch police methods. The unfortunate aftermath of the affair was that, on seeing the big splash that the press had made of the case, the successful lawyer produced an invoice for a sum large enough to have covered the defence of a murderer and which, of course, Colin refused point-blank to pay. Later the lawyer travelled to London in an effort to sort out an agreement with Colin, but unhappily he electrocuted himself while shaving in the bathroom of his hotel on the morning of his appointment, so that was the last that was heard of it.

In fact, Graham Gauld reminds us in his book* that in 1963 Jim Clark also had a brush with the Dutch police at Zandvoort. He had walked out on to the circuit infield to watch practice, when a policeman, who did not recognize him, accused Clark of not having the correct pass. Clark was marched off, and later released after lengthy explanations. The consequences were, happily, less serious – Jimmy went on to win the race and, later, his first World Championship.

Following the horrific crash which had taken place the previous year soon after the start of the Indianapolis 500-mile race, the regulations had been extensively revised in order to improve some of the safety aspects. The main change was the mandatory use of alcohol-based fuel which, in case of accident, was much less volatile than gasoline. In addition, pressure refuelling was also banned so that tanks would have to be replenished by a gravity feed system. Always ready to apply his inventive genius, this was a godsend to Colin, who came up with a transparent mock-up of a scheme for a fuel tank which enabled Len Terry, who was designing the car, to shape the tank in a way that would permit quick refuelling. During the race, Clark's pit were able to put 44.4 gal of fuel into the car in the space of only 19.8 sec, which was almost as fast as when fuel was forced into the tank under pressure! It became an established record, quoted for some years in the 'Guinness Book of Records'.

The car itself, the Lotus 38, was completely new and for the first time since the 1962 Lotus 25 the monocoque shell was no longer in the shape of a bathtub but was a full monocoque. It was made up, ahead of the dashboard, in the form of a complete tube with detachable panels giving access to the foot controls and with separate inner panels forming the fuel tank bays. This scheme greatly improved strength and rigidity. At one point Chapman had contemplated providing this new car with de Dion rear

---

*   'Jim Clark Remembered' (Patrick Stephens, 1984).

suspension, which he had given up using in his single-seater racing car designs after the initial tests of the Lotus 12 back in 1957. Since then, tyre width had increased considerably and he felt that it might prove worthwhile to put up with the usual de Dion handicap of road shocks from one wheel being transmitted to the other, in order to benefit from the increased traction because the near-vertical position of the wheels allows a wider expanse of rubber to be in contact with the surface of the track. However, after some tests Colin decided, probably for the best, not to proceed with the idea. Following the fiasco of 1964, he also decided to drop Dunlop tyres in favour of Firestone, in view of their special and extensive experience of the Indianapolis track.

The first two Lotus 38s were shipped to the USA in time to take part in a race at Trenton, New Jersey, in April, where Jimmy Clark and an American, Roger McCluskey, were entered to drive. However, a faulty assembly of the linkage caused McCluskey's throttle to jam in practice and the car was badly damaged in the resulting crash. It was therefore decided to withdraw Jimmy's entry because there would have been insufficient time before the Indy race in which to rebuild more than one car, should something similar have happened to the second car, so the team went straight on to Indianapolis.

Apart from the two Team Lotus 38s there was a third new car for Dan Gurney who, it should be remembered, had initially arranged for Lotus to appear at Indy three years earlier. However, this time Dan had decided he wanted to run the car himself and so, in partnership with Carroll Shelby of Cobra fame, he started his own team under the name of 'All-American Racers' and entered his Lotus 38, bought with the support of Yamaha. Colin was not too happy about this at the time and he was especially disappointed later on when it turned out that the following year AAR were destined to benefit exclusively from the Ford Indianapolis budget. But on top of stealing Colin's main sponsor, they also poached his Chief Designer, Len Terry, who left Lotus immediately after the '500' to join Dan Gurney and take up residence in California.

Following the debacle of the previous year, Ford had now changed their policy somewhat and Leo Levine, the American writer, described one particular conversation which took place between Ford's Leo Beebe and Colin Chapman. '"Cut the budget and don't come back without Clark", were Iacocca's instructions to Beebe in mid-September (1964), and Beebe flew to England to negotiate.

'Although Chapman is undoubtedly one of the great talkers of modern times, as a negotiator he met his match in Beebe. (Although the Ford man had the edge, Colin was also very anxious to win the race he had almost won twice before.) Beebe didn't waste any words: "Colin, I'll tell you what I am going to do. I'm not going to make a contract with you like we had last year, I'm going to take my wallet out and lay it on the table and you can have all that to race on and no more – and I'm not going to tell you how to spend it." Beebe named a figure and Chapman said it was too low, and besides, he had other offers. "I'm either going to work out a contract right here this afternoon," Beebe replied, "or I'm going to leave and get someone else and that will be the end of it. If you've got a better offer, then by all means take it and let's both save time." Chapman agreed – at Beebe's figure!'

Ford had sold 25 of their 4.2 litre engines – now converted to run on the regulation alcohol-based fuel and developing 505 bhp – and of the 33 cars qualifying for the race, 17 were using Ford engines! But for the 'rail-birds' – the traditional Indy fans – there was worse in store when only five of their beloved 'roadsters' qualified for the race. Without any doubt Lotus had changed the shape of American motor racing. The cars from Cheshunt were out in force in 1965. Apart from the three new 38s, all the previous 29s and 34s still in existence took part, most of which had been extensively modified by their owners. Two of those using last season's 34s were currently the best American drivers, A. J. Foyt and Parnelli Jones, winners of the two previous Indy races. Foyt was using Goodyear tyres, which enabled him to qualify fastest and take pole position alongside Jimmy's 38, whose Firestones were somewhat less effective. But the previous year's Dunlop drama was re-enacted when the Goodyear users found out that their tyres were unlikely to last the distance between each refuelling stop. This time it was Goodyear's turn to produce some more tyres in a hurry and as these were, in fact, slightly different from the original supply, they had technically infringed a rule. However, since they proved somewhat slower than the Firestones, no objection was made.

The front row of the grid was an all-Lotus affair, with Foyt's 34 ahead of the 38s of Clark and Gurney. Parnelli Jones in his 34 was in the middle of the second row and Al Miller in the old 29 was in the third. Team Lotus's second entry, a steady stock-car driver named Bobby Johns, managed no better than the eighth row of the grid.

During the days preceding the big event, the atmosphere was as tense as ever, if not more so, because this time everyone at Lotus knew they could not afford to let victory escape them for a third time. The Americans were not being very friendly either, and Jimmy did not conceal the fact that it had taken considerable persuasion on the part of Ford to convince him to be there at all. His mother was scared of this race, his father's health was deteriorating and he was, in fact, contemplating the possibility of withdrawing from motor racing entirely in order to devote his time to the family's farm in Scotland.

To cap it all, after practice the Ford men told Colin that in the past, the Lotus pit work had been sloppy and they insisted that refuelling should be entrusted to their 'star' stock-car team, the Wood brothers. Colin knew that the small problem which had caused some confusion the previous year had been incorrect handling of the jack by Danny Jones of Ford Motor Company and it was the same Danny Jones who was now asking for the Wood brothers to join in! Anyway, reluctantly he had to give in and the next day the lanky Southerners arrived and soon they had built a dummy of the car to practice refuelling and wheel changing. The American press were, of course, lapping it up and the Wood brothers probably received as much publicity as the rest of the team.

Jimmy took the lead at the start and by the end of the first lap the first five places were occupied by Lotuses. Foyt's car had a slightly more powerful engine than Clark's and had been fitted with bigger fuel tanks because it was running on nitro-methane. This gave him a slight power advantage at the expense of somewhat higher fuel consumption, and by the end of the second lap he had forged ahead of Jimmy's green and yellow car. This did not disturb Clark in the least, for a lap later he overtook Foyt

Right *At his third attempt Jimmy Clark triumphed in the 1965 Indianapolis 500 Miles Race, winning for the team the then enormous sum of 150,000 US dollars. Colin's happiness was never so evident and Dave Lazenby looks pretty pleased too!*

Below *The entire 1965 Indy crew pose with the winning car. Left to right: Chief Mechanic Dave Lazenby (sitting on front wheel), Graham Clode (mechanic), Peter Jackson of Specialized Mouldings who was attending for the fun of it but also helping the crew, Bob Sparshott (mechanic) now of BS Fabrications and still involved in motor racing, Alan Moffat (Alan sometimes drove Team Lotus Cortinas and is now well known for his racing exploits in Australia) and sitting on the rear wheel is Jim Smith, an Australian and previously a ship's engineer. In front of them are Colin Chapman, Mike Underwood (known as Charlie Chins!) who later became Indy Chief Mechanic when Dave Lazenby became General Manager of Lotus Components, and Jimmy Clark.*

and from then on he was out on his own, only relinquishing the lead for a period of nine laps following his refuelling stop. After 116 laps, when he was still lying in second place but a lap behind, Foyt's gearbox broke, so he was out of it. Parnelli Jones and Gurney were then fighting over second place until Dan's engine blew up in a big way and Jones eventually managed to hold on to his second place, although towards the end he did have to slow down somewhat to avoid running out of fuel. Third place was taken by a young man named Mario Andretti in a Ford-engined Brabham, whilst Al Miller was fourth in the old Lotus 29 and Bobby Johns finished in seventh place with the second works Lotus 38.

I rarely saw Colin happier than on this day. Not only had Lotus racing cars proved their utter supremacy in this most prestigious American racing formula, but also his car had won more than 150,000 dollars. The only thing he was sad about was that the Wood brothers had rather deprived the Team Lotus mechanics of their full share of the glory. Certainly the pit stops had been very quick indeed, but much of this was due to the design of the fuel tanks. That evening we celebrated in style at an Italian restaurant in the town but, as the State of Indiana was 'dry' over the Memorial Day weekend, our red wine was served in coffee cups!

For all this, back in England Lotus were not quite so successful, especially in the field of sports car racing. A Series 2 version of the Lotus 30 had appeared using 15 in wheels in the interests of improved brake cooling. The engine was now fuel-injected and was giving 360 bhp. However, with a cast-iron cylinder block the engine was much heavier than the alloy GM power units used by the main rival McLaren, thus offsetting any advantage gained by the lighter weight of the Lotus chassis. They tried enlarging the capacity to 5.3 litres but to no avail and so, in the end, after building only twelve Series 2s, a new type 40 appeared with a stronger chassis and a massive Hewland LG500 gearbox in place of the previous ZF box. But the Lotus 40 met with no more success, and Richie Ginther – who drove it in the States later in the season – summed it up by describing it as 'a 30 with ten more mistakes'!

Things were going very much better with the Lotus-Cortina, now equipped with a 150 bhp engine specially prepared by BRM. It also had leaf-spring rear suspension in place of the coil springs of the earlier models, the locating A-bracket of which was found to be putting so much stress on the differential casing that the subsequent distortion caused serious oil leaks. With this car, entered by Alan Mann, Sir John Whitmore won the European Touring Car Championship against mounting opposition from the Alfa-Romeo GTA.

Team Lotus had now grown into a very complex organization and, with a budget approaching almost two million pounds, Andrew Ferguson was co-ordinating no less than six separate operations. The Formula 1 team, under Chief Mechanic Dick Scammell, was the mainstay, of course. Dave Lazenby was in charge of both the Indy race team and Lotus 30/40 sports car operations, while Ray Parsons was responsible for both the preparation and the driving of the Team's 26R, the Lotus Elan. Then there were two separate Lotus-Cortina teams, both under the technical eye of Bob Dance. One was the Ford/European Touring Car Championship entry based in Britain, whilst the other was pursuing a very active racing programme in the United States. There were no less than 27 drivers signed up, some of those in the States on a

The Ferodo Gold Trophy was again presented to Colin Chapman in 1965.

'one-off' deal which at times became very confusing, and even Colin would have been hard pressed to list the names of all his drivers! For Andrew, the worst time was the month of May when it was necessary for him to handle his logistical work at Indianapolis, taking all his files and paperwork with him and operating directly from his hotel room. Needless to say, the resulting phone bill was enormous!

Finally, there were the Formula 2 and 3 teams, again entrusted to Ron Harris, which this year were running the Lotus 35 in both formulae, a new model evolved from the earlier 27 and 32. With victories for Jim Clark at Pau, Rouen and Albi, the team managed to win the most coveted F2 championship, the 'Grand Prix de France' series. Jimmy also won the less prestigious British Formula 2 championship. Curiously, the highly aerodynamic Lotus 35, with inboard front suspension, was never as quick as the more box-like Brabham, and Harris's successes were due more to Clark's skill as a driver than to the quality of the car itself. Although the Ron Harris Team Lotus entry, driven by the American Peter Revson (of the Revlon cosmetics family), did win the important Monaco GP Formula 3 curtain-raiser, the Brabham F3 car was again generally much more successful than the Lotus 35 and a total of only 22 examples were built.

So with the great days of Lotus Components slipping behind somewhat, and with – in Colin's view anyway – the Lotus Seven becoming a little long in the tooth, he realized that he had to look for some additional new activities for this division of his company. He decided that the time was appropriate for the introduction of a small coupé with what was then a very rare feature, a rear engine. The problem was finding a suitable power unit. Technical reasons militated against using the trusty twin-cam engines – although eventually one did find its way into one of these cars – but the main reason why Chapman wanted to find an alternative was because he was anxious to avoid becoming too dependent upon Ford. At the 1964 Motor Show he had spotted the new front-wheel drive Renault 16 saloon and with his usual foresight quickly came to the conclusion that this engine could prove to be 'just the job'. This mass-produced unit had a light-alloy cylinder block, with a high camshaft allowing the use of short pushrods with the consequent reduction in inertia permitting higher engine speeds. Above all, though, the engine was installed longitudinally and some way back in the Renault chassis, with its rear end positioned right up against the main firewall bulkhead. Because all the accessories were fitted on the gearbox side, accessibility for repairs would be excellent since the gearbox and transmission were at the front end of the engine. Colin could immediately see that this arrangement would be eminently suitable for his rear-engined sports car because the unit could so easily be installed in the reverse position.

On 27 January 1965 Colin wrote me the following letter:

> Dear Jabby,
>
> I was very interested indeed to see the specification of the new 1½ litre engine recently announced by Renault.
>
> I am in the process of evolving a very inexpensive lightweight sports road car as an eventual replacement for the Lotus 7 and would like to consider the possibility of offering this Renault engine and transmission as a power unit.
>
> Do you have any contacts at Renault, and if so, could you approach them with a view to finding out whether they would be prepared to grant us extremely advantageous terms over the purchase of, say, 500 engine-gearbox units per year?
>
> I realize that these would probably be handled through the Renault (England) outlet but, as price is the prime consideration, no doubt the special policy decisions in this respect would have to be made in Paris, and I am hoping that you can help me here.
>
> Yours etc

I immediately contacted my friend Bob Sicot, then head of public relations for Renault, who quickly realized the potential of such an arrangement with the world's most successful Formula 1 racing car manufacturer. A meeting was quickly arranged, for which Colin flew to Paris, and a deal was soon made at what were very advantageous terms. During the months following we had several meetings with top engineers from Renault but, to ensure absolute secrecy, not one of these ever took place at the Renault factory. Instead, Colin would fly over in the morning in his own plane to a small airfield at Toussus-le-Noble, south-west of Paris and not very far from Versailles. I would meet him there and we would then drive to l'Aubergade, a very good restaurant at Pontchartrain, some forty miles from Paris, where the Renault people would be waiting for us. I remember on one occasion one of my press colleagues suddenly appeared in this restaurant, where on the previous day Bentley cars had given a press lunch. He had mixed his dates and arrived on the wrong day, but, seeing Bob Sicot and me, he came over to say hello. Little did he realize the scoop he missed by not recognizing Colin Chapman in deep discussion with Yves Georges, the head of engineering at Renault! The new rear-engined sports car appeared in 1966 – and it was called the Lotus Europa.

Right *A reproduction of the letter Colin Chapman wrote to the author in January 1965, having realized that the engine and transmission unit for the new Renault 16, which had then just been announced, might prove ideal for use in a rear-engined sports car. This was to become the Lotus Europa which, although very successful, did not become a replacement for the Lotus Seven, despite what is said in the second paragraph.*

Below *An all-Lotus celebration display at Brands Hatch to mark the winning of the 1965 Formula 1 World Drivers' and Constructors' Championships.*

Chapter 11

A Lean Year Preparing for Hethel

During the five years of the 1½ litre Formula 1, which ended in 1965, Team Lotus had been by far the most successful entrant. Despite the first year, when all the 1961 users of the four-cylinder Coventry Climax engine were so handicapped against the V6-engined Ferraris, out of the 46 Grand Prix races in which Colin Chapman's cars had been entered they were victorious in twenty of them, with two more going to the credit of Rob Walker's privately entered Lotus. In the non-Championship events Lotus also scored the most wins with 33 out of a possible 65. In fact, their F1 record over the period was only a little short of achieving wins in 50 per cent of the races entered. Quite an incredible performance.

But in 1966 – as in 1961 – Lotus were to face a very lean year indeed. Keith Duckworth and Mike Costin were working very hard to produce their new Ford-financed V8 3 litre engine for which, as part of the development programme, Cosworth had designed a new 1,600 cc unit to be used for the new Formula 2 due to come into force in 1967. Two of these engines, arranged in V-form would, in principle, make up the new F1 engine. However, there was no way that the V8 could possibly be ready for use during the first year of the new formula, so Chapman had little alternative but make a deal with BRM to use their new H16 engine and gearbox unit. This had been designed by Tony Rudd, BRM's chief engineer, who had opened up the 'vee' of their 1,500 cc engine to 180 degrees and then put one bank of flat-eight cylinders on top of the other, hence the 'H' designation, although strictly speaking the letter should really be placed on its side! As can well be imagined, the mating of the separate crankshafts was an absolute nightmare and Rudd had to rely heavily on his technical experience gained with Rolls-Royce, his former employers. Initially there were some serious problems caused by vibration, which made it necessary to change the firing order, ensuring that Lotus would have to start the season without their BRM engine.

When this became obvious to Colin, he was immediately in touch with old friends Coventry Climax who soon succumbed to his convincing ways and agreed to prepare, purely as a stop-gap, a special version of their World Championship-winning V8 FWMV engine. What Wally Hassan did was to take one of the extra-large-bore engines and fit it with a crankshaft from the small-bore one. The result, called the Mk IX, gave 1,974 cc (72.3 mm x 60 mm) with a power output of 240 bhp at 8,800 rpm. Of course, this was a long way from the 400-odd bhp which could be expected from the new generation of 3 litre engines. However, most of the

Above *Chapman had contracted to use the BRM H16 3 litre engine for 1966, while the new V8 Ford-Cosworth was being developed. The BRM engine, which scored only one victory, in Jimmy's 43 at Watkins Glen, was designed by Tony Rudd (seen here talking to Colin at the 1966 Monaco race) who eventually joined Lotus in 1969.*

Right *In 1966 Lotus did not yet enjoy the use of a full 3 litre engine for the new Formula 1, so the faithful 33 was equipped with a V8 Coventry Climax brought up to 2 litre capacity. Despite this eminently suitable combination, once again Jimmy was unsuccessful here at Monaco, his unluckiest circuit.*

competitors were also finding their feet at the time and, indeed, even the highly-favoured Ferrari also proved a failure. Eventually the World Championship went to Jack Brabham in one of his own cars, using a Repco engine of Australian origin with a power output of only 360 bhp.

Under these circumstances, Jim Clark generally managed to hold his own in the Lotus 33 with the Mk IX Climax engine. He secured a third place in the Dutch GP, having once again failed to finish at Monaco, the one race for which his under-powered car was most suited, when he was forced to retire with a broken suspension upright after holding fourth place. It seemed that Jimmy was 'jinxed' at Monaco, because in six attempts he never managed to win. His best performance was in 1964, when he was classified fourth – though his car was not running at the finish!

Clark was unable to take part in the French GP at Rheims, due to being hit in the face by a bird during practice whilst going full-chat down the long straight. By a sheer miracle, and no small amount of skill, he was able to keep the car on the road and bring it safely to a stop. Colin was very shocked by this incident as he had not forgotten the loss of Alan Stacey at Spa from a similar mishap some years earlier, and he immediately flew Jimmy home for medical attention to his eye which, very fortunately, was only slightly injured. Pedro Rodriguez took over the car, only to retire on lap 41 when lying fourth because an oil pipe fractured and the engine seized. It was in this race that the H16 BRM-engined Lotus made its debut in the hands of Peter Arundell, having originally been entered for the Belgian GP where Peter failed to qualify. Mike Spence, who had deputized for Peter after his serious accident in 1964, was driving a BRM V8-engined Lotus 25 for Tim Parnell's private team which was receiving some support from the Lotus factory. Arundell's Lotus lasted only four laps before it retired with gear selector problems.

The new car, the Lotus Type 43, was designed by Len Terry's successor, Maurice Phillippe, who had been known to Colin for a very long time. He had once worked at de Havilland at around the same time as Mike Costin and 'Mac' McIntosh, who remembers that Phillippe was probably first bitten by the 'special car bug' when Mike Costin arranged to drive the original Mk VIII Lotus past the office window at Hatfield so that everybody could see it! Since Maurice did not have the right equipment in his workshop at home, he had become a frequent visitor to Tottenham Lane when he needed parts machined or welded for his car. In 1954 he had actually designed a car with a monocoque chassis for the 750 Formula. He had then moved on to the Ford Motor Company, where further opportunities for brief meetings with Colin occurred during the planning stages of the Lotus-Cortina project.

Maurice was a Lotus owner himself at that time, racing a Series 1 Seven which he had bought from Keith Duckworth, who had been using it as a mobile test bed for his Formula Junior engine. Maurice was also racing an FJ car of his own design and construction, and not dissimilar to the 'Terrier' FJ designed by Len Terry and driven by Brian Hart. Brian was then working for Cosworth Engineering who, in those early days, were at Edmonton in North London, close to where Lotus had built the Elite prototype. In fact, quite a substantial racing community thrived in that area for some time! This explains why, when Len Terry asked Colin if he could be released from his contract in order to join Dan Gurney's All-American Racers team, Colin agreed provided Terry could introduce him to a suitable substitute. Len immediately came up with Maurice Phillippe who then joined Lotus in September 1965.

Phillippe's first brief had been to modify the one-off 39, the car originally designed to take the flat-16 Climax engine. Since this never went further than the test bed, the chassis was superfluous and Chapman had it adapted to accept an old four-cylinder FPF Climax engine for Clark to use in the 1965/6 Tasman series in Australia and New Zealand. His next job was, in fact, two different cars because Lotus's arrangement with BRM, as we shall see later, was 'double-pronged'. Colin had made a deal with Andy Granatelli – the boss of the STP oil additive company in the States – to field a team of 4.2 litre H16 BRM-engined cars at Indianapolis in 1966. So Maurice was, at the same time, working on designs for both the Type 43 F1 car and the 42 Indy car.

It was during this period that the Lotus company was about to move into a brand-new factory just outside the city of Norwich, in East Anglia, the designing of which was keeping Colin very busy indeed. Maurice Phillippe remembers the time very well: 'I was amazed to see so little of him while I worked on the H16 cars. Obviously he had a tremendous amount to say on the way he wanted the car, but our contacts were very brief and few at the time. Working for Colin was a constant challenge, and because he was such a good, sharp engineer, you needed to come up to him with ideas. We might have some hand-drawn sketches but he would mostly come up with written instructions. Sometimes he would arrive in the drawing office and say, "I want this," but in the final analysis it was up to me to design the car. I knew his theories on suspension design which at the time were to have plenty of wheel movement and also plenty of steering lock. This was one of his pet ideas and he was always bringing out his classic photograph which showed Jimmy in a 33 in a full-blooded 90-degree slide and because the car had a lot of lock he was able to catch it. Personally, I think maybe that was OK for Jimmy, but with most other drivers it would have caught them out before they would have known what to do!'

The Types 42 and 43 were monocoques with a fully stressed bulkhead, similar to the Len Terry-designed Type 38 Indy car, but the chassis terminated behind the driver's backrest because the engine and gearbox unit was strong enough to take the rear suspension loads. Unfortunately, there was some early indication that all would not be well with this engine when the team of four men sent to collect it from the BRM truck shouted for two more strong men to give them a hand with the unloading! Lotus knew then that they were going to be in big trouble and, in fact, it turned out that the weight of the engine, gearbox and rear suspension alone added up to the minimum weight demanded by the regulations! Rather amazingly, this car did manage to win one Grand Prix during the 1966 season – at Watkins Glen, in the hands of Jim Clark of course – and that was the only GP victory for the ill-fated H16 BRM engine.

Following the introduction of 15 in tyres, specially made for Lotus at Indy in 1963, as explained earlier, Goodyear had made up their minds to become involved in motor racing and to challenge the supremacy of Firestone, their closest competitor in the USA. This sparked off a tremendous battle which became fiercer still when Ford decided they were going to race at Le Mans. Both manufacturers were determined that if Ford were to win the world's greatest endurance race it would be with their tyres. During this period, tyre research, design and development proceeded by leaps and bounds.

Goodyear soon entered Formula 1 and it was not very long before a car using their tyres won them their first GP – the last race of the 1½ litre formula at Mexico, where Richie Ginther was victorious in a Honda. Firestone were, of course, keen to follow them and so this became a highly profitable period for the best teams and their drivers, as the tyre manufacturers lured them into their respective camps with promises of large amounts of money and juicy testing contracts. Knowing how poor his chances of success were likely to be in 1966 – and as Dunlop had been left behind on the technical side – Colin agreed to use Firestone tyres for the Grand Prix races, in the hope that during the season both organizations would make progress together in getting their respective products right.

As could only be expected, there were initial difficulties and there was the classic story of Jim Clark coming into the pits during practice for the Tasman series race at Pukekohe in New Zealand. It was raining hard and Jimmy was most upset because he had just been overtaken down the straight by a train running alongside the track. To rub salt in his wound, the driver had blown his whistle as he shot past the Lotus!

It took some time for Firestone to produce really good tyres, especially the intermediate 'all-weather' variety, and in the end Colin designed the pattern himself. The tyres which were finally manufactured became the famous R125s with which Clark's BRM-engined Watkins Glen-winning car was fitted and were used by several teams for the next three years.

It was after the Italian Grand Prix in 1966 that Colin, Jack Brabham and I were arrested at Milan's Linate Airport! The day after the race Colin had decided that he would fly to Bologna in his twin-engined Piper Comanche to visit one of his great fans, Gian Paolo Dallara, Chief Engineer of Lamborghini, and he invited me along for the ride. Unfortunately, when Colin reported to air traffic control and was asked to show his pilot's licence he discovered it had been allowed to lapse. He did have a current medical certificate and all fees had been paid up to date, so it was really a matter of 'rubber stamping' and the British civil aviation department agreed by telex to renew it. But this was not good enough for the Linate airport controller, so we went over to the commercial terminal thinking that our only course of action now was to take a scheduled flight, when who should appear but Jack Brabham who was about to do the same! 'Do you want to be my pilot?' asked Colin. This suited Jack perfectly because he really wanted to go to Corsica where his family were on holiday, and that was also where, ultimately, Colin wanted to end up that evening. For some time he had owned a villa in Ibiza, to where he would fly quite frequently when time permitted but, having become rather tired with Spain, he had rented a house in Corsica to see if he would like that better, and Hazel and the children were already there waiting for him. So Jack, having agreed to the plan, took his own pilot's licence to the controller and then went to a telephone booth to announce his change of plans.

Unfortunately, while he was away doing this, someone stole his small travelling bag that he had left lying on their pile of luggage and it so happened that this contained the starting money from the Monza race. Colin was most embarrassed that Jack should suffer such a loss while he was helping him and he suggested that, like him, Jack would surely be insured. Never a particularly well organized person, Jack had no idea but agreed that it was possible and, if this was the case, he would have to report the loss at the airport police station. So all three of us marched off to do just that, following which we boarded the Comanche. However, immediately more police arrived saying they wished to search the aircraft and the first thing they found was another travel bag containing Colin's starting money, which just happened to be the same amount as Jack's! Now the officer thought he had discovered a perfect case of insurance fraud and the three of us were promptly taken off the plane and locked up in the police station. It took quite a while to contact the race organizers, the Milan Automobile Club, to obtain confirmation that Brabham and Lotus had each been paid the same amount of starting money and when we were finally cleared to leave it was much too late in the evening to go to Bologna.

It was very obvious when the first prototype was tested that the H16 BRM Indy engine was not going to be ready for the race so Lotus had to rely on the previous year's Ford-engined 38s, of which some customers had ordered replicas although not all of them qualified. Of the 33 cars which did line up on the grid, five of them were Lotuses – three 38s and two 34s. The latter were in the hands of George Snider, the fastest qualifier, and Al Miller, while two of the 38s, painted in STP's 'Day-Glo' red, were for Jim Clark, (the second fastest qualifier) and Al Unser. The third 38 was to be driven by the great A. J. Foyt.

The 1966 Indy '500' was famous for a massive and most spectacular startline pile-up and to this day nobody really knows exactly what happened although every driver was quick to blame the other. It would appear that it was initiated by Billy Foster whose Vollstedt-Ford used a four-speed gearbox while most of the other cars were equipped with the two-speed transmission more commonly used with this form of oval circuit racing. As soon as the green starting light came on, Foster took advantage of his car's superior acceleration to weave through the field from his place on the fourth row of the grid. Unfortunately, in doing so his car touched Gordon Johncock's Gerhardt-Ford, which had been on the second row of the grid and which then promptly hit the wall – triggering off a whole series of collisions, with wheels, cars and bits of cars spinning around all over the place. The net result was a restart with a total of eleven cars eliminated from the original line-up, including the Lotuses of both Miller and Foyt, with the latter gentleman being very upset because millions of TV viewers all over the world had seen him escaping the mêlée by climbing the chain link fence surrounding the circuit in a somewhat undignified fashion rather reminiscent of a monkey! Amazingly, and miraculously, Foyt's finger, lacerated by the fence, was the only injury sustained by any of those involved.

At first it looked as though Clark might well repeat his 1965 success, but then it was noticed that the track was becoming slippery. Now, for the first time, the organizers were allowing entrants to use additives in their oil and STP had offered cash bonuses to everyone using their product. Therefore there was a large percentage of cars, apart from the two bright red works machines of Clark and Unser, sporting STP decals and running on somewhat thinner oil. As soon as the engines began to tire the track became incredibly slippery due to so many cars dropping oil. In practice the Lotus 38 had not handled as well as the previous year (possibly the new tyres were a contributory factor) and also an adjustment had been made to the suspension. But the moment the track became so slippery the 38 became practically unmanageable and even Jim Clark was caught out when he spun on the 64th lap. Usually a spin at Indy ends up with a crash into the outer wall and almost certain retirement, but the incredible Scot managed to 'keep it on the island' without even stalling the engine though he did have to come into the pits for a tyre change. Within 20 laps he was back in the lead only to spin a second time, but again he held it although he did brush the wall slightly, necessitating another pit stop to change the battered wheels. By now Jimmy had come to the conclusion that he should ease off a little and concentrate on finishing as well up as possible.

The leader became Lloyd Ruby in the new Lotus 38 lookalike, the Eagle-Ford, but then his car sprang a serious oil leak and the Clerk of the Course did what he should have done with Parnelli Jones three years earlier – he black-flagged Ruby. It then looked as though Jackie Stewart in a Lola was going to be the winner, but his oil pressure dropped to zero and he was out. At that point, the official leaderboard – a large illuminated tower in front of the pits – had been giving completely wrong positions so that it had finally been switched off. When it came on again it showed Graham Hill was leading with Jim Clark in second position. In the Lotus pit there was complete consternation because Cyril Audrey, the highly respected RAC timekeeper from England, was sure that Jimmy was ahead of Graham. The race was concluded but in Victory Lane complete chaos reigned when Clark, thinking he had won, tried to wheel in his Lotus only to find that Hill's Lola was already occupying the winner's position. Meanwhile, Andy Granatelli was having a furious argument with the organizers who finally decided to wait until 10 am the following morning before posting the final result, by which time all the records would have been checked.

I was sharing a room with Cyril Audrey, who always came to the Indy race with the Lotus team, and we spent the evening checking his lap chart against mine, which I had done from the press balcony, quite independent of the Lotus pit, and which afforded a much better view of the track. My chart clearly showed that Graham was the winner. Finally it transpired that during the confusion following one of Jimmy's spins, Cyril had missed one of Graham's laps. The next day we went to the organizers to tell them that they were right after all.

For Formula 3 racing Lotus Components had come up with an entirely new car, the Type 41, which oddly enough had an elaborate multi-tubular space frame instead of the then more normal monocoque. The simple reason for this was that such a frame was much cheaper to manufacture and more convenient for the customer because of the ease of repair. The main virtue of the monocoque chassis was that it presented the maximum rigidity for the minimum weight. However, as the minimum weight limit for Formula 3 was so high that the cars were having to carry ballast anyway, strength was all that mattered. Two salient features of the new car were that the Ford-Cosworth engine was inclined to the right by 30 degrees and the track was much wider than on the earlier cars.

The 'official' works team for 1966 was run by Charles Lucas and his first team driver was a young man named Piers Courage, of the brewing family, who in fact won the Craven 'A' series of French F3 races. Ron Harris retained his control of the 'official' Formula 2 team using another type variation, the 44, which was similar in most respects to the previous year's 35 except that it had the wider track of the Type 41. Unfortunately, neither the team nor the car met with much success because Brabham virtually annihilated all opposition, thanks to their exclusive use of the Honda engine.

In 1966 also came the joint announcement by Chapman and Alessandro de Tomaso of a new engine, built at Modena with the help of Lotus's engineering expertise. This was a light-alloy V8 of 5,512 cc, said to be good for over 500 bhp. It had two large in-line valves per cylinder actuated by very short pushrods. Unfortunately, this engine did not get very far, and Alessandro de Tomaso told me recently that only a small batch was delivered to Ford America. Although it was first commissioned when it was still thought there was a future for big sports cars, by the time it came out the Lotus 40 had been shelved and the trend in European motor racing had moved away from this type of car.

However, probably due to the adoption of the leaf-spring rear suspension the previous year, the Lotus-Cortina was proving sufficiently robust and powerful enough to tackle rallying with a considerable measure of success. It won the Acropolis and the British RAC Rally in the hands of Bengt Soderström, and Gilbert Staepelaere of Belgium won the Geneva Rally. Even Jim Clark tried his hand at rallying one, and was doing very well in the RAC Rally until he managed to turn it over on to its roof! The Lotus-Cortina also continued to excel in circuit racing, with the Team Lotus cars. Now equipped with a full-race wishbone suspension system and a new dry-sump BRM-prepared engine pushing out 180 bhp, it won the British Saloon Car Championship.

The search for a site for a new factory outside London had actually begun some time earlier when, as Fred Bushell has already explained, the difficulties over the construction of Elan body shells first arose and Cheshunt Town Council had reluctantly granted permission for an extension to the factory warning Lotus that no further development of the site would be allowed. 'At the time we first decided to move,' says Fred Bushell, 'Lotus was not enjoying a particular commercial success but, by the time we found Hethel, Cheshunt had just completed a year making its best-ever profit which helped. Once Colin decided we should move, he produced a concept which said that we would need to have our own test track because one of the complaints levied at us by the local government authorities in Cheshunt was the testing of cars taking place on the adjoining roads causing too much noise. It may well have been that Colin could also foresee the desirability of a runway for his own use, doubling as a test track, but in all other respects the acquisition of a disused airfield was seen to be the cheapest way to come up with a site which incorporated a ready-made test track.

'This had to be within about 100 miles of Cheshunt and also had to be near a town that was a desirable place to live. The criteria for 100 miles and a pleasant environment were associated with the requirement to transfer a large number of people from Cheshunt to the new site. We believed that if it was within 100 miles and was a pleasant place to live, it would be possible to uplift Cheshunt almost intact.

'At this time, the Government were disposing of a number of disused airfields and Colin obtained a list of available sites and we flew together over quite a number of them, starting with the South Coast as we were very keen on being near Chichester or somewhere between there and Dover. A number of places were identified and we flew down to liaise and visit with the local authorities. Because these were non-industrial areas, most of the authorities we spoke to would obviously have been pleased to receive Lotus's R and D operation, but showed no enthusiasm over getting the whole factory. As we progressed round the compass to the East Coast, we then flew into Norwich and met with the planning authorities for Norfolk. These were the first people to receive us open-handed and they said they would do everything possible to help us find a site and would offer every co-operation, other than money!

'We found this friendly approach so refreshing that we looked particularly carefully in Norfolk and found that there were three disused airfields on the market. Whilst two of the others had recently been renovated and were in better shape, Colin preferred the Hethel site because it was closer to the city of Norwich. At that time Hethel had been unused for many years and was a War Department scrap dealer's site, covered with old army equipment, lorries, gun carriers and so on. The actual airfield was in the process of being returned to three or four neighbouring farmers, the original pre-war owners, who were being given the opportunity of buying back their land. This was a most opportune moment since these farmers needed funds to buy their part of the land and therefore, by Colin offering to buy the area that we wanted, the farmers could see the opportunity of obtaining enough cash to buy the rest of their entitlement. Dealing with three or four different farmers presented a major problem and we found them to be very cautious and unwilling to move at the speed at which Colin usually did business! Very many meetings were held and Colin and I must have had more farmers' teas and hospitality than we would normally have had time to enjoy in a lifetime. Colin was on his best behaviour and most charming, and eventually his enthusiasm and salesmanship persuaded the farmers to fall in with his plans although not without reservations that they demanded should be overcome. These covered rights of access, poaching of farming staff, restrictions on the running of racing cars and general noise abatement, plus understanding as to aircraft noise, etc. Eventually the deal was done and the land was acquired in 1965.

'Again blind faith was shown that Fred would somehow find the cash flow to effect the purchase of the land and provide the funds for building the factory. Once the land had been acquired, negotiations commenced to design the factory and prepare a general programme covering the layout, the persuasion of personnel to move and generally plan the complete operation. We interviewed and finally engaged a firm of architects, Chaplin and Ferrant, a firm specializing in factory layouts and the control of costs. They made many visits to the Cheshunt factory in order to get to grips with Lotus's business and Colin was personally involved in planning every detail of the new factory. Meetings were often held late into the night whenever Colin could find the time and, whilst the architects took this in good part, the number of changes of mind were such that they began to show signs of wear and tear. Eventually, a contract was placed with the large firm of Costain for completion in the autumn of 1966.

'We decided that the management team needed strengthening and that another new era for Lotus was to commence with a top man being brought in from the motor car industry. During our dealings with the Ford Motor Company's engineering division we had come to know Dennis Austin very well and were impressed by his vigour and obvious skills. Eventually Dennis was persuaded to join Lotus with the assignment of overseeing the building of the new factory, a role he shared with Colin, and then to take over the running of the operation as Managing Director following the impending move.

'During 1966, Dennis and Colin concentrated on building the new factory layouts and production facilities and I was running the Cheshunt operation as profitably as possible to generate funds for the move. I was able to arrange a very advantageous loan of £300,000 which was on an interest-only payment basis, which was intended to cover the cost of the land and the new factory. I felt this was a major success, since it solved the problems associated with the funding of the new Hethel site.

'As a team we initiated a full information programme to our staff, explaining the reasons for and the effects of the move. We consulted with the Greater London Council over the general level of success met by other companies in moving staff to new sites outside London and we were told that the highest level had been achieved by the Dexion company who had removed to the outskirts of London and had persuaded ten per cent of their staff to make the move. This, in their book, was an immense success. Lotus on the other hand, employed some 500 people and were looking to transfer virtually the entire staff to Norfolk and our friends at the GLC thought we had to be mad to plan on such a basis.

'Our Sales Director at the time, Graham Arnold, was charged with mounting a campaign to promote the benefits of moving. Visits were organized by coach so that staff could look over the area and questionnaires were circulated concerning accommodation. Apparently a large number of people were renting or they lived with their relatives or in-laws. The price difference between London and Norfolk was very wide and a lot of new housing was being built quite close to Hethel, so we arranged for a presentation to be made to all the staff in the Town Hall at Cheshunt, which was also attended by a large number of Norfolk traders, furniture suppliers, finance, education, medical services and so on. Diagrams and tables were prepared to show the differences in housing costs and the costs of living. One of Graham Arnold's gimmicks was to send a girl out shopping in Hethel with ten pounds and then to shop in Cheshunt with another ten pounds, comparing the size of the respective shopping bags to show that the one from Hethel contained much more than that from Cheshunt. Whether or not this was a fair comparison, only Graham would know!

'Just prior to this presentation, on one of my own regular visits to Norfolk, I went to new housing sites and put down deposits on 24 bungalows at prices from £2,500 to £3,000. I offered these at the presentation to the staff and by the end of the afternoon twenty of them had been taken up.

'On the Hethel site there were some old RAF buildings and, during the early part of 1966, these were hastily reconditioned and used for the lamination of body shells which were then transported to Cheshunt to be finished and painted. It served the purpose of meeting the increased volume which we required.

Left Colin Chapman, assisted by Jimmy Clark and the Mayor of Norwich, lay the foundation stone of the new Hethel factory in July 1966.

Below Colin and Hazel being interviewed before the TV cameras in the new open-plan offices at Hethel. The interviewer is journalist and motoring writer Gordon Wilkins.

'We recruited our first local trainees in the summer of 1966 when 25 office staff living in the Norwich area were engaged and brought down to work side by side with the staff there until the move in November 1966. Of the original 500 staff, by June some 100 already worked at Hethel. Allowing for the fact that some people were locally committed to stay, 250 people moved and only fifty actually had to leave the company. After the move a small vehicle service unit was retained at Cheshunt but this was eventually closed after a year. The actual move of the factory was carried out over one single weekend. The manufacturing of cars stopped at Cheshunt on the Friday night; those in progress were moved by transporter and work started again in Norfolk on Monday morning. It was with great relief that we saw the first Hethel-manufactured vehicle finished by 4 pm that Monday afternoon.

'The factory was not fully finished due to delays by the builders, although it has to be said that Colin had some role to play in this. On every occasion he returned from a motor race, he spotted some new angle or alteration which he wanted to incorporate. I remember, for instance, the time he inspected the gents 'loo' being built for the use of the workers. Quite logically the architect had stipulated that the urinals be set into the wall at two different heights. "None of this," said Colin, "I want complete symmetry." And so the builders had to tear them down and start again. More delay! The main area not completed at the time was the executive offices and for a few months we all worked in the general office, which made for a very friendly atmosphere, which was particularly good at the time of such a major move.

'One of the ideas that Colin had picked up in his travels was the open-plan office concept which, at the time, was fairly novel. Few other examples existed and those that did were often badly executed. Colin learnt that the BP company in Germany had adopted this approach so he visited their offices and as always came back full of enthusiasm. The basic concept was that, in an open-plan office, services could be provided in such a way that you could change the location of people's desks at the drop of a hat, and they would have a better communal spirit than if they had been segregated in little boxes. We had found at Cheshunt, with the development over the years of 'rabbit hutch' offices, scattered all round the factory, that there were barriers erected between the various office departments, engineers, finance, stores and so on. By bringing the staff together in one big room a better spirit of co-operation would prevail. This, in essence, is what Colin had seen at BP in Germany – what they called 'Büro Landschaft'. This was to be an office in a garden with flowers and plants used to create natural barriers or divisions of attractive appearance. We were able to lay out a general office with fully-fitted carpets and curtains at the windows. Under the floor, at intervals of twelve feet, we put down services such as internal and outside telephone systems and electricity, so that any desk could be 'plugged-in' to these at six-feet intervals. In other words it was a grid system enabling complete flexibility to be achieved.

'The move was completed in November 1966 and all continued to go well until Christmas Eve when our architects demanded a meeting, together with the contractors, at which they presented a bill for the factory which was some one hundred per cent above the quoted price. All of the careful funding that had been achieved and which was meant to enable us to start off with a clean sheet was in

Left *The new Norfolk factory was opened by The Rt Hon Peter Walker, MP, then a Shadow Minister in the Conservative Opposition.*

Right *A factory photograph of the early Lotus Europa.*

disarray. It is difficult to imagine the seriousness of the situation when the additional money demanded was also demanded immediately, and it was clearly beyond the company's ability to pay. Since the architects had charged a special fee for cost control and Lotus people had been monitoring the building of the factory so carefully, it was one hell of a surprise. The contractors stated that, because of the speed of the job, they had incurred vast costs to meet the time schedule and there had been many changes in specification which, because of deficiencies in their site management, had not been costed as the job progressed. This claim was the subject of a running battle that lasted some 18 to 24 months, during which Dennis Austin and I had to learn much detail about the construction business and an awful lot about the legal system, and such new words as "Scotts schedule" came to be part of our vocabulary. In the end the claim was settled and the additional costs were shared between the builders, the architects and Lotus. However, this meant that the contract with the architects was terminated after the Christmas Eve meeting and a new firm, Lambert and Innes, were engaged to finish the factory with a new contractor, R. J. Carter & Co. This was a very fraught period but, whilst it was all going on, Colin's attitude was – "You deal with that while I go motor racing"!'

The new Renault-engined Lotus sports car was developed during 1966, to be introduced at the end of the year and to be built from the outset at the new Hethel factory. Originally it was to be called the 'Elfin', and then 'Concorde' was suggested. Finally the name 'Europe' was agreed – the French translation for the word Europa – because the first batch of cars was for export only, to France. Later, when the car went on sale in England, it was known there, of course, as the Europa. 'It was really meant to be a replacement for the Seven,' says Fred Bushell. 'Colin saw a requirement for

filling the spare production capacity of Lotus Components. Personally, he wanted a simple vehicle and found himself somewhat at odds with Ron Hickman, the Development Director, who Colin felt had over-complicated the Elan. Also our experience with Ford over the supply of the 116E block for the twin-cam engine was felt to be a potential return of the Climax syndrome when both the supply and the price could be adversely affected at the whim of Ford and possible changes in their management structure. Colin thought that the most simple package would be a mid-engine car offering excitement with economy. When the programme developed though, the simplification theory was overtaken by the reflection of the growing Lotus image and eventually, instead of being produced by Lotus Components as a Seven replacement, it became a main line product.'

Designer John Frayling had styled a very pretty little coupé, albeit at the expense of rearward visibility, hampered by two side fins which in later models were deleted for this reason. Although it was wider than the Elan, space in the cockpit of the Europa was more restricted, with the seat backrests right up against the firewall bulkhead between the cockpit and the engine compartment. If you wanted to take even a briefcase with you in the car it had to be carried in the luggage compartment at the front, which in itself was not very large – the eternal problem of all mid-engined cars. In his quest for simplicity and low cost, Colin had insisted on fixed side windows, which created quite a problem when turning up at a toll gate where the pavement in front of the booth was too high for the door to be opened! The seats themselves were fixed, all adjustments considered necessary to accommodate different sizes of driver being made to the pedals, for which – of course – a couple of spanners were required. This was not a very welcome feature where the car doubled as the wife's during the week and the husband's fun car at the weekend.

The Europa used the same 'backbone' chassis concept as the Elan except that, because of the rear engine, it was the other way round with the forked part for the engine at the rear. The suspension was independent with disc brakes at the front and, although the front suspension was similar to that of the Elan, at the rear it was completely different, with the half-shafts playing the part of maintaining transverse wheel location. Unfortunately, this resulted in some bump-steer from the back axle because the engine and gearbox unit, to which the suspension was directly linked, had to be rubber-mounted to avoid excessive vibration.

The Renault 1,470 cc engine was specially tuned to give 82 bhp at 6,000 rpm and the Renault four-speed box modified to cope with the rear-engine installation by transferring the crown wheel to the other side of the pinion. The completed Europa weighed 1,344 lb (610 kg) and was good for a maximum speed of around 110 mph (177 kph). Unfortunately, the original target price of £650 was not reached and, despite all the efforts to simplify the car, the final price had to be nearer £1,100, which was approximately the same as the Elan. This explains why, initially, Lotus did not want to sell it in England for fear of hurting the exisiting Elan market.

The published road tests of the original S1 Europa were not devoid of criticism either, although, despite some instability on bumps, the roadholding was adjudged to be excellent. Journalists generally found the car a little cramped, hated the ventilation system and found the gear linkage was not very accurate and failed constantly. However, worse came from the insurance companies. Because the chassis was encased within the glass-fibre bodyshell for increased rigidity, in the event of accidental damage it proved necessary to replace the entire unit – a most expensive undertaking. Under pressure from the insurance companies, the next model was to incorporate a separate body and chassis. Other modifications were also made like electrically-operated windows, adjustable driver and passenger seats, and the side fins which obstructed the rearward vision so much were removed. Later, the Europa was fitted with the same twin-cam engine as the Elan and received a five-speed Renault gearbox. The use of the Renault engine had to be given up after the initial batch of 500 had been taken up because Renault had no desire to renew the deal at such favourable terms. Also Bob Sicot had left them to join Ford France, and Renault themselves were under pressure from Jean Redelé – the maker of the Alpine-Renault – who was loath to see a rival foreign company receiving Renault engines to use in a sports car. At one stage a possible deal was contemplated where Redelé would build the Europa under licence for the Continental market, and Colin even paid a visit to his factory in Dieppe but, in the end, the deal fell through.

As was usually the case with new Lotus models, a racing programme for the Europa was set in motion with a special batch of cars built by Lotus Components, all equipped with twin-cam engines. This 'racing' Europa – the Lotus 47 – made its debut at the 1966 Brands Hatch Boxing Day meeting when, in the hands of John Miles, son of famous actor Sir Bernard Miles, it won the prototype class in a race for sports cars. Due to international regulations, the car was not permitted to run in the GT class until the minimum quantity of fifty had been built, and it would appear that to shorten the length of time it was taking to reach this number some cars received a plain Ford Cortina engine!

The Lotus-Cortina deal with the Ford Motor Company came to an end in May 1966, after the car had been in production for over three years. The close ties with Ford over the project had been very important for Lotus and, particularly in Fred Bushell's view, it made a considerable contribution towards the company's success. 'The entire Lotus-Cortina project, and our involvement in it with Ford, did a great many good things for Lotus. They gave us support with buying, and taught us such things as quality control, and they virtually forced us into developing the management structure so obviously necessary to cope with the increase in output by encouraging us to hire the right type of senior managers and experienced quality controllers. A production line system was introduced, the standard of paint and quality of finish was very much improved and with Ford's help Lotus really matured as a car manufacturer, albeit a small one. The initial quantity run of Lotus-Cortinas was increased on at least a couple of occasions, and nine months before our move to Norfolk we asked Ford if they would like us to provide space for the assembly of cars at Hethel, but they decided that the main factory at Dagenham should take it over. In fact, we continued to provide them with engines for another two years.' A total of 1,250 Lotus-Cortinas were built at the Cheshunt factory before the move to Hethel.

Initially, the twin-cam cylinder heads had been machined for Lotus by the JAP engine firm, J. A. Prestwick, but then they were taken over by another well-known motor cycle engine manufacturer, Villiers, and moved to Wolverhampton so finally Lotus bought the jigs and tools and, from 1968, these engines were machined and assembled at Hethel by Lotus themselves.

Production of the twin-cam engine ceased in 1975, after the Elan +2 was phased out, but only recently Graham Nearn of Caterham Car Sales – who took over the manufacturing rights to the Lotus Seven – bought these jigs, together with the rights to manufacture these twin-cam cylinder heads, so perhaps we still have not heard the last of this highly successful power unit.

Chapter 12

Ford Power for Formula 1

After such a difficult Formula 1 season, Chapman – determined to see his drivers, especially Jim Clark, climbing the winner's rostrum again rather more frequently – faced up to the 1967 season with considerable optimism and in a confident mood. At long last the new Ford Cosworth F1 engine – the DFV, as it was to be designated – would be ready for use and, with Colin's guidance, designer Maurice Phillippe had come up with the Lotus 49. 'I wanted to design a simple car,' Colin told me at the time, 'because this was Keith's first Formula 1 engine and, with teething troubles likely to occur, the last thing we wanted was problems with the chassis as well. The 49 was really a mobile test bed!' And, indeed, the Lotus 49 featured none of the Chapman innovations which could normally be expected – these were to come in the following years . . !

The car itself was, of course, another monocoque – Jimmy Clark would not drive anything else anyway – and followed the general lines of the Type 43, except that it was slimmer because the new V8 engine was obviously much narrower than the H16 BRM. 'The 49 was basically a very simple car,' says Maurice Phillippe. 'We were interested in minimum weight and minimum frontal area. You have got to bear in mind that this was a period when the exploitation of aerodynamics had not yet come to the fore. Aerodynamics at that time really consisted purely of what was frontal area, so you had very narrow cars and, of course, you had very narrow tyres as well. The 49 was literally a banana-shaped monocoque, the outer profile of which was really determined by the shape of the engine.'

The suspension of the 49 was also conventional. As with the 43, the monocoque chassis terminated at the bulkhead behind the driver's backrest where again, under the seat, was a triangular-shaped fuel cell, with the rear suspension once more attached to the gearbox.

The most important factor about the Lotus 49 was that for the first time Chapman was able to enjoy the luxury of using an engine which had been designed to suit the car. Although this is obviously the case with some manufacturers, for example Ferrari, who build their own engines, it had never been like that before with Lotus. And also, the Ford-Cosworth association was originally started by Colin when he advised Ford that if they did not help with the financing of his engine they would be '. . . missing out on the best investment you have ever made'. This proved to be very true and, consequently, not only was he able to work very closely with Keith Duckworth through all the design and test stages, but also Team Lotus enjoyed exclusive use of the engine for the 1967 season.

'When Climax withdrew from Formula 1,' says Keith Duckworth, 'Colin decided that his best hope of getting a Formula 1 engine was to try and see whether he could get the money to support me in making one. We decided that £100,000 would be sufficient to design, build and maintain five engines for a year. (£100,000 – I can't believe that now!) I said: "We will make this in two stages. I will make the four-valve 1.6 litre engine for Formula 2 and, provided that looks reasonable, I will go straight into making a V8, incorporating the knowledge and principles learned and achieved with that."

'Originally there was going to be a three-way contract between Colin Chapman, Ford and me but that subsequently proved unworkable and finally there were two separate agreements with Ford for each of us, with a third one between Colin and me. It took a long time to work out and by the time the agreements were actually signed, the FVA 1.6 litre engine was already running and giving 208 bhp and that was a year before the V8 started. We considered that this engine was worth £25,000 out of the £100,000 with which we had started. After a fairly short discussion with Colin, we

One of the men that made the Ford-Cosworth engine possible. Harley Copp (left), Ford's Engineering Director, with Keith Duckworth who designed it.

A rare shot of a bare-headed Colin Chapman driving one of his own Lotus 49 Formula 1 cars in 1967 at the introduction of the V8 Ford-Cosworth engine.

decided that although we could probably make a 12-cylinder engine, it was always an advantage to have a small lightweight car. Also, I did know something about four-cylinder engines and I felt that if I made a V8 with a common-plane crankshaft, I could be fairly sure of it being in the 400 bhp category, whilst the Repco-Brabham, which was then winning, was giving only 360 bhp.

'Colin always was a "small and light" man so that is why we really decided we would make a V8. There was also some influence by Ford who had always been involved with V8s for a very long time. Because we couldn't get anything like a chassis round the engine, we designed this to be a stressed member of the chassis. The position of the two mounting bolts at the base of the engine were dictated by the width of Jim Clark's bottom. The centres of these bolts were nine inches apart, the seat width being eight inches. We then had to have a gearbox, so the first thing needed was a drawing of the back end of the engine which Colin could then take to ZF. While all this was going on, we used to call each other to discuss the odd things like water pump mountings, suspension pick-up points and so on. Many of these discussions took place with Maurice Phillippe.'

It will be remembered that Chapman had developed and long enjoyed a special relationship with the ZF gearbox people, although he had later gone over to the Hewland gearbox simply because of the ease with which ratios could be changed. However, Colin was never very fond of this British box and was often critical of it. Later, when the Hewland had become traditional wear on most F1 cars – except Ferrari, of course, who always built their own – Colin tried to get away from it and, as we shall see, briefly revived his own Ansdale-designed gearbox dating back to the Lotus 16. This perhaps explains to some extent why he returned to using a ZF gearbox on the new car, despite the handicap of having to use fixed ratios, which turned out to be an especially severe restraint for the Lotus 49. This was because the DFV delivered the very high power output of 405 bhp but, in its initial form before a revised throttle linkage system was designed, it proved extremely difficult for the driver to cope with the sudden surge of power coming in at 6,500 rpm. Therefore, it was particularly important for the car to be properly geared to suit each corner at particular circuits.

The other failing of the 49, lasting most of its career, was a serious shortage of brakes. At first it was equipped with large ventilated discs, but they were found to cool so well that the pads would glaze. Halfway through the first season they were replaced with solid discs, with some noticeable improvement, but the Lotus 49 was never very strong in this area.

Ford, with their investment in the Cosworth-designed engine, were now taking a sharp interest in Lotus's racing activities and, quite rightly, they decided it was unwise to invest a large sum of money and then rely on only one driver. Walter Hayes therefore insisted that Colin have a second driver of the very highest calibre and was instrumental in bringing Graham Hill back into the team with which he had made his Grand Prix début nine years earlier. Fortunately, Colin had made his peace with

The team that created the Lotus 49. Left to right, Maurice Phillippe, Chief Designer; Keith Duckworth and Mike Costin of Cosworth Engineering; Graham Hill and Colin. Jimmy Clark was by then a tax exile living in Bermuda and was not able to pose for this 'family' picture.

Graham quite soon after he had sued him for leaving Team Lotus for BRM in 1960, but nevertheless, in the back of his mind, there always seemed a slight trace of bitterness.

For the first GP of the 1967 season, the South African held at the Kyalami circuit just outside Johannesburg early in January, Clark and Hill had to make do with H16 BRM-engined Lotus 43s – although they were looking forward to having their new 49s ready in time for Monaco four months later – but both retired quite early in the race. Unfortunately, the new engine was still not available for Monte Carlo so they used 33s – Clark's with a V8 Climax engine whilst Hill's was equipped with a V8 BRM engine. Again Jimmy retired with rear suspension trouble but Graham finished second to Denny Hulme's Brabham at what was always his luckiest – and Jimmy's unluckiest – circuit.

Testing of the new car was entrusted to Graham Hill only because, at the time, Jimmy had become a temporary 'tax exile' in Bermuda and was sharing a flat with me in Paris during the peak of the season. By arrangement with the tax authorities, during the mandatory first twelve-months period, he was allowed only one stay in England and, obviously, that had to be reserved for the British Grand Prix.

The Lotus 49 made its début at the Dutch Grand Prix at Zandvoort and the result went straight into the history books. Although Graham Hill initially led from pole position in the development car, he retired on lap eleven with a broken camshaft drive. Jimmy fought hard from his lowly eighth place on the grid (due to troubles in

practice) and went on to win first time out in the new car. This was a fairy tale result and Ford, who up to then had kept a fairly low profile, celebrated it quite loudly. However, the fact was that Jimmy finished the race in a very sick car, suffering from failing brakes and clutch as well as from a defective timing gear. The latter was especially serious because that had also been the reason for Hill's retirement and, with only two engines in existence, Keith Duckworth was going to have to work very hard if he was to succeed in putting things right.

Nevertheless, the DFV-engined Lotus made an explosive arrival on the motor racing scené and it turned out that it was not until the Spanish GP in May of the following year that another make of car was seen in pole position at the start of a Grand Prix race, the 49 having achieved that honoured spot in eleven successive events. Regrettably, Jimmy Clark was not destined to win the World Championship in 1967 because, apart from teething troubles with the engine, the chassis was not short of faults either, with the suspension having to be beefed-up and the gearbox playing tricks because the side plates were flexing too much. The battle for the Championship was close though, being finally decided between Jack Brabham and Denny Hulme in the last GP of the season when Denny beat his boss in Mexico. Jimmy finished third in the Championship, five points behind Hulme, although he did win four GPs to the others' two each. It was the unreliability of·the car which let him down in too many of the other races. With points in only three GPs, Graham Hill shared sixth place with Pedro Rodriguez.

Left *Colin Chapman checks over the new engine and rear suspension of the 49 during one of its early outings.*

Right *A pit stop for Jimmy Clark at Monza in 1967 during practice, hence the relaxed expressions! On the right is Harley Copp, Ford's Engineering Director in Europe. Dick Scammell is talking to Jimmy, while the author and an Italian colleague, Enrico Benzing, look on. John Standen, one of the original team of Lotus helpers in 1954, and later a director of the company, is on the left at the back in dark glasses.*

The highlight of the season was probably Jimmy's achievement at Monza in the Italian Grand Prix where, although he did not win, he nevertheless drove a tremendous race – probably one of his very best. Delayed by a pit stop after twelve laps to change a punctured tyre, he restarted in 16th place – a whole lap in arrears – and eventually fought his way through the field to regain the lead by lap 61 of the 69-lap race. He broke the lap record several times then, on the last lap, he ran out of fuel and had to settle for third place. The reason for this apparent oversight by his Team Manager was that, in the interests of safety, Colin had filled the fuel tanks with a special anti-explosive foam which had been specially developed by Firestone for use at Indianapolis, where it was obligatory. Unfortunately, he had failed to allow for the fact that a small quantity of fuel would always be retained by the 'mesh' of the foam!

Throughout the season, no set team orders were given to the two Lotus drivers, with one exception and that was before the US Grand Prix at Watkins Glen. Graham Hill told the story in his book[*]: 'That night I remember, Walter Hayes called a meeting . . . There were four of us in Colin's room – Colin Chapman, Walter Hayes, Jimmy and myself. Although this was an English Ford enterprise and nothing whatsoever to do with American Ford, Walter was particularly anxious that we should do well in the United States Grand Prix and, therefore, he didn't want the two of us scrapping together. We agreed that the fairest thing to do was to toss a coin to decide who should cross the line first if the two of us ended up dicing in front of the field; the one who lost would have the privilege, assuming we were both in front, of winning the Mexican Grand Prix.

'I won the toss and so, if we were sufficiently far in front of the field that we could then go round at our own speed without scrapping, it fell to me to win the American Grand Prix. This was just team tactics – though they didn't quite work out in practice; there was no sense in the two of us blowing ourselves up. This was actually the first occasion on which we had discussion about team tactics before a race, but we realized the importance of this race to Ford, and it was up to the drivers to do their best for Lotus and Ford.'

Jim Clark took the lead at the start but soon allowed Hill to pass and the order remained until lap 40 when Graham began to slow with clutch problems. Jimmy slowed down, too, to hold station but then came under pressure from Chris Amon's Ferrari, so Colin signalled him to forget the 'agreement' and forge ahead. Amon then retired and so Jimmy again slowed down, but as he was by then 45 sec ahead of Graham with only 13 laps to go, it was just not on to hang around waiting for him. Two laps from the end, however, it began to look as though the original plan would be followed after all when Jimmy's suspension virtually collapsed and he had to slow down dramatically. Finally, he finished only 6 sec ahead of Graham Hill whose car was also, by then, in a pretty terrible state. But Ford were happy – they had their one-two finish, but only just!

Lotus's 1967 Indianapolis effort was low-key indeed. Although Chapman was still enjoying STP's sponsorship, he had been too tied-up with the 49 to design a new car for the '500'. Having abandoned the 4.2 litre H16 engine, he again used the trusty

---

[*] 'Life at the Limit' (William Kimber, London, 1969).

For the 1967 Indy race, the 4.2 litre version of the BRM engine was still not ready and Clark once more had to use the two-year-old Lotus 38 with the Ford V8 engine. He retired with a broken piston and was classified 31st – his worst performance at Indy, where he was not to be seen again.

American Ford V8, with Jim Clark driving an old 38, while Graham Hill used the only existing Type 42 chassis – the one originally designed to take the H16. This had been hurriedly converted with a tubular structure to carry the V8 engine which, unlike its British counterpart, could not be used as a stressed member of the chassis.

Jimmy qualified at a slower lap speed than the previous year and was in 16th place on the grid. The race was stopped by heavy rain after only sixteen laps and the restart delayed until the following day, soon after which Clark was among the first to retire – with a broken piston. Graham was even lower down the starting grid in 31st position. He had actually qualified at a higher speed than his team mate but had done so during the second weekend of qualifying whereas, at Indy, times achieved in the first weekend take precedence. Graham retired even earlier in the race than Jimmy – and for the same reason. However, there was some satisfaction for Colin and the team: the race was won by A. J. Foyt in a Coyote-Ford, a car which was nothing more than a blatant copy of a Lotus 38.

Certainly, though, 1967 was a decisive year for the Indy race because, apart from the two Lotuses, STP's Andy Granatelli fielded a brand-new turbine car for Parnelli Jones, and it would have won the race but for a minor mechanical defect only four laps from the end. This STP-Paxton turbocar, equipped with Ferguson four-wheel drive transmission, was actually designed by Ken Wallis, an expatriate Englishman, although there was a story going round at the time that Colin Chapman had lent a hand with the suspension design. There was some credence for this because, in April, Jimmy had been allowed to test drive the car during one of the early practice sessions at Indy. Having flown directly back from there to Pau for the Formula 2 GP, I remember him saying to me on arrival, 'I have just driven the car which will win the 500 Miles this year!'

In Formula 2 racing, Lotus were obviously among the first to use the new Cosworth engine (the basis of their new V8, of course) for which Chapman came up with a nice new but conventional monocoque chassis – the Lotus 48. In fact, this was ready before the 49 F1 car and actually first appeared during the early part of the year – driven by Graham Hill – in the Tasman races, which Jimmy won in a 2 litre Climax-engined Lotus 33.

The two Lotus 48s driven by Clark and Hill entered most of the F2 races that year but, although Jimmy managed to win a few of them, it was really Brabham's year again, albeit using a Ford-Cosworth FVA engine rather than the Honda. Actually there was also a third Lotus 'works' entry that year, a car referred to as a 41B and basically a beefed-up space-framed 41 fitted with the FVA engine. It was entered by Lotus Components and driven by Jackie Oliver.

Lotus Components also entered their own Formula 3 car driven by John Miles, but Mo Nunn – an ex-Lotus mechanic later destined to become a Formula 1 team owner – was really the most successful of the Lotus F3 drivers, in a season where Brabham again took the lion's share of victories. Lotus Components, however, were not unduly perturbed by their lack of success in Formula 3 and their consequent poor sales of Lotus 41s, because the new Formula Ford had just come into being and they were turning out cars in vast quantities for this new class.

The new Formula Ford Lotus 51 was a space-framed car based on the 22/31 but modified to accommodate the mildly-tuned Cortina engine which was the basis of the new formula. In 1968 this became the 51A and during those two years a total of 218 Formula Ford cars were built.

Elan production was now in full swing, and during the year Lotus celebrated the manufacture of their 5,000th example. Also, the new Elan +2 was introduced, similar to the original but with a wider track and a wheelbase one foot longer to accommodate two occasional seats in the back. The shape was quite distinctive and was based on a prototype the Metier designed when the company was still at Cheshunt. A much flatter bonnet line and engine compartment resulted in a more efficient aerodynamic shape, which helped greatly in retaining an acceptable level of performance, despite the extra weight of the +2 compared with the 'standard' Elan.

The appearance of the Elan +2 was a pointer to some of Colin's future ideas. More luxuriously appointed than the two-seater (priced at £1,923 including purchase tax) and with Lotus having now become a household name, Colin had dreams of going 'up-market' with the +2 in order to fill the gap beyond the Elan, which had appealed so much to the younger enthusiast. In fact, the +2S version which was to appear the following year was no longer made available in kit form.

However, before moving into the higher quality car market, Lotus had to have an engine of their own, and not only for reasons of prestige but also because of the genuine concern over the continuing availability or otherwise of the Ford block, the basis of the twin-cam engine. 'We had to thank Ford for a lot of the successes we had with the twin-cam,' says Fred Bushell, 'but we never knew how long they would continue to be available. There were difficulties in boring out the blocks, because of which there was a tremendous scrap rate and unless there was pressure from very senior management it was highly likely that they would cease production altogether, so we just had to have our own engine.

'The project was supposed to begin at the time we moved to Hethel and we engaged two engineers especially for it. Colin believed that, compared to the twin-cam, a 2 litre engine could be manufactured for a very low cost penalty, provided it was built in-house and with the latest automated equipment. This engine was to be the first stage of a V8.'

When Coventry Climax ceased the manufacture of racing engines one of their engineers, Ron Burr, became available, so Colin quickly hired him to work on the engine under Steve Sanville, who was in charge of the powertrain development. Burr, of course, was very conversant with the design of four-valve cylinder heads, which was what Chapman wanted to use. As Fred Bushell has already explained, the intention was to follow Keith Duckworth's philosophy and start with a four-cylinder unit before doubling it up to make a V8. Originally, some thought had been given to producing a V6 designed by BRM, but an engine of such a configuration, with twin overhead camshafts to each bank of cylinder heads, would have been either too wide if inclined at 120 degrees, or too high at 60 degrees, to be accommodated within the traditional type of Lotus chassis which Colin wanted to retain, along with a low bonnet line. It is interesting to note that there was a possibility of a V8 version being enlarged to 4.2 litres in order to compete at Indianapolis. But nothing came of the proposal and it was settled that the new Lotus engine was to be a four-cylinder 2 litre with the block inclined at an angle of 45 degrees, to suit both a low bonnet line and a future V8 version. The twin overhead camshafts were to be driven by a toothed belt and the four valves of each cylinder actuated in a similar way to that of the Coventry Climax unit which Ron Burr knew so well.

At the 1967 Motor Show, which Colin Chapman, Steve Sanville and Ron Burr visited together, Vauxhall introduced a new car powered by a four-cylinder 2 litre engine inclined at 45 degrees and with a specification very similar to the new Lotus project. Chapman therefore lost no time in negotiating with Vauxhall when he found that the cylinder head they were in the process of designing could be fitted to the cast iron block of this engine with very little modification. Invaluable development time was thus gained.

Chapter 13

The Heartbreak of Hockenheim

For Colin Chapman, 1968 was destined to be both a triumphant and a tragic year. On the one hand, the company of which he was practically the sole owner was tremendously successful, producing 3,048 cars and bringing in record profits of £731,000. This enabled him to sell shares to the public and become a millionaire in his own right. On the racing side, he was equally successful with the Lotus 49B – aided by aerodynamic devices which he was the first to introduce into Formula 1 – with which Lotus won its third World Drivers' Championship and fourth Manufacturers' Cup. On the other hand, this was the year in which Jim Clark was fatally injured in an unexplained accident during a relatively unimportant Formula 2 race in Germany. The links between Jimmy and Colin were far stronger than the usual driver-constructor relationship. There was a deep and very genuine friendship between the two men, and both owed a great deal to each other. Jimmy's loss was felt profoundly by Colin.

At the end of the 1967 season everyone had been shocked when the Esso Petroleum Company announced that they would be withdrawing their support for motor racing. Traditionally, it was always the fuel and oil companies who were the mainstay of European motor racing from long before the Second World War but, in recent years, they had watched while the tyre companies assumed more and more importance until they were almost forgotten, even though they were still spending considerable sums of money in support of the teams. Esso's withdrawal was not entirely unexpected, but it was clear that something significant would have to be done to ensure the future of motor racing. Accordingly, the CSI (Commission Sportive Internationale) of the FIA (Fédération Internationale de l'Automobile) decided that they should follow American practice and rescind the rule which banned any form of commercial advertising on racing cars. The way was then open to the sponsorship of motor racing – a quite monumental decision at the time.

Although it was a little while before the full effects were felt, Lotus were the first to benefit from the decision. The first thing Andrew Ferguson did was to draw up a list of the 200 most important companies in England and he then sent each of them a proposal outlining the advantages and benefits of sponsoring Team Lotus. The results of this mailing were not very promising, and it became fairly obvious to Andrew that sponsorship was only likely to be forthcoming after personal contacts had been made, and it was quite impossible for him to reach directly all the people who just might be interested.

However, by pure chance, Dave Lazenby (the former chief mechanic for Lotus at Indianapolis, who was then managing Lotus Components) was looking, quite independently of Andrew Ferguson, for a relatively small sponsor for his two racing Europa Lotus 47s. One of Lazenby's mechanics used to go out with a secretary who was working at Sales Link, the company that handled the Imperial Tobacco public relations account, and she tipped him off that Imperial were thinking of sponsoring motor racing. The prospect was so good that Lazenby took it to Andrew. It very soon transpired that Imperial Tobacco were indeed very keen, and were prepared to spend a really large sum of money to promote their Gold Leaf brand of cigarettes. They were prepared to make a deal with Team Lotus and, of course, with Lotus Components, too! The whole thing was arranged very quickly. The F2 cars destined for the Tasman series in December being already in transit, they had to be repainted hurriedly, in red and gold, as soon as they arrived 'down under'.

Geoffrey Kent, then the Chairman of Players and later in the top job at Imperial Group, recalled for me why they had decided to sponsor motor racing. 'Things were not going too well for England at the time,' he said, 'and it seemed that the only sport in which the British were doing well was motor racing. So we thought, "why don't we sponsor motor racing?" I really think that patriotism played a large part in making this decision.' Of course, this partnership was destined to become extremely successful and the personal relationship between Colin Chapman and Geoffrey Kent became so close that Colin asked him to join the board of Team Lotus.

Although the Lotus 49 was to be extensively modified for the coming season, it was with a 'standard' 49 that Jim Clark won his 25th and last Grand Prix race on New Year's Day at the Kyalami circuit in South Africa. He won quite easily from pole

Jimmy's last Grand Prix victory – the South African at Kyalami on New Year's Day 1968.

position, having been a whole second faster in practice than his team mate, who was second fastest – and led throughout, winning from Hill by a margin of over 25 sec. Simple confirmation of his absolute superiority.

Early in the season Alan Mann had flown over to Paris to talk with Jimmy about driving his new P65 Ford DFV-engined sports car in the BOAC 500-mile race at Brands Hatch, which was due to take place on the same day as the Hockenheim event. Since this new car had the full backing of Walter Hayes and Ford, Jimmy felt he had a commitment and he therefore agreed. Unfortunately, Alan omitted to confirm the arrangement to Jimmy who was the type of person to take such omissions very seriously. For instance, he was never late for appointments: for him everything had to be done 'by the book', and he would just not tolerate someone who did not do what they said they would do. Probably Jimmy thought that Alan had changed his mind and so he told Andrew to go ahead and enter him instead for the Hockenheim race. When Alan Mann finally did confirm the sports car drive, it was too late and Jimmy was already committed to Hockenheim, so he turned him down flat.

The date was 7 April 1968. The weather was lousy. Jimmy had metering unit problems in practice and he started the first race of the two-heat event in seventh position on the grid. Graham Hill, with incorrect gear ratios and a handling problem, too, was even lower down the grid. The slight rain had all but stopped when the race began and Jean-Pierre Beltoise took the lead immediately. Jimmy was not able to improve on his seventh position and, in fact, soon dropped back to eighth place. Clearly, there was a problem somewhere.

I was not at Hockenheim that day, but Doug Nye described what followed most graphically. 'On lap five he was a lonely eighth as he disappeared beyond the pits and accelerated into the woods building up to near maximum speed on a virtual straight which led into a tightening right-hand curve. A lone flag marshal heard the car approaching after the leaders had screamed by, and then the red, white and gold machine burst into sight twitching from side to side with the driver fighting the wheel. It slewed broadside at around 140 mph and careered off the road, slithered over the verge and took down some saplings before smashing into a larger tree which caught full in the cockpit.'

Jim Clark was killed instantly.

The cause of the accident was never officially determined but Colin, who was away on a ski-ing holiday in St Moritz with his family that weekend, initiated a full enquiry. As soon as the wrecked car was back at Hethel he invited the RAC scrutineer, Peter Jowitt, Senior Engineer of the Experimental Aircraft Department at Farnborough, specializing in military prototype aircraft accidents, to examine it. In the second edition of Graham Gauld's book 'Jim Clark Remembered'* his report, which follows, was published for the first time since the accident.

> 'I was initially quite surprised to have a telephone call from the RAC to the effect that Colin Chapman had asked whether I would assist in the investigation of the accident. At that time the relationship between Colin and myself could best be

---

*	Published by Patrick Stephens, 1984.

described as armed neutrality. I had rejected a number of his cars, including at least one from the start line. I knew that Colin was aware of my background at Farnborough, and I immediately agreed to go. At Hethel I found Keith Duckworth, who did the engine strip examination, and Chris Parry, of Firestone, who looked principally at the tyres.

'The car had been in the original Lotus green and yellow livery, but had been overpainted red and white, the new sponsor's colours. It had sustained a very heavy impact to the left side, and it was fairly clear that it had struck a tree at the point where Jim's left elbow would have been. The direction of impact was such that the car must have been going sideways at the time. The car had started to wrap around the tree. The left side structure had bent around the tree, and the right-hand side had failed in tension. No form of driver restraint could have saved Jim.

'We had a piece of evidence of enormous value. A statement had been taken from the marshal who had very nearly been hit by the car, and it had been taken whilst he was still white-lipped and trembling, and before he had had time to rationalize. He said that he had seen the car, whilst coming towards him, start to break away at the rear end. There had then been a correction which caused a sharp breakaway the other way, followed by another correction which caused a further, fairly gentle but progressive breakaway in the original turning left mode, which continued until the car hit the tree.

'Any oversteering accident will focus attention on the rear of the vehicle, and I found an oddly shaped cut in the tread of the rear right-hand tyre. This cut went completely through the tyre, and I could not find any part of the wreckage which could have caused it. If the tyre had been punctured, there is an odd effect which I had seen before. At high speed in a straight line, centrifugal force will in fact hold the tread out so that it looks as if there is no puncture and the driver will not know that the tyre has deflated.

'As soon as a side load is put on, in cornering, the tyre becomes unstable, and cannot generate the cornering force that the driver would expect. With the right-hand rear tyre deflating, the effect in a right-hand corner would be some oversteer. Correcting this by steering left would put a heavier cornering load on to the unstable right-hand tyre, which would give rise to a fairly vicious right-hand oversteer. Correction in the opposite sense, at high speed on a very wet track, would clearly be difficult. The tachometer in the car, a mechanical type, indicated that Jim had had power on right up to impact, clearly trying to hold the car. There are, however, situations in which even the unearthly skill of Jimmy Clark will not suffice.

'This rear tyre was off the rim, and half inside out. There was, however, mud right across the width of the tread. Photographs taken of the undisturbed wreckage showed the same thing, indicating that the tyre had been in place when the car left the track. There had been a suggestion that the tyre had left the rim, and that this had been a factor in the accident. I have no doubt whatever that the tyre leaving the rim was a result of the impact.

'This accident investigation left a greater impression upon me than any other that I have ever done. There are not too many men of the calibre of Jimmy Clark. I had to revise my view of Colin Chapman. He must have known that he could expect nothing but the unvarnished result of the investigation, but he was absolutely determined to have the truth, no matter how hurtful. He was not the

Chunky Chapman that the world normally saw. I felt that he was being tortured (not a word that I would use very frequently) by the thought that he had in some way contributed to the death of a man who was to him very much more than his team leader. I am fairly sure that if there had been some short-coming which in any way had caused this accident, he could have simply turned away from racing. Colin's grief was very private. He did not want the results of the investigation published, and I think that they never were. The odd bald statement was put out, but that was Colin's way.

In later years I investigated the Jochen Rindt accident for Lotus. It is fair to say that this did not have the same shattering effect, even though it at one time made it appear possible that Colin Chapman could face manslaughter charges in Italy. After Jimmy's accident I saw a Chapman I think very few people saw, or even suspected existed.

'Even now, I can remember driving away from Hethel, feeling absolutely miserable, and thinking very bitterly that a small piece of debris picked up in a race which really did not matter one tiny bit had cost the life of one of the finest men in motor racing. On today's tracks, this accident would have meant nothing more than an engagement with the barriers, and some ribaldry from the mechanics, when the driver walked back to the pits. Hindsight is too damned easy.'

Colin was absolutely shattered by Jim Clark's death and did not attend the Spanish GP where Graham Hill, driving the sole Lotus entry, raced and won in the old '49'. The new 49B should have appeared but Colin gave instructions that it was not to be used in his absence. Since there was so much that was new on it, he wanted to oversee its first race personally.

However, Team Lotus were back in force at Monaco, with Jackie Oliver now the second driver, and Graham Hill had the new 49B. In many ways the car was very different from the previous model. The weight distribution was altered, with the oil tank now in the form of a 'saddle' and positioned over the gearbox, thus giving more rear weight bias and aiding traction. The wheelbase had been lengthened simply by raking the front suspension arms forward by three inches. The rear suspension geometry was also modified and the car now sported a Hewland gearbox to allow easier changes of ratio. The width of the wheels was increased to accept the latest Firestone YB11 tyres and the engine power had been marginally improved to give 410 bhp, but still at 9,000 rpm. However, the most important innovation was to the bodywork for here, for the first time, was a Grand Prix car with a body expressly designed to provide downforce by using the air flowing over it. It was equipped at the front with two small horizontal fins, made to an aerofoil section, one on either side of the nose cone, and at the rear with a new engine cover in the shape of a scooped-out wedge.

Recently, I was able to talk with Jackie Oliver about his years with Lotus. 'After racing the Elan 26R,' he said, 'my chance to drive for Lotus came about through a visit to Snetterton where I was testing a Formula 3 Brabham which I had just bought myself. When I arrived I found that the Charles Lucas-Team Lotus F3 team was also there and they were running a third car for Andrew Cowan who was really a rally driver. I was pretty angry about this and I remember saying to the Engineering

Director of Team Lotus, Jim Endruweit, "If you want to get on in motor racing it is no good being a successful customer with a Lotus Elan, or even doing quite well as a private entrant in Formula 3. You have no hope of ever having the chance of a works drive unless you are a ping-pong champion or a rally driver." I think Jim must have passed on this caustic comment to Colin Chapman because soon afterwards he suggested to Charles Lucas that I should be given a test drive.'

Actually, to be fair, Andrew Cowan – a very successful long-distance rally driver and winner of the famous London to Sydney Marathon – was a farmer and near neighbour of Jim Clark, who was trying to get him into Team Lotus. It was, in fact, at Jimmy's request that he had a few fruitless drives in the Lucas team but Andrew realized that this was not for him and he soon returned to rallying.

I asked Jackie how his drive in Formula 2 had come about. 'That,' he explained, 'was because Colin had said that if I wanted to run a Formula 2 car I would have to find my own sponsor – which was nothing new in this business – and I came up with the Herts and Essex Aero Club. What used to happen was that Lotus effectively supplied the car and sent the bills for its preparation to the Club. This arrangement lasted about a year.'

I also asked Jackie Oliver about his early meetings with Colin Chapman. 'When I went for a test drive to Snetterton,' he answered, 'I had not met Colin and I didn't know Jim Clark, not even by sight. I never had any adulation for top sportsmen, but I did know that Colin Chapman produced good cars.

'I never really came to know Colin properly until I started to drive for him in Formula 1 and that was not until much later. Up to that time he always conducted all negotiations through Jim Endruweit and Andrew Ferguson. He didn't even turn up on Formula 2 test days.

'Of course, I did meet him sometimes at the factory because I did quite a lot of testing for Lotus before I ever started to drive for them in Formula 1. But Colin had no real reason to talk to me because Jim Endruweit or Andrew Ferguson always dealt with the less important racing formulae. He would walk past sometimes and I would then say "Hello" to him but we had no dealings together at all. The only negotiations I ever had with him were after Jimmy's death. Jim Endruweit then suggested that the young Oliver should be given an opportunity and that was the first time I ever had any real contact with Chapman.

'He started to explain to me the importance of Formula 1. "Now lad," he said, "you are in Formula 1 and this is what it is all about. All the other stuff is not really important." And then he gave me his philosophy on what was and what was not important. It was not until I was going to be driving one of his Formula 1 cars that he felt it was worth spending any time with me imparting his philosophy.

'It was, of course, a very bad time for him because he had just lost Jimmy and I don't think his heart was really in it. I had come along really as a stand-in for Jimmy, for whom – in Colin's eyes anyway – I was quite rightly no substitute.'

I asked Jackie whether, when testing in Formula 1, he found Colin to be helpful. 'He was actually quite aloof,' he replied. 'He was astute enough to know that any answers he got from this young driver would be of no value, so why bother to ask? That's the way he was – he was very hard. I remember the first thing he said to me at the start in Monte Carlo was, "Now lad, if you finish here, in the whole history of Monte Carlo, you finish sixth. Let's stay out of trouble and don't have an accident on the first lap." Those words were still ringing in my ears when, as I came out of the tunnel on the first lap, I collected Scarfiotti and Bruce McLaren who had just had an accident before I arrived!

'That made the old man furious and he fired me on the spot. It was only through Jim Endruweit's efforts (he was a good supporter of mine, and he had Colin's ear) that I was given a second crack of the whip in Belgium. This was very much Colin's way of handling a young driver; there were no subtleties with him, and you had to be very tough to survive in the team after Jimmy's death.

'I think Jimmy's death made Colin a much harder person and people like Rindt and Andretti managed to survive in such an environment where perhaps the younger and more sensitive drivers did not. Looking back on it now, and from what I gathered from my own experience at the time, I think there was a "Phase One Chapman" which existed before Jimmy died, followed by a "Phase Two Chapman" afterwards, who took a complete change of direction.'

Jackie Oliver led the British Grand Prix at Brands Hatch in 1968, until his transmission failed just after half distance. 'That was my last year,' he said. 'I had a four-year contract with Lotus and it was in the fourth year that I was in the Formula 1 team with Graham Hill, when he won the World Championship.'

I asked Jackie if Colin was inclined to take more interest in him once he was in the Formula 1 team, and whether he was generally more friendly. 'Colin always wanted to own things,' he replied. 'He wanted to make everyone part of the Lotus family and I very much fell into that mould. Quite rightly, he saw that I was never going to be a true champion like some of his drivers, but on the other hand he clearly thought I was good enough that he did not want to lose me. He didn't want me to go to BRM and yet he could not offer me anything tangible. He was very angry when I left but that was the style of the man; he had given me an opportunity for four years and then, even though it was he who had set his sights higher and was no longer able to offer me a Formula 1 drive, he still found it difficult to actually let me go.

'Generally, he was always friendly, and also his humour was always laced with the truth. For instance, if I had a crash with the car, he would dig me in the ribs and say, "Another one like that and you'll be looking for a job. Ha, Ha, Ha!". All the time there were innuendos in his humour. "You are not getting the job done lad!" he would say. That was his way with people. Colin would never sit down with me and say, "Now young Oliver, I understand all the difficulties . . ." He wasn't that sort of person. He was too brash.

'Whilst Ken Tyrrell was probably the best team owner when it came to bringing on new young drivers, Colin was probably the worst. He would never spend time considering other people's difficulties and problems because he was too impatient. On the other hand, I think he was the only team owner to possess the three most important elements for success. He could find the money; he could design the cars; and he could run the team. Those three qualities in one man are quite exceptional, even today.'

Chapter 14

The Wonders of Wings

The first car to race with any form of aerofoil was the big American Chaparral F2 sports car, which first raced at Daytona, Florida, early in 1967. At Indianapolis that year there were also several cars which had been fitted with spoilers and later Jim Clark had been invited to drive an American Vollstedt in the Riverside Grand Prix, a race run under Indianapolis rules, and where Lotus were not taking part. (This was only the second time that Jimmy ever drove a single-seater other than a Lotus.) The Vollstedt had been fitted with a large flap mounted on struts at the rear of the car and, although Jimmy was not successful in the race, he was sufficiently impressed to ask his mechanics to fit a similar aerofoil to his car for the Tasman races. When Colin heard about this he blew his top! To him, car design was very much the domain of the engineers and not the drivers. But he had been thinking along the same lines because, at that time, he was busy on the design of a Lotus turbine car for the 1968 Indianapolis race and was in the process of giving it wedge-shaped bodywork in order to generate some downforce. The need for this was becoming acute because racing tyres were now so wide that they were developing a great deal of 'lift' of their own.

'The very first wing that I ever knew about,' Colin told me, 'was fitted by Jim Clark in the Tasman series. He used an old helicopter blade which just happened to be lying about in the garage. We took a 49 with wings to the Spanish Grand Prix but we never actually ran it. No one else had wings at the time and ours stayed in the truck. There were wings on each side of the nose and a big sort of scoop at the back. Not a wing as such but a downforce creator. But on the front they were proper wings of aerofoil section and we actually ran the car in that form at Monaco.'

Maurice Phillippe explained to me that Colin was first made aware of the lift problem when, during a test session for the 1967 Indianapolis race, they fitted a special 'recorder' to the Lotus 38. In those days, the miniaturized electronic equipment now used was not available, and this was a large aircraft 'black box' running off 24 volts, so space had to be found in the car for a couple of batteries. The results of this test indicated definite signs of aerodynamic lift to the car, which was what set Colin thinking about ways of combating the problem. His first thought was the wedge-shaped body and this was tested in a wind tunnel but, although it did reduce lift somewhat, it did not overcome it entirely.

The appearance of the 49B at Monaco, and its success, started a frenzy of work, with all the other constructors experimenting in one way or another. But it soon became apparent to Chapman that the efficiency of an aerofoil was much higher than that of the wedge-shaped body and so he concentrated his attention on wings. (Of course, it was not until about ten years later that the idea of a 'negative lift body' would recur, and then Chapman was again the instigator.)

Strangely enough, it appears that Colin was not as quick in following up the initial lead he had gained at Monaco. At the next Grand Prix, held on the very fast and demanding Spa-Francorchamps circuit where downforce would be needed most, the 49B was unchanged – although there was a second one for Jackie Oliver. Both the Brabhams and the Ferraris appeared with proper aerofoils at the back, albeit very small ones, but by the French GP at Rouen the 49Bs both had large rear aerofoil-section wings. These were mounted on struts, not acting on the chassis like the others, but directly upon the suspension uprights – as those on the Chaparral sports car did – which was a distinct advantage.

The 1968 season saw tremendous developments in this direction with a race between the various team designers and engineers as to who could bolt on the most effective wings and spoilers. Wings were made so that their angle of attack could be adjusted by the driver for 'feathering' when travelling fast down the straight. The French Matra people even drew on their knowledge of aerospace technology and actuated their wing by means of a small electric motor originally designed for use in a missile! Lotus were somewhat less sophisticated, with their wing being adjusted by the driver operating a pedal and cable mechanism.

The World Drivers' Championship was disputed by only two cars – Jackie Stewart's Matra-Ford, owned by the private entrant Ken Tyrrell, and Graham Hill's Lotus. After Clark's death some had forecast that Team Lotus would fall apart because, 'after all, it was really Jimmy's team', they said. But Graham rose to the challenge and fully justified Walter Hayes's earlier suggestion that he should be in the team. By winning the next two Grand Prix races after the tragedy of Hockenheim it was Graham who restored the team's spirit. Later, he scored seconds in the German GP and in the USA at Watkins Glen, whilst Swiss driver Jo ('Seppi') Siffert won the British Grand Prix in a Lotus 49 which Rob Walker had bought.

With rear wings becoming ever larger and more efficient, and with the consequent enormous increase in traction, one of the team's major problems had been to find constant velocity joints for the rear drive-shafts strong enough for the job, and it was not until almost the end of the season that Chapman solved the problem by fitting Lobro CV joints.

On the other hand, Jackie Stewart had the big advantage of being the spearhead of Dunlop's attempt to restore their supremacy in Formula 1 racing, when they asked Ken Tyrrell and his team to help with tyre development and testing. In dry weather conditions the new British tyres were no better than the Firestones used by Lotus, but in the wet the Dunlops definitely had the edge. These were designed so that, when they revolved at high speed, the centrifugal force created would distort them in such a way that they would assume a triangular section. This would therefore reduce the area of tread in contact with the road surface and so decrease the chances of aquaplaning. It so happened that the weather in Europe during the spring and summer of 1968 was very poor and Stewart was able to make full use of his Dunlop 'wet' tyres on several occasions, including an unforgettably wet Nurburgring where fog, cutting visibility down to fifty yards in places, made conditions even worse. Graham Hill, driving with even more determination than usual, filled second place after a magnificent drive. At one point he spun when his Firestones aquaplaned on a stream of water, whereupon he got out and pushed the car back on to the track, climbed in, started the engine and rejoined the fray – without losing his position. The conditions were so bad that no one would have blamed him had he just left the car on the side of the road and walked home!

The title was eventually decided in the Mexican Grand Prix, between three possible candidates – Stewart, Hill, and Denny Hulme, now driving for Bruce McLaren, who still had an outside chance. It was in this race that Chapman introduced his adjustable wing. However, to keep the other teams guessing, before practice, Team Lotus displayed the 'T' (training) car without wings at all! Practice and the race were very much dominated by Jo Siffert in the blue Lotus 49B belonging to Rob Walker (now partnered by Jack Durlacher) although initially the race was led by Stewart and Hill. Siffert, who was on pole, soon looked as though he would quickly pass them both, until he had to stop for a broken throttle linkage to be repaired – losing two laps in the process. Undaunted, 'Seppi' then put up not only fastest lap but also a new lap record and eventually finished in sixth place.

Meanwhile, Graham was able to get the better of Stewart, by which time Hulme was out, having crashed earlier. Then Stewart's fuel pump failed and he was only able to cruise home in seventh place, so Hill came out the winner and with that became World Champion for the second time, but the first with Lotus. Colin rejoiced in the victory although for him it had been such a sad year and he could not help remembering that, but for a defective oil pipe, Jim Clark would have won his second World Championship at the same circuit four years earlier.

In a way, Graham's victory had been lucky because during most of the race he was worried by the possible complete failure of his 'feathering' wing system and which he wrote about in his book:

> 'On the third lap, as I came into the straight, I pushed the pedal to flatten the wing – and the pedal went light. Crumbs, I thought, we're in trouble. I turned my mirror – I always have them mounted fairly loose – and had a look: there was the old Bungee rubber band waving in the breeze. I had a look in the other mirror, slightly despairing, because if that one was gone, I was sunk. Without the rubber bands to pull the wing into the maximum downward load position, the car oversteers like a pig, but it was all right and it held all through the race. With only one rubber Bungee, it couldn't come back to the maximum download position for braking at the end of the straight when I let off the pedal, but, as the speed dropped, it came into the right position of its own accord and stayed there. It was all a bit hairy under braking, but it held.'

It was at the previous Grand Prix at Watkins Glen that Colin first invited Mario Andretti to drive a Lotus, when he took over the team's spare third car. Colin had met and been much impressed with Mario at Indianapolis and the American was keen on buying a Lotus for the following year's race. This was Mario's very first Grand Prix drive and he was most excited about it. Although he was now an American citizen, and living in Pennsylvania, he had not forgotten that his enthusiasm for motor racing had been fired soon after the War when, as a small boy living in a camp for displaced persons at Montona, near Trieste, he had first heard and dreamed about the exploits of the great Alberto Ascari.

In fact, despite his lack of Grand Prix experience, Mario's performance was quite shattering to say the least. In the first practice session he just drove the car round to get used to it and to learn the circuit. Afterwards, he told Colin, 'Now I am going to put it on pole' – and put it on pole he did. Colin, of course, was tremendously impressed and from then on his friendship with Andretti began to blossom, although it was to be some time before he would take part regularly in Formula 1 races, simply because he was already pursuing a very profitable career in the States.

One factor about the 1968 Formula 1 races was that Chapman's exclusive use of the Cosworth-Ford DFV engine finished at the beginning of the season, and it was therefore offered to the other teams at the price of £7,500. However, because it was in short supply for some time, only McLaren and Tyrrell – for his Matra – had been able to take advantage.

Although Andy Granatelli's STP-Paxton turbine car may not have been the first to appear at Indy, it was certainly the most successful and, in fact, its performance was such that the United States Auto Club – very much under the control of many of the car owners themselves – decided to alter the rules for fear that everyone would have to change over to turbines. So, in June 1967, USAC announced that the inlet annulus should be restricted to 15.999 square inches, a drastic measure since this would mean a loss of about 200 bhp, and when two stages of the three-stage axial compressor were removed the output dropped to around 430 bhp.

By 1968 the Ford was no longer the latest thing in Indy piston engines. One reason for this was that they had only sold their engines on condition that Ford's own brand of spark plugs, Autolite, was used, which virtually meant that Champion were out in the cold as far as Indy was concerned. However, with Champion having always been so dominant, especially in that race, they were not prepared to put up with such a situation without a fight. One of their research engineers then persuaded a Californian-based turbocharger specialist to try out a unit on one of the 'old' four-cylinder Offenhauser engines, even though this would mean reducing the capacity to only 2.8 litres to meet the regulations. Despite this, the Offys – even in '67 – gave 600 bhp and with more to come in 1968 the Ford V8 engine was very soon outpaced. From this it was pretty clear that the handicap which had been placed on the turbine engine was unfair and would make things particularly difficult for Granatelli, especially as he was also having to cope with the tremendous battle between the tyre giants, with the STP team backed by Firestone and the turbo-Offy supported by Goodyear.

Granatelli went to court over the USAC decision to change the rules, the case involving about twenty lawyers and costing around 200,000 dollars. Although he lost the action, he never lost his faith in turbines and, despite the restrictions imposed, he decided he would still come back with a new turbine-engined car for 1968 and, to be quite sure it was a good one, Colin Chapman would design it.

Of course, it is not simply power and top speed which matters in motor racing, whether at Indianapolis or anywhere else. Roadholding is really the key to success and Colin believed that, apart from the tremendous torque which gave it such superior acceleration, the turbine would be especially effective in obtaining optimum cornering speeds on such a high-speed track as Indy, because of the smoothness of the power curve. In addition, if he could take care of the high-speed lift – indicated so clearly during the special tests with the Lotus 38 earlier in 1967 – he was sure the increase in stability would be substantial, hence his research into the wedge-shaped body.

In November 1967 Chapman signed a contract with Andy Granatelli to design a turbine-engined Lotus (the Type 56) for him. Four cars were to be built. Two would be Team Lotus-STP entries for Jim Clark and Graham Hill, the third would be looked after by Granatelli himself for a, so far, un-named American driver, the fourth would be a spare, while Parnelli Jones would be back driving the old STP-Paxton car, affectionately known as 'Samson'.

The new car, like the old, would be equipped with four-wheel drive transmission and for this Colin turned to Harry Ferguson Research, a firm with considerable experience in this field. They were also well known to Granatelli because they had provided him with a four-wheel drive transmission for his Indy entry back in 1964 – the 700 bhp Novi-Ferguson supercharged V8. It is also worth noting that the Ferguson P99 four-wheel drive racing car, driven by Stirling Moss, had actually won a race at Oulton Park some years earlier. Indeed, it was on Stirling Moss's recommendation that Granatelli had first turned to Ferguson.

As a turbine needs no gearbox – because, like a steam engine, it develops sufficient torque at all engine speeds to be able to accelerate from rest to maximum speed in one gear – the transmission consisted of two crown wheel and pinion assemblies, one at the front and one at the rear, linked by a shaft driven from the engine. There were three differential gear units, one for each cwp and one, acting as a torque splitter, governing the distribution of power between the front and rear axles. These differential gears were very special units and it was in their design that Ferguson's expertise was so valuable.

Maurice Phillippe recalls that, when he and Colin discussed the initial brief, the biggest problem was whether to drive the shaft from the turbine with gears or a 'Morse' chain. 'The race was in May, there was testing to be done at the beginning of March and we had got to the stage by early January that we had still not made a decision on the transmission. The ZF axles were well under way and so was the car, but for the transmission we were going to do a deal with Ferguson Research led by Major Tony Rolt, a former Le Mans 24-Hours race winner in a Jaguar. So Colin said, "Right, we had better go and see them and make a decision with them". There were two possibilities; a Morse chain transmission which, at the rpm that we envisaged and the high loads, was a bit beyond the limit for which it was designed. The other alternative was a gear train, but we needed a system where we could alter the ratio.

'On the day of the appointment we took off from Hethel in the Twin Comanche and Colin said, "We will discuss what we are going to do on the flight up." During the discussion we decided that we probably favoured the gear transmission. We knew what to expect from that. We all sat in the boardroom at Harry Ferguson Research

Chapman tries out the 56 for size. Note its funnel-shaped exhaust behind the driver's head.

with Major Rolt at the head of the table. Derek Gardner was the engineer responsible for the transmission. Colin then introduced what he thought should be done but after we had been going for about half an hour, he suddenly got up saying, "Excuse me, but where is the toilet?" He then left telling them, "Continue the discussion with Maurice." We were going along smoothly, dealing with the schedule which was going to be very tight because we wanted to test in less than six weeks – this was going to be a very hectic programme. When we had the 'Is' dotted and the 'Ts' crossed and Colin had been gone for half an hour, there was a little bit of concern.

'Finally, he came charging in and took over the meeting in the way that he had always done – to the point, clear, quick and very precise. Whilst he had been in the loo, he had prepared – on one sheet of notepaper – a contract for the transmission. The only thing was that it was not for a gear transmission but for a chain transmission! He had obviously said to himself, "Now wait a minute, I must give this some more thought," and had gone away to mull it over. He then told them, "You have two weeks to design it, then you need the trial castings in aluminium and in three weeks it will have to be finished. You can do that, can't you Derek?" He didn't even give him a chance to say yes or no. This was in front of the entire Ferguson board and not one of them said a word! And the punch line read – "Four transmissions, four hundred pounds"! This was nothing – well under cost. Then Colin said, "There it is Tony, sign that." And he signed it!'

In order to reduce the frontal area, Chapman decided against positioning the turbine 'sidecar' fashion as had been the feature of the STP-Paxton car. So, in the new car, this was behind the driver who, as a result, was seated some way forward in the chassis. The Lotus 56 was a complete departure from the then-current Lotus monocoque design because the side pontoons were so wide, and they imparted so much rigidity in themselves, that there was no need for a stressed bulkhead as well. The 61-gallon fuel tank was contained entirely within the left-hand pontoon so there was no need for asymmetrical suspension, as on the earlier Lotus Indy cars, because the weight distribution took care of this requirement instead. The suspension was also entirely new because of the four-wheel drive transmission. Air was fed to the turbine through NACA ducts positioned in the top of each body pontoon just by the driver's shoulders, and it exhausted through a chimney, similar in shape to a ship's funnel, in the centre of the body just behind his head.

Painted in the usual STP dayglo red, the Lotus 56 was a very impressive car indeed

It was at Indianapolis that Chapman first fitted recorders to a car during a testing session and he was staggered by the amount of aerodynamical 'lift' which was evidenced. Before he adopted wings, his first solution was the wedge shape he gave to his turbine-engined Type 56, which was later raced in Formula 1 as the 56B. Colin reckoned that the failure of this car was due to the four-wheel drive transmission.

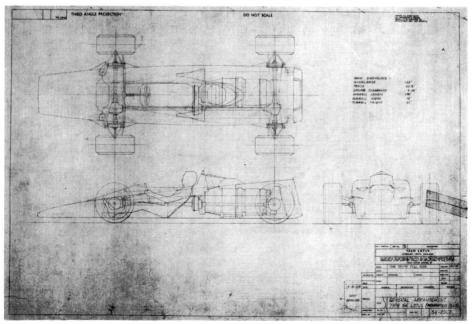

and I flew over to Indy to see its first tests in March 1968. When Jimmy took it out on the track there was a problem with the fuel pump which was not working properly, so it was quickly taken off and Colin himself took it to pieces. Jimmy and I found this most fascinating because it was obvious he had never seen the inside of the pump before and yet, by working from basic principles, he was able to recreate in his mind the way in which it functioned. Later that evening, in 'The Cove', a restaurant across the road from the Speedway where most of the racing people went for dinner, he gave us a lecture on the turbine which showed just how much knowledge he had acquired by reading anything and everything on it that he could find. Finally, of course, the pump was repaired using some parts 'borrowed' from a turbo-prop airplane out at the airport, so that Jimmy was able to test the car properly. Sadly, he would never race it, as he was to die only four weeks later.

Left *Although he died almost two months before the 1968 Indy race took place, earlier that year Jimmy Clark did the initial testing of the turbine-engined Lotus 56. He is seen here behind the car with, left to right, Andy Granatelli, Parnelli Jones, Andy's brother Vince and Colin.*

Below *Andy Granatelli, the head of the STP oil additive company, commissioned Lotus to build two turbine-engined cars for the Indianapolis 500 mile race in 1968. Team Lotus would also run two cars. However, after Jimmy's death Mike Spence took over, only to suffer a fatal accident in practice. In the end, Granatelli ran two cars for American drivers (who were deprived of victory by the failure of a pump driveshaft), while Team Lotus ran this one car for Graham Hill. This Type 56 hit the wall after a failure of the front suspension, and fortunately Graham was uninjured.*

RACE STRATEGY.   30 WAY

① 3ʳᵈ Man slows field under the yellow.   ✓

② Race after the last pit stop.   ✓.

③ Pool lap money for whole race.   ✓

④ 1ˢᵗ man forward Graham, Pollard. Race.

⑤ Leader not more than 30 secs ahead.   ✓

⑥ All signals are ahead of 1ˢᵗ poster ced. only.   ✓

⑦ Do not drive below white line.

⑧ The objective is to win the race as slowly   ✓
   as possible.

⑨ When running together never closer then say 100 yds.   ✓

⑩

Left *Colin Chapman's race strategy notes made before the 1968 Indianapolis 500.*

Below *The 1968 World Championship-winning team. Lotus had weathered the terrible loss of Jimmy Clark.*

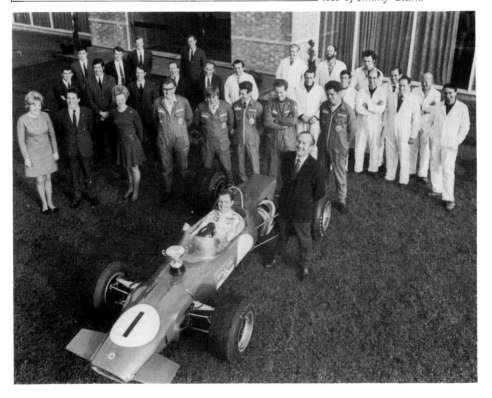

Finding a replacement for Jimmy was an almost impossible problem but Jackie Stewart agreed to take his place at Indianapolis only to injure his wrist in a crash during the Spanish GP, which side-lined him for Monaco as well. So Colin invited Mike Spence along and the Indy team was then Graham Hill and Mike in the Team Lotus-STP cars and an American driver Greg Weld in the STP-prepared third new car. Parnelli Jones had by then withdrawn 'Samson' since it had proved too slow because of the new restrictions. In fact, Granatelli had actually enticed Jones out of retirement the previous year but this time he finally retired for good and eventually became a Formula 1 team owner.

Tragically, Mike Spence crashed while testing the Granatelli car. He had been very fast in his own car and it appeared that with this one he changed his line slightly, coming out of the corner 'on the marbles' – the tiny granules of rubber usually to be found on the outside of corners. According to eye-witnesses, it seemed that he sensed he was about to spin off and so perhaps had decided to slow himself down by deliberately grazing the wall. He managed to do just that and, although the damage to the car was relatively light, the right front wheel was partially torn off. It remained attached by one of the links, swung in the air and caught Mike's crash helmet, fracturing his skull. He died four-and-a-half hours later.

Coming as it did so soon after Jimmy's death, this was too much for Colin, and Andrew Ferguson remembers Colin saying to him at the hospital, 'This is it, I quit motor racing, I'm leaving right now – sell the equipment, pay the bills and come home.' But Andrew knew Colin well enough and decided to proceed as though he had said nothing. Nobody knows where he went to when he disappeared, but a few days later he was back as though nothing had happened and never a word was said to Andrew about disobeying his instructions.

So for the race the team had to be altered again and now two cars were to be entrusted to Andy Granatelli (in fact, he actually bought them) for Joe Leonard and Art Pollard, while Graham Hill remained the sole Lotus entry. Leonard qualified on pole with Graham on his right in second spot and Pollard was in the centre of the fourth row. Graham Hill retired with broken suspension soon after half distance, and the race became one between Joe Leonard's 56 and Bobby Unser in a turbo-Offy-engined Eagle. Leonard was leading Unser when the yellow lights came on only 21 laps from the finish. Unser was then in a desperate situation with no overtaking being allowed under a 'yellow', yet amongst the backmarkers separating him from the leader was the other Lotus 56 driven by Art Pollard and being given pit signals by Andy Granatelli telling him to slow down. Eight laps from the end the green light came back on, but the moment Leonard floored his throttle the fuel pump drive failed and he coasted to a halt at the same point by Turn 1 as Pollard's car did a few seconds later. Unser, of course, went on to win and the era of the Indy turbocharged cars began. The turbine, much to Andy Granatelli's consternation, was soon to be banned altogether.

In Formula 2 for 1968 the Lotus 48s wore the same F1 red and gold livery of Gold Leaf cigarettes, while Jackie Oliver's 41B was sponsored by the Herts and Essex Aero Club. Of course, the season was completely marred by Jim Clark's death and only very few successful results were achieved in this class.

Chapter 15

Failure of Four-wheel Drive

Two important developments came about because of Jim Clark's accident. The first was that Dunlop, although they did not supply tyres to Team Lotus, felt there was a real possibility of such an accident happening again. At the following year's Spanish Grand Prix they introduced a system of safety pegs on the wheel rims – now mandatory on racing cars – which prevent the tyre coming off the rim in the event of deflation. The second development came about because it was fairly clear that if the Hockenheim circuit had been protected by guardrails Jimmy might have escaped unhurt or with only light injuries. The drivers all realized this and Jackie Stewart took it upon himself to mount an energetic safety campaign to improve all forms of protection given to drivers. Ironically, the high point in this campaign came in 1970 when the Grand Prix association members refused to take part in the German Grand Prix if it was to be held on the Nurburgring circuit, which was not lined by guardrails. The CSI backed the drivers and the German GP duly took place at Hockenheim where, in the meantime, the guardrails had been installed.

In October 1968 shares in the company were floated on the London Stock Exchange and Lotus Cars Ltd became a public company. This was entirely Chapman's idea, as Fred Bushell explained. 'In the spring of 1968 Colin made the suggestion that maybe Lotus should be floated on the Stock Exchange. At the time, it was very much the vogue; the thing a successful business should do if it wanted continued growth. It was also a time of very high personal taxation and therefore while Colin remained almost the only person with a substantial shareholding, and with Lotus making quite large profits, the company had to make sizeable distributions in the form of annual dividends which were then very heavily taxed when they reached Colin's hands.

'He and I flew off abroad for a weekend's relaxation and he spent the entire time persuading me that we should go ahead with the idea. I told him about the drawbacks of public involvement in the company's affairs and I said that I felt he would not be particularly happy since it would place considerable restraints upon his own freedom of action which, from experience, I felt he would be unwilling to accept. Although he listened to my warnings, he said that he was changing and was quite sure he could rise to the challenge. Finally he succeeded in persuading me that we should proceed.

'I told him that it could well take up to two years to complete all the arrangements and that we would also have to meet certain profitability criteria. Colin's reaction was that I was being over-cautious and that he wanted to see everything completed within six months. In fact, everything was completed in about that length of time although it meant a virtual seven days a week schedule for me because I had to provide all the necessary information required by the sponsoring merchant bankers, Hill Samuel and Co and the brokers, Joseph Sebag.

'Colin threw himself into the undertaking with his usual drive and enthusiasm, and many most enlightening meetings were held with our various advisers, at which he insisted on being instructed in every aspect of City of London financial operations. Quite often his attempts to over-simplify what they were telling him caused some measure of resentment from the professional financiers, who were embarrassed by being questioned and by everything they said being examined and dissected in Colin's inimitably critical and analytical manner. However, so obvious was his enormous enthusiasm that nobody could be put out for long by his inquisitive approach, as this was usually followed by a very strong dose of Chapman charm.

'The final meeting with the merchant bankers was held with the object of fixing the price at which the shares would be offered to the public, and here Colin produced reams of notes and calculations as to how he felt the shares should be valued. I felt that the financiers were rather mesmerized by this mass of logic and, since Colin's figure was higher than they were recommending, they had some difficulty in balancing his logic with what, in all honesty, was only their gut feeling for what the market might stand. This meeting lasted several hours, I remember, and eventually the chief representative of the merchant bank had to leave us to attend another appointment. In the end, after more discussion, Colin wrote down a figure on a piece of scrap paper and this was sent in to the other meeting for final approval. Almost in desperation I believe, the paper was sent back to our room initialled as OK and as a result the shares were offered at a figure giving a magnificent price/earnings ratio of 26! Despite all sorts of forebodings on the part of the bankers, the high price proved no deterrent to the successful initial placing of the shares.

'Then followed an orgy of effort to ensure that the profit forecast for 1968 was met, with Colin out on the shop floor every day monitoring progress with production and with Sales Manager Graham Arnold being given a small incentive to meet sales targets.'

Colin had retained 52 per cent of the shares himself, which then valued his personal stake in the company as being worth four-and-a-half million pounds, quite an achievement since those days in Hornsey fifteen years earlier. However, it must be emphasized that it was only the car manufacturing side of the business which became a public company – now known as Group Lotus – and not Team Lotus, which has always been a separate company. It remained very much a Chapman family affair, and still does to this day.

Ken Tyrrell remembers that, shortly after the successful flotation of the company, during the Mexican Grand Prix period, he and his wife along with Colin and Hazel visited some pyramids – one of the local tourist attractions. He clearly remembers saying, 'So Hazel, now you are a millionairess then,' to which she replied, laughing, 'It's only paper Ken . . .!'

At the US Grand Prix in October '68, in the Technical Center where the cars were garaged, Chapman took Maurice Phillippe to one side to tell him that next year's

Formula 1 and Indy cars were going to have four-wheel drive. They would both use Ford engines – the DFV in F1 and the 2.6 litre V8 at Indy. This particular project was the most extensive ever launched by Team Lotus and the two new cars – the Type 63 for F1 and the 64 for Indy – were the most complicated and expensive they ever built.

Colin explained to Doug Nye his reasons for deciding to use four-wheel drive in Formula 1 racing as well as at Indianapolis. 'Our Indy experience with four-wheel drive was good, we had all the sophisticated and complicated lumps of stuff [sic] laid in and, since we had the bits, we thought OK, we will have a go. At the time, tyres were relatively lousy and we did not have much down load, and we had a problem handling the 3 litre power, so putting it down through all four wheels seemed the way to go. The front-engined Ferguson had been heavy and the experimental BRM was cobbled-up, and although BRM said it wasn't the way to go, we were conceited enough to think they hadn't done it right . . . and everybody else seemed to follow us!' At the time every F1 engineer and constructor turned to Colin for their inspiration. The moment he embarked on the four-wheel drive project, they started thinking that they should do the same and the 1969 season saw such cars built by McLaren and Matra. Even Cosworth, who commissioned a design from Robin Herd, built a car but never raced it.

The Lotus 63 again used an open monocoque chassis but with the engine in the reverse position, with the output shaft and clutch facing forward. This was mated to a five-speed Hewland gearbox with the transmission offset to the left and Type 56 final drives were fitted at front and rear. It is interesting that the drive from the left to the

Left *When Lotus Cars became a public company in 1968, Colin Chapman's co-directors bought him a fully restored Austin Seven 'Chummy' just for old times' sake. It was presented to him at a special celebration at the Hethel factory. Here, crammed into it with Colin, now a millionaire several times over, are (left to right) Peter Kirwan-Taylor, a financier also keen on body design who came up with the superb shape of the Elite, Fred Bushell and John Standen.*

Right *Colin Chapman delivering his opening speech at the 1969 BRSCC Racing Car Show at Olympia, in West London.*

Below *Seven-year-old Clive Chapman tries the Formula 1 Lotus 49 for size.*

right of the car passed through a tube positioned above the driver's legs. A similar arrangement had been applied to the 56 and, to make sure that this would not hamper the driver, a dummy tube had been fitted to Jim Clark's Lotus 49 at Kyalami in 1968, when he reported that it did not bother him at all. In 1969, however, the drivers were not so accommodating and they complained bitterly! The suspension was different from that on the Type 56 Indy car although it was on the same principle, with inboard suspension units, and the steering was a most complicated affair using bell-crank systems. The 63 was a large and cumbersome car. It was not ready until the middle of the season and it never achieved any of Colin's hopes.

While the Type 63 was being designed and built, an improved version of the 49B was used at the beginning of the 1969 Formula 1 season, becoming a full 'biplane' with aerofoil wings fixed to both front and rear suspension uprights. By then the DFV engine was developing 430 bhp, with an increased rev limit to 10,000 rpm. Jackie Oliver had left the team for BRM and Colin had replaced him by signing the Austrian driver, Jochen Rindt. He had just spent a painful season at Brabham where they had been experimenting with a most unsuccessful four-valves-per-cylinder Repco engine.

Jochen had yet to win a Grand Prix, but he was the undisputed master of Formula 2 and clearly had terrific potential, so Colin made him equal Number One to Graham Hill. Unfortunately, Jochen had a rather abrasive character and he was very outspoken, which was made worse by the fact that he did not have full command of the English language. When he criticized something or someone, which he was quite prone to do, he would aggravate people with the involuntary use of too strong words. As a result, his relationship with Colin was not particularly good. It started off on the wrong foot at the South African GP when Jochen discovered that a third 49B was entered for a 'guest appearance' by Mario Andretti. On top of this, Jochen's car was the only one without the highly efficient 'four into one' exhaust manifolds. To cap it all, his former boss, Jack Brabham – having finally got the message and fitted DFV engines into his cars – notched up pole position on the grid!

In the race both Rindt and Andretti retired but Graham Hill took second place. Jackie Stewart led from start to finish in his Matra-Ford – the beginning of his first successful attempt at the World Championship.

During practice for the next race, the Spanish GP on the beautiful but demanding street circuit of Montjuich in Barcelona, Colin began experimenting by widening the rear wings and immediately times improved. Jochen gained pole position, while Graham Hill was third fastest on the outside of the front row, with Chris Amon's Ferrari separating them. At the fall of the flag Jochen jumped into the lead, and only Amon succeeded in hanging on to the Lotus for a few laps before his engine went sour. Graham was third, when on the ninth lap there was a flurry of yellow flags just after he had gone past the pits. At this point there was a fast but quite easy left-hander, compounded by a dip and a hump which tended to throw the cars into the air. The Lotus had crashed into the guardrail on the inside of the curve and only a few hundred feet past the hump.

Graham was not hurt and, realizing that something must have gone wrong with his car, he set about examining it to see if he could locate the problem. His mechanics

Graham Hill's crash during the 1969 Spanish Grand Prix at Barcelona. The accident was caused by the failure of the rear wing which folded up when stresses upon the car were inverted as it took off over a notorious bump. Graham – who was unhurt – quickly realized the cause of his crash and ran to warn his team mate Jochen Rindt, but he was too late. Jochen had already lost it at exactly the same spot and was seriously injured.

also came up to take a look and then, as Jochen Rindt's car flashed past, Hill noticed that a crease seemed to have formed in the centre of the rear wing. Immediately, he realized that this was probably what had happened to his own car. The wing, not being stressed to take a negative load, could have folded when his car had 'taken off' over the hump. Graham quickly sent the mechanics back to the pits to warn Colin, while he ran towards the hairpin to warn Jochen. Alas, it was too late. The next time round the Lotus's wing folded up completely in the same way that Graham's had and, devoid of downforce, Jochen spun. He clouted the wreckage of Graham's car, and in the process turned upside-down. At first Rindt looked as though he might be very badly hurt. In fact, his head injuries were relatively slight but he was moved to the local hospital which, it so happened, was run by Professor Soler-Roig, the father of Alex – Spain's best racing driver and a friend of Jochen's.

It would be fair to point out here that Rindt, on behalf of the Grand Prix Drivers' Association, had inspected the course and had specified that guardrails should be erected along that very part of the circuit where he had crashed. The organizers had duly fitted these and there was little doubt that they certainly saved Jochen's life – perhaps Graham's, too. He was so grateful to them that the following year he presented them with a gold miniature of the guardrail mounted on a plaque, designed and made by a jeweller friend of his in Vienna.

Immediately after the race I went with Colin to the hospital. Although Jochen had

Dour-faced and somewhat abrupt in manner, the Austrian Jochen Rindt was one of the most gifted drivers of his generation, but for a long period his success was limited to F2 racing, which he dominated. He had to wait until the end of 1969 before he won his first Grand Prix. A year later he was a posthumous World Champion.

only a slight hairline fracture of the skull, it was pretty certain that he would not be racing again for at least a few weeks. His manager and a great friend, Bernie Ecclestone, was also at the hospital and from what was said it seemed fairly obvious that the relationship between Chapman and Rindt would, for a while anyway, be soured as a result of this accident. In fact, afterwards Colin would phone me when he had something to say to Jochen and I would have to relay a message. Conversely, Jochen would get in touch through Bernie!

Jochen Rindt, amongst others, was not very fond of wings on racing cars, especially when it became clear that their design was perhaps beginning to get out of hand. Indeed, only a week after the Spanish race, at the Pau F2 Grand Prix, a wing fell off one of the F2 Brabhams right at the feet of Maurice Baumgartner, the President of the CSI. Meanwhile, from his hospital bed, Jochen composed an 'open letter' which he then had circulated to the press. This further aggravated the tension between himself and Chapman, whose philosophy was always that no restrictions should be placed on technical innovations and developments in Formula 1 racing car design.

The letter began as follows:

'This is an open letter to all people who are interested in Formula 1 racing. I want to show up a few points about the aerofoils, which at the moment are used on most F1 cars, in order to convince the so-called experts that they should be banned.

'Basically I have two reasons why I am against them:

'1. Wings have nothing to do with a motor car, they are completely out of place and will never be used on a road-going production car. Please note I mean wings and not spoilers, which are incorporated into the bodywork. You can say they bring colour to racing, I cannot argue against that, but after all F1 racing is meant to be a serious business and not a hot rod show.

'2. Wings are dangerous, first to the drivers, second to the spectators.'

This, obviously, made Colin furious.

At one point it was hoped that Rindt would be well enough to drive at Monaco, but he was not and his place in the team was taken by the British driver Richard Attwood, while Jochen continued his recuperation at his home in Begnins, near Geneva.

Even before the first practice session at Monaco, on the Thursday before the race, Paul Frère, who was the Clerk of the Course and also a member of the CSI Technical Committee, gathered all the entrants together and asked them either to reduce the size of their wings, or remove them altogether. Colin Chapman was not there to argue because he was at Indianapolis, but Ken Tyrrell pointed out that if this was done the race could not count towards the World Championship. So the first practice session took place with the wings still in position and Jackie Stewart proved fastest, ahead of Graham Hill, the great master of Monaco.

The CSI President, Maurice Baumgartner, arrived at midday, and what with his own experience at Pau, coupled with Rindt's open letter, he had also become a strong opponent of wings. He called for an urgent meeting in the afternoon of all those CSI Executive Committee members present in Monte Carlo. They decided that wings should be banned there and then, that the results of the first practice session would be cancelled, and that an extra practice session would take place on the Friday morning. The decision created an uproar amongst the entrants because, although it was the duty of the CSI to take all measures necessary to preserve the safety of the drivers and, even more so, the spectators, it was felt that the meeting should have taken place immediately after the Barcelona race so that the teams would have had more time to modify their cars properly.

In the second practice session Stewart's Matra once more put up the fastest time, but some seven-tenths of a second slower. Again, Hill was second fastest, although after the third and final practice session he had been relegated to the second row by both Amon's Ferrari and Beltoise's Matra. However, Graham won his fifth Monaco Grand Prix, taking the lead after Stewart and Amon both retired.

Richard Attwood stepped in and took over Rindt's car for the Monte Carlo race, the first and only time he ever drove for Team Lotus. He finished fourth despite a brief stop to replace the gear lever knob which had fallen off. With Jo Siffert finishing second in Rob Walker's 49B, Colin was well pleased with his three places in the first four. It was probably one of the best results he ever had.

Rindt was back at the wheel for the next Grand Prix, the Dutch at Zandvoort. All the cars appeared there with what aerodynamic systems were allowed under the temporary rules set at Monaco, pending a joint meeting between the constructors and the CSI scheduled for the Monday after the race. As a result of that meeting, it was agreed that wings would be allowed but their dimensions were to be limited; they could not be moveable, nor could they be fixed to unsprung parts on the car.

Although the four-wheel drive Type 63 was now ready and was taken to Zandvoort, neither of the Team Lotus drivers was very keen to race it. Rindt flatly refused even to sit in it, while Graham Hill just circulated slowly for a few practice laps. In the race Jochen proved to have lost none of his form by storming into the lead only to retire with broken transmission. Graham, unhappy with the roadholding of his car, finished a lowly seventh.

The French GP was held on the twisty Charade circuit at Clermont-Ferrand and here Rindt found that, probably as a consequence of his earlier head injuries, he was troubled with sickness due to the constant cornering. He was forced to call it a day after 22 laps. There was also a third entry of a Type 63 four-wheel drive car for John Miles, now in the Formula 1 team, but the fuel pump drive broke after only one lap and while it was running it displayed very excessive understeer.

Colin was very annoyed with his drivers for refusing to drive the new 4wd car, and when they all arrived at Silverstone for the British Grand Prix they were told they would have to race the 63s because there was only one spare 49B, the other two having been sold to Jo Bonnier and John Love! The drivers were furious and, with Bonnier being a close friend, Graham persuaded him to lend back the car, while Jochen insisted on driving the one remaining 49B. The two 63s were then to be driven by Bonnier and Miles. But the race brought no successes to Team Lotus. Although Rindt was fastest in practice, he finished only in fourth place, with Graham Hill seventh and John Miles tenth – nine laps behind Stewart the winner. Bonnier retired his 63 with engine trouble after only six laps.

At the Nurburgring, Colin tried another tack. 'OK,' he thought, 'If they don't want

The son of actor Sir Bernard Miles, John Miles was Jochen's number two. An engineer by profession, he now works at Lotus Cars.

the 63, they can have the 49B and I will give a 63 to Mario Andretti who will show them!' Mario was a great supporter of four-wheel drive and he looked forward to driving the car. Unfortunately, his practice was marred by continual engine problems and there was no time to carry out any tests with full fuel tanks. He started from a poor grid position but managed to pass a couple of rows, only to fly off the road when the car 'bottomed' as it came out of the Karussel. So much for Colin's bright idea! Graham Hill was fourth and Rindt again retired, this time with engine trouble.

Following this race Colin had a heart-to-heart talk with Jochen Rindt, who finally agreed to drive the Lotus 63 in the Oulton Park Gold Cup race, a non-Championship event. Although he managed to finish second, the result was not very conclusive and Jochen, who was contributing a regular column to my magazine *Sport-Auto* wrote, somewhat gleefully, 'I tried the four-wheel drive 63 for the first time at Oulton Park. Very soon after the beginning of practice I realized that the distribution of power between the front and the back had to be modified; a long-winded operation as one needs about a month to cut the necessary gears!'

So for the Italian Grand Prix at Monza it was back to 49Bs for Hill and Rindt, with Miles in a 63. After a tremendous scrap with Jackie Stewart – who clinched the world title there – Jochen finished second. Hill and Miles both retired with broken camshafts.

In the Canadian Grand Prix, Goodyear tyres had everything going for them and Brabhams finished first and second, ahead of Rindt who had yet to win a Grand Prix. However, all came right for him at Watkins Glen, where he dominated the race, finishing over 45 sec ahead of second place man Piers Courage in a Brabham. Unfortunately, his success was marred by the very serious accident which befell Graham Hill. The track was oily and Graham spun at the loop, so he undid his safety harness, push-started the car down a slight slope and rejoined the race. As it is not possible for a driver to secure his harness without help, Graham should really have stopped at the pits to have this done, but because there were only a few laps to go he carried on. Then a tyre suddenly deflated and the Lotus spun off, hit a bank and turned over. Graham was flung out, breaking his right knee at the joint, dislocating his left knee and tearing all the ligaments. At the time there were some doubts as to whether he would ever be able to resume his racing career. Mario Andretti gave the 63 yet another chance in this race, but found it too slow and it became quite clear that four-wheel drive was never going to be suitable for Formula 1 racing cars.

Later, Colin explained to me the reasons for this failure. 'Four-wheel drive,' he said, 'is ideal for conditions where you need to transmit low torque from the wheels to the ground, in other words on mud or ice or super high-speed tracks like Indianapolis. But where you are transmitting a lot of torque to the ground the car becomes inadequately controllable. A driver has to be able to control his car by steering the front end with the steering wheel and the rear end with the throttle. The trouble with four-wheel drive is that the throttle affects both ends of the car and therefore you don't have the ability to balance the car through a corner on the limits of adhesion, which is necessary to go quickly.'

The original plan for the 1969 Indianapolis race was for Team Lotus to enter two 64s, while a third – with some help from Firestone – would be bought by Mario Andretti. Unhappily, a restriction was placed on the tyre manufacturer's budget so the deal fell through. However, Andy Granatelli stepped in, took over the car and retained Mario to drive it, although it was to be prepared by Mario's team under Jim McGee. The Lotus 64 was an even more impressive-looking machine than its Formula 1 counterpart, with its huge radiator aperture at the front. The maximum permitted engine displacement of the turbocharged cars had now been reduced to 2.65 litres but the V8 engine was still pushing out around 700 bhp. On the 64 the Schwitzer turbocharger was mounted lower than on any of the other cars, to provide a lower centre of gravity.

Andretti's car was tested early in the season at Hanford, after which Mario produced a 'job list' of about 95 items which, in his view, required improvement. Most were dealt with and when the car arrived at Indianapolis at the beginning of May it was clearly the quickest on the track, with Mario achieving an incredible lap speed of 171.657 mph (276.25 kph). The Team Lotus entries were slower and Jochen, who did not like the track, spun his car. Then, in a practice session held only three days before the second qualifying weekend, Andretti crashed very heavily following the failure of his right rear hub. Valiant efforts to make new stronger hubs failed by only an hour and a half, so Mario took over his reserve car – the Brawner-Hawk, basically a copy of a Brabham – and the two Team Lotus entries were scratched.

This was a great relief to Jochen Rindt, who later wrote in his *Sport-Auto* column – 'The doctor forbade me to race at Monaco but on the day following I flew over to

Indianapolis and arrived just in time to see Mario Andretti lose a wheel. This crash convinced Colin Chapman of the danger and, despite opposition from his sponsors, he withdrew both his cars when it became evident that there was not enough time to machine new hubs for Graham and me to test before qualifying. I was most relieved and fully agreed with Colin's decision.'

Maurice Phillippe later explained to me the reason for the hub defect. 'Because of their similar layout and the disposition of the engine in the 63 and 64, the transmissions had many common characteristics. It was therefore possible to avoid making totally new parts for each type of car, so saving valuable time which was already very short, and especially so in the case of the Indy car. But we should really have used individually designed and manufactured parts for it.'

Although the Hawk was slower than the Lotus, Mario went on to win his first Indianapolis 500 Mile race. Maurice Phillippe stayed on to see the race and it was really because of this that he eventually left Colin Chapman and Lotus. During carburation tests two days before the race, the Hawk had been fitted with a supplementary oil cooler positioned outside the body in the airstream. The very strict Indy rules forbade not only a change of tyres but also any change to the car's configuration once qualifying had begun, so A. J. Foyt lodged a protest. Mario met with the scrutineers and they agreed he could relocate the oil cooler, provided it was contained within the bodywork. Mario asked Maurice's advice and, quietly behind locked doors, he designed and fitted a scoop to draw in air to the cooler. As there was no time for testing, it was a good job it proved successful. Mario was so impressed that, two years later, when he was planning to drive an all-American Formula 1 car for Parnelli Jones, it was suggested that the design should be entrusted to Phillippe, who then left Lotus to live and work in California.

The original agreement was for Granatelli to buy all three Lotus 64s but in the end the deal never went through, as Doug Nye explained: 'The STP and Lotus men were able to meet at the Speedway Motel to finalize the deal and sign over the cars. Andrew Ferguson was late by a couple of minutes and as he walked into the motel car park he was nearly flattened by a white-faced Chapman furiously reversing out. "We're not selling the cars," he roared. "Hide them, take them away and don't let Granatelli have them. Don't let him find them!" He then floored the throttle and screamed away to the airport and home.'

What had happened was that Granatelli had upset Colin by questioning the cost of the spare parts, but the fact is that the relationship between the two men was not at its best anyway. Colin had been going through a difficult time. There were the Barcelona crashes, the lack of progress with the Type 63 F1 car and then the forced withdrawal of the 64s from the Indy race. Andrew Ferguson then had to find somewhere quiet and secluded where the engines – which were only on loan from Ford – could be removed from their chassis. The cars were taken there on a trailer after making a wide detour to ensure that they had not been 'tailed'! The three cars were eventually returned to Hethel, where Colin threatened to 'personally put a hacksaw through them, personally dig a hole and personally bury them'!

Needless to say, Andrew Ferguson was beginning to become rather tired of working for Lotus. It had never proved easy to keep up with the tremendous pace and pressure at which Colin Chapman worked, and quite suddenly he made up his mind that he could endure it no longer.

While Andrew was still at Indianapolis he had received a letter from Peter Warr, the former Managing Director of Lotus Components, who had left the company when it moved from Cheshunt to venture into the commercial model slot-car racing track business which, at the time, seemed to have a big future. Unfortunately, their popularity had not lasted very long. Peter had sold out his interest and was now keen to get back into motor racing. He had written to Ferguson for advice because he had heard that there might be an opportunity with the Surtees team. Ferguson replied, 'You can have my job'. So Peter Warr finally took over the job he had always wanted, becoming Team Manager of Team Lotus.

For Formula 2 and 3 in 1969, Lotus Components had produced another space frame car, this time designed by Dave Baldwin and labelled the Type 59. Both Rindt and Hill drove in a series of Formula 2 races for an 'unofficial' works team under the name Winkelman Racing which, in effect, was Jochen's earlier team that had been run by Alan Rees. The two drivers met with some useful victories, Jochen winning at Thruxton, Pau, Zolder and Langenlebarn while Graham won at Albi. Although the F2 team did not receive any sponsorship from Gold Leaf, the F3 works cars, driven by Roy Pike and Morris Nunn, did carry the red, white and gold colours. Indeed, it was at the wheel of one of these that the promising newcomer from Brazil, Emerson Fittipaldi, first made himself known in Europe.

Lotus Components, now run by Mike Warner, had a very successful year with the Type 51 Formula Ford car, fitted with wedge-shaped bodywork and called the Type 61. This became the 61M for 1970 – and, in fact, 248 of them were manufactured and sold between 1969 and 1971! They also tackled another project – a new prototype sports car, the Lotus 62. The main object of this was to try out the new Lotus-Vauxhall engine LV220. Unlike the Europa, with its Elan-type backbone chassis, this car reverted to a space frame, but Colin insisted that it must bear some resemblance to the Europa which had been launched on to the British market in June. However, it was not long before it became obvious that with modern technology advancing at such a pace, there was an ever-widening gap opening up between racing cars and road cars. When the racing 62s began to sprout all sorts of air scoops, flaps and spoilers they soon lost their close resemblance to the road-going Europa. These two cars, also painted in Gold Leaf colours, were driven by John Miles, Roy Pike and Brian Muir, who succeeded in winning their class in the BOAC 500 at Brands Hatch. The new 2 litre Lotus engine, using the Vauxhall cylinder block which was not originally designed for racing anyway, gave a great deal of power (220 bhp at 8,000 rpm) but also its fair share of problems.

One very important milestone for the company in 1969 was when BRM's Chief Engineer, Tony Rudd, joined Lotus. 'I first met Colin at a Goodwood Easter meeting when he was entering his single-seater Type 12,' says Tony. 'It had no fireproof bulkhead and Colin had hurriedly concocted one in hardboard, covered with aluminium paint! The scrutineers were loath to pass it but they asked my opinion and I explained that, in my view, this did represent a proper fireproof protection. Later Colin was to help us on the BRM's rear suspension and two years after that the situation was reversed when I became his consultant on carburation for his inclined engines for the Types 15 and 16. When Colin was finally established in Formula 1 we saw a lot of each other. There was a very friendly atmosphere in Grand Prix racing at the time and we often used to borrow each other's equipment but, of course, we would cut each other's throats once the flag fell!

'In 1964 Colin asked us to modify the twin-cam engine for the Lotus-Cortina and in 1966 we made the deal over the H16 engines. By 1968, Sir Alfred Owen's policy at BRM became, "You must earn money to pay for Formula 1 racing by finding outside consultant work". I disagreed with him as my personal opinion was that we should win Grand Prix races first and that would bring us customers. At the Motor Show, Colin offered me a job. This was not the first time, mind you, because in 1960 I had terrible troubles with the BRM drivers who were refusing to drive the cars at Zandvoort, and then Colin had proposed that I join him. I declined then but this time I took his offer.'

Tony Rudd's first assignment was to oversee the development of the new 16-valve engine and to prepare it for ultimate quantity production. As he explained, 'The development of this engine was going to be most important to the company's future because, in its original form, the twin-cam would not continue to meet the new emission rules which were becoming more and more restrictive, especially in the USA. The idea was that this engine should be capable of powering a whole family of cars: the M50 was to be a four-cylinder four-seater; the M51 a V8-engined version of the same car; the M52 would be a four-cylinder 2+2, with the M53 again a V8-engined version of that. Then there was to be the M70 and M72, both mid-engined cars. When I arrived there was already an M50 in model form but after wind tunnel tests it had to be dropped because, as Colin had suspected, it had serious aerodynamic lift problems, besides many other things wrong with it.'

It was in August 1969 that Lotus experienced their first and only strike. It happened when Colin was away motor racing and Managing Director Dennis Austin was on holiday. Fred Bushell was the only senior director around and he was in charge. The factory was partially shut down anyway, for the annual holiday period, but some departments were functioning to enable those members of the staff not entitled to take annual leave then to continue working. It was a very convenient time for a backlog of work to be cleared up. The trim shop was working and one of the chargehands was acting as a temporary foreman when he had cause to discipline an operator for refusing to accept his authority. As a result, a few people stopped work. Although this particular problem was quickly dealt with, it transpired that the real cause of the unrest was that a number of employees had recently joined the Transport and General Workers' Union. They had sent a representative to deal with the problem but, because they were seeking recognition, it merely escalated the stoppage.

Both Colin Chapman and Dennis Austin had to return to the factory to give support to Fred Bushell and the dispute took six weeks to settle. However, production never stopped completely, due to volunteers being prepared to cross the picket lines. After long and difficult negotiations in London with the union, the problems were finally solved and, in an effort to avoid any repetition, the management wrote a Lotus employee's charter, issued to the staff in the form of a

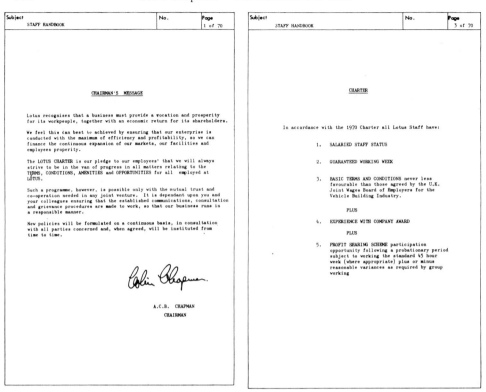

Subject		No.	Page
STAFF HANDBOOK			1 of 70

CHAIRMAN'S MESSAGE

Lotus recognises that a business must provide a vocation and prosperity for its workpeople, together with an economic return for its shareholders.

We feel this can best be achieved by ensuring that our enterprise is conducted with the maximum of efficiency and profitability, so we can finance the continuous expansion of our markets, our facilities and employees property.

The LOTUS CHARTER is our pledge to our employees' that we will always strive to be in the van of progress in all matters relating to the TERMS, CONDITIONS, AMENITIES and OPPORTUNITIES for all employed at LOTUS.

Such a programme, however, is possible only with the mutual trust and co-operation needed in any joint venture. It is dependant upon you and your colleagues ensuring that the established communications, consultation and grievance procedures are made to work, so that our business runs in a responsible manner.

New policies will be formulated on a continuous basis, in consultation with all parties concerned and, when agreed, will be instituted from time to time.

A.C.B. CHAPMAN
CHAIRMAN

Subject		No.	Page
STAFF HANDBOOK			3 of 70

CHARTER

In accordance with the 1970 Charter all Lotus Staff have:

1. SALARIED STAFF STATUS

2. GUARANTEED WORKING WEEK

3. BASIC TERMS AND CONDITIONS never less favourable than those agreed by the U.K. Joint Wages Board of Employers for the Vehicle Building Industry.

   PLUS

4. EXPERIENCE WITH COMPANY AWARD

   PLUS

5. PROFIT SHARING SCHEME participation opportunity following a probationary period subject to working the standard 45 hour week (where appropriate) plus or minus reasonable variances as required by group working

The Chairman's Message and the 'Charter' in the Lotus Staff Handbook, issued in 1969 after Colin Chapman's first experience of labour problems.

booklet. A Staff Council was also formed, made up of elected representatives who were responsible for feeding back to the management the views of the employees. The charter and the introduction of this system was quite advanced for such a relatively small firm but they have since proved an enormous help in dealing with industrial problems without recourse to union involvement.

On moving to Norfolk it had been Colin and Hazel's intention to build their own house. A site (incorporating a farm of about 200 acres) was eventually found a couple of miles from the factory, in the village of East Carleton. As usual, Colin wanted the design of the house to be perfect and, as he had been impressed by the American Colonial-style houses he'd seen on his travels, the design was based on this. He did many of the drawings himself and it took three years before the house was completed. During this time, the family lived in a house nearer to Norwich, from which Colin and Hazel could make daily checks on progress! As the new house stood on the exact site of the old manor house, they called it 'East Carleton Manor' and eventually moved in during May 1969.

'Colin really loved this house and its surroundings,' said Hazel. 'He had been evacuated to Wisbech during the War and had become used to liking flat, open spaces. We both worked hard on the design of the house with Colin putting

The beautiful East Carleton Manor was a completely new house, designed in a colonial style almost entirely by Colin himself, using many ideas picked up during his trips to the USA. It was built on the site of an earlier manor house which had been demolished some fifty years previously. Hazel took charge of the extensive gardens with considerable skill and great taste.

everything down on paper and then getting the architect to do the detail work. But there were several things he couldn't do which Colin had to take on, mostly to do with such things as window and door seals. The architect said he could not put the water tank under the roof where we wanted it, so Colin had a special glass-fibre tank made. We used to sit evening after evening working on the designs.'

The house was also fully air-conditioned because throughout his life Colin suffered badly with hay fever, and during spring and summer the windows had to be kept permanently shut. This ventilation system even incorporated special pollen filters. It was only late in his life, with the help of a special vaccination, that he found some relief from this complaint, which used to be especially bad at motor races when his hands were often covered in grease and oil.

Between them, Colin and Hazel gradually redeveloped and landscaped the dilapidated grounds of the Old Manor House – although Colin was never quite as keen on the actual gardening as Hazel! He did most of the planning, and even incorporated a grass airstrip right near the house for his own use.

Chapter 16

Tragedy at Monza

By the middle of the 1969 season, when Colin Chapman had finally realized that the four-wheel drive concept would not be successful in Formula 1 racing, he began to discuss plans with Maurice Phillippe for the next Lotus Grand Prix car. He recalls their conversation. 'Colin said, "I am going to write down a series of requirements for the new car and I'd like you to do the same." We then went away and independently produced our lists. That made it possible to come up with individual ideas and then to discuss them together. It was a real challenge and you just felt that you had to come up with good ideas. He insisted that he wanted a rising rate suspension. I wasn't convinced but then he was the boss. On the other hand the idea of inboard front brakes came from me.'

Lotus were now enjoying a very close relationship with Firestone and they were undoubtedly the top F1 team using their tyres. This enabled Chapman to design the new car, the 72, knowing that Firestone would produce tyres especially suitable for it. He thus had a free hand to apply very radical changes which, once again, would affect the entire shape of Formula 1 motor racing. The Lotus 72 was destined to become the most successful F1 Grand Prix car in history.

Some years ago, Colin explained to me the philosophy behind the Lotus 72. 'We started designing the 72 in the middle of 1969. This car was built to make the best use of its tyres, because tyres were assuming more and more importance in Formula 1. The wings had been temporarily banned since the Monaco GP, and this prompted us to give it a wedge shape which we had successfully experimented with on the turbine-engined 56 at Indianapolis. But the 72 was really going to be a step into the unknown with five features entirely new to Formula 1 racing:

'1. The wedge shape which prompted us to put the water radiators on each side of the cockpit.

'2. A weight distribution biased towards the rear which allowed us to put a lot of wing at the back to get good traction.

'3. Inboard front brakes to reduce unsprung weight and enable us to maintain a good grip at the front end despite its light weight.

'4. A rear wing with multiple slots giving a better drag/downforce coefficient.

'5. A rising rate suspension which could be very flexible without bottoming. It also enabled us to do away with the over-fastidious practice sessions in which Graham Hill played with bump stops!

'All this enabled us to use very efficient tyres which would have been quickly destroyed on a conventional car.'

Due to the wedge shape, the monocoque was very complicated and was made from a very soft magnesium alloy. Two side ducts fed air to the side-mounted radiators and this arrangement became the main feature to be copied by all the constructors in the years to come – before the Lotus 'wing' (or ground effect) car changed everything again! Apart from helping the rear weight bias, the advantages were that it reduced the overall weight because of the shorter water pipes; the coefficient of aerodynamic penetration was lowered by the sharply pointed nose cowl; and the driver's comfort was improved by the lower cockpit temperature.

There were three bag-type fuel tanks, one on each side and a third between the seat and the engine. At the front, a sub-frame of square tube grafted to the tub carried the suspension, the steering and also the magnesium bearers for the inboard disc brakes, which were linked to each wheel by small universally jointed half-shafts. A space frame of very light, thin tubes extended to the front to carry the nose, inside which was the battery and the fire extinguisher system. The Ford-Cosworth DFV engine was bolted straight to the back of the monocoque, and the rear suspension was attached to the Hewland DG300 gearbox. As with the 49B, the saddle-shaped oil tank was positioned over the gearbox. There were inboard Armstrong dampers at front and rear and springing was by torsion bars linked by a bell crank system to apply the rising rate. These torsion bars were of the compound type, made in two parts; the outer section was tubular and attached to the chassis but linked by an internal joint to the concentric solid bar, the end of which was linked to the hub.

Another feature of this suspension, which was to create some problems, was that the wishbones were not horizontal. Their mountings were 'angled' in such a way as to provide 'anti-dive' characteristics at the front and 'anti-squat' at the rear. The magnesium wheels were of 13 in diameter at the front and 15 in at the rear. The wing was, in effect, three small winglets mounted on top of each other in a staggered formation. Initially, these were set at 30, 20 and 10 degrees to the horizontal, although it was possible to vary these angles.

Following his serious crash at Watkins Glen, Graham Hill had spent much of the winter in hospital, and John Miles was signed up as the regular number two driver. This helped in easing the tension with Jochen Rindt, who by now considered himself to be the number one and was demanding much of the Team's attention. Chapman had agreed to this because he could see that Jochen was such an exceptional driver and it was a similar arrangement to that with which he had achieved so much success with Jim Clark.

There was also to be a 'works-assisted' third car in the form of a Lotus 49 for Alex Soler-Roig. The reason for his inclusion in the team – apart from some financial backing – was probably because it was a way of thanking his father, the surgeon, for dealing so well with Rindt's injuries in the previous year's Spanish GP. New Team Manager Peter Warr was very surprised by what he felt was something quite uncharacteristic of Colin, especially at a time when the team would need all its energies to develop the brand-new Lotus 72.

Since it was obvious that the car could not be ready in time for the first Grand Prix, the South African at Kyalami, Type 49s were run there but with new front suspension allowing the use of 13 in wheels and tyres. Coincidentally, this solved one of the big

Colin Chapman, complete with the sideboards and drooping moustache so fashionable at the time, briefs Rindt on race strategy. Colin was always troubled by the language problem with foreign drivers which, in the case of Jochen, he found particularly difficult at times.

problems encountered with the 49 – its instability under braking! These cars were designated 49Cs.

The Lotus 72 took to the track for the first time in March, and by chance I was at Hethel that day. *Sport-Auto* was track testing the new Lotus Seven Series 4 when someone asked us to stop because another car wanted to use the track. Talk about a scoop – it was the 72!

The car made its debut at Jarama for the Spanish GP but it proved a disappointing race, with neither Miles nor Soler-Roig qualifying amongst the sixteen starters allowed, and Rindt retiring the new 72 with ignition trouble after only 10 laps. For Monaco, both Rindt and Miles reverted to their 49Cs fitted for the occasion with the 72's rear wing. Jochen was not very fast in practice and started from the fourth row of the grid. He was somewhat disillusioned, feeling that he had very little chance of success with this old car. Gradually as the race progressed, his confidence returned and by the time the halfway stage was reached he had worked himself up to third place. By three-quarters distance he was second, behind the leader Jack Brabham, with twenty laps to go.

Although his chances of catching Brabham were slim, the Austrian drove like a man possessed. By the beginning of the last lap he was only a couple of seconds behind Brabham, who had been involuntarily delayed by Jo Siffert. On the very last corner Jack made a mistake: momentarily losing his concentration when lapping Piers Courage, he left his braking too late at the Gasworks hairpin, locked up a front brake and slid into the straw bales. He restarted immediately, but in the meantime Jochen Rindt had passed him to win his second Grand Prix. It marked the swansong of the Lotus 49, originally conceived as a test-bed for the Ford-Cosworth engine, but which had raced so successfully for almost four seasons, winning twelve Formula 1 Grand Prix races in the process.

Jochen established a new lap record on his last lap. 'I never drove quicker than I did on that day,' he told me, 'and probably than I ever will, but I couldn't have won if Jack hadn't made that small mistake. He braked too late, thinking that I was actually closer than I was, and he lost it because he was on the right-hand side of the road to stop me going through on his inside and he found himself on the "marbles".'

At the Belgian Grand Prix Rindt again tried the new 72 but without the anti-squat suspension at the rear. Following more mechanical problems, he again raced the 49C, only to retire with piston failure after only eleven laps. Colin said later, 'The suspension on the first cars was built with both anti-dive and anti-squat, but when we started to race them there were a number of problems with the roadholding. As always in the case of a new car, we didn't know what to blame but everybody immediately suspected the anti-dive. We then built a new chassis with parallel suspensions, but while we were doing this we looked at the uprights – they were those we had been using on the four-wheel drive 63. We then realized that one of the problems was a lack of rigidity, so we built up some new stronger ones.

'We then went to Zandvoort to carry out some back-to-back tests between the two cars – one with anti-dive and the other without. During these tests Jochen's times were comparable but at the end of the session he told us that he liked it best without anti-dive and from then on all the 72s were built like that. We even modified the first car. Knowing what we know now, I'm sorry we didn't stick with it as I'm convinced we would have had even better results if we had. But there are so many new things on this car – anti-dive, anti-squat, the rising rate torsion bars – and each time one came up with a problem it was so difficult to know just where to start.'

According to Maurice Phillippe, the trouble with the anti-dive suspension was that it gave the driver very little 'feel'. He could lap as fast with it as without it, but less consistently. Rindt went to Zandvoort for the Dutch GP without the anti-dive suspension and virtually destroyed the opposition with what was the first in a succession of four victories. He also won the French, British and German GPs. His win in the British race was lucky, Jack Brabham running out of fuel on the last corner whilst in the lead, having overtaken Jochen some ten laps earlier.

Rindt was almost disqualified at the Brands Hatch race because the scrutineers found that his wing appeared to be a fraction of a millimetre too high. 'This was due to the fact that Colin Chapman had an argument with the Chief Scrutineer because,' wrote Jochen, 'the latter had been late in arriving on the first practice day and the Lotus mechanics had been forced to wait around for half-an-hour. What happened

was that after the race one of the wing stays was found to be bent and the scrutineer contended that if it had not been bent, the wing would have been too high. So he disqualified me without even telling Colin or me. Obviously, as soon as we were told about it, we had the stay straightened up and the height of the wing was still 2 mm under the legal maximum, much to the embarrassment of the scrutineer!'

Jochen was absolutely delighted with the car and would not allow Colin to make any more modifications to it for fear that they would spoil it. When we congratulated him on a win, he would answer, 'I have no merit, this car is so good, a trained monkey could win in it!'

'It was an incredible summer,' Peter Warr remembers. 'We turned up at Clermont in such a terrible state that, with all the business over the 72, there was no time to change the gear ratios of the 49C from those used in the Spa race. Soler-Roig was driving it and he came into the pits with this 200 mph top gear and said to "Rabbit" Bartles, the mechanic on the car, "I don't seem to be able to get into fifth gear." "Rabbit", who assessed the situation immediately, said, "Well, go out and get a tow then!"

'One of the worst races was at Zeltweg because Jochen came to the Austrian circuit with everyone expecting him to become Austria's first World Champion and he failed to finish in the race. So when he came to Monza it was already a bit of a pressure situation.'

Right *The revolutionary 72 did not begin its career very auspiciously, but when it did get going it was uncatchable. Here Jochen Rindt is about to win the 1970 French GP at Clermont-Ferrand, in the car in which he was killed five weeks later at Monza. Note the special disc coolers being used on the brakes.*

Left *Rindt was at first disqualified after his win in the British GP at Brands Hatch in 1970. Here, during the post-race drama in the scrutineering bay, Colin Chapman talks with Louis Stanley (GPDA and BRM) while two scrutineers deliberate and Team Lotus mechanics, Peter Warr (in glasses) and designer Maurice Phillippe (on the right with arms folded) await a decision.*

Despite all his enthusiasm, Rindt was becoming rather fed up with motor racing but was desperate to win the title because he wanted to cash in on it by starting a business, for which he was equally gifted. At a Formula 2 race at the Paul Ricard circuit in France, I remember Jochen asking me what I thought he should do and I said, 'If you don't enjoy motor racing any more you must retire on the spot.' To which he replied, 'In that case I should not be driving here today!'

Victory at Monza would have assured him of the title, but it was not to be. He crashed with fatal results during the second practice session. 'I am not sure if anyone will ever completely get to the bottom of the Monza accident,' explains Peter Warr, 'but for what it is worth, my own opinion is that Jochen felt he just had to win that race and had built himself up mentally in order to do so. He had been out on the Friday and had been very quick, although it had taken about six laps to warm up the tyres. It was obvious he was becoming bolder and bolder and intended to give the opposition no chance at all. He just wanted to destroy them.

'We all had dinner together in the Hotel de la Ville on that Friday night and Jochen was telling everybody about his plans for using his name to build up a sports clothing company, and that he was going to make a fantastic success of this. Then the car became the subject of conversation and he would keep coming back to the fact that he wanted to race it without the wing, as he had tried it in the afternoon. So the following day we fitted it with different gearing, giving a top speed of 205 mph – 15 mph more than anyone had ever used before.

'My own feeling is that, considering the no-downforce configuration, he started to go quickly much too soon. Denny Hulme, who was actually behind him when the accident happened, said he couldn't believe it when he went past him. I believe that he was caught out because the tyres had not warmed up and the aerodynamic and brake balance was miles out due to having no rear wing. On the previous day they had been very slow to warm up. Also the Monza circuit then consisted almost entirely of right-hand corners, so the left-hand tyres would be the first to warm up. I think that the first time he hit the brakes really hard the car became totally out of balance and that was when the accident happened.

'What actually killed Jochen was the environment in which he found himself once the car left the track. He hit the Armco barrier extremely hard, although no-one could tell just how much damage was inflicted by this initial impact. What is certain is that after the impact the car spun and carried on in contact with the barrier. This was lifted out of the ground by the left front wheel, which then went underneath it. The right wheel, which also passed beneath the Armco, then caught the next supporting post – one carrying a public address loudspeaker, and therefore somewhat stronger and heavier than the others. As a result, this tore the front bulkhead off the car, together with the suspension and the steering. The steering wheel itself was prised though the instrument panel and it was this that had torn the front bulkhead out of the car. Because he refused to wear the crotch straps of his seat harness, Jochen was forced down into the cockpit with his feet tangled up with the pedals and, in the process, his throat was cut by the harness.'

Denny Hulme, who had seen the crash take place, immediately drove round the circuit to stop and report the accident to the Lotus pit. We then all ran over to the mobile hospital unit, only to find that they had taken Jochen straight to the Niguarda Hospital in Monza. I had my hire car handy and so drove Colin, Hazel and Nina, Jochen's wife, to the hospital, at first going to the wrong one. When we arrived, Louis Stanley of BRM – the man behind the Grand Prix medical unit – was already there. He took Nina Rindt to one side to break the sad news to her. Actually, Jochen had probably died instantly but, by Italian law, if this happens all proceedings at the track must stop and an inquiry be initiated immediately, so he was not declared dead until he was in the ambulance.

Colin immediately flew Nina back home to Geneva in his plane and all the Lotus cars were withdrawn from the race – including Graham Hill, who was driving Rob Walker's brand-new 72. The inquest started straight away and the inquiry lasted several years, a repeat of Colin's unfortunate experience after Jim Clark's Monza crash with von Trips in 1961. It was a bitter blow for Colin, coming only two years after the deaths of Jimmy and Mike Spence. In the case of Jimmy's fatal accident, there had been no accusations and Chapman's personally arranged independent investigation had proved that Lotus could not be blamed for the crash in any way. Also, he was not present on the day it had happened. In the case of Rindt's accident, he was actually there and, following the practice under Italian law, he was accused of homicide.

He went home and for a few days he did not go anywhere. The inquest was finally terminated with the charges being dismissed on a technicality. However, Chapman was not very happy about being cleared on a technicality, and wanted to establish that he was not making unsafe cars. So another investigation was started, this time entrusted to Sandro Colombo, the former Chief Engineer of Ferrari. Colin also put the matter in the hands of Tony Rudd who went to Italy, together with RAC Scrutineer Peter Jowitt. 'Colombo said he was very pleased to see us,' recalls Tony Rudd, 'because there were certain aspects of the evidence surrounding the accident which he could not understand, and the ideas we put before him helped a great deal.'

Tony was asked to return to England as quickly as possible to obtain a sworn statement from Denny Hulme, together with one from John Miles, who had also driven the car in practice without the wing. He was to be back by the following Monday. Rudd had flown to Italy in the company plane only to find that they could not refuel for the return trip due to an Italian tanker drivers' strike. However, they had just enough fuel left to fly across the border to Lugano, in Switzerland, where they were able to refuel and fly on to England. Tony managed to locate a Notary Public who he then took on to Silverstone to find Denny Hulme. Having just decided to retire from motor racing (temporarily as it turned out) they found Denny amongst the spectators and obtained the sworn statement. They then flew straight back to Italy.

Tony Rudd's understanding of the accident was that '. . . the car had an inboard brake shaft fail but Rindt did not even try to take the corner. One of the things about it which Sandro Colombo couldn't understand was that, although there was a large sand-filled run-off area available to slow the car down, Rindt did not allow the car to go into it but instead he veered off and hit the Armco. Denny Hulme said that, when Jochen went past him on the back straight, the car was weaving badly which does indicate that it was aerodynamically unstable.

'In his affidavit, John Miles also said that, when he had driven his car without the wing, he had the same problem. What we don't know is how the car came to be out of control aerodynamically at the end of the straight. Although it had lost the braking on one wheel there was some braking effect left and somehow Jochen should have been able to get the car round the corner. Even then, having hit the barrier, had that been properly secured the car would not have gone underneath it. Had he also been wearing the harness crotch strap, he would have had a very good chance of survival.

'There was a reason for the failure of the brake shaft. This was made of a special very high-grade steel peculiar to the aircraft industry and which at the time was unknown to the motor industry. We always crack-tested these between each race, but in order to get the best out of this steel it has to be shot-peened, which gives it a smooth matt surface. This process makes it difficult to give it a magnaflux test and as we did not have the right facilities we always sent them away for the crack-testing. It would appear that, in this case, when the testers polished it prior to crack detection it became scratched, and it was this scratch which started the failure.'

More recently I was able to talk with John Miles about Rindt's accident. His memory of the whole unfortunate episode remains vivid: 'The three cars arrived late so there was a hell of a panic,' he recalls. 'In such a situation the best thing to do is to get on with things on your own without bothering anybody else.

'Towards the end of the Friday's practice I had arrived at a wing setting which, oddly enough, was the same as Graham Hill was running on Rob Walker's new 72. He had been there since the day before and had done more testing. We were still running the three-tiered wing at the back and, as I recall, we knocked the centre section out and ran the two remaining aerofoils at a very flat angle of incidence. The front aerofoils were also set very flat.

'Just before the practice session was due to end I found myself with Jochen, who by this time – and probably at Colin's instigation – was running without wings. For the first time in my life I had actually been able to keep up with Jochen although his car looked quite a handful, particularly in places like the Ascari Curve, on to the straight and at Lesmo, where I plainly had much more grip but lost some speed down the straight. For me the trade-off seemed well worthwhile.

'What happened then was that I came in just a few minutes before the end of practice, and Colin came over, I think to look at my times. Although generally about half a second slower than Jochen's, our comparative times were somewhat closer than they usually were after that amount of practice. Colin then said, "You've got it wrong with that wing. You've got to take the wings off your car." "I don't really want to Colin," I replied, "the car already feels a little spooky." However, at his insistence, I took off the wings and drove only a lap and a half or so before practice ended for the day, and it wasn't a flying lap. I had never driven such an awful race car in my life. It was very, very unstable with what felt like a huge amount of lift at the back.

'Afterwards we had a conversation in the truck when Colin said, "The only way you are going to be quick is to run without wing." I replied, "I don't want to run without wing because this is the first time in my life that I was really frightened in a racing car." But he then said, "You have got to run without wings and I am taking them off your car tomorrow." And so it went on. I replied, "I don't want you to take the wings off my car," and he said again, "I am going to take them off."

'The next morning I arrived at the track for practice after a miserable night and the wings were off my car! However, I never got to practice in it because, by the time it had been fuelled up and was ready for me, Jochen had had his accident.

'I remember that when we were discussing it in the truck, Colin had said to me, "We have sorted cars before which didn't have wings," and I replied, "Yes we did Colin, but we had more time then than we have now, and I don't feel confident enough to gain back the practice day we have lost."'

The case in Italy was eventually dismissed because it was clear that, even though the brake shaft had broken, it was not this which had caused Jochen's death. Two questions were never answered though: why were the bolts missing from the Armco barrier, and why was the wheel able to pass underneath it?

The Brazilian, Emerson Fittipaldi, had first been invited to join Team Lotus in the middle of the season, taking over Soler-Roig's third team car in time for the British Grand Prix. He finished eighth and, even before practice at Monza, Peter Warr had signed him as the Team's Number Two. With John Miles leaving the team after the Monza tragedy, Fittipaldi was catapulted overnight into the position of Team Leader.

John Miles drove briefly for BRM in GP racing the following year and then he

Young and inexperienced, Emerson Fittipaldi bravely took over the number one spot after Jochen's death, and by winning at Watkins Glen two months later he made sure that the World Drivers' Championship remained Rindt's.

turned to sports car racing with some success. However, he had lost his desire to race in Formula 1. 'It wasn't the Rindt accident in isolation,' he told me, 'it was just that that year had been sort of so gory, what with Piers Courage, Bruce McLaren and Paul Hawkins – with whom I was very close – all being killed, too. I had also had a lot of nerve-racking failures on the car and in the early development of the 72 there were many things I found kind of daunting. Together it all absolutely devastated me.

'What happened then, after Monza, was that I saw Colin and said that it was my mistake but that I found it hard when people were dying. He said, "Yes, I understand. I don't know quite what we are going to do now but just go away for a couple of weeks." About ten days later, I had a call from Peter Warr saying, "I am sorry to have to tell you that Reine Wisell has replaced you in the team.'

'I never actually resigned my drive. All I needed at the time was some confidence, as I was just shattered. Mike Warner offered me the Lotus 70 Formula 5000 car which I refused, somewhat fortunately because, with Alan Rollinson driving, it broke in half two weeks later! It really was the end of my career with Team Lotus. I am sure Colin didn't want the responsibility of a driver who had lost confidence in the car. Bringing back that confidence was not his job; he had enough on his plate at the time.'

Team Lotus scratched from the Canadian GP, but turned up at Watkins Glen for the US Grand Prix with two Lotus 72s for Fittipaldi and Reine Wisell, a new boy from Sweden, who had been successful in Formula 3 racing. By then no one had exceeded Rindt's points total, but if Jacky Ickx had won the US race he could still have been World Champion if he had won Mexico as well. But the race was won by Emerson Fittipaldi – with Wisell third – thus ensuring that the title would go to Rindt posthumously, no matter what the outcome of the Mexican GP, which Ickx won. And so Colin Chapman and Team Lotus concluded the 1970 season with yet another Formula 1 Manufacturers' Cup – their fourth – and another World Champion driver – but under very sad circumstances.

In a recent talk with Rob Walker, I asked him to tell me about his dealings with Colin Chapman, particularly as far as the 72 which he bought for Graham Hill was concerned. 'Right from the first Lotus 18 my deals with Colin were always as straight as a die. Even at the end, when he sold me the 72, he only charged me £5,000 and it must have cost him a good deal more than that. This car, of course, was for Graham Hill to drive and there was quite a story in that.

'We were both taking a long-distance commercial flight back home in 1969, when Colin came down to the rear of the aircraft where I was sitting and said, "Why don't you have Graham Hill as your driver?" So I replied, "But I already have Siffert, a perfectly good driver, and anyway Graham drives for you." Whereupon Colin said, "Well I think it would be a good idea. I could help you a bit. I'll give you the best equipment if you'll take Graham on." So I said, "I am not going to take Graham on as long as I have Siffert, but if he leaves me, which he might do because he really wants to drive for a team where he thinks he will get a better deal, then I would consider it." Of course, this conversation was quite a revelation to me, as I had always thought Graham would be a Team Lotus driver to the end.

'In 1970, when the Lotus 72 first came out in Spain, Graham was by then driving for me. During practice Jochen Rindt went off after only about five laps with a broken driveshaft. He came back to the pits, saying, "I am never going to drive that f-----g car again!" I turned to Graham and said, "What happens now?" He replied, "You'll see. Colin will take him into a corner and will talk to him for about ten minutes, and the next thing is he will get back in the car and drive off." And that is exactly what happened!'

In Formula 2 racing, Alan Rees had joined Robin Herd and Max Mosley to form a new company, March Engineering, and at one point they actually tried to persuade Rindt to join their team. The Lotus F2 team was therefore taken over by Rindt, under the name Jochen Rindt Racing Ltd, in partnership with his friend and manager Bernie Ecclestone, who was to look after the organization. Some new regulations now applied to Formula 2, one of which was mandatory bag fuel tanks, as already stipulated for F1, and this entailed redesigning the cars. The F2 Lotus 69 was therefore a new car, again designed by Dave Baldwin, and now incorporating a central monocoque section. Rindt, with John Miles as team mate, won four of the Formula 2 races that year.

In Formula 3, the Lotus 59 was still in use, although it was modified as a 59B with a similar nose to the new 69. The team drivers, running under Gold Leaf colours, were Bev Bond and Dave Walker, the latter proving very successful.

For the new Formula 5000 (Formula A in the United States) Lotus produced the 70, but this did not prove very successful and only six were built. Nevertheless,

Lotus Components, now known as Lotus Racing Ltd, had a very successful year because the new Series 4 Lotus Seven was selling so well.

However, the situation with Lotus Cars was not so brilliant. Sales of the Elan had been dropping, and after a meeting of the Sales and Technical Departments it was decided to increase the power of the engine and to apply a different paint scheme. This car became the Elan 'Sprint' and was introduced in the red, white and gold livery of Gold Leaf to emphasize their link with motor racing. Tony Rudd had produced a 'big valve' engine, giving 120 bhp and increasing the maximum speed to 127 mph. The price, in kit form, as were most Elans, was £1,663. This engine was also made available in the Elan +2, never available in kit form and thus more highly priced at £2,627.

Chapter 17

Success with the 72

In 1971 Team Lotus failed to win even a single Grand Prix, the first time this had happened since 1960. There were some good reasons for this, and for a start neither of the drivers was really up to form. Wisell's performances were rather disappointing and Emerson Fittipaldi had a road accident soon after the start of the season. Fortunately, his injuries were not sufficiently serious for him to have to miss even one race, but it clearly took some while for him to get back into top form. The cars were not in particularly good shape either. Firestone had introduced a new low-profile tyre which necessitated some revisions to the suspension, although the original lower wishbone was retained which in itself caused a recurring problem that took some time to iron out. Peter Warr explained, 'The expansion and contraction of the gearbox and bell-housing due to heat from the engine would cause the wishbone to break as it became narrower or wider. It also used Armstrong shock absorbers and it was not until we fitted Konis that it really started to go right.'

The new suspension appeared at Monaco on Fittipaldi's car. Called the 72D, it finished fifth. (The 72B was built without anti-squat suspension and the 72C without either anti-squat or anti-dive.) Later the Brazilian managed to finish second in the Austrian Grand Prix and third in both the French and British GPs.

Another contributory factor to 1971's disappointing performances was that both drivers were inexperienced. I remember Emerson telling me on one particular occasion, 'It was very difficult for Colin to trust us because neither Reine nor I had much experience. When we were explaining a problem to him we had a job to convince him that it was a real one and not simply our lack of experience. On top of this Colin was really more interested in the turbine car and we were doing a great deal of testing with it.' It is, of course, possible that the drivers' foreign languages may have compounded this particular problem.

Once again, Chapman had introduced something revolutionary into Formula 1 racing – a turbine-engined car. This was one of the 1968 ex-Indy type 56s, adapted to suit Formula 1 and designated 56B. In 1968, Graham Hill had taken part in an 'Indy Formula' race driving a Lotus 56 on the Mosport road circuit in Canada, and he had been very impressed with its behaviour. The main problem was that of throttle lag. This meant that in order to accelerate quickly out of a corner, the driver had to make sure that the revs did not drop too low. To do this he had to keep his right foot on the throttle pedal when entering the corner and at the same time brake furiously with the left foot!

Maurice Phillippe assures me that when the Type 56 Indy turbine car was originally designed, it was intended to produce a Formula 1 version, but somehow it was forgotten until 1970 when Colin by chance met up with the Canadian Pratt and Whitney engineer who had looked after the turbines two years earlier. He confirmed that it would be possible to produce a version of the P & W ST6 engine to comply with the FIA's rules for the use of turbines in Formula 1 racing. This fired up Colin's enthusiasm again and he duly ordered one to be fitted into the spare 56 chassis which had been lying idle at Hethel.

The turbine F1 car made its debut at the Brands Hatch 'Race of Champions' meeting in the hands of Emerson Fittipaldi. Unfortunately the rear suspension broke after bottoming badly. In another non-Championship race at Hockenheim the turbine blew up and Peter Warr recalls how he flew it back to London in the company's Piper Cherokee Six in order to have it airfreighted to the USA for repair: 'When we landed at Heathrow, the chap at Air Traffic Control said, "Where do you want to go?" and we replied, "Seaboard World Airline cargo." So he then said, "Left, right, down runway so and so . . ." When we eventually arrived at the cargo terminal, back came the Controller to say, "Congratulations, you now hold the record for the greatest taxying distance at Heathrow!"

'We had the turbine back in time for the Dutch Grand Prix, where the car was driven by Dave Walker. After practice he was 22nd out of the 24 cars that lined up on the grid. On race day it was pouring with rain, and in its favour the car was carrying a fair amount of weight with 75 gallons of Kerosene on board. It also had four-wheel drive and Firestone wet-weather tyres, which were immeasurably superior to the rival brands. The last thing I said to Walker on the grid was, "For Christ's sake take it easy. This is a 70-lap race so don't even race anybody for 25 laps." At the end of the first lap Walker was 19th. He was 10th by lap five but as he tried to outbrake Graham Hill with 65 gallons of Kerosene still in the tanks, he slid off the track and filled the turbine with sand. It was so silly – he was in a perfect position to win his first Grand Prix.'

The drivers very soon found out, as Graham Hill had in the 1968 Mosport race, that the easiest way to drive the turbine was to keep the foot on the throttle when on the over-run. Unfortunately, the enormous weight of the fuel meant that the brakes became overloaded, so these had to be increased in size as a result of the Dutch GP episode, about which Dave Walker talked to me only recently.

'I remember,' he said, 'I had to start almost from the back of the grid but we quickly began to move up through the field and by about the seventh lap I remember seeing a pit signal telling me that I was tenth, or something like that. I was also lapping faster than Jacky Ickx and Pedro Rodriguez who were leading the race.

'However, I was having a little trouble braking as the track was very bumpy and also it was very wet. A couple of times I had been outbraked by the conventional cars and I then had to repass them again, so at the Tarzan corner I left my braking a little bit later than usual. Every time I had taken my foot off the brake the car would accelerate again because the idle speed was set at around 80 mph. To cut a long story short, I came into the corner rather too quickly, and with the four-wheel drive it was impossible to spin the car so I went off into the sand. At one stage or another almost every driver had been off at this particular corner, but I was out of the race and Colin

wasn't at all happy about it. He was particularly upset because he had felt sure I was going to win. As I would have been one of those rare drivers to win the first Grand Prix in which he had been entered, as you can imagine, I felt pretty bad about it too.'

At the Italian Grand Prix, due to possible problems with litigation over the previous year's accident to Jochen Rindt, Lotus fielded only one car, the turbine, which was entered in the name of Worldwide Racing and painted gold and black . . . the first Lotus to appear in these colours. The reason for this was that, had Team Lotus made the entry, their cars might have been impounded. The race itself was held on a very hot day, which upset the performance of the turbine, and Fittipaldi finished no better than eighth. The Lotus 56B appeared only once more, in a Formula 5000 race at Hockenheim, when Emerson managed to take second place.

Later, Colin Chapman explained to me his reasons for not continuing with the turbine. 'I think this was a blind alley because if we had eventually become successful with it, it would promptly have been banned and then a great deal of money would have been wasted. It has happened before, at Indy, when the four-wheel drive turbine cars were banned as soon as they started to be successful. Unfortunately the innovator in motor racing is often penalized the moment he produces something of benefit to himself and which makes his cars go faster than those of other competitors. If I could have been sure of at least two years' stability, I would have carried on with developing it, because the turbine is a very good converter of torque. What was wrong with it in Grand Prix racing was that we ran it with four-wheel drive. If we had built a two-wheel drive turbine I think that, with its smoothness, its very high torque at low rpm and the power it was capable of producing under the Formula equivalence, it would have been very competitive. I think that what really killed the turbine-engined Formula 1 car was more the four-wheel drive than the turbine itself.'

During the season Team Manager Peter Warr was being kept extremely busy, for Grand Prix racing had not then reached the level of affluence it enjoys today. He found that not only did he have to do the timing of both cars, but he also had to be available to talk to the drivers when they came into the pits. (Compare this with today's Longines electronic timing monitors and one race engineer to each car!)

Also at this time Chapman was becoming worried by the increase in the output of the Ferrari V12 engine. Although the Cosworth engine was giving about 430 bhp, the Ferrari was now developing a good 460 bhp. So, as Matra were also producing a V12 engine, Colin asked me to put him in touch with Jean-Luc Lagardere, the head of the French firm. This was very easy for me to do because I was then Technical Adviser to the Matra Racing Department. However, in the end, nothing came of it, but Peter did manage to convince Colin that Team Lotus could not survive in the

Above left *In the 1971 Dutch Grand Prix, Dave Walker took the Lotus 56B turbine car from 22nd place on the starting grid to 10th by lap five. The next time round he put it into the sand at the Tarzan Hairpin.*

Left *The 56B was also driven by Emerson Fittipaldi in the Italian Grand Prix at Monza, but this time it appeared in strange gold and black colours and entered under the name Worldwide Racing. It was the single Lotus entry and finished only eighth.*

The start of a race for Lotus Sevens at Monthlhéry. Sport-Auto promoted an operation in France where 17 Lotus Sevens in kit form were offered by Ford for use by automobile clubs. They were assembled, maintained and driven by young members. Amongst the drivers who were discovered through this promotion were four times Le Mans winner Henri Pescarolo and GP driver Johnny Servoz-Gavin.

environment of the car factory, so the team moved into the premises of the defunct Lotus Racing Ltd in nearby Potash Lane.

The reason for the demise of Lotus Racing Ltd – formerly Lotus Components Ltd – was that Managing Director, Mike Warner, had handed in his resignation after hearing rumours that Chapman had decided to sell the company. It was said that Chapman was no longer keen to carry on building racing cars for sale to the public as he felt it was not in keeping with the 'up-market' image he was seeking for the Group. Although a batch of cars had been built earlier in the season, the Formula Ford Lotus had not been selling well and the new Merlyn car was cornering most of the market. Lotus Racing Ltd carried on officially for a while after Warner's departure, although all activities had virtually ceased. The Series 4 Lotus Seven, although not having quite the same appeal to enthusiasts as its predecessors, was by no means a commercial failure. Production was transferred to the main factory for a time, until the manufacturing rights were acquired by Graham Nearn of Caterham Car Sales.

The closure of Lotus Racing Ltd proved a severe blow to many customers. In Formula 2 racing the official colours were carried by London International Racing Associates, a company run by former journalists Justin Haler and Chris Witty. Unfortunately, LIRA was under-financed and it was not long before it went out of business, although their driver Reine Wisell did score a somewhat lucky win at Pau in a Lotus 69. Emerson Fittipaldi also did very well in his own 69, driving under the sponsorship of Bardahl, the oil additive company. In Formula 3 racing – then run under a new engine formula decreeing the use of an inlet restrictor – the Gold Leaf Team Lotus 69 of Dave Walker did tremendously well, earning him a Formula 1 drive after a fantastic series of wins.

Even though Mike Warner's misgivings were somewhat premature, there were grounds for his concern because Chapman had turned his thoughts to an entirely new subject – boats. He was not really a boating enthusiast and when his father had owned a sailing cruiser Colin had never been very keen on joining him, although they had spent several holidays together on the Norfolk Broads in earlier days. What was attracting him now was the challenge of building something which was new to him, of applying his skills to an industry which seemed to be lagging behind in technical development and manufacturing techniques. So, on his own account and quite independently of Group Lotus, he bought a company called Moonraker Boats which had belonged to David Buxton, a former Sales Manager of Lotus (and an Elite Le Mans driver). Although their range of boats remained basically unchanged, Colin introduced a number of modifications and improvements to the Moonraker cabin cruiser. Later he designed a 46-foot luxury cabin cruiser, the Marauder, for another company he had subsequently acquired, JCL Marine Ltd. This in itself had a far-reaching effect on that company because of Chapman's introduction of a new and revolutionary vacuum moulding technique for boat hulls. This was eventually used in the manufacture of Lotus car bodyshells, and patents were applied for from all over the world. In fact, through this development, coupled with his earlier experience, he

In 1972 Colin Chapman bought Moonraker Boats Ltd from his former Sales Manager David Buxton. This was the Moonraker high-speed cruiser (below), 350 examples of which were turned out before the company was closed down in 1980. By then the cost of producing new designs was just too much for the market, which had been seriously affected by the fuel crisis and the introduction in the 70s of Value Added Tax.

Left and below *The Moonraker yard was on the River Yare not far from Norwich. In June 1972 Earl Mountbatten of Burma paid a visit.*

Below right *The 'Marauder 46' used a GRP (glass reinforced plastic) hull of very advanced design. At the time it was the largest-ever one-piece injection moulding and was manufactured using a process specially developed by Colin Chapman.*

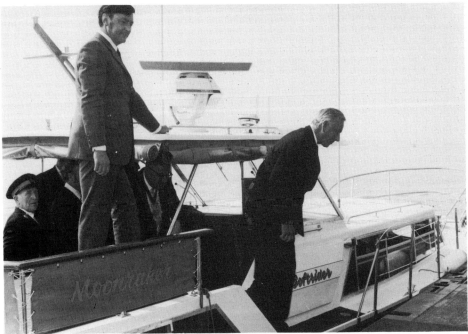

soon became one of the world's leading authorities on the manufacture and use of glass-fibres.

'Moonraker Boats was bought by Colin, personally, in 1972,' says Fred Bushell. 'It cost him £100,000 and it operated for two years at a profit. By reorganizing production and introducing quality control, the boats were produced at reduced cost. After about six months, the existing design was modified with the attachment of a flying bridge, which was done very quickly and without having to interfere with the structure integrity.

'Soon, because he wanted to develop his own line of boats, Colin bought another company, JCL Marine, and he then carried out a complete investigation into the market. He wanted to produce a boat which could be operated either in the North Sea or the Mediterranean. As always, he sought to reduce weight as he looked for higher speed.

'The first new model was the Marauder which was offered at a price of £90,000, and which actually represented extremely good value for money. Unfortunately, it was two years before the boat was in a saleable condition, by which time the costs had escalated. It had been on sale at the Boat Show at a fixed price, which led to a number of legal actions with customers who would not pay the final price. Production was stopped in 1980.

'Apart from the Marauder there was also the Mirage, the basic design of which had been acquired from Italy, where it had been manufactured in wood. The idea was that JCL would redesign it in glass-fibre for the Italian market, but then that collapsed suddenly so JCL were left trying to market the boat themselves, outside the Mediterranean. That, however, turned out to be virtually impossible because the

design of the boat was totally orientated to that area. Moonraker Boats was also closed down because the enormous cost of introducing a new product line had to be funded entirely in-house. Sufficient volume could never be generated to produce such funds because the Moonraker was an old design anyway. Also the Government introduced VAT on boats.'

I recently came upon Colin Gething, still with Lotus Cars today, who for some years worked in Colin Chapman's boatbuilding companies. He told me something of his experiences. 'I came to Lotus in 1973,' he said, 'ostensibly to join the car company. However, at that time Mr Chapman had just taken over Moonraker Boats and he asked me if I would like to transfer over to it as an engineer. In fact, it was to JCL Marine – or rather Technocraft – that I was eventually transferred.

'We were very involved in developing the process of moulding the hull. At that time we had a prototype of the Marauder built in wood which had just been exhibited at the Boat Show, where many orders were taken for it. The knowledge we had already gained was then incorporated into the manufacture of the boat.

'In all we built about eighteen Marauders and there were also about twelve Mambas, fifteen Mysteres and nineteen Mirages. The Mystere was also originally developed from an Italian design, the Magini, and was then marketed in Italy by a company called Versilcraft. From the wooden prototype we turned out a product in glass-fibre using our special resin injection system. The Mystere was a twin cabin design but then, using the same hull, we produced a new superstructure, and by changing the interior entirely, we ended up with a three-cabin boat with two bathrooms. This model was called the Mirage.

'In all, I think about 350 Moonrakers were produced. At the beginning it was selling for about £30,000 but when it was stopped the price had risen to nearer £70,000 although, of course, during the period in which it was manufactured the design was revised several times.

'We had quite a few problems with the JCL boats because we were breaking new ground in their design and construction, not only with the hull but with the whole system. We had various methods of reducing noise and vibration, very much the same as with car design, whereby we were flexibly mounting the engines with universally jointed propeller shafts, the thrust being taken by the hull and not the engine itself. On the hull, we were using the flexible membrane theory, where instead of having a single stiff thick hull, this was made up by using a number of stiff 'boxes' with each particular panel between these being able to flex. We consulted with Lloyds on this at all times but there were obviously some areas which really required much further development but, with the cost of this being extremely high, a number of educated guesses had to be taken. We had two instances where the outer skin of the double-skin construction had peeled off, basically because it had punctured and water had been introduced under pressure into the punctured area, which then de-laminated the outer skin, although the inner skin always remained intact. These boats were much lighter than normal – about 40 per cent in fact. In its wooden form, the Mystere weighed all of twelve tons, whereas when we produced it in glass-fibre using the sandwich skin construction technique that figure came down to around seven-and-a-half tons.

Above *The Mamba was another cabin cruiser built by JCL Marine Ltd. Only about a dozen were produced.*

Below *The Mystere was an Italian 'Versilcraft'-designed boat. Originally built in wood, JCL Marine acquired the design in order to manufacture it by the revolutionary vacuum-injected plastic system developed by Chapman.*

'Greater weight means heavier fuel consumption and higher cost. Using a lighter hull meant smaller engines and lower fuel consumption and therefore less fuel had to be carried.

'We also introduced new technology into the interiors with many of the panels using a light cardboard honeycomb form of construction. All this new technology was introduced into a boating world which up to then had no idea whatsoever that such developments existed.

'Certainly Colin Chapman treated it all like racing car design, on the principle that you never engineer anything to be light in weight in the first instance without it breaking, and therefore you should engineer it on the borderline. Then, once that particular item breaks, you beef it up until it is strong enough. However, we never had a proper development boat and that was always the major problem.'

During the year Lotus also introduced a new road car when, at last, the twin-cam engine was made available in the Europa chassis, to become known as the 'Europa Twin-Cam'. This car was developed by a young engineer who had joined Lotus two years earlier from Jaguar Cars, where he had been working on the exciting V12 5 litre XJ13 sports-racing car project. His name was Mike Kimberley.

Meanwhile, Tony Rudd – now promoted to Technical Director – was making good progress with his task of preparing for the production of the all-Lotus 4-cylinder light-alloy engine. This had been a major undertaking – the machine tooling alone cost over £550,000 – but it was vitally necessary because the twin-cam engine would not be able to meet the new exhaust emission laws then beginning to come into effect all over the world. In fact, this engine was not as much of a luxury as might at first have been thought. Due mainly to the efficient manufacturing processes that Rudd had introduced, its cost was very little more than the twin-cam. In 1969 the cost of the material for the twin-cam unit amounted to £160. In 1972 – when it was in full-scale production – the material cost of the 16-valve type 907 Lotus engine (developing 160 bhp against the 128 bhp of the twin-cam) compared very favourably at £200.

However, the all-new Lotus road car, coded M50, for which the 907 engine was intended, was far from ready. The final designs had only just been approved by Colin Chapman and it would be three years before it could be in full-scale production. He therefore came to an agreement with Kvell Qvale, a Californian who had acquired control of the well-known Jensen Car Company, to provide the new Lotus engine for use in their Healey-designed two-seater open sports car. This version of the engine, developing 150 bhp, appeared in the Jensen-Healey quite some time before it was seen in a Lotus.

In 1972 Team Lotus sported an entirely new livery when their main sponsors, Imperial Tobacco Company, decided to bring out a new brand of cigarettes, for which they had conceived a very clever marketing plan. The brand name was to be 'John Player Special' and the packaging – to emphasize the quality – was to feature a gold motif and lettering on a high-gloss jet-black background. The cars themselves were no longer to be called Lotuses but became known as 'John Player Specials'; they were to be entered under the name John Player Team Lotus and, of course, they were to be painted black and gold in the style of the cigarette packaging. (Later the gold was replaced by yellow, because this showed up better on television screens.) Apart from

Colin and Team Manager Peter Warr proudly posing with the entire Team Lotus for 1972, with two Type 72 Formula 1 and two Type 73 Formula 3 cars. This was the first time Lotus racing cars became known as John Player Specials and everyone, including the cars, wore the black and gold livery matching the packaging of the new brand of cigarettes introduced at the same time.

the obvious financial incentive to Lotus, the reason behind the adoption of such a strategy was that in the event of cigarette or tobacco advertising being banned on cars – or in sport generally – the brand name, as part of the cars' name, would have to be accepted. Of course, in America, the brand names of products had been applied as names of racing cars for many years.

This was going to be a memorable season indeed. Reine Wisell had gone, to be replaced by ex-Formula 3 driver Dave Walker, and Emerson Fittipaldi, by winning five Grand Prix races, became Lotus's fourth World Champion driver. Maurice Phillippe had been replaced by two new designers, Martin Wade and Ralph Bellamy, and the Lotus 72 appeared with very little modification. Apart from the fact that Colin's ambitions for Dave Walker did not materialize, it was a dream year for Colin and it was probably the last Formula 1 season he really enjoyed until he next won the

After a difficult 1971 season in which he was hampered by an injury he sustained in a road accident, Emerson Fittipaldi – much to Colin's delight, as indicated in this cap-throwing sequence – hit form again in the 1972 Spanish GP. He went on to win the World Championship that year.

World Championship with the 'ground effect' car in 1978.

Although Team Lotus were still absent from Formula 2, the John Player Special colours appeared in the shape of a new and very advanced Formula 3 car boasting, like the 72, inboard front brakes. The cars were driven by Tony Trimmer and Bernard Vermilio but, although Trimmer took second place in the Monte Carlo F3 race, the Type 73, as it was known, did not fare so well during the remainder of the season. And to rub salt in the wound many of the races were won by a new make, the GRD, introduced by Mike Warner, the former Managing Director of Lotus Racing Ltd . . !

For 1973 John Player Team Lotus replaced Dave Walker by the young Swede Ronnie Peterson – a real 'charger' from the same mould as Rindt. 'Ronnie had been on our shopping list for some time,' recalls Peter Warr, 'but the problem was that he had a three-year contract with March which tied him down for 1970, '71 and '72, and which he had signed when he hardly understood a word of English, other than "Formula 1". And when Max Mosley uttered those words – Ronnie just signed.

'He finished second in the World Championship in 1971, for which he was paid only about £10,000, or something equally ridiculous, so even in early 1972 he was very unhappy indeed. We tried hard to find a way of taking him over, but there was no way round that contract. When he became free at the end of the 1972 season – having finished only ninth in the Championship – we jumped in quickly and signed him up for another three years. He really was a most fantastic bloke.

'Emerson, by this time, had already been World Champion and was now assuming the attitude consistent with that high office. He was no longer the 'tiger' he had been when he first joined the team. Ronnie, on the other hand, was every man's dream of a "racer". He just breathed, walked and talked motor racing the whole time. He was a marvellous guy to work with, the only difficulty being that he was so good he was able to "drive around" any problems which arose with the car!

'We very quickly ran into a problem of a different sort when everywhere we went Ronnie demonstrated that he was basically quicker than Emerson. In some places he was staggeringly quicker, like at Barcelona where he was 1.7 sec faster in practice than anybody else in the field, and 1.9 sec faster than his team mate! I feel sure that, without a shadow of doubt, Ronnie would have won the World Championship but for gearbox trouble at both Barcelona and Zandvoort.'

Obviously, Fittipaldi did not particularly enjoy having such a quick team mate, especially when there were such incidents as the one that happened at Monza. Here the two JPSs dominated the Italian GP from start to finish, yet Ronnie beat Emerson to the flag despite the fact that, had Fittipaldi won, he would have had a good chance of taking the Championship, while Peterson's chances were virtually nil even if he had won the race. The Brazilian was furious. He had hoped that Chapman would deliberately slow Ronnie down in order to let him through, but this Colin would not do. As it was, Jackie Stewart became World Champion by clawing himself back into fourth place following an early puncture.

'What people didn't understand,' says Peter Warr, 'is that a deal was struck in Brazil at the beginning of the season, where it was agreed that Emerson would have the Brazilian race while Ronnie would take the Swedish. And, of course, Emerson did

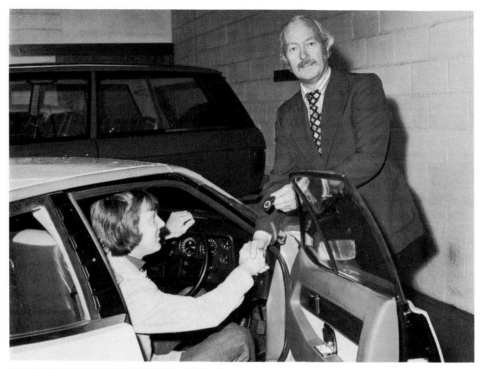

win in Brazil whereas Ronnie lost out in Sweden when he had a puncture on the last lap and Denny Hulme passed him to win. When we came to the halfway point in the season the situation had got so bad that in practice sessions Ronnie's car would be prepared in one way while Emerson's would be set up in another. Then, with only about five minutes' practice left, Ronnie would be totally confused and so we would have to adjust the settings of his car to those of Emerson's. Things would then become very tense because not only would Ronnie then be quicker but he was doing it by pinching Emerson's settings as well!

'What actually happened was that it had been agreed that if Emerson had any chance of taking the World Championship, Ronnie was to be prepared to give up the lead. But all this came to an end in the Austrian Grand Prix where Ronnie was giving the race to Emerson in order to help him win the Championship, when Emerson dropped out due to a broken fuel pipe so that Peterson won the race after all.

'At that point Emerson still had a chance of winning the Championship, albeit a remote one, but when it came to the Monza race the main problem was that had we given it to Emerson he would also have to be allowed to win in both Canada and at Watkins Glen. This would have meant that he would have been 'given' a total of five races. Despite what people said at the time, what happened was that I briefed Colin on the up-to-date points situation at the stage of the race when Stewart had fought his way up to fourth place after his puncture. We then realized that the Championship would be his unless Emerson won at Monza and at the other two remaining GPs. Colin, quite rightly, felt that the chances of Emerson winning all three races were so remote, particularly in view of Ronnie having to agree, that it was pretty obvious we would not be winning the Championship.'

The supremacy of the Lotus 72 was still clearly evident throughout the season, and even though neither of the drivers won the title, Lotus once more won the F1 Manufacturers' Cup – the sixth time they had done so. However, things were now becoming tough for the tyre business, and Firestone – soon to pull out altogether – were showing signs of indecision over their future racing activities. So Lotus switched to Goodyear who had just introduced the 'slick', or treadless tyre, into motor racing.

On the fuel side Lotus were now supported by the Texaco company, with whom they formed a new Formula 2 team to race the Type 74. This car was designed by Ralph Bellamy and borrowed some of the features of the all-conquering 72, such as the inboard front brakes and the torsion bar suspension. It used a special racing version of the Lotus 907 engine, prepared by a company called Novamotor, represented in England by none other than Steve Sanville, the former Lotus power train engineer. This engine was reputed to give 275 bhp at 9,200 rpm. The two cars were to be entered under the name 'Texaco Star' but, despite the talents of Emerson Fittipaldi and Ronnie Peterson, they proved a dismal failure.

Above left *When Ronnie Peterson joined the Team, Colin presented him with an Elite.*

Left *Despite the happy atmosphere evident in this picture, there was often antagonism between Ronnie Peterson and Emerson Fittipaldi, especially by the end of the 1973 season. Ronnie was potentially the quicker driver, but did not enjoy the same knack with chassis tuning as his team mate.*

Above *The famous Monza finish in 1973, where Peterson kept his team mate Fittipaldi at bay. They finished first and second but Stewart became World Champion. Furious that his co-driver had not protected his position in the Championship, Emerson there and then made plans to leave the team.*

Below *The Texaco Star (Type 74) was a very unsuccessful Formula 2 car built in 1973. It used a highly tuned version of the Lotus slanted 4-cylinder 16-valve engine. Despite the talents of its drivers, Fittipaldi and Peterson (above), it never scored any successes and was soon dropped.*

At the factory, both the Elan and the Lotus Seven had now been phased out, one of the reasons being that, with Britain having joined the European Economic Community, a Value Added Tax had been introduced in place of the old Purchase Tax and it was no longer worthwhile selling cars in kit form because they were subject to the new tax however they were sold. There were other reasons, of course, such as the costs which would have been incurred in adapting the designs to fall into line with the new safety certification rules in the USA, and also they no longer suited the image which Colin Chapman and Lotus were now trying so hard to create.

Because of the change, output dropped sharply with only the Europa remaining in production. This was now called the Europa Special, and featured a Renault five-speed gearbox. Work on the new M50 road car was still proceeding, although at a painfully slow pace. Nevertheless, despite the problems, 1973 had proved a very good year for Lotus with profits before tax of £1,155,700.

However, Fred Bushell was becoming very worried over the new car. 'The brief was,' he says, 'that it should be priced at little more than the Elan +2, selling at that time for £3,500, and I began to get very worried by the costs. I persuaded Colin that we should recruit a marketing manager and eventually we took on a man who had previously worked for Lyons, the big catering group, and who arrived amidst great enthusiasm on both sides. However, it was not very long before he ceased to have any contact with Colin and after only six months he left, during the course of which he never did have a full hearing with him! Whilst he was with us I got him to extrapolate the market situation for fifty cars a week and to examine the market at higher prices.

The upmarket Lotus. The prototype M50 finally became the new Elite, but it was introduced at the worst possible time – during the 1973/4 fuel crisis. The hatchback design gave it good aerodynamic performance.

He came up with a forecast of only ten cars a week if the price was £5,000! I tried hard to persuade Colin to review the situation because, whilst I thought the price would have to be somewhere in that area, he stuck to his figure of £3,500.

'It was at this time that Sir Leonard Crossland joined us as Deputy Chairman of Lotus Cars. He was brought into the company to help with the pretty monumental step forward we were taking with the M50, which was to move us out of the kit car era and into fully automated manufacturing. The relationship we had enjoyed in the 'sixties with Ford of Britain, when Sir Leonard was their Chairman, was one of the main factors behind our invitation to him to join us. Apart from this, though, he had taken early retirement and therefore had the time to spare and could live more or less wherever he chose. From acting initially in a purely advisory capacity, as the seriousness of the M50's programme developed, and the very real extent of the changes in attitude by the bringing together of plans for design, development and production became apparent, Sir Leonard grew much more actively involved in the company. Soon he was personally controlling the activities of the Managing Director, and was therefore performing the monitoring, motivating and target setting which on previous new model launches Colin would have carried out himself.'

'It was when we were preparing the M50 that Colin decided we should investigate the possibility of buying Aston Martin. He was concerned that with the retail price of the M50 having to be so much more than we had originally envisaged, and with a rate of production of fifty cars a week, we would be wiser to market it under a name more losely associated with an up-market luxury high-performance car image.

'When the approach was made I understood from Colin that his prime interest was because, unlike Lotus, Aston Martin's product was already being marketed to a more affluent type of customer and one who would probably be more receptive to the new M50 than the traditional Lotus owner.

'I am not sure whether David Brown himself was still the owner then, and I certainly never spoke to him myself. However, our general view was that there were other aspects of Aston Martin which had to be considered, apart from the name. For instance, there was the fact that their workshops, situated just off the M1 motorway, might have made an ideal Lotus and Aston Martin maintenance department. However, when we went to look over the manufacturing facilities, we found them to be very much attuned to hand-made construction methods, with much metal work and "tin bashing". They also seemed highly disorganized and eventually, having reviewed the situation very carefully, we decided that leaving the maintenance at Hethel had considerable merit and the whole idea went no further.'

In fact, there was already another new model in the pipeline, to which Colin was devoting a great deal of time. In 1971 he had met the famous Italian stylist Giorgetto Giugiaro who had suggested to Colin that he should be allowed to design a 'dream car' based on a Lotus Europa chassis. Later he was duly supplied with a chassis although it was one which had already been much modified, since it was going to be the basis for the new M70. In his Ital Design factory Giugiaro built a very beautiful wedge-shaped car which was then first shown at the 1972 Turin Motor Show and called the Lotus Esprit.

Everybody immediately fell for this superbly styled sports car and so Colin quickly initiated a crash programme to get it into production as soon as possible. He sent his own stylist, Oliver Winterbottom, to Turin for eighteen months, with some other engineers, in order to make this dream car into a commercially acceptable proposition. Engineer Mike Kimberley was put in charge of the project and he flew to Turin each week in one of the company's planes, often accompanied by Colin, to monitor progress.

Later the car was brought back to Hethel so that Chapman could personally supervise its development at Ketteringham Hall, an old Gothic-style mansion in a country estate only a mile or two from the car factory, which the company had acquired and leased to Team Lotus. 'Colin was quite exasperated over the length of time being taken up with the development of the new Elite,' (the name chosen for the M50) Fred Bushell told me, 'and particularly by the amount of work having to be carried out in order to secure simultaneous certification both in America and on the Continent. I believe he felt this was weakening the whole concept and he then became very excited by the Esprit and the prospects for its future.'

With the Lotus 72 having started the 1973 season so well by winning both the Argentinian and Brazilian races, Colin returned from South America to give Ralph Bellamy a brief for the next Formula 1 JPS Lotus. It was a simple one – another 72, only a hundred pounds lighter! Bellamy worked on the car throughout 1973 and it was eventually introduced not long after the beginning of the 1974 season. It was, in fact, the first Lotus to be built from the outset in the JPS colours and its official designation was JPS/9 or Mk I, although the Type number 76 was discreetly retained for in-house use.

Over the past year, Chapman had spent a great deal of time working on his boat designs and on developing the Esprit version of the M50. It was clear that he had not applied himself as much to the 76 as he had to his earlier Formula 1 cars. In this case he simply wanted a lighter 72 and he was content to let Ralph Bellamy get on with it. At the time of the 76's introduction I can remember Colin saying to me: 'The era of radical innovations has now passed. From now on we will proceed by detail improvements.' Coming from such a man as Colin Chapman, this was indeed a surprise but it just goes to show the frame of mind he was in at what was a critical time for all car manufacturers, but especially for Lotus, due to the fuel crisis which had struck throughout the world a few months earlier. He knew this could have a serious effect on his company, and he was reluctant to devote too much time to the racing cars when he had so much on his plate at Lotus Cars.

'You can see that the basic philosophy behind the new John Player Special,' he said at the launch of the 76, 'is similar to that we evolved over the four years of racing the Type 72s. There are a number of features which are similar; it has the same basic dimensions; the same configuration of torsion bar suspension with inboard brakes and so on, which we felt were those aspects of the 72 which gave us the best performance advantage. However, the 72 has evolved through four years of extensive development with a great many detail changes, and this always tends to make a car heavier than it need be. We therefore took the opportunity of a complete rethink around several of the basic concepts, and to build a car which would not only be stronger but also considerably lighter than the 72. This new car is therefore something like one hundred pounds lighter than the most recent examples of the 72 which we have been running.

'At the same time it incorporates a number of new features, the most obvious of which are the new tub with the now mandatory deformable structure; the new type of side radiators which we first introduced on last year's Formula 2 car; and a rather new aerodynamic system. But probably most important of all is that for the first time we are introducing a Formula 1 car with two-pedal control. This is a major new feature which we have been experimenting with now for nearly a year, and which we believe is going to give a very substantial advantage in performance. You will see that the driver actually has four pedals to operate. One is the clutch pedal which he only uses to set the car in motion on the start line. Then he has two brake pedals so that he can use either foot – although normally he would only use the left foot and the left-hand pedal, with the right foot and right-hand pedal being available as an alternative. And then finally there is the throttle pedal. Gear shifting is done by an electric-hydraulic mechanism, operated by a switch on the gear lever, driving to a conventional fixed-ratio gearbox. This is not an automatic transmission – merely an automatic clutch.'

There is no doubt that Chapman felt there was something radically wrong with current racing car design, when it was still necessary for a driver to use only one foot, alternating between two pedals, during the most difficult phase of positioning a racing car before a corner. He probably had this in mind at the time of the early Lotus gearbox, designed by Richard Ansdale, which incorporated a motor cycle-type sequential gear-change mechanism where the driver simply pushed the lever in one direction to change up and pulled it in the reverse direction to change down. Of course, with Colin having been such an accomplished racing driver himself, he had the edge over other engineers not so familiar with the techniques required.

In answer to a question about the new clutch, he explained: 'On entering a corner, particularly a fast one, the disruptive element of taking the foot off the throttle automatically produces engine over-run braking. Then applying the right foot to the brake produces quite a severe change of pitch, which in turn causes a change in the torque applied to the rear wheels, all of which tends to unsettle the car. This new system makes this transition between off-power and on-power both smoother and more gradual, and the increased stability enables the driver to negotiate the corner at a higher speed.

'We first fitted this system to a Formula 2 chassis last year when Ronnie did quite a lot of running with it and saw its potential advantages. There were some detail technical problems, such as the speed at which the clutch released and the speed of the change itself, but we have worked on its development and now that the system has been fitted and run in this chassis, Ronnie is very satisfied with it and sure that there will be a performance advantage. It does mean that the driver can have his left foot on the brake and his right foot on the throttle, and thus concentrate on keeping the car steady at the same time as he is braking. The temptation, of course, is to use both pedals at the same time and then you are liable to get into all sorts of problems with the brakes. There is no power loss involved whatsoever because this is not an automatic transmission. It is a development of Automotive Products' automatic clutch with which we are using our normal Hewland gearbox.'

One of the most striking features of the car was the twin superimposed wings at the back. Although each one used on its own would have been only slightly less effective than a larger single wing, it was hoped that their combined effect would be greater. The reason for this type of wing was that the regulations, originally evolved after the total ban on wings at Monte Carlo in 1969, now stipulated a maximum height and overhang. So, with the double wing, Colin sought to make the best use of the space the dimensions allowed under the new rules.

Unfortunately the Lotus 76 proved a total failure. It was extremely unreliable, primarily due to the way the systems had been designed, while the automatic clutch itself never received proper development due to lack of time caused by all the other problems. On top of all this, when the car was put on the weighbridge it was found to be heavier than the 72, rather than 100 lb lighter!

The drivers all loathed it and Ronnie soon demanded to get back to a 72, with which he then proceeded to win three more Grand Prix races – in the model's fifth year of racing. His team mate, now the Belgian driver Jacky Ickx, was less successful although he did succeed in winning the Brands Hatch Race of Champions in pouring rain – conditions in which he always revelled. Throughout its short career the 76 only ever scored one fourth place, and even then it was not a 76 as originally designed, but a 76 tub on to which had been grafted the rear end of one of the 72s which Ronnie had shunted in practice.

Colin Chapman and Peter Warr during a somewhat heated exchange of views in the pits in 1974. This was a lean year for Lotus. Colin had told Ralph Bellamy, 'I want you to design a lighter version of the 72'. Instead, the 76 was not only unreliable but it was heavier! So the old 72 was pressed back into service again.

Far left *'A penny for your thoughts!' An evocative shot of Colin in the cab of the JPS transporter.*

Left and below left *Another black cap is hurled into the air, this time at Brands Hatch when Jacky Ickx, replacing Emerson Fittipaldi in the team for 1974, gave his expected display of rain mastery by winning the Race of Champions in a downpour. This cap was retrieved for another day!*

Despite being overweight, the 72 had proved it was still a power to be reckoned with, although more problems were beginning to loom up. It is important to remember here that this car was actually designed around the special low-profile tyres made for their Number One team by Firestone. However, the Goodyear tyres they were now using had been developed around the other teams' cars which were of more conventional design than the Lotus 72.

At the end of 1974, Maurice Phillippe's new Parnelli F1 car appeared and it turned out to be just what Colin had wanted his 76 to be – a lighter 72 – and as a result he became even more frustrated. However, the Parnelli soon began to suffer from similar tyre problems, despite the team purchasing their entire stocks when Firestone pulled out of F1 racing in 1975. (Although it was entered in all but two of the 1975 season's fourteen GPs, driven by Mario Andretti, the Parnelli was to be classified as a finisher in only six of them, with fourth place in the Swedish GP being its best result.)

Meanwhile the factory was now beginning to feel the effects of the fuel crisis and the last link with the company's early days had been severed when the Europa was finally phased out to make space for the production of the M50, due to be introduced in March. There was little doubt that the Europa had played a very large part indeed in the growth of the company, as is clearly indicated by the production figures of all the road cars built up to that time. There were 1,030 Elites, 12,224 Elans, 5,200 Elan +2s and 9,230 Europas – a grand total of 23,180 cars, to which it would be fair to add approximately 3,300 Lotus Sevens.

Fred Bushell talked to me about this difficult time. 'We had been producing around three to four thousand vehicles a year up to then. With the Elan being terminated in 1973, we were able to carry on with the Europa for another year or so by making it almost exclusively for the American market, but finally they came to an end too. Of course, by that time we should have had the new M50 on stream, but this was well behind schedule and so there was actually a period when we did not produce any cars at all. Then, almost the night before the new car was launched, the costings were checked and it was found that the price would have to be around the £5,000 mark, whereas it had always been intended that it should be no more than £3,500. And this was after we had already committed ourselves to launch it with a production volume of fifty cars a week based on the intended price. Having reconsidered the costings Colin realized that it would have to be sold for at least £5,000 and, of course, this immediately jeopardized the launch and exposed the company to selling a product with inadequate marketing and also, to some extent, inadequate quality control. This was despite the introduction of Sir Leonard Crossland and all the attempts made in upgrading the company's image.

In order to enable the traditional Elan customer to remain faithful to the make, even after the advent of a young family, Colin introduced the Elan +2, for which additional seats were provided by lengthening the wheelbase by a foot. The lines of the car were rather sharper than those of the original Elan.

'Whilst the car was enthusiastically received – as all new Lotus models usually were – with the effects of the 1974 fuel crisis, the output never rose above fifteen cars a week, whereas all the planning had been based on the figure of fifty. In fact, the factory was quite capable of producing eighty cars a week, so the effects of all this were pretty diabolical. We had to reduce staffing levels quickly and do everything possible to control expenditure.'

Originally the launch date of the M50 had been planned for mid-March, but the miners' strike forced the Government to impose a three-day working week throughout industry, which delayed the introduction until May. Ironically, Lotus had already booked an expensive full colour advertisement, with a long lead-time, for the new car in *The Sunday Times Magazine*, which duly appeared two months before the car was finally announced!

Now formally called the Elite, the M50 was certainly a very striking car. Stylist Oliver Winterbottom had successfully managed to combine a sporting appearance and a good aerodynamic line (its Cd was 0.34) with comfortable accommodation for four passengers, headroom for the rear seat passengers being achieved with the aid of a hatchback roof line.

The body was moulded under the revolutionary – and very secret – vacuum process that Colin had evolved and used for the manufacture of boat hulls. There was a backbone-type chassis along similar lines to that of the Elan, and of course, independent suspension on all four wheels, with disc brakes at the front and drum brakes at the rear. The gearbox was the Lotus five-speed which had first been developed for the Elan +2 and which used the gear cluster from the Austin Maxi. The 907 engine, now developing 160 bhp, gave the car a maximum speed of 125 mph. The general performance was only a little better than the 128 bhp Elan Sprint but, of course, it weighed-in at 2,500 lb against only 1,400 lb, the increase in weight being due to the much greater luxury afforded and also to numerous additional items required for the purposes of certification. Two versions of the Elite were offered; the 501 was the basic standard model priced at £5,445, while the 502 came with air-conditioning, quartz halogen headlights and stereo cassette radio for £5,875.

By the time of the launch there had also been some changes in management personnel at the factory, with Dennis Austin having relinquished his position as Managing Director in favour of Richard Morley, while Mike Kimberley had been appointed Chief Engineer.

Due to its rather unusual appearance, and perhaps also because of the marque's good reputation, the new Lotus Elite did not do at all badly in its first year of production. Despite its much-higher-than-expected price and the poor economic climate then existing, a total of 687 were sold, a far cry from the fifty a week originally forecast but nevertheless quite promising.

However, 1975 was to be another story with Colin also being severely restricted in Formula 1 for financial reasons. 'At the end of 1974,' Peter Warr explained, 'Players suddenly told us that they were going to quit! So what we did was to tell them, "Hey, hold on a minute. There are only six weeks before next year, you can't do that to us because we will have no chance of finding another sponsor." So they agreed to come back in but with a vastly reduced budget – something like 40 per cent of what we really needed. It was an enormous cut. In the end, having talked it over together, we decided that the only thing to do would be to ask Ronnie if he would drive for less money. This he wasn't prepared to accept because he had gone through similar problems at March. Basically, he was told that if he agreed to drive for less money there would be a new car, but if he couldn't agree to that, there would be no new car.

'As it happened we were already well down the road with the 76, which was a disaster. Ralph Bellamy was a great ideas man but not so good at detail. He drew up a marvellously elegant yet simple tub, but then forgot to allow somewhere for the wiring and plumbing to go! In the end this all had to be added and it became a total mess. The real problem was that Colin was too busy with other things and didn't spend enough time looking over Bellamy's shoulder. Actually, even if he had done, he would have had a job to read the drawing because Ralph's lines were always so fine that you could hardly see them!'

So here was Team Lotus starting yet another season with the type 72 – its sixth – and it was telling. 'When we moved to inboard front discs,' Colin told me, 'we had worked very closely with Firestone and so were getting a tyre which was ideally suited to the low unsprung weight provided by such an arrangement, and taking advantage of the improvement in roadholding. But over the years, after we left Firestone and went over to Goodyear, we were the only team running with inboard front brakes and the standard Goodyear racing tyre was really developed to suit all the other cars

If 1974 was a bad year, the situation was even worse in 1975 when John Player cut their financial support so severely. Jacky Ickx left the team and several drivers took turns in trying out his cockpit, including John Watson (above) for a single but unsuccessful attempt at the German GP.

which all had outboard brakes. I suppose we persevered too long with trying to make the tyre suit the car and in the end, of course, we had to make the car suit the tyres. The basic problem was due to the dramatic difference in inertia of the unsprung front wheel assembly. The fact that the wheel revolved without the added weight of the brake assembly meant that its total weight was considerably less than a wheel with brakes, and therefore the spring frequency of the tyre needed to be completely different. When we were with Firestone they gave us tyres which suited us but when we went over to Goodyear they didn't, and that is what really caused the demise of the 72.'

During the summer, Peter Warr suffered a very serious car accident and was out of action for three months. Nigel Bennett, a race tyre engineer who had become available when Firestone gave up F1 racing, deputized for him.

During the season, in an effort to improve the 72, the suspension was modified by the addition of coil springs to the torsion bars, and then later the torsion bars were dropped altogether. Halfway through the season Jacky Ickx left the team by mutual agreement and a new driver, Jim Crawford, took his place for the British Grand Prix, while another newcomer, Brian Henton, drove a third car in that race. Then, for the

German Grand Prix, John Watson – who had been driving for John Surtees – took over the second JPS Lotus.

Jim Crawford was a new recruit who had been signed by Peter Warr on the strength of his promising performance in lesser formulae. Peter's idea was to offer a small token sum of money, and a Formula 1 test drive, to a couple of these 'stars of tomorrow' in exchange for their exclusive services for a limited period of time, during which they might just prove good enough for Formula 1. The French driver René Arnoux signed a similar contract and, immediately after he received the money, he went out and bought a dog. It was a Basset Hound just like mine and, also like mine, he called it 'Lotus'! Unfortunately for both Crawford and Arnoux, this was a lean time indeed for Team Lotus; the former drove a couple of unsuccessful races and the latter never even sat in a Lotus, although the limelight in which he basked for having been singled out by Colin Chapman doubtless helped him secure a contract with Elf, which ultimately took him into Grand Prix racing. It was a sad ending for the Lotus 72's career which, with twenty Grand Prix wins, three Manufacturers' Cups and two World Drivers' Championships remains the most successful Grand Prix car in recent history.

Chapter 18

Leading the Way with 'Ground Effect'

By the beginning of 1975 things were not looking too good and the factory at Hethel was very much in the doldrums. After the fairly encouraging initial sales figures achieved by the Elite, demand dropped. The country's economy was in a poor state and the new car was not yet sufficiently reliable for the different type of customer Lotus were trying to attract with their new image. Having to tighten up the odd nut and bolt from time to time was something which the average Elan owner thought nothing of. He was happy to accept this in return for the sheer pleasure of owning and driving such a nice handling sports car. However, the Lotus customer was now more affluent, more demanding and certainly less mechanically inclined. The word 'unreliable' spread, and sales fell to such an extent that the company made a loss in 1975 totalling a staggering £488,000!

At the Motor Show another version of the Elite – a sister car called the Eclat – was exhibited. It was a lighter, simpler and cheaper fastback model, offered with a four- instead of a five-speed gearbox, at a price of £5,729. This was £700 less that the cost of the Elite, the price of which had now been increased. Stylist Oliver Winterbottom had found a way of changing the styling at the rear, while still using the same mouldings, with the exception of the rear part of the roof which now sloped down to a conventional boot lid. Although it was 120 lb (54 kg) lighter, the Eclat was rather less efficient aerodynamically than the hatchbacked Elite, which was now available in two other model forms – the 503 with power-assisted steering, or the 504 with automatic transmission as well, which proved particularly un- successful.

However, the high point of the London Motor Show was without doubt the introduction of the long-awaited Esprit, the design prototype of which had originally been seen at the 1972 Turin Show. One of the problems contributing to the delay was the difficulty experienced in finding a suitable gearbox. Eventually, Citroen agreed to supply their five-speed box, which had originally been made for the Citroen SM and the Maserati Merak. With its striking lines, the Esprit attracted an enormous amount of attention at the Show. The retail price, at £5,844, was only fractionally higher than the basic Elite. For almost the same price, here was a more glamorous-looking vehicle, but being a pure mid-engined two-seater with very little luggage space, it was somewhat impractical. It was no quicker than the Elite, it did not handle as well and it was noisier. Despite the big splash at the Show, it did not become ready for sale until June 1976 because there was just not sufficient money available for the tooling required!

Apart from the technical deficiencies, which were mainly due to the haste with which it had originally been conceived, it seems that the early Esprit was a 'market misfit' in much the same way as the Europa had been. Both cars were originally created for a completely different type of customer from those who were finally to buy them. Fred Bushell explained how this happened: 'Colin believed that the Esprit should initially only be sold in the UK market. It was to be very much after the style of the Europa, that is to say simple to manufacture yet good-looking and with plenty of performance. But the Europa had matured over the years mainly because of what the marketing people said was necessary, and so it ceased to fit into Colin's basic concept, by virtue of things like electrically-operated windows and other similar refinements. While he believed these were of some consequence, they were not as important to him as outright performance and style – albeit, to a degree, impractical style – and the same thing was now going to happen with the Esprit.'

In the early stages it seemed that Chapman was inclined towards building the car with complete disregard for the marketing requirements. Then, once the car was designed or in the initial stages of being sold, the marketing people would finally have their say and get the better of him. He would then have to turn his car into what they thought the public really wanted.

'Basically this was so,' continued Fred Bushell, 'but you have to modify that slightly by saying that Colin always believed there was a market for the car as he had originally conceived it, but normally it turned out that the market was either already saturated, or was going to be within the first year of production. In other words, he was really only looking at the novelty market.'

Another example of a Lotus finally fulfilling another purpose was the Eclat, originally conceived as a lower-priced Elite and therefore first offered with a reduced specification. Very soon, though, it was found to be attracting a similar type of customer to those wanting the Elite, except that they preferred the more conventional lines of the Eclat. Eventually, therefore, the Eclat became an Elite without the hatchback and was sold for the same price. (In fact, later the Elite was the model to be axed, with the Eclat then continuing in production under a new name, the Excel.)

After the pretty disastrous 1975 season, Chapman simply had to build a new Formula 1 car, even though Players were still being frugal with their financial support. Dubbed the 'fully adjustable car', the new Lotus 77 (JPS Mk II) was introduced to the press at a London Airport hotel, when Colin explained the reasons for the design. 'We feel that motor racing is becoming more and more competitive as each year goes by and it is obvious that the circuits have different characteristics; some are fast, some are slow; some are twisty, some have open bends; some are smooth, some are bumpy; and so on, so that different configurations of racing cars do better on certain circuits. For instance, McLarens, because of their very wide track, might be ideal on some circuits, while the Brabhams, being very narrow and with a short wheelbase, would do better on others, and the Shadows, with their softer suspension, would be good somewhere else.

'It was obvious that to optimize the design of a car to suit all circuits was becoming much more difficult. Although we have all been capable of making minor adjustments and changes to things like springs and rollbars, dampers and so on at each circuit we go to, it has not been possible up to now to change the basic configuration of the racing car to suit each particular circuit's requirements better. This car therefore is an attempt to produce what could be described as a 'variable geometry racing car' in that the major dimensions are adjustable. For instance, we can alter the front track very easily by moving the whole of the suspension system out on the very simple sub-frame. We can carry a number of these sub-frames in our transporter and it is only a matter of an hour or so to alter the track over the quite large variation of nine inches. It is also very easy to change the rear track. In fact, this is achieved simply by swopping over the rear wheels, which varies the track by four inches. We can alter the wheelbase by up to ten inches because there are five inches of adjustment at both the front and the rear, and so we can have either a long or a short wheelbase car. At the same time, depending upon how it is set up, it is possible to change the location of the centre of gravity, a fairly major adjustment which normally cannot easily be effected once any particular design of racing car exists.

'So the basic concept of the Lotus 77, apart from trying to produce a light, strong and efficient racing car, is to attempt to effect quite large geometry changes very easily. This is not to say that we will go to a circuit and immediately start altering the car, although that could be done quickly. The idea is that if we are going to a circuit where we know that a long wheelbase car would probably perform best, we will set it up in the workshop as a long wheelbase car. If we felt that a wide track would be beneficial for a particular circuit, then we will set up the car in that form. Then, if we found we were mistaken, we could very easily and very quickly change it.

'Going into more detail, another feature which will be immediately apparent is the rather unusual brake configuration. This has come about because tyres are becoming better and better in terms of traction and grip, and the cars are becoming steadily heavier because of the various safety features which are having to be incorporated, and therefore it is becoming necessary to have bigger and better capacity brakes. We really are now at the limit of the size of brake which can be accommodated inside a wheel. On this car, these are 13 in wheels and the maximum size of brake disc which they can accommodate is about 10½ in, whereas these discs are 11½ in, and there is provision to go to 12 in if we feel it is necessary. The disc is now away from the wheel and out in the air stream where it will be better cooled.

'At the same time we felt it would be beneficial to use two calipers to each disc; two lighter and smaller ones instead of the one big one, because this gives a more symmetrical grip on the disc. Instead of just clamping on to one side of the disc and grabbing the brake against the caliper and the hub bearing over a distance of only five inches, we are now able to react the torque over ten inches, giving a better opportunity of producing smoother and more efficient braking. Also, by having these dual calipers we have managed to incorporate the whole of the front suspension – and, incidentally, the rear suspension, too – into the calipers themselves. This saves a lot of structure and immediately provides hard points on to which we can mount the wishbones; usually quite tricky to provide on a lightweight fabricated sheet-structured tub and, of course, the whole suspension is moveable as a unit. If we wish to increase the track, it is simply a question of undoing these four bolts and taking the whole thing out before bolting on another, different, frame. We can get a certain amount of wheelbase adjustment by setting the frames forwards or backwards, and we can also adjust for anti-dive characteristics, if we feel that will be beneficial, by producing a frame that rotates the whole lot by a couple of degrees. We have almost infinitely variable front geometry merely by the substitution of a very inexpensive sub-frame.

'The same thinking is carried on at the rear where we again use dual calipers mounted on our special gearbox side-plates, and again carrying the track control links into the calipers which are stiff points, easy to mount on and capable of taking the load and, in fact, very adjacent to the through-bolt which goes right across the car. The normal tubular frame structures, crossbeams and such things which are required on other racing cars can therefore be done away with. This is one way of making a lighter yet at the same time stronger car, two very difficult things to do.

'The fuel is largely centred behind the driver, so there is less change in the centre of gravity due to consumption of fuel and, because most of the fuel is actually situated between the driver and the engine, it is possible to have a fairly slim tub containing quite small yet efficient radiators.'

Perhaps one of the reasons for this 'variable geometry' idea was that, having hung

Chapman never wasted a moment. Here he is keeping up with some reading matter and sheltering from the hot Brazilian sun in the pit at the Interlagos circuit, site of the Brazilian GP.

on so long to the 72, Chapman had been overtaken by others in the development race. With this design he would quickly establish the best weight distribution, wheelbase, track and so on, to arrive more quickly at the current state of the art. However, it is a fact that the setup of the Lotus 77 did not appear to change very much during the season, little use being made of its adaptability, and once a satisfactory setting was found it more or less stayed that way. Certainly, with the huge front brakes positioned midway between the wheels and the tub, it was never a very good-looking car.

'In 1976 we were still very hard up for money,' recalls Peter Warr, 'and we thought our last remaining asset was Ronnie Peterson, so I spent the whole of the early part of that year trying to sell his contract. That didn't really work and after the Brazilian race he left anyway to return to March.

'In the Autumn of 1975 I had been to Mugello, near Florence, where BMW were testing their turbocharged touring cars and I signed up the Swedish driver Gunnar Nilsson because I felt he was a good prospect. Actually I think he was potentially a very good driver. Mario Andretti had made another of his 'guest appearances' in the Brazilian GP driving our second car, and ex-BRM driver Bob Evans joined Gunnar for the South African GP on a trial basis. At Silverstone, for the BRDC International Trophy race – a non-Championship event – Gunnar Nilsson had a good drive and amongst those he passed was Mario Andretti, this time driving the new Wolf. By that time the 77 had been greatly improved and Mario was very impressed.

'Colin asked me to phone Mario and offer him a place in the team, which I did, and

Below left *Gunnar Nilsson was signed up for 1976 and he did extremely well, winning the Belgian Grand Prix in 1977. Unfortunately he was to die after a courageous fight against cancer. Here he is seen in his car talking to Colin and Peter Warr at the South African GP in 1976.*

Right and below *After the disappointments of 1974 and 1975 salvation came in the shape of Mario Andretti. He, too, was in the doldrums at the time and was just as motivated as Colin to get back to the top. He drove the new 77, a simple 'adjustable' car, which finally won the last Grand Prix of the 1976 season in pouring rain in Japan.*

he said "Yes" he would be interested. So we got together and I signed him up. Actually this in itself was another landmark because Mario's contract was the first we ever signed that was basically open-ended, and it is still the type of contract we use today. Mario wanted a lot of money but we didn't have a lot of money, so it was decided that he would not be paid a huge retainer but would be paid a substantial amount for every point he scored in the World Championship, and so Mario Andretti joined us.

'It was a very hard season and we had some problems indeed. I remember, from the Hornsey days, an occasion when we pushed the Type 16 on to the trailer to go testing and the chassis was so light and flexible that the car put itself in gear! Now, in 1976, when we pushed the 77 round from the sheds in Potash Lane to the front of the factory for the announcement photographs to be taken, the front top wishbone bent! We had to get Len Terry to redesign the front suspension, which he did just in time for Silverstone.

'The car in its modified form was not bad at all. It was a bit too heavy because Len Terry had gone overboard with some of the structures, but gradually we did better and better as the season progressed and we finished with Mario winning the last Grand Prix of the season, in Japan – and in pouring rain too.'

However, the fertile brain of Colin Chapman had not lost its edge because during the really disastrous 1975 season he had been giving very serious thought to the problems the team was experiencing, and once again he made one of his so-called 'monumental decisions'. He told me about it later. 'It was in Ibiza, in August 1975, when I was there on holiday. I was sunbathing at the time and thinking about various ideas and in my mind I drew up some lines of investigation that I thought were necessary in order to decide what could be done to produce a negative pressure beneath the car which was greater than that above it. Then, if you could do that, it would produce the stabilizing forces necessary to hold the car down on the road without the need for wings.

'When I got back from my holiday, we started an investigative programme, not really with a car but using various shapes such as flat plates and deflectors, aerofoil sections, oval sections and so on, just trying to study what happened between the body moving over the ground, and the ground itself. What had always made this type of work so difficult in the past was that usually it had to be carried out in a wind tunnel. Almost all wind tunnels were principally designed for aircraft use and were really unsuitable for the experiments which we wanted to do. We needed to analyse the effect properly in a wind tunnel with a rolling road. Eventually we got permission to use such a wind tunnel and began some work with it which had never been done before. We found that some shapes applied to the underside of a car would produce a small negative pressure, although not very much. And it is still impossible to produce as much negative pressure beneath the car to equal the amount produced by the wing. Although the car itself is a relatively large object, it is not as efficient as a wing in terms of the total download it can produce. However, what it does produce it does with less drag and that is important. So what we have been working on is to use a contoured underside to the car so as to run less conventional "wing" and by doing so produce the same downloading but with less drag.

'We produce a depression underneath the car by taking the air in at the front, accelerating it through a throat – rather like in a carburettor choke – and then expanding it again as it goes out through the back. The negative pressure created at the throat thus forces the car down on to the road surface.

'Once we'd done the pure research, we built a model of the car. We decided that if we were going to have negative lift side pods, which themselves were virtually aerofoils, we must obviously build a fairly narrow tub so that the contoured pods could be as wide as possible. Actually the amount of download these pods produce is quite small really and can be rapidly dissipated by any inflow of air from the outside to the inside of the car, so you have to create a barrier which, in effect, stops this crossflow of air. These are the skirts.'

When Chapman returned to Ketteringham Hall from Ibiza, he soon initiated a development programme, putting Tony Rudd in charge now that he had completed his work on the Esprit and the 907 engine. Tony's assistant was to be Peter Wright, an aerodynamicist who had worked for Rudd when he had been at BRM. Wright had first joined Lotus early in 1974 as a manager of Technocraft, a subsidiary company very much involved with plastics for boat hulls and car bodies. It was this company which, under Colin's direction, had evolved the VARIP vacuum moulding process which was such a major breakthrough for the plastics industry.

Tony Rudd remembers very well the birth of the 'ground effect' car. 'One of our ideas was to investigate the difference between what is called a chisel nose, as on the Tyrrell for example, or a nose carrying an aerofoil. Which was best? Then, having found the answer to that, if an aerofoil worked best at the front, was its effect in part related to the rotating wheel behind it, and therefore could we put an aerofoil in front of the rear wheels?

'I put together a project team which consisted initially of Peter Wright, Ralph Bellamy, and also Charlie Prior – the man who made our models – and we went to work with the wind tunnel at Imperial College, in London. This is a quarter-scale tunnel which does not give totally accurate results, but it does have a rolling road and we discovered – or rather we confirmed what Colin already knew! – that if we moved the nose aerofoil closer to the road surface, say to within six inches at full scale, the downforce it produced increased dramatically. When we reduced the gap to only four inches, it became much greater still, in the order of twice as much. When we first noticed this the "road" actually lifted up to meet it! In fact we had to rework the tunnel so as to hold down the "road's" surface and that is when we really found out the true importance of "ground effect".

'We used to do this work during the week and would then report to Colin each Saturday morning and at one of these meetings we described it all to him. He was, of course, very intrigued so Peter and I trotted out the idea that we felt the answer was to make the whole car like an inverted wing and he latched on to this immediately. One of the key factors was that, although it was a large wing, it was also quite a narrow one, so that when the car was at a yaw angle the air would slide off, so we had to put end plates on to prevent this. Colin showed a great deal of initiative with the direction of all our investigations. He would hear our reports at the weekend and then would say, "I think we should investigate this or that." He really was the stimulus – the catalyst –

that got us all going. As the thing evolved, I came up with the idea of putting the radiators in the leading edge of the wing, like on the wartime de Havilland Mosquito aircraft. When we first tested this we agreed we would send back a coded message – "the Mosquito flies" – when we had proved it to be successful. That came on the day of Graham Hill's funeral in early December 1975. We also then discovered that heating the air created thrust.'

Becoming involved in this project marked Tony Rudd's return to motor racing. Since 1969, when he first joined Lotus from BRM, he had always worked only on the production car side of the business, apart from a short period during which he was involved with the boat companies. When Colin Chapman first asked Tony to take on the 'ground effect' project, he told him that he thought he'd had a long enough holiday from motor racing!

Another assignment which Rudd was supervising at the same time concerned the original Lotus gearbox because, following the lack of success with the electric clutch on the 76, Colin decided that it might be worthwhile resurrecting this. 'He told me about his idea,' Tony explained, 'to develop the original Lotus gearbox of the 'fifties, which operated by pulling a sliding dog through the gears. We discussed together how this might be converted into the form of a "clutchless" gearbox, and I came up with the idea of having a collection of steel balls inside the shaft which were forced outwards by a cam, which then drove the gear. The loads were pretty high and I spent a considerable time working out mathematical formulae to ensure that the balls would fly out, but under centrifugal force the gears would push them back again. It was a pretty complex piece of engineering.

'Colin wanted ZF to produce it for us and when we were going to a race at Hockenheim we visited ZF beforehand, but they were not very keen. I was then sent to see Getrag, another possible manufacturer, who smiled and showed me patents which went back many years, to just after the war when they had used the principle in the transmission they had made for the little Messerschmitt three-wheeler. So they knew that the idea would work but they were not so sure that it would do so on the scale we were talking of. Nevertheless we worked on it with them for some time and in the end the gearboxes were made.'

This turned out to be a very interesting period in racing car development because, as Peter Warr put it, 'By that time we were beginning to get involved in all sorts of things which we didn't even know existed until then, like friction-free suspension. That is why the Lotus 78 had needle roller bearings, and bearings everywhere, instead of the rose joints. In fact, by the end of the Type 77 era, we even had a recognized procedure for boiling all rose joints in oil for a certain length of time in order to loosen them up and so make the suspension as friction-free as possible! It was an exciting time, too, and the time when, in my view, motor racing ceased to be a black art. What was happening was that people were now devoting themselves exclusively to the engineering side.'

It was at this time that Colin Chapman decided he wanted the racing team all under one roof and as close to his own office as possible. So, between 1976 and mid-1977, the whole operation was moved over from Potash Lane into the Gothic splendour of Ketteringham Hall.

Above *Ketteringham Hall, the headquarters of Team Lotus and the car company's 'think tank', a mile or two from the Hethel factory.*

Right *The drawing office in the almost 'chapel-like' Gothic surroundings of Ketteringham Hall. The estate dates back to before William the Conqueror and it was once the home of Lady Jane Grey, England's shortest-reigning monarch, who was beheaded at the age of seventeen. Parts of the building date from these Tudor times but much restoration and rebuilding was carried out in the mid-19th century. During the last war it served as the headquarters of the 2nd Air Division of the 8th US Army Air Force and from 1950 to 1965 it was a preparatory school.*

Construction of the Lotus 78 'ground effect' car was completed by August, when it was secretly tested by Gunnar Nilsson at the Snetterton race circuit in Norfolk, not very far from the Ketteringham Hall headquarters. The test proved so effective that Chapman decided against using the car in any of the remaining races that season. Lotus were way behind in the championship anyway, and he knew that if the car was raced and seen to be as successful as he expected, the opposition would have all winter in which to copy it.

Colin thought that this decision would probably disappoint Tony Rudd, who had put so much time and effort into the project, and Tony well remembers the day on which he was told. 'In his office there were two chairs for visitors; a comfortable one which he would offer you if the conversation was going to be relaxed, and a hard one on which you had to sit if he was going to give you bad news. He made me sit on the hard one, saying, "this is going to be disagreeable". I was wondering what was the matter when he then said, "I know we will have the new car ready in time for Monza but I have decided not to race it this year." I replied that I had been thinking about it myself and I completely agreed with him!'

At the factory, the situation was beginning to look a little better, with the 1976 accounts showing a small profit of £17,000. Although sales of the Elite continued to drop, the effects had been offset by the Eclat coming on to the market and, in addition, the Esprit was now beginning to sell. It was actually the best year since the launch of the new range, which was now at last complete except for the V8 engine, development of which had been curtailed because of the fuel crisis.

Christmas 1976 was itself a sad time for Colin, Hazel and the family, for Stan Chapman was killed in a road accident when travelling to Norfolk from his home in Torquay on his way to stay at East Carleton Manor for the Christmas holiday. Apparently he fell asleep at the wheel of his Mini, probably due to over-tiredness because his own father – Colin's grandfather – had only just died at the age of 96, and Stan had been working long hours dealing with the subsequent clearing up of all the family matters that arise at such a time. Colin felt that the result of the accident might not have been so serious, indeed it might not even have happened, if Stan had been driving the large Bentley saloon which Colin had given him some years earlier.

One piece of bad news for the factory was that Jensen-Healey had been forced to call in the receivers, but not before they had built 10,453 cars, each with its Lotus 907 engine providing a worthwhile source of revenue during the preceding difficult years.

It was at this stage that Sir Leonard Crossland decided that the time had come for him to resign his chairmanship, and Richard Morley the Managing Director, also left, so a reshuffle of responsibilities took place. Tony Rudd became Group Technical Director and Colin decided that he would insulate himself completely from the hassle of the car factory by permanently settling his own office at Ketteringham Hall, leaving the running of the production side entirely in the hands of Mike Kimberley.

There is little doubt that Colin Chapman had now become disenchanted with the factory, happy to leave things there to other people. Motor racing was what mattered most to him, especially now that he was on the brink of this breakthrough with the 'ground effect' car. In fact, Mike Kimberley reckons that the Esprit was the last of the Lotus production cars with which Colin was seriously involved.

The JPS Lotus 78 was first seen officially at a testing session at the Paul Ricard circuit in southern France. It was then immediately flown to Buenos Aires for the Argentine GP, the first of the 1977 races, to make sure there was insufficient time for it to be copied by anyone. The truth of the matter was that, at first, nobody thought of copying it anyway, because they were all wondering whether this rather large and obviously heavy car would actually be any good! The real significance of the closeness of the car to the road surface was not fully appreciated; people thought that Chapman had put two extra wings on the side of his cars at the expense of extra weight and volume. There was no doubt that the car looked very nice indeed – in some eyes it was the best-looking Lotus F1 car of all. With the extra-large side pods, its appearance was certainly somewhat different from any of the others. Little did any of those present at that first test session realize that within two years every competitive Formula 1 racing car would virtually be a copy of the 78.

The fact that the new car was ready in such good time for the 1977 season enabled there to be two brand-new cars at Buenos Aires for Mario Andretti and Gunnar Nilsson. But Peter Warr was now no longer in the team. Walter Wolf, the Canadian owner of the new Wolf Formula 1 team, had made him such an attractive offer that he felt he could not turn it down, especially at this stage of his career. When Peter first told Colin Chapman about this, towards the end of the previous season when they were together at Monza, Colin replied, 'OK. Treat it as leave of absence and then you can return whenever you want to.'

By the Argentine race Peter's place had been taken by none other than Andrew Ferguson who, after a stint in America with STP and Parnelli Jones, had returned to England where he had been messing about with boats while unemployed. He had his own sailing boat and wanted to make some extensive modifications to it. His wife had suggested that, as these would be very expensive, he should take the opportunity of attending a Government course in boat building, so that he could then carry out his own modifications! Some time afterwards Fred Bushell paid a surprise visit to Andrew's home for a quiet word with his wife. 'Colin always liked to talk to the wives first,' Andrew points out. So Fred, having made sure that it would have the approval of Andrew's wife, offered him the job of managing one of the Chapman boat companies.

'I went to see Colin,' reports Andrew Ferguson, 'and I said, "As long as it doesn't mean me going back into motor racing, that's fine," and he said, "No, no, of course not, whatever makes you think that?" Then, the very day I started, Peter Warr came over to see me, and over a cup of coffee he said, "How are you going to enjoy being back in racing?" "I'm not going back into racing, I'm in boats," I replied, and Peter then said, "Don't you be so sure, I've just handed in my notice!"'

There was also a new Chief Racing Mechanic in the team. Another old hand from earlier days, Bob Dance, rejoined after a period with STP and Brabham.

The 1977 season certainly started with a bang, quite literally in fact, when Andretti's onboard fire extinguishing system exploded while he was passing the pits during practice for the Argentine race, and the monocoque was unfortunately wrecked. Ever fearful of terrorist activities, the Argentine police were so nervous and sensitive to explosions of any sort that, on hearing the bang, some drew their guns!

More cap throwing to celebrate Gunnar's victory in the Belgian GP . . . and Mario's at Monza.

For the race Andretti took over Nilsson's car and put up a fine performance from fourth place on the grid, only to be forced into retiring due to a collapsed wheel bearing when just about to take over second spot only two laps before the end of the race. Although he failed to finish, he was nevertheless classified in fifth place two laps behind the winner – Jody Scheckter, driving the brand-new, first-time-out Wolf!

Nevertheless, the car which quickly established itself during the season as the force to be reckoned with was the JPS Lotus 78. It did not win the championship that year, but Mario Andretti did win four Grand Prix races, while Niki Lauda and Jody Scheckter (who were first and second in the championship) only won three each. The main reason for this state of affairs – apart from two first-lap collisions, which could be attributed to Andretti's over-exuberance – was that five engines blew up at one time or another. This was never clearly explained, although there was a theory that the oil capacity of the 78 was less than that of the other Cosworth-engined cars.

The roadholding of the 78 was a revelation – 'the car feels like it's painted on the road,' Mario used to say. It was somewhat lacking in straight-line speed, because it was found that the side pods were applying their pressure rather too much towards the front of the car. To balance this, more wing had to be applied to the rear, increasing the drag and thus slowing the car down on the straights.

The situation with the car company was now showing some signs of a slight improvement, although Fred Bushell was looking for a way of recapitalizing the money which Lotus had borrowed for the development of the Elite. In October, he succeeded in arranging a five-year loan of £2.2 million from the American Express Company.

However, production and sales were still not showing a satisfactory increase, and

Chapman decided that other sources of revenue would have to be found if he were to ensure the future of the company. Already the Lotus factory boasted its own emission test laboratory, set up so the company could ensure that its cars conformed to the very strict Californian emission laws. At the time, it was one of only two such labs in the country. Now, though, if the company were to earn more revenue from sources other than the manufacture and selling of cars, something more ambitious was needed.

'Colin and I were flying to Turin in the company aircraft in 1977,' recalls Mike Kimberley, 'and we were talking about the enormous investment cost of the new model range, which had amounted to six million pounds. Our conversation developed into a discussion as to how we could find ways of recovering some of that investment by making available to industry a highly technical consultancy service, providing advice on all those aspects of automobile engineering at which we excelled, from composite construction to combustion, ride-handling and so on. We were already looking at another future investment programme for new types of vehicles; Colin wanted to produce a four-door four-seat car with the V8 engine to compete with Mercedes, and I wanted to produce another Elan. We believed that by setting up as consultants we would be able to employ more engineers and provide ourselves with a larger engineering budget. This was discussed at a board meeting soon

The Lotus 78 introduced ground effect to Formula 1 racing. Despite four victories to Mario and one to Gunnar, it failed to win the Championship for 1977.

afterwards and the scheme went ahead. There is little doubt that the income from this source saved Lotus by offsetting the losses made by the car division.'

For the 1978 Formula 1 season, JPS Team Lotus were no longer able to enjoy the services of Gunnar Nilsson. Now bravely fighting the cancer from which he eventually died, he was not fit enough to drive. His place in the team was taken over with the return of Ronnie Peterson who, despite his great talent, was not to be highly paid this time. Colin knew that Mario was quite capable of becoming World Champion on his own and that he did not need, nor could he afford, such a brilliant second driver, but Ronnie's friend and guardian angel, Count Zanon, helped him in getting the drive. Although the relationship between the two drivers might have been expected to develop into a situation similar to that between Ronnie and Emerson Fittipaldi back in 1973, this was never to be the case. While Ronnie was often just as quick, and on occasions quicker than Mario, the American went on to win the Championship with a series of six wins to Ronnie's two. The Swede behaved like the gentleman he was, although by the time they came to the Italian Grand Prix he was perhaps becoming just a little tired of taking the back seat.

Team Lotus was by now using the new 79. The main difference between the 79 and the 78 was that the side pods could now be changed, thus enabling the use of different underbody profiles, in order to provide the right amount of downforce, and also the correct distribution of the download. In doing this Colin was helped by the new regulations which no longer stipulated the minimum three fuel cells. Now he was able to fit just a single fuel cell between the seat and the engine, and position the driver further forward in the car, keeping the pods empty to facilitate the change of underbody profile.

Left *Jackie Stewart was allowed to drive the 78 for a TV programme, hence this autographed photo which he presented to Colin.*

Right *Colin with Mario Andretti at Long Beach in 1977 shortly before the latter achieved his second victory for Lotus, and a most popular one for this American driver on an American circuit. Mario repeated the feat at the next GP in Spain but narrowly failed to win the Championship that year.*

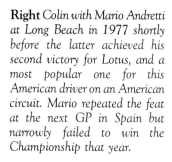

The Lotus 79 was another extremely good-looking car and was soon given the nickname of 'Black Beauty'. Most of its success was due to the technology of its ground effect principles and although some competitors had also adopted identical principles, they had not yet reached the same advanced level as Lotus. Unfortunately, it soon became apparent that, while Chapman had spent most of his time perfecting the ground effect technique, he had neglected the rest of the design. It was not obvious at first but it certainly contributed to the 79 not enjoying such a long and successful life as the earlier World Championship-winning Lotus 72.

During practice, Ronnie had met with some problems on his Lotus 79 and he started the race from the third row of the grid. He had suffered a brake problem during the morning warm-up session and crashed his 79, which could not be repaired in time for the race. There was no alternative but for Ronnie to drive the spare car, one of the previous year's 78s. The start was a very ragged affair, the starter dropping his flag before the cars at the back of the grid had come to a halt after their pace lap. This meant that those backmarkers went straight into a flying start, so causing a large bunch-up of cars where the track becomes narrower just after the pits. Peterson's car was hit from behind by James Hunt's McLaren and pushed into the guardrail, and all hell broke out with cars spinning in all directions. The outcome was that, on hitting the Armco barrier, both Ronnie's legs were badly broken. Although he was obviously seriously hurt, his injuries were not considered to be critical so it was a great shock to everyone when he died in hospital the following morning for reasons which have never been very clear.

Lotus were not involved in the inquest this time, and as far as the accident itself was concerned, many years later, according to the Italian magazine *Autosprint*, the

Italian justice blamed James Hunt, although the case has yet to be settled. Why Ronnie Peterson died after suffering only broken legs was a matter for conjecture, and there were some who felt it might have been due to medical negligence. Whatever the reason, Ronnie was dead and once again Colin Chapman had lost one of his drivers. He felt very bitter about this; especially as the footbox on the new 79 was much stronger than that on the 78, and if Ronnie had been driving a spare 79 instead, it is quite likely that his injuries would have been less severe. What made Colin particularly angry was that the spare 79 was not ready to take to Monza.

Andrew Ferguson recalled this rather difficult period for me: 'Although most people outside our team would agree that 1978 was, on the face of it, a good year for us, the more we got into the season the worse the atmosphere became within our organization. I was no longer travelling with the team but was working from the office, and at the races Nigel Bennett was acting as both Engineer and Team Manager, with my assistant Peter Hemming to help him with the organization. Every time Colin came back from a race, even though we might have taken both first and second places, he was like a bear with a sore head and the situation got steadily worse as the season went on. I could only put it down to success. I had known a similar situation with Charlie Cooper some years previously, although in his case it was probably because he thought that numerous victories would merely result in his people asking him for a rise!

'Then came the Monza race and Ronnie's accident. Colin returned from the hospital and said that Ronnie was going to be all right. Then on the Monday lunchtime we heard that Ronnie had died. Colin really couldn't accept the events leading up to the tragedy, saying that there was something seriously wrong with the medical profession when a simple thing like a clot of blood could kill someone and yet people were walking about on the moon. It was typically Colin.

'From then on it was almost as if he blamed everyone on the team for the accident simply because Ronnie had had to drive a 78 in the race instead of his spare 79, which we were still repairing at the time. He said that he, personally, had been let down by everyone on the team because they were not pulling their weight; if they had been then they would have produced the other 79 on time and Ronnie would still have been with us.

'Eventually Colin decided that we would have a time clock installed, into which everyone would have to punch a card when they came in and punch it again when they left. This was duly put up on the wall and instructions on how to use it were issued to everyone, but *en masse* they refused to use it.

'We had used a time clock some years previously and Colin had it taken out because he had caught some employees playing cards late one night in company time. Perhaps he now thought they were getting their own back by refusing to use this one.

'The dispute was a very long-running one and involved myself, Nigel Bennett and our Chief Accountant Manning Buckle in almost constant meetings negotiating between the two parties. It went on for around three months in all and there were so many misunderstandings on both sides that it was apparent the whole affair could very easily be brushed under the carpet if only Colin would have had a word with everyone at a group meeting. "Why should I," he said, "I am the boss. Such a meeting is your job; if you can't do it then you're not a manager."

'Colin's invaluable ability to be able to smooth things out very quickly by reason of his charismatic personality was unfortunately not brought to bear for some considerable time. Eventually a meeting was arranged for him to talk to everyone and Eric Gray, a team fabricator, was then selected as spokesman by our shop floor workers. At the time it was called, our production output had become very seriously curtailed mainly as the result of so many meetings going on left, right and centre. Some time after the meeting had taken place, Manning Buckle, Nigel Bennett and I were called into Colin's office and we remained there until about 9 pm, pleading with him to do something positive. We produced various sets of figures showing just what a good job had been done during the season, but he just shut his mind to it all. Manning said later that he felt we three had made the mistake of going to see him as a group; because we all had the same attitude Colin probably felt we were supporting the rebellion.

'From that evening onwards none of us was spoken to again about the problem; we all three were passed over in the meetings that followed. Tony Rudd and Tim Enright (another Director at that time) were brought in to deal with it and eventually various contracts and agreements were produced for everybody to sign.

'A number of people left us as a result of these problems, including Eric Gray. It was a very unfortunate episode for Eric as he had accepted everyone's request to take on the task of spokesman, but by the time the meetings were over he was regarded as the leader of the rebellion. Eric had also called Colin by his first name at the meetings rather than "Mr Chapman". Colin had mentioned the fact to me later, saying, "Who was that fellow with the moustache? I don't like his attitude; far too familiar." So eventually Eric left, together with five or six other good people.'

Another chance event, significant for the future of Lotus, took place in Monte

Recognition of Colin Chapman's achievements by the British Racing Drivers Club. The club's President, the Hon Gerald Lascelles, presenting Colin with the BRDC Medal for 1978.

Carlo, when both Andretti and Peterson were driving 78s. In order to promote his new luxury development, the 'Monte Carlo Park Palace', a man called Pino Camperio had taken advertising space on the front of both cars. A friend of his, former racing driver François Mazet, suggested that he also hold a dinner at the fashionable Restaurant Septime for the team. Amongst the list of invitees was a friend of Mazet and Camperio, an American resident of Monaco, where he dealt in oil, called David Thieme. It was at this dinner that Colin and David first met and both were extremely impressed with each other.

Thieme was on his way up the ladder: with oil prices rising rapidly, this was the time to make money, and he was making it in enormous amounts. (His 1979 net profits were estimated at 70 million dollars!) This first meeting of the two men was to play an important part in the following year, when John Player decided at the end of the 1978 season that they could no longer spend their money on so many different sporting activities. Lotus were then going to be in need of a new sponsor.

In 1978 the Esprit became the Esprit S2. The car's shortcomings have already been mentioned and, although some had been rectified on the new model, most of the modifications were only cosmetic – apart from an improvement in stability. However, the engine had been greatly improved by the fitting of a new camshaft which lifted the middle-range torque, leading – amongst other things – to an enormous increase in driving pleasure. The engine modification was extended to the entire range of Lotus cars, total production of which rose that year to 1,200.

Another feature of the year was an interesting deal made with Sunbeam, who wanted a competitive car to use in international rallying. The idea was to squeeze a Lotus 2 litre engine into one of their cars to beat the Ford Escort RS. Des O'Dell, the Sunbeam Competition Manager, was the one who first thought up the idea and he went to see Mike Kimberley with it, who was very receptive to the proposal. Apart from supplying the engines, Lotus did considerable development work on the car and the prototype actually succeeded in taking second place in the French 1000 Pistes Rally, driven by Tony Pond.

However, O'Dell wanted more torque than was available from the standard 2 litre engine and he managed to convince Tony Rudd that it should be enlarged to 2.2 litres. Rudd feared that this would cause severe vibration so, instead of fitting a balance shaft as Porsche do with their large capacity 4-cylinder engine, which he believed would add weight and be totally against Lotus's philosophy, he turned to his Rolls-Royce experience and dealt with the problem by using a flexible flywheel, which dampened the vibrations. This version of the 907 engine developed 150 bhp at 5,750 rpm.

Above right *After winning the 1978 World Championship, Lotus were also presented with the Freedom of the City of Norwich, and even allowed to drive several racing cars through the city streets!*

Right *Team Lotus parade against the background of Ketteringham Hall, celebrating four World Championships for Drivers and five Manufacturers' Cups since the beginning of the 3 litre GP formula in 1966. Lotus also scored two titles and two cups between 1961 and 1965 during the 1,500 cc formula.*

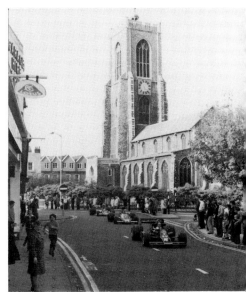

Chapter 19

Skirts and the Thieme Lotus Era

For the first time in twelve years the Lotus Formula 1 team was back in its national colour of British Racing Green for the 1979 season. This was in line with the policy of their new sponsor, Martini, who encouraged the manufacturers they supported to keep their chosen colours (preferably their national ones), to which the Martini stripes would then be added. Shortly afterwards the 'Essex' logo appeared on the cars' side pods and David Thieme's company soon became more and more a part of Team Lotus. He and Chapman got along well together: indeed, it seemed at times that Colin was almost mesmerized by Thieme.

The confrontation with the factory-based staff appeared to be forgotten as the season got under way. Andrew Ferguson continued as Competitions Manager, although still in a non-travelling role, apart from making overseas visits to sponsors with Colin. One of his tasks was to find an Assistant Competitions Manager and this resulted in Peter Hemmings being taken on in 1978. He was then replaced by Peter Collins in 1979. Andrew's position remained like this until the end of the 1981 season when Peter Warr returned. By this time, at Colin's request, Andrew had set up a Public Affairs Department in order to provide sponsors with a better service. Part of his activities included the production of a monthly magazine for Lotus enthusiasts around the world. This incorporated news of both the Team and Lotus Cars, as well as a new organization, Club Team Lotus. The magazine, entitled *Lotus World*, first appeared in April 1982 and continues to be published to this day.

Colin was undecided as to who should replace Ronnie Peterson as Mario Andretti's partner. In September 1978 I had flown over to England to visit the Hethel factory with a team from my magazine in order to road test the Esprit S2. While we were there Colin sent a message to say that he wanted me to join him for lunch. A car was sent to collect me and take me to Ketteringham Hall, where he told me: 'I have here on my desk two contracts, one of which I have to sign this afternoon. One is for Carlos Reutemann, the other for Gilles Villeneuve. If you were in my shoes, which contract would you sign?' I replied: 'Mario is one of the most frequent travellers on Concorde, as he has kept his home in America. I cannot see him doing this for many more years and I feel he may soon retire from Formula 1 racing. Carlos Reutemann is also close to the end of his career and, if you pick him, you may have to find two new drivers by the 1981 season. This would seriously disrupt the smooth running of the team, and therefore I think you should sign up Villeneuve.'

As it came about, Colin signed Reutemann, but there were rumours at the time that Lotus had received some financial inducement to do so from Goodyear. They were keen to have under their wing a driver who had just come across from a team (Ferrari in this case) which had successfully been using the Michelin radial tyres, a technology with which Goodyear were not familiar in competition.

The new Martini-Lotus 80 was introduced in the Kentagon at Brands Hatch on a chilly April day. The transporter bringing the new car was late arriving, and while we waited Colin told me about some of its features. 'What we have tried to do with this car is to go as far as possible in cleaning up the underside, so as to make the whole of the body's surface negative lift-producing. We have also altered the mechanical layout to suit the skin profile, rather than the other way round which is what most people normally do. The result is that we now believe we have sufficient download from the basic body surfaces to dispense with wings altogether. All we feel is necessary is a device for controlling the total download (a flap at the back which has a pretty evenly distributed effect), and also a device for controlling the differential download (a front trim tab). These two should be sufficient to provide enough trim control to give us the download we need more efficiently than using wings. While we are not getting more download than with the 79, we are hopefully going to produce it with less drag. That means we will be able to make up for some of the horsepower deficiency we suffer through not having a twelve-cylinder engine.'

The Lotus 80 was another impressive-looking car. Devoid of wings, it was very long, with the nose at the limit of the overhang allowed by the regulations. The skirt system ran from the nose of the car right back to the rear wheels, and to maintain the 'seal' around the wheels the skirts were actually curved to follow the line of the wheel wells. The rear suspension was redesigned to improve the airflow at the rear of the car and, for the same reason, the gearbox casing was of a new, narrower design. The car itself was almost 60 lb (27 kg) lighter than the 79, and to achieve this a considerable amount of honeycomb had been used for the first time by Lotus in the construction of the tub. The brakes were conventional at the time the car was first introduced, although Colin did tell me that it was possible to fit either inboard or outboard rear brakes, and also that provision had been made for carbon-fibre discs to be used.

When Chapman had said that he was not looking for more downforce than was already possible with the 79, he made the mistake of believing that the 79 had developed the maximum possible downforce and that therefore the way to go was to minimize the drag. The previous year, Brabham had introduced their Alfa Romeo-engined 'fan-car' in which download was obtained by a revolving fan at the back, driven from the gearbox. Niki Lauda won the 1978 Swedish Grand Prix with this car, and immediately caused an uproar. Colin Chapman was amongst several constructors who protested to FISA (Fédération Internationale du Sport Automobile), the new international body that had now superseded the CSI. They maintained that the system should be banned immediately on the basis that the regulations clearly stated that the use of 'moving devices as aerodynamic aids' were prohibited. So Chapman went to Paris with Bernie Ecclestone, the Brabham team chief, for a special meeting with FISA which I attended in my position as the French representative to the Technical Commission.

When it came to Colin's turn to put his case he explained that if such a system

The Lotus 80 – the 'wingless wonder'. Despite its promising looks, this car proved a complete failure. Mario Andretti raced it only three times in 1979 before reverting to the Type 79 which, by then, was too short of development.

were allowed it would become possible to take a fast circuit like Silverstone absolutely flat-out, which would be tremendously dangerous. He won his case, and from then onwards fan-cars were banned, but before the meeting he had said to me: 'Ground effect is a marvellous system for giving a new lease of life to the Cosworth engine which we are all using, except for Alfa Romeo and Ferrari, who have the edge over us on power. But really, with the 79 we are 95 per cent there, and there is little more to gain.'

This, of course, was not the case and, with hindsight, we now know that his time would have been better spent by carrying on with further development of the 79. With the 80 he was once again launching into the unknown and met all manner of problems. Meanwhile, Frank Williams was scoring success after success with his FW07, a complete crib of the Lotus 79, although lighter, better engineered and better developed. It was only because this car was not ready for the beginning of the season that Australian driver Alan Jones was not World Champion in 1979. The title went to Jody Scheckter whose Ferrari, although deprived of the advantage of a full ground-effect system due to the width of the flat-12 engine, nevertheless scored because of its superior power.

The Lotus 80 was not ready to be raced until the Spanish GP at Jarama, so Mario Andretti and Carlos Reutemann were driving 79s now completely outclassed by their carbon copies! Only Andretti ever drove the 80, with which he had considerable problems, so it was only used for three races, in Spain, Monaco and France.

'During last winter,' Colin told me at the end of the 1979 season, 'we concentrated on building and developing the 80, and particularly in constructing enough of them. This was because one of our problems the previous year was that we never had enough 79s and were always working from hand to mouth. So I was determined we were going to get enough new cars built to be able to run them properly and always have sufficient spare parts available. We concentrated all our efforts on the 80, with the result that when we started to race it we found there were certain problems which we had not foreseen, and to which we could not readily find answers. The only alternative we had was to go back to using the 79, on which we had done no further development work whatsoever. The major problem was with the tyres, because over the winter they had been altered and of course we had not adapted the 79 to accept a change of size.

'The problem we had with the 80 was the car equivalent of aerodynamic flutter, and the only way we could cure it at the time was by killing a large amount of the downforce, which was one of the advantages the 80 was giving us. We stopped working on it at the halfway point of the season because, at that stage, it does become very hectic and very difficult to keep up with everything for race after race. Development really has to come to a halt. When we went back to using the 79, we worked on the suspension but we hadn't fully adapted it to suit the new tyres. We think the 79 could be more competitive than it is even now, but it does mean some fairly substantial changes which we did not have time to do during the season.'

Oddly enough, the Lotus 80 had its best result on its first appearance at Jarama, when Mario Andretti finished third, but even then it did not run in the same shape as it did when it was introduced at Brands Hatch. Now there were wings at the front and back and the skirts did not extend further than the pods. Regrettably, it failed to finish either of the last two races, and from Jarama to the end of the season Mario Andretti – then the current World Champion – scored only two more Championship points! However, Carlos Reutemann, not having wasted time with the 80, was better placed – achieving sixth. Only once in the first seven races had he failed to score points, but then his luck turned. For the second half of the season he never scored again, and he left the team at the end of the year to join Williams.

Certainly one of the worst characteristics of the 79, which Colin did not mention in his talk with me, was that with the continual increase in ground effect and downforce (brought about by the constant development in trying to keep up with the other constructors) neither the tub nor the suspension were now sufficiently rigid. The monocoque had to be reinforced, but still 'Black Beauty' wilted under the tremendous pressure inflicted by the enormous download developed by the side pods, and the roadholding was seriously affected.

There was now another new face in the team, too. Besides Peter Collins, an Australian who had started his career working at Ron Tauranac's RALT factory, Peter Wright, who had been attached to Team Lotus since the beginning of the development work which had eventually led to the 78, was now accompanying it to look after aerodynamics.

At the factory, the Chrysler-Sunbeam-Lotus had now matured and the car was announced during the year. It was a very quick little car, topping 120 mph in standard form. The arrangement was that bare shells were transported from the Sunbeam factory to Lotus, who had organized special premises at Ludham, an ex-RAF fighter station twenty miles from Hethel. It was here that they were assembled. This was a most useful contract which, in a similar way to the Ford/Lotus Cortina deal of the 'sixties, helped enormously in keeping the company's head above water when sales were particularly badly affected by the collapse of the US market.

'From January-February 1979 until May 1983,' explains Fred Bushell, 'we had no US market whatsoever. Although it is different and extremely costly to service, it nevertheless provided a potential 40 per cent of our total car business, and made the whole manufacturing thing possible and viable. You have to recover overheads and your original R & D (research and development) costs. Until you have recouped the costs of your present model, you cannot get on with the next!'

The problem with the American scene for Lotus was that, throughout its history, there was never a properly effective distribution network. In 1979 Lotus thought that they had the answer when they came to an agreement with Rolls-Royce to market Lotus cars alongside their own through their dealer network. Apart from the anticipated increase in sales, it was felt that such a move would also considerably boost the Lotus image in the States. A batch of new cars was duly shipped but, unfortunately, a second fuel crisis developed. The sales of Rolls-Royce cars themselves were badly affected, so much so that they devoted most of their energies

Left *After the breakthrough in 1978, with the discovery of the application of ground effect, Colin went through a lean period over the next four years. The main reason was that, instead of concentrating (as did his rivals) on the further developments of his own concept and a successful car, he tried to go one step further and paid dearly for it. This was a difficult time for Colin. He was also worried with financial problems at the car factory, and with his boat business which he later had to close down in 1980, a year after this 'pit-side' photograph was taken.*

Below *The Sunbeam-Talbot-Lotus proved a winner in rallies and took the World Rally Championship in 1981. It also helped to keep Lotus Cars in business during a very difficult period.*

to selling their own vehicles and the sales of Lotuses were virtually nil.

At the end of the 1979 season Colin Chapman had become so taken with Essex that he pulled out of the deal with Martini. During the season, Martini had been distinctly low-key and Essex had assumed more and more importance and the moment full sponsorship of the cars became available, David Thieme snapped it up and once more the Lotus F1 cars changed colour, to adopt the metallic blue, red, white and silver of the Essex Petroleum Company. One of the Lotus 80s was specially rebuilt to show standard and presented to Count Rossi, head of Martini and Rossi.

To find a replacement for Carlos Reutemann, Chapman held a test session at the Paul Ricard circuit during the winter. He tried out five new young drivers – the Englishmen Stephen South and Nigel Mansell, the Italian Elio de Angelis, the American Eddie Cheever, and Dutchman Jan Lammers. The eventual choice was de Angelis, although Nigel Mansell was given a contract to take part in a few events.

Left and below left *In 1980 Lotus's principal sponsor was Essex Petroleum. Accordingly Chapman painted his planes and helicopter in Essex's colours of dark blue and red with silver trimming. He flew the Jet Ranger helicopter himself with considerable skill.*

Above right *The Essex-Lotus equipe. Left to right, American David Thieme, Monaco-based chairman of the Essex companies, Mario Andretti, Colin, Elio de Angelis and François Mazet, former driver and Thieme's assistant.*

South was originally Colin's choice, but his contractual situation was not clear. I attended this test session as a guest of Essex, and when it was over Colin asked me to join him and Peter Wright in the motorhome as he wanted to ask my advice on some points to do with the F1 regulations. It transpired later that it was during these tests that Colin and Peter had been discussing the idea of a 'twin-chassis' car, and they were wondering how it would stand as far as the regulations were concerned. They wanted to ask my opinion but, of course, it was difficult for them to put the question in such a way that it would be possible for me to answer, without my being made fully aware of the type of vehicle they actually had in mind! Anyway, the principle was described to me and, after checking the regulations, I came to the conclusion that as such a design had been unforeseen when they were written, there was nothing which could specifically ban it. However, I did not believe that Colin would be able to get away with it, and I reminded him of the Brabham 'fan-car' which, although basically not exactly at variance with the regulations, had nevertheless been banned immediately after its first victory.

A new Formula 1 Lotus – the 81 – was launched with a lavish party at the 'Paradis Latin' cabaret in Paris. This car was actually purely a stop-gap in order to give Colin more time to develop the new concept now germinating in his fertile brain. What he had done in order to produce the 81 quickly was to clothe the tub of the 80 with bodywork evolved from the 79.

It was during 1980 and 1981 that what might be fairly described as a 'war' developed between FISA and FOCA (the Formula One Constructors' Association) over the F1 regulations. This created considerable instability within the sport, so that Chapman felt it would be unwise to come up with a brand-new car, hence this interim model.

Once again the lack of rigidity of the tub was the problem. 'Because of the disputes over the regulations,' Colin explained to me later on, 'we have not produced our new car and we ran all through the season with the 81, which was mainly an interim car. On some tracks it did not behave at all badly but we have a serious problem with traction coming out of slow corners. I don't think it is an aerodynamic problem, I feel it is due to the way we are making the rear tyres work.'

In the Austrian Grand Prix Nigel Mansell drove the team's third car, an 81B with a lengthened wheelbase, but this did not prove to be the solution to the problem. For the last GP, at Watkins Glen, the rear suspension was modified somewhat and certainly the cars seemed better behaved, with Elio de Angelis finishing fourth and Andretti sixth.

Mario Andretti had a quite disastrous season, scoring only the one Championship point throughout the entire year. After that last race he decided to leave the team and return to racing in America, though he continued to make the occasional Formula 1 guest appearance, as he had often done in the past. All the same, his five seasons with Team Lotus had enabled him to fulfil his ultimate ambition of becoming the Formula 1 World Champion. Colin was most unhappy to see him go; he had developed a strong technical *rapport* with Mario and together the pair of them had made a good recovery from the time in 1977 when both had been at a rather low ebb. For Lotus it had been pretty short-lived though because, for the first time in its 23-year Grand Prix racing history, Team Lotus had not scored a single victory for two full seasons.

However, thanks to a second place in Brazil and finishing in the points in three other GPs that year, new boy Elio de Angelis achieved seventh place in the World Championship. This was the beginning of a very sound relationship between Elio and Colin who, at first, had been somewhat reluctant to have another driver in the team whose mother tongue was not English. He would really have preferred South or Mansell, but David Thieme had pushed him into favouring the more charismatic Italian, who he felt would fit in better with the type of 'jet set' guests he was bringing to watch the Grand Prix races.

I recently asked Elio about his early days with Colin Chapman and Team Lotus. He told me, 'In 1979 I was driving for the Shadow team and the first time I met Colin was at Silverstone. He was surprised by my eleventh place on the grid, in front of both Ferraris, and I found him in our garage kneeling down and looking underneath my car, obviously wondering what had made it go so quickly. I said "Hello" to him, and then he complimented me on my grid position.

'I next saw him at Watkins Glen, the last race of the season. Peter Collins was the Team Manager then and he told me that there was a possibility of a test drive for Lotus, with four other drivers – Nigel Mansell, Jan Lammers, Stephen South and Eddie Cheever. I remember we were given a set of tyres each and we all drove the same car, a 79. We had a long run at the Paul Ricard circuit and it so happened that I was the fastest.'

I asked Elio how Colin had behaved during the tests. 'He looked like a godfather watching over all these young guys,' he said. 'He was trying to get at our personalities; talking with each of us in turn, trying to get some idea as to the types of drivers we were. After the test was over he didn't say a word, but I knew I had been the quickest.

I went to the motorhome and he said to me, "Quite a good time." I replied, "Whatever happens, Colin, I want to thank you for giving me the opportunity to drive your car."

'Then I met him again at Ketteringham Hall. Of course, there was this big problem over my three-year contract with Shadow. Although they were going bankrupt it was not easy to get out of it. At this time Colin seemed really involved, thinking perhaps he had discovered another good driver. He told me, "We have a good programme and we still have Mario in the team, but although you are going to be number two you will have all the help."

'The first really good impression I made was in Brazil when I came second. After the race finished I could see Colin running along behind my car. For me it was an unbelievably good feeling.

'Gradually, he began to talk with me more and more and I think that perhaps his feelings for me were deeper than he showed. Although he would be talking to Mario, more often than not he was coming over to my car to get more information from me to help in setting up Mario's. Of course, the following year, Colin was working on my car and then it was not so good; not because we didn't understand each other, but because we both had our own ideas and sometimes we did not get on quite so well over this.'

The season had seen Essex lavishing tremendous hospitality. They had built a special three-storey bus for guests, in which all the seating was upholstered in the best quality Connolly leather and from which they could watch the racing in comfort. Lunch was served on the top deck – covered by an awning in Essex colours – and guests, mostly the cream of the oil industry, flew in from all over the world. The catering was in the hands of the famous chef, Roger Vergé of the 'Moulin de Mougins', and it was here that some of the Formula 1 'regulars' were first introduced to eating caviar with a spoon!

Colin Chapman revelled in it all. He had now become a great admirer of David Thieme, somehow trying to emulate his affluent lifestyle and never travelling anywhere without a copy of 'Guide des Relais et Chateaux' in his briefcase. Although he could well afford such extravagance, it unfortunately gave the impression that, if the performance of his cars was disappointing, it was because he did not devote enough of his time to them. Although there was some truth in this, it must also be said that things were still not going too well with Lotus Cars and that certainly distracted his concentration from racing. On the other hand, he had now wound up the two boat businesses, mainly because the fuel crisis had narrowed the market too much and they were not making profits. Perhaps, however, he had been rather too hasty in some of his conclusions. Although his boats were certainly lighter than their competitors, capable of higher speed and lower fuel consumption, this had its drawbacks and the hulls could not always withstand rough treatment from the sea.

When Frenchman Jean-Marie Balestre had first been elected president of FISA in October 1978, his election manifesto was to restore the authority of FISA over Bernie Ecclestone, the President of FOCA, who was being accused of running the whole Grand Prix scene himself.

One of the problems which FOCA members were having to face was the emergence of the turbocharged engine. Renault had first initiated turbo technology into Formula 1 racing in 1977, originally with little or no success. They had steadily developed it to the point that they were now enjoying a definite power advantage over the somewhat dated Cosworth DFV, even though the latter's power output had improved from 405 bhp to around 500. Ferrari had quickly got the message, unveiling their own 1,500 cc V6 turbo engine in 1980, although it did not race until the following season. FOCA was now staging a running battle with FISA to have the turbocharged engines banned, but Balestre found it was more convenient to side with the 'grandee' manufacturers in order to try and topple Ecclestone from his perch. One of the points at issue was the ban which Balestre was trying to impose on skirts in order to reduce cornering speed, which was now frightening both the FISA Safety Committee and the race circuit owners. Obviously, such a ban would have put more emphasis on engine power and imposed an even greater handicap on those teams which did not enjoy the use of turbos.

The conflict really flared up at Jarama for the Spanish GP at the beginning of June. Some drivers had not attended the mandatory Clerk of the Course's briefings before the Belgian and Monaco races, even though Balestre – trying to establish his authority – had forewarned them that they would incur a heavy fine should they not do so. The constructors had openly encouraged them to miss the briefings and, when the fines were imposed, to refuse to pay. FISA then announced just before the Spanish GP that any driver who had not paid his fine would not be allowed to practise. In an effort to salvage the race, the organizers offered to pay the fines themselves, but Balestre would not hear of it. Finally, there was a split within the organizing committee itself, part of which then sided with FOCA and decided to ignore the FISA ban and get on with the race. Balestre announced immediately that the Spanish race would not count towards the World Championship! The 'grandee' constructors – Renault, Ferrari and Alfa Romeo – withdrew altogether, so taking much of the interest away from the race.

Following this there was great confusion and FOCA decided to retaliate by refusing to take part in the next Grand Prix, which just happened to be the French at the Paul Ricard circuit. By doing so they hoped to put Balestre in a difficult position in his own country.

There were four weeks between Jarama and the French GP and during this period a tremendous amount of negotiating took place. It so happened that halfway through this period was the Le Mans 24-Hours race, where Essex were sponsoring the works Porsches. David Thieme invited Colin Chapman to come to the 24 Hours of Le Mans – his first visit since the 'affair' of 1962. He duly turned up, only to spend virtually the whole time in negotiations with Balestre, for which I did the interpreting since the latter's knowledge of English was then not so good.

Finally, agreement was reached: Colin Chapman was to take over the Presidency of FOCA and there would be a great reconciliation between the members of this body and the dissenting manufacturers who had resigned over the Jarama troubles. Balestre hoped that this would then be the end of Bernie Ecclestone in Formula 1 racing. It was also agreed that Chapman would fly to Maranello the following week to arrange everything with Ferrari.

The face of Formula 1 racing was nearly changed by this meeting, lasting many hours, in the caravan of FISA's President Jean-Marie Balestre (right) during the 1980 Le Mans 24 hour race. It had been decided that in order to end the feud between the constructors and the sporting power, which had led to FISA cancelling the points scored in the Spanish GP, Colin was to topple Bernie Ecclestone and take over as FOCA's new president. He would then make peace with Enzo Ferrari. In the event, upon returning home Colin changed his mind.

In exchange for this the skirt ban would be rescinded in favour of a ban on slick tyres, which Colin was adamant would bring about the same effect. However, it seems he changed his mind when he arrived back home. He felt so much in sympathy with Ecclestone that he refused to go to Maranello on his own, and when he arrived he was accompanied by Bernie's main adviser – lawyer and former March co-owner Max Mosley! Certainly Chapman's leadership would have been acceptable to the other FOCA members, but he obviously realized that he was already far too tied up with his other responsibilities and he would not have been able to devote sufficient time to the job.

Finally, a temporary truce was established and the French Grand Prix duly took place, but the tyre restriction was judged by the tyre manufacturers to be impossible to police and that was dropped. Everything was now back to square one! FISA then re-introduced the ban on skirts for the following year, thus starting the FISA/FOCA 'war', which continued until March 1981.

After Chapman's fruitless discussions with the President of the Automobile Club de l'Ouest in 1962, who had refused to compensate him adequately for the losses he incurred through the incompetence of the Le Mans scrutineers, he had sworn he would never go back there again. On the other hand, David Thieme had great plans to extend his collaboration with Colin, and was adamant that there were only three motor racing events of which a world-wide public were aware. They were any of the

F1 Grand Prix races, especially Monaco, the Indianapolis '500' and Le Mans. By now Thieme was already in Grand Prix racing with Team Lotus, at Indy with Roger Penske and now he had sponsored Porsche at Le Mans. Immediately after Le Mans, David Thieme talked with Colin about designing an Essex-Lotus sports car for the following year's race. He wanted this to be propelled by a turbine engine, for which Essex would supply a very special high-energy content fuel, and which would in itself attract a great deal of attention towards Essex.

I was asked to prepare an analysis of the Le Mans regulations, and Tony Rudd carried out a feasibility study of all available turbines. As a result of this it appeared that the only engine capable of providing sufficient performance to win the race would have been a Rolls-Royce GEM 41-2 Series 2 turbine. That was assuming Porsche did not improve on their previous performance by more than five seconds a lap. Although there would have to be several extra pit stops, costing a total of 18 minutes in wasted time, the power advantage of 750 bhp in race trim would have produced an overall gain of 24.9 minutes and a net saving of 6.9 minutes, or virtually two laps. To save fuel the turbine would have been equipped with a shut-off valve so that it could be flamed-out on braking and re-lit as the car came out of the corner, this alone being worth one lap for each tankful of fuel. In his extensive analysis, Tony Rudd outlined the fact that the turbine would have expelled 165,000 cubic feet of air per minute, which could have been harnessed to improve the aerodynamics – 'similar to aircraft blown flaps,' as his report stated. The project, interesting as it was, went no

Lotus's public relations man Don McLauchlan often managed to arrange for James Bond to use a Lotus in his films. Here is 007 Roger Moore with the Esprit.

further than the planning stage before Essex had to give it up.

In February 1980 Essex and Lotus gave a fantastic party to introduce the new Esprit Turbo, the first hundred of which were to be called the 'Essex-Lotus' and painted in the same colour scheme as the racing cars. The party was held in London's Royal Albert Hall, which had been specially transformed into one huge dining room. The Essex-Lotus Turbo – rising up from the stage in clouds of carbonized snow – was flanked by the 81 Formula 1 car and the Essex-Penske Mario Andretti was to drive at the Indy '500' in May. Naturally, the food was to be prepared by Roger Vergé, who made use of the kitchen facilities at the Dorchester Hotel, and the 1,000 guests were later entertained by Shirley Bassey. Prime Minister Margaret Thatcher even attended the pre-dinner cocktails, although she did not stay on for the later 'extravaganza' which was rumoured to have cost nearly one million dollars!

The Essex-Lotus Turbo was much more than simply an Esprit to which had been added a turbocharger. A number of important technical changes had been made to the car. At last, the rear suspension had been altered so that the wheels were now positioned by links instead of by the half-shafts. With the earlier arrangement, a legacy from the Europa, the choice was either to have very rigid mounting points for the engine-gearbox unit (resulting in a large volume of noise and vibration filtering through the chassis to the cockpit), or suitably soft mounting points (when the whole unit would move, thus introducing bump steer and producing a strong tendency for the car to wander over uneven road surfaces). The front suspension was also changed from that supplied by Opel to the type already being used on the Elite and Eclat.

These were by no means the only changes made to the car. The bodywork was also modified to provide air scoops for the turbo engine and to give better aerodynamic balance. The interior was greatly improved, with heavily padded upholstery in very supple red leather giving the cockpit an air, and smell, of luxurious opulence. As for the engine, the big news here – apart from the turbo – was that the original 2 litre 907 unit had gone and in its place was the 912, a derivative of the 2.2 litre 911 engine originally developed for the Sunbeam Lotus. The increase in displacement had been achieved by lengthening the stroke from 69.2 mm to 76.2 mm.

In turbocharged form there was not an enormous gain in power but the driveability was dramatically improved. Peak torque on the 2 litre 907 engine had been 140 lb/ft at 4,000 rpm, but whilst the 912 was now producing a maximum of 160 lb/ft at 5,000 rpm, it was actually also giving 140 lb/ft at only 2,400 rpm! The engine was fed by a single Garrett T3 turbocharger through two dell'Orto carburettors. One big problem often experienced by the smaller volume car manufacturer has been to persuade makers of fuel injection equipment to supply them. Lotus were no exception to this rule, hence the carburettors, but despite this an extremely satisfactory result had been achieved. With the turbocharger blowing through the carburettors there was some measure of inter-cooling. With the length of the inlet tract having been deliberately kept very short, the driver would hardly have been aware of the presence of the turbo had it not been for the tremendous increase in performance. One other notable change was the adoption of a dry-sump engine lubrication system.

Thus endowed with 210 bhp and a maximum speed in excess of 150 mph, with the

Essex Turbo Esprit Colin Chapman had at last stepped into the 'super car' category. It was just as well that it was so luxuriously appointed, for the price was no less than £21,000, a figure which – I suspect – was purposely kept on the high side because Lotus knew that, initially anyway, they would not be able to build very many. They also wanted to be able to follow the career of those they did sell, if only because David Thieme was so anxious to promote a jet-set image for the car that bore the name of his company.

The Elite 2.2 sold for £16,142 and the 2.2 Eclat for £15,842. Although the increased displacement and improved torque transformed the performance of the car, it did absolutely nothing for the sales, and 1981 turned out to be an all-time low with only 345 cars being sold during the whole year. It was indeed most fortunate that the engineering consultancy side of the business was now proving so successful, for without doubt it was that side of the business which was keeping Lotus going.

One such consultancy contract at around this time, and which no doubt helped the company to maintain its solvency, was that placed by the now somewhat notorious De Lorean Motor Company, based in Northern Ireland and heavily subsidized by the British Labour Government. Even at the time of writing, a number of questions relating to this contract are still unanswered, and may remain so for a long time to come.

It was also in 1980 that Colin Chapman renewed his interest in aircraft design and began to think about producing a microlight aeroplane. Colin Gething, who had been working as an engineer in the boat companies, also became involved in this. He recalls, 'In 1980 we went into microlight aeroplanes. We looked at several basic designs, but the most suitable for our particular method of composite construction was the Rutan.

'Colin wanted side-by-side seating. He felt that by using composite materials we could achieve the required weight of a fully enclosed two-man aircraft and yet remain inside the microlight regulations.

'Rutan produced an aircraft using known methods of construction, which was a help to us, but his aeroplane was designed for home construction and not for commercial production. It was extremely labour-intensive and relied upon the fact that the builder is prepared to spend many hours in his garage to produce the finished aircraft. We looked at the design and decided that we could produce as light an aircraft – if not lighter – by using our own production techniques.

'The aim was to carry two passengers at 100 mph for one gallon of fuel used in one hour's flying. We decided to build our own engine, too, because of the distinct lack of any other suitable equipment. We were not convinced of the reliability of two-stroke engines and considered that a four-stroke would be a much better bet, but there was no known suitable four-stroke on the market at the time. So Tony Rudd designed the engine, the salient feature of which was the camshaft drive which doubled as a reduction gear for the propeller. It was also a modular engine and was designed to be produced in either two or four cylinder form.'

Chapter 20

The 'Twin-chassis' Controversy

During the winter of 1980/81 the FOCA members tried to split away from FISA completely by creating their own sanctioning body, to be known as the WFMS (the World Federation of Motor Sport), for which Colin Chapman had written the Technical Regulations. Colin explained to me what he had in mind when he wrote these rules: 'Formula 1 should be the pinnacle of motor racing. It should have the minimum of parameters controlling performance. There are only four parameters which control a racing car; one is the power from the engine; the second is the aerodynamical download it can produce; the third is the amount of grip which can be obtained by the tyres and the fourth is the weight. Then there should be some second category of regulations concerning the passive safety of the cars in the event of an accident. I think this should be controlled by some form of crash test, rather than by myriads of little regulations which, in themselves, very rarely produce the objectives they were set up to achieve.'

The FOCA constructors went to the South African GP at Kyalami, which should have been the opening race of the 1981 F1 World Championship season, but it was not recognized by FISA and so lost its status. Deprived of entries from the big manufacturers like Ferrari, Renault, Alfa Romeo and Talbot-Ligier, who had all stayed loyal to FISA, the public lost interest and the race was a dismal flop. The future was now very grim. Sponsors were threatening to withdraw their support and the smaller teams were living from hand to mouth, dependent on start money to pay wages. Their very existence was now in jeopardy. Finally, FOCA realized they had lost the war and initiated talks with FISA.

This was well-timed, for Jean-Marie Balestre was not in a very strong position either. He knew that the FOCA members were feeling the pinch and his strategy should have been to cancel the first two or three GPs of the season and really have them crying out for mercy. However, it just so happened that the first Championship race (after the South African fiasco) was scheduled to be the US Grand Prix West at Long Beach, California. The American market was, of course, very important to Renault, due to their close links with American Motors. When they realized that the race at Long Beach might not take place, Renault panicked and spread the word that, 'with or without Balestre, we shall be in Long Beach'. Balestre thus lost his support and knew he would have to make a deal with FOCA.

The discussions took two weeks and finally a pact was signed called 'The Concorde Agreement', enabling Grand Prix racing to resume at Long Beach on 15

March 1981. However, on one thing Balestre was intransigent – there would be no skirts on the cars. This was bad news for the manufacturers, most of whom had already prepared their new models over the winter – and Colin Chapman was one of them. He had now finally put his Type 86 on the road, a car which was every bit as revolutionary as the 78, for it incorporated two separate chassis. However, now that skirts were to be banned, a somewhat modified design was called for and this was the Type 88 which appeared in February. Once again, it was officially launched at another Essex party at the Albert Hall. If the previous year's festivities had been memorable, this one was even more lavish. The number of invited guests was now well over 1,000 and there was a tombola for which the first prize was an Essex Esprit Turbo! Top of the bill this time was Ray Charles at the piano.

There was sound logic, of course, behind the extravagant parties held by Essex Petroleum during the time when the leading figures in the oil industry were in London for their annual conference. After the previous year's gathering the Essex party had become the talk of the whole industry, and attending future ones was the social ambition of the year. It certainly helped enormously to put David Thieme's name on the map in oil circles and, in an industry where just one good deal can easily bring in several million dollars in profits, what is a mere 'million bucks' if it helps to acquire the right connections?

Nobody could get close to the new 88 at the party, but a very elaborate 'press kit' was presented to journalists. In this Colin Chapman devoted seven pages to an explanation of his latest revolutionary design. Before this function, though, the 88 was tested secretly at the Paul Ricard circuit and Colin invited me to take a look at it. He then showed me the draft of his press release and asked for my comments. He also asked me to translate it into French for him. I read it through and told him that I thought it was a most interesting document which would fascinate about a dozen journalists, while the rest would be totally confused by the technical jargon when the time came for them to write their stories! 'All right then,' he answered, 'you write me an abbreviated version that they will understand.'

I duly wrote the piece, but unfortunately the people in charge of the printing managed, firstly, to sign it with my name, and secondly to place it immediately following Colin's document. As a result of the *faux pas* my signature appeared on the very last page of this thick wadge of paper, which was then handed out at the press launch. When it was seen by those present, they immediately said: 'This car must be legal. If Crombac, who is a member of the FISA Technical Committee, has signed this document, then it is obvious that FISA is giving the car its blessing'!

This caused considerable consternation amongst the constructors, and immediately Frank Williams sent a telex to Balestre complaining about my signature appearing on the press release. Obviously, everybody in the business knew that Chapman had been working on a new and once more revolutionary car. It had been further tested at Jarama in great secrecy during the winter and these things soon get around in such a fairly close-knit community, although the details were scarce. At one stage, through the grapevine, there had been a rumour that the new car had no suspension at all, whereupon the Royal Automobile Club's representative at the December meeting of the FISA Technical Committee asked us to incorporate a new clause in the regulations banning any cars without suspension!

Of course, it is important to realize that after the introduction of the ground effect Lotus 78 and 79s, every Formula 1 manufacturer had been forced to scrap his own current model and to build an entirely new one to a totally different design, throwing away all the existing aerodynamical data acquired at great expense. This had been a tremendously costly operation and they were all loath to go through all that again only two years later. No new Formula 1 car's first appearance has ever been less welcome, and clearly Colin Chapman was going to have to work extremely hard to convince people to accept it. For sure, there was no rule against it specifically, as we had found out at the time we had first checked the regulations that day at Paul Ricard when Colin and Peter Wright had first thought about it. But no one in the 'establishment' wanted that car, whether they were FOCA members or 'grandees' and they would soon be happy to have some help from Jean-Marie Balestre.

Disgusted at having been let down by Renault, just at the time he was about to win his long war with Bernie Ecclestone, Balestre turned around completely and became very friendly with him. Having lost most of the battles, the wily Bernie was on his way to win the peace. One very important thing Bernie did want was to have the twin-chassis Lotus ruled illegal, while his own telescopic suspension system would receive official approval to the point that, instead of everyone having to copy Lotus, they would have to copy Brabham. This was of great satisfaction to Ecclestone and – let's face it – a darn sight cheaper for everyone concerned.

But Colin Chapman was not one to give up easily. He could be extremely persuasive and at the press launch he explained his reasoning for the car's design in the following way. 'In late November 1979, at the Paul Ricard circuit in the South of France, a frustrating year of trying to develop the Lotus T80 into a competitive racing car was concluded. Stephen South drove the car and in a last desperate attempt to control the unique aerodynamics of the 80, even stiffer springs had been fitted. They were over five times stiffer than in pre-ground effect days and the stiffest kept in the Team Lotus inventory.

'South needed only a few laps to make an assessment: "Definitely better, but the car still moves around too much. These super-stiff springs cause so much vibration that I have difficulty in keeping my feet on the pedals and my backside's pretty bruised." That was on Ricard's almost billiard table surface: obviously there would be a big problem on bumpier circuits.

'Still, if only the car could be sprung even stiffer and yet isolate the driver, and the fragile parts of the car, from the shocks and bumps that would result, maybe the concept would work. Thus the Lotus T86 was conceived. It was an attempt to resolve the mutual incompatibility of suspension requirements between those parts of the car which affect its aerodynamics and those parts which insulate the driver from the road shocks. So the concept of two separate chassis with two separate suspension systems was born.

'It was evident by now that the aerodynamic loads exceeded the inertia loads on the car, and that the primary structure must be designed to absorb and distribute these loads, and the suspension to feed the loads to the wheels while maintaining body attitude.

'So the first chassis of the T86 is a ladder-type frame in steel and carbon fibre, on to which all the coachwork, cooling system and some mechanical elements are mounted, and which is suspended by separate springs and dampers. The movement of the primary chassis is thus controlled to keep aerodynamic changes to a minimum. The driver, fuel tank, engine-gearbox unit and all other parts that benefit from insulation from the road surface are mounted on the second chassis which is of carbon fibre/honeycomb construction. This is sprung to the wheels to give optimum mechanical handling and is thus sprung and damped softly enough to give a good ride. The concept can be likened to a modern truck where the suspension is stiff enough to take the payload and the driver is insulated in a "sprung cab". The T86 has a "sprung cab". The T86 was built as a "technology demonstrator" arising out of three years of research and development, starting with the T80. It was conceived to meet the FISA regulations of that period which included the permitted use of skirts.

'Many useful lessons concerning suspension and aerodynamic stability were learned from it, in testing at Jarama and elsewhere, some of which were incorporated into the T88 designed to race under the 1981 FISA regulations. The T88 which is on show here today incorporates the same fundamental concepts as the T86, the main difference being that no moving skirts are fitted. The two-chassis arrangement, with individually optimised suspension systems, is beneficial in maintaining constant aerodynamic characteristics by regulating the ground clearance under all aerodynamic and dynamic loadings.'

Looking at the car from a distance, you were hard put to detect any sign of the novelty. Getting closer, however, you could see there was a slight gap between the monocoque and the side pods, so that the former could move up and down between them on its flexible springs, while the pods, interlinked from one side to the other by the undertray, rode on tiny little suspension units which went solid on their bump-stops as soon as the car got going and aerodynamic downforce took effect. But the Lotus 88 was not interesting just because of its twin-chassis layout. It was also the first Lotus to have a moulded carbon-fibre tub.

Only the week before, McLaren had introduced their own new MP4, which also incorporated a carbon-fibre tub, and they made quite an issue of the fact that it had been manufactured for them by the Hercules company in Salt Lake City, one of the largest American aerospace specialists. However, the new Lotus tub had actually been moulded in their own small glass-fibre workshop at Hethel and cured in the oven at the car factory nearby. This was made possible because Colin had already acquired a considerable amount of technical knowledge of composite construction. Also, the division of Lotus responsible for the work was Technocraft, in charge of which had been Peter Wright, now with Team Lotus, so there was no shortage of expertise and the transition to carbon-fibre went very smoothly indeed.

Originally, the 86 had incorporated an alloy tub, but while testing at Jarama it had become pretty obvious that carbon-fibre was the way to go in the future, especially as it was quite a heavy car. So, for the 88, a complete carbon chassis was built with material consisting of a mixture of carbon-fibre and Kevlar to give more resistance to impact, since carbon-fibre itself is very brittle.

The Lotus 88 was shipped to Long Beach, California, for the US Grand Prix West, the first race of the 1981 season, where everyone was much relieved that the political battles seemed to be over at last, to make way for some sport. Unfortunately this was not to be. As soon as the car appeared, people gathered round it and said, 'The springs on the primary chassis go solid the moment the car moves, and therefore all aerodynamic elements are not, in fact, suspended, which is against the regulations.'

There was a long drawn out session at scrutineering where John Timanus, the Chief Scrutineer of the race organizing club, declared the car to be eligible. But immediately protests were entered by every constructor except Ensign, Tyrrell, Theodore and Wolf – the latter's Team Manager being Peter Warr!

During the first day Lotus were allowed to practise the 88, pending a firm ruling from the stewards, but this was rescinded under more pressure from some of the constructors. So after de Angelis had done only a few laps, the car was black-flagged and Elio then had to get into the spare 81. Nigel Mansell, now having replaced Mario Andretti, had been using an 81 from the beginning.

The stewards considered the matter at a long meeting later that day. It was generally known that most of the competitors had threatened to withdraw should the Lotus 88 be allowed to run. If the race had been cancelled, the matter would have ended in some difficult litigation, but the mere threat was very damaging to the size of the 'gate', so the organizer, Chris Pook, was fairly openly pushing for the 88 to be excluded. It was a very strange stewards' meeting because some of them had not seen the car at close quarters and they had not even talked about it with the Chief Scrutineer who was not invited to their meeting!

We were all awaiting the result in the Lotus motorhome and finally we were told that we had lost. It was strange that, during the hour or so following the meeting, most of the stewards involved sheepishly appeared out of the darkness one after the other to explain to Colin '. . . it wasn't really my fault, but . . .'

Colin Chapman was absolutely shattered by the decision. He was so sure his car did comply with the regulations, and now to see it banned by a 'kangaroo court' such as this was just too much for him to stomach. In despair he told François Mazet, David Thieme's friend and business associate, 'This is too much for me, please take the matter into your hands, I am too disgusted!' That night we tried to get an American lawyer to take the case to court immediately, but to no avail. It all concluded so late in the evening that even the restaurants were closed on the old *Queen Mary* where we were all staying. We ended up in a miserable sailors' pizza joint in derelict downtown Long Beach. It was a very sad dinner from every point of view.

Immediately after the race – in which neither 81 finished – Colin decided to appeal against the decision to the American motor sporting authority ACCUS (the Automobile Competition Committee for the United States). They met in Atlanta four days after the Long Beach race and declared the 88 to be legal, and that it should have been allowed to run! This was too much for Balestre, who immediately issued a press release threatening action against any other organizers supporting that decision. Nevertheless, Lotus turned up with the 88 at Rio for the Brazilian Grand Prix two weeks later, only to be turned down again, once more after the scrutineers had judged it to be eligible. However, as they were not feeling too confident about their decision, they had qualified it with the words, 'There is no text to rule it out but we leave the matter in the hands of the stewards'! These gentlemen met again during practice and turned the car down just after Elio de Angelis had taken it out on to the track, resulting in yet another black flag.

This time Chapman was better prepared, having brought along a very efficient American lawyer, Bob Hinerfeld from Los Angeles, who had successfully fought the matter with the ACCUS Court of Appeal. There was nothing that Hinerfeld could do on the spot over this latest rejection, because he realized that if the matter was again put into the hands of the national sporting power – in this case Brazil's – Ecclestone's influence with them would carry too much weight as he was also the promoter of the Grand Prix. So, instead of appealing, he decided to take the issue straight to the FIA Court of Appeal. To make quite sure that this would happen, Chapman phoned through from Rio to Teddy Mayer, the McLaren team chief. He was at home, not having attended the race, and Chapman asked him as a favour to protest against the ACCUS Court of Appeal's decision, so that the matter would have to be passed over to the FIA. While he was preparing the case, Bob Hinerfeld even managed to obtain an affidavit from one of the stewards, who certified that he had been offered a job by the President of the Brazilian Automobile Confederation provided he would vote the right way at the hearing!

But the final straw came in Argentina where, for the first time, the scrutineers rejected the car. However, they were obviously not very pleased at having to reach this decision as they added to their announcement, 'this Committee wishes to express its admiration for the creative ingenuity of those who designed the Lotus T88.' By then, Colin was thoroughly fed up and, when we had dinner together that Friday evening, he asked me to prepare a really scathing press release. We met very early the following morning to get this down on paper, as Colin planned to catch an early flight out of Buenos Aires, having decided that he wanted to get away from it all. (It was to be the first Grand Prix he had missed since 1968.) After he had finally approved the text, I typed it out. Colin had already given a specimen of his signature to François Mazet to add to the foot of the release before photocopying it. Unfortunately my English is by no means perfect and, although Lotus Team Manager Peter Collins looked it over, he did so rather hastily and there was not enough time to make any corrections. So when it duly appeared in my somewhat clumsy English, it could quite obviously only have been written by me. Whereupon Monsieur Balestre, thinking it was a machination engineered by François Mazet, issued a further strongly worded press release announcing that a fine of 100,000 US dollars had been levied against Essex Team Lotus for having published our press release!

Here is the text (unedited) of that press release:

> 'For the last four weeks we have been trying to get the new Essex-Lotus 88 to take part in a Grand Prix, to no avail.
>
> 'Twice it was accepted by the scrutineers, twice it was turned down by the stewards under pressure of lobbies. The USA national Court of Appeal ruled this new car eligible and gave a firm recommendantion it should be allowed to race, it was still forced off the track by protesters and the black flag.
>
> 'And now we have been turned down again from participating in the Argentine Grand Prix, even though the Argentine Automobile Club's technical

commission commented on the innovative design it features and the worthiness of its technological advances.

'At no time throughout this ordeal had any steward or scrutineer come up with a valid reason for the exclusion consistent with the content and intention of the rule.

'It is a particular disappointment for this to have happened at the Argentine Grand Prix which has marked more pleasant points in the history of Team Lotus. It is here, in 1960, that we were welcomed into the band of sportsmen competitors with our first full Formula One car, which was as innovative then in its way as the Essex-Lotus 88 is today. It was also here in 1977 where we ran the first ground effect car ever in motor racing, a principle which every Formula 1 car has since copied.

'Throughout these years, we have witnessed the changes which have taken place in Grand Prix racing and unfortunately seen what was fair competition between sportsmen degenerate into power struggles and political maneuverings between manipulators and money men attempting to take more out of the sport than they put into it.

'We have a responsibility to the public of the Grand Prix and to our drivers and this has stopped us from withdrawing our cars from this event. But for the first time since I started Grand Prix racing, 22 years ago, I shall not be in the Team Lotus pit during the race for this reason. During this period no team has won more races, more championships than we have, nobody has influenced the design of racing cars the way we did, through innovations which are already finding their way into everyday motor cars, for the benefit of increased safety and energy conservation. And yet we are being put under the unbearable pressure by our rival competitors who are frightened that once again we are setting a trend they may all have to follow.

'The matter shall go to its next stage at the FIA Court of Appeal in two weeks time. We shall defend our case with all the arguments we can muster for the defence of a cause we consider worthy.

'When this will be over I shall seriously reconsider with my good friend and sponsor David Thieme of Essex Motorsport wether Grand Prix racing is still what it purports to be: the pinnacle of sport and technological achievement. Unfortunately, this appears to be no longer the case and if one does not clean it up, Formula 1 shall end up in a quagmire of plagiarism, chicanery and petty rule interpretation forced by lobbies manipulated by people for whom the sport has no meaning.

Buenos Aires, April 10th 1981
9 am

COLIN CHAPMAN

'PS: When you read this, I shall be on my way to watch the progress of the US Space-Shuttle, an achievement of human mankind which will refresh my mind from what I have been subjected to in the last four weeks.'

These were pretty powerful words, to say the least, but FISA's sanction was pretty powerful, too. One hundred thousand dollars! I claim to hold the record for the most expensive press release ever written!

The Argentinian race was won by the Brazilian Nelson Piquet, whose Brabham was fitted with skirts – now supposedly banned – and also a telescopic ride compensator. This was a device which enabled the suspension to be adjusted so that the car was kept well clear of the road surface when it was stationary. The minimum regulation gap was 6 cm (2.36 in). But as soon as it was on the move, the body could then be lowered in order to make full use of the skirts, thus restoring the ground effect! The second Brabham, driven by Hector Rebaque, and equipped with the same system, stopped out on the circuit during the race and was still in the lowered position when it was later retrieved. The Williams team immediately lodged a protest but nothing more was heard of it even though Piquet had beaten local hero, and Williams driver, Carlos Reutemann.

During the evening when we were all discussing the press release idea, François Mazet had tried several times to contact David Thieme, who had not attended any of the first three races. Although he was quite unable to make contact, he certainly kept any thoughts and observations to himself. It was not until I arrived back in Paris on the following Tuesday that I heard the news that the Essex 'empire' had collapsed and that David Thieme had been imprisoned in Zurich!

At the next meeting of the FISA Executive Committee, Balestre used the collapse of Essex Petroleum as the pretext to revoke the ludicrous fine imposed and change it to a reprimand. He knew he would be criticized for applying such a large fine without first referring it to the Committee and, besides, he had now realized that the press release was actually Colin Chapman's idea and it had not come from François Mazet and me, as he had at first assumed. This was particularly aggravating for me because, until then, I had always been one of his advisers, and for a while he had been managing the magazine which I am still editing.

Eventually David Thieme was released from prison on bail, put up by Chapman and he then successfully sued the Swiss bank which had arranged for his imprisonment. But his business had well and truly collapsed, and this just added to Colin Chapman's worries. Thieme still had hopes that he would be able to save the company and asked Colin for the Essex name to remain on the cars, promising that he would soon be able to pay his sponsorship money.

As for me, I was very soon relieved of my responsibilities as Chairman of the Technical Board of the FFSA (the Fédération Française du Sport Automobile, the French national motor sporting authority), and as the French representative on the FISA Technical Commission. Colin first heard about this when we were both in Monte Carlo for the Grand Prix a month or two later, and he immediately fished a set of keys out of his pocket, saying, 'the least I can do for you is to give you my own Eclat'! I was, of course, completely taken aback by this solid indication of his deep-down generosity and I thanked him profusely before realizing that he had actually presented me with the ignition keys of the company's Cessna aeroplane! In fact, I still have that Lotus Eclat and use it regularly, especially on my frequent trips to England.

The FIA Court of Appeal was due to meet on 23 April and on the previous Saturday, which happened to be the Easter weekend, Colin phoned me early in the morning to ask, 'Can you be at Le Bourget Airport in a couple of hours, if I send a plane to pick you up? Bob Hinerfeld has arrived and he feels we should have our case translated into French as the judges don't seem to be familiar with the English language. There will also be a French lawyer on the flight.' I duly rushed off to Le Bourget and met this very pleasant French barrister, only to find to my horror that he was Bernie Ecclestone's lawyer, too! Of course, Colin was convinced that it had been Bernie who had first pushed Balestre into banning the 88 and yet he had still turned to Ecclestone to recommend him a good French lawyer. I was dumbfounded by his naivety. In the end he was only used for the purpose of making the introduction.

When I arrived at Ketteringham Hall later that day, I found the whole place in a turmoil. Bob Hinerfeld had prepared what he thought to be a rock-hard case, going back to the reasons why the fitting of aerodynamic attachments upon unsprung parts had been forbidden, and he was able to prove that the T88 was actually well within the spirit of the regulations. The documentation for our case was complete by Saturday evening and, so that the noise from my typewriter should not disturb anyone, I spent almost the entire night translating it in the kitchen at East Carleton Manor. My only company was Hazel Chapman's budgerigars, who chirped away most of the time, happy to have an unexpected companion!

Back in Paris on the following Thursday, after the case had been heard but before the Court had reached a verdict, Colin, Peter Wright, John Timanus (the SCCA scrutineer, who had come over specially from the USA to give his evidence), Bob Hinerfeld, his assistant, another journalist and I, then went out to dinner together. It was a large although somewhat subdued party. Afterwards, we returned to the FIA offices and waited for what seemed to be a very long time before we were ushered

Peter Wright, the aerodynamicist, was also Technical Manager of Team Lotus in 1981-82. Here he is (right) talking with Nigel Mansell, another of Colin's discoveries.

into the 'courtroom'. There we were told that, since the verdict had not been translated into English, would I please translate it. I did not have to get very far with it before Colin realized that, once again, he had lost the case. He looked like a man who had just been stabbed to death. Ashen-faced, he stood up and, without a word, rushed off back to his hotel, leaving Peter Wright to listen to the complete facts.

However, I had warned Colin that this was what I had expected to happen because I knew only too well the way FISA functioned. The Court's ruling was that the wings were, in fact, acting directly on an unsprung part of the car. However, in order to prove their point, the judges had dug up a regulation in the International Sporting Code which applied to touring cars, and was certainly not in the Formula 1 technical regulations appended to the Concorde Agreement. This, in itself, was enough to invalidate the judgement, except that in the FIA's rules final jurisdiction always remains with their own Court of Appeal!

Team Lotus did not turn up at the first European race, the San Marino Grand Prix at Imola, where the constructors met with FISA and agreed to legalize the new Brabham suspension system.

Two weeks later, at Zolder, Essex-Team Lotus were back with two 81s when Nigel Mansell finished third and Elio de Angelis fifth. At Monaco, Colin Chapman introduced a new car, the Lotus 87. Basically, this was made up of the tub of the 88, to which conventional bodywork had now been fitted. Unfortunately, due to the restrictions imposed by the earlier double chassis, it was not possible to make the side pods as large as they should have been. Nevertheless, the cars remained in this form for the remainder of the season.

David Thieme's financial situation showed no signs of improvement, so Chapman was very happy to have John Player back as main sponsors in time for the Spanish Grand Prix. There the two 87s appeared again in the black and yellow JPS colours, although the Essex logo still featured on the side pods. Unfortunately, the relationship between Colin Chapman and David Thieme was now deteriorating rapidly and, in fact, by the end of the season they were no longer talking to each other, with Essex still owing Team Lotus several million dollars in unpaid sponsorship fees.

Chapman, however, could not dismiss the T88 from his mind, and remained quite adamant that it was legal. The irony of the matter was that he later realized the stewards could actually have disqualified the car anyway, for a minor technical infringement concerning the positioning of the oil cooler! So this was moved and the revised machine – now referred to as the 88B – was then submitted for examination by the RAC scrutineers, prior to being entered for the British Grand Prix at Silverstone.

This action proved to be just what Basil Tye, the Director of the RAC's Motor Sports Association – the organizers of the race – needed. The following October, Jean-Marie Balestre would be seeking re-election as President of FISA and Tye had decided some time before that he would stand against him. He reasoned, therefore, that if he allowed the car to run in the British GP, even if there were to be a protest and the FIA Court of Appeal disqualified it afterwards, the mere fact that it would have raced would be proof of his power over Balestre! After the scrutineers had examined the car and approved it, Tye issued a press release to this effect, so that

Return of the black and gold. After Essex ran into financial problems in 1981, Team Lotus was very happy to be able to renew its links with John Player Special. The drivers were Elio de Angelis (left) and Nigel Mansell (right).

everyone knew the Lotus 88B was going to be accepted for the Silverstone race.

Unfortunately, Basil Tye was outflanked at the next FIA Executive Committee meeting. Bernie Ecclestone was leaving Paris before the end of the meeting and he offered Basil Tye the opportunity of a lift back to London in his aeroplane which, of course, he jumped at since the meeting was virtually over anyway. Unbeknown to him, though, the matter of the RAC's press release was suddenly introduced after his departure under the item of 'Any Other Business', and Balestre then obtained the permission of the Executive Committee to prevent the Lotus 88B from appearing at Siverstone, by using an article in the International Sporting Code which gives the FISA representative on the spot the right to impose his own decision over that of the race organizers. So, when the 88B arrived, passed scrutineering and duly practised on the first day, Ferrari, Alfa Romeo and Talbot-Ligier immediately lodged protests. When these were examined by the stewards of the meeting, Balestre declared that he would exercise the right which the Executive Committee had given him, and promptly rejected the car!

Tye was prepared for this to happen and was quite ready to go to the High Court immediately to obtain an injunction against Balestre – all good stuff just before the FISA election – but the stewards chickened out and so that was that. The history of the Lotus 88 ended with one practice session at Silverstone in which de Angelis was ninth fastest, and yet throughout the career of this car, no-one ever produced a valid article in the rules which justified the ban.

Although Colin Chapman must have by then realized that continuing the fight would be in vain, he nevertheless went through the whole rigmarole again. He appealed against the decision of the stewards; the RAC held another meeting in the presence of Lord Shawcross, the famous barrister, at which the 88 was again declared eligible, and the meeting severely criticized the judgement of the FIA Court of Appeal, issuing the following statement. 'The Stewards of the Royal Automobile Club regret to have to say, and they do so with the utmost respect, that even if the decision of 23 April was directly applicable to the Lotus 88B, which it is not, they would for their own part feel unable to apply it as a binding precedent since they are forced to the conclusion that its details are, in many cases, inaccurate, and its *ratio decidendi* [the general reasons or principles of a judicial decision] as indicated above is unjustified by the regulations and is mistaken.'

Nevertheless, the FIA Court of Appeal met again on 6 November and did not

Late in his life Colin became tremendously interested in microlight aircraft and he owned several examples which he insisted the whole family should learn to fly. On his land at East Carleton there was a special hangar for them, and a landing strip. The factory's runway at nearby Hethel was also at his disposal. This machine is an Eagle and is being flown early one morning by his daughter Jane.

Colin Chapman with Nigel Mansell, who has often since said how much he owed to Colin for having given him the opportunity of breaking into Grand Prix racing.

even consider the technical aspects of the modified car; they simply decided that the earlier judgement still applied. Of course, with Basil Tye having failed in his bid to be elected President of FISA – by 17 votes against 33 – it was a foregone conclusion.

The whole lengthy business was all very unsavoury and my feeling is that these events had a deep effect on Colin Chapman's enthusiasm for motor racing – and who could blame him? I remember the following April having what could have been called an 'old comrades dinner' with him and lawyer Bob Hinerfeld during the 1982 Long Beach Grand Prix meeting, when Colin hardly mentioned motor racing the whole evening. He had just returned from visiting some aircraft company in California, and it was clear that building aircraft was really what was in his mind for the future.

I asked Elio de Angelis whether he felt that Colin was still as concerned with Formula 1 racing or did he perhaps notice an increasing interest in aeroplanes. 'Not in my first year with him but in the second, yes definitely, he was not concentrating on motor racing nearly so much. I think the double chassis 88 was his last try, in the motor racing sense. I think he knew he was at the limit of the regulations but as it was a breakthrough in modern technology he was going to go for it and yet I don't think he was following it up as thoroughly as he could have done. I believe he could have designed that car in a completely different and much better way.'

I also asked Elio what the 88 was like to drive. 'It was very short of development,' he told me. 'The only time it worked well was in free practice at the Riverside circuit

just before the Long Beach race. We finally got it working well during official practice for the race itself and then it was banned. We did have to change the springs as the car wasn't going down low enough. It also went quite well in free practice in Brazil, but the main problem with the car was that it was not very well made and it was sucking in air between the two chassis. In the fast corners one chassis tended to go one way and the second chassis went the other. I crashed it in Brazil!'

Due to the lack of ground effect, the Lotus 87 drivers scored very few Championship points during the 1981 season, Elio de Angelis finishing eighth and Nigel Mansell fourteenth in the Championship. Now Team Lotus had not scored a single Grand Prix victory for three years, a sad state of affairs to say the least. The only saving grace for Colin Chapman was that he had succeeded in signing a new two-year contract with his old friends John Player, which would enable him to produce a new car for the 1982 season. He would be keeping the same two drivers but there was to be a new Team Manager, with Peter Warr returning from his 'leave of absence' to claim back his old job.

At the factory, production had fortunately picked up somewhat, mainly due to the appearance of the 2.2 litre engine and the fact that work put in over the past year or two to improve reliability was now paying off. The range of Lotus cars was, at last, again worthy of the name.

To speed up the sales of the Esprit, once the limited-edition Essex cars had been completed, the Turbo had been marketed at the much reduced price of £16,917, achieved partly by making some of the luxury equipment like air-conditioning an optional extra. Also the Esprit S3 model had now been introduced: this was an Esprit Turbo chassis and body with the 2.2 litre unsupercharged engine, selling for only £13,461. This was cheaper than the previous model by a large margin, even though it was a much better car. All this helped considerably towards a total production in 1982 of 541 cars – 96 more than in 1981. This was especially satisfactory considering that there was no American market whatsoever, the agreement with Rolls-Royce having already been severed.

It was also during this period that the Sunbeam-Lotus deal came to an end after a total of 2,298 cars had been made, its swansong being a victory in the 1981 World Rally Championship.

Chapter 21

Renault Power for the Turbo Era

Although Colin Chapman's 1982 GP contender, the Lotus 91, looked very similar to the 87 – which still had to be used for the first GP of the year in South Africa – it was a definite improvement. 'It was a much cleaner car,' explains Peter Wright, 'and it was lighter, too. Our biggest problem in that period, though, was that we were still suffering severely from the effort we had wasted on the 88. We had two years of lost time to make up and it was with the 91 that we began the process. When it was running properly the 91 was incredibly fast, but when it wasn't it was diabolical. What we lacked that year was the ability to make it run properly all the time.'

As had been the case with the 87, the 91 again used the tub which had originally been designed for the 88. The main drawback with the car was that although it was a very good chassis for use on the faster circuits – where, of course, it was hampered anyway by the lack of power from the non-turbocharged engine – it did not work so well over the more twisty courses, where the lack of power would not, if anything, have been such a disadvantage.

Nevertheless, the Lotus 91 did manage to win one Grand Prix in 1982, the Austrian at Zeltweg, where most of the turbo-engined cars blew up left, right and centre. Elio de Angelis led the non-turbocharged cars right from the end of the first lap, eventually taking over the lead on the 48th lap of a 53-lap race when Alain Prost's Renault retired with engine problems. However, he was then forced to slow down a little due to some fluctuation in fuel pressure, thus enabling Keke Rosberg in a non-turbocharged Williams to catch him up during the last lap. Rosberg made a tremendous bid to pass Elio just before they crossed the finishing line, but failed to do so by less than 1/125 sec! At last, after more than three years, Colin was again able to jump out on to the track to throw his cap in the air, as he had so often done in the past.

Elio told me about Colin's reactions to his win at Zeltweg: 'I think that at that moment I had the closest relationship with him that I have ever had with anyone in Formula 1 racing. I saw him almost crying, he was so happy, and I was happy, too. It was my first victory and for me a victory with Colin Chapman meant more than one with anybody else. I thought this was the beginning of a new era because after that win we talked together many times about various projects. He even used to phone me up at home, which he had never done before. When he died I was very shocked and saddened so much that I cried for almost an hour. It changed my whole outlook on motor racing.'

It was after the Zeltweg victory that Innes Ireland began to feel that perhaps the

Above *After a brilliant second place in Brazil in 1980, only his second time out in a Lotus, Elio de Angelis finally managed the great victory in Austria which did so much for Colin's morale after three previous seasons in the wilderness.*

Right *The last victory! Colin throws his cap high in the air for the last time in his life. Elio de Angelis had just beaten Keke Rosberg to the finishing line by only a few inches to win the Austrian GP at Zeltweg in August 1982.*

gulf which had existed between him and Colin since 1961 was finally bridged. I asked Innes to explain how this came about: 'Becoming friendly again with Colin was actually a very gradual process,' he said. 'In all the time that I had been writing Grand Prix reports for *Road and Track* magazine, and even earlier for *Autocar*, he never asked me out for a meal or to anything else of a social nature. When Elio won in Austria, it was the mechanics who included me in the celebrations. The first thing they said was, "Come up to the hotel and join us," and we had a terrific evening together. It was a very happy occasion and, with time being a big healer, I was once again able to talk to Colin, although we never recaptured the close relationship we had enjoyed in the late 'fifties. We had a lot of fun together then, and with me having an aeroplane as well we had plenty of common interests and much to talk about always.'

I asked Innes if he thought that Colin Chapman had changed much in his later years: 'I can't give you an honest answer to that,' he replied. 'I think that latterly he had a lot of problems, many of them probably of his own making. I think these were bothering him more and more, and obviously, having to live up to all the JPS money, or whoever's money it was at any particular time, the pressures were much greater than in the early days. After his enormous successes in 1978, things did not go right and he then had all the problems of the ingenious 88 two-chassis car which, incidentally, I never thought to be illegal. I think he became very disillusioned when this was finally chucked out. It was almost as though he said to himself, "Sod it. Who needs Grand Prix racing?" I think it really got him down and from then on I always had the impression that his heart was no longer totally in motor racing.'

The Austrian Grand Prix victory came at a very opportune moment, as Chapman had just reached agreement with Renault for them to supply Lotus with their V6 turbocharged engine for the following season. For some time Renault's racing manager, Gérard Larrousse had been keen to supply the French engine to a non-Renault F1 team. His reasoning was that the incredible reliability of the Cosworth engine was principally due to the fact that, because so many examples were in use, any potential weaknesses showed up quicker and could therefore be dealt with more promptly.

The offer was made on the evening after the second practice session for the French Grand Prix at Paul Ricard, when Gérard Larrousse summoned me to the Renault motorhome to organize a quiet rendezvous with Colin Chapman. This was tremendous news for Colin because he knew that John Player were going to be adamant that they could not continue their sponsorship in 1983 unless Lotus had a turbo engine. To begin with, the performance level of the Cosworth engine was now no longer sufficient to win the Championship, and also turbocharged engines were now the fashion anyway. Although Peter Warr had started talks with BMW they had made very little progress, so a deal with Renault was quickly struck and announced before practice started for the Swiss Grand Prix at the Dijon Prenois circuit at the end of August.

Gérard Larrousse explained to me why Renault-Sport had decided to supply their engines to Lotus. 'The plan we had originally set up was a simple one,' he told me. 'Renault-Sport was attempting to win the World Championship and we had

Above *Prince Michael of Kent – like his older brother the Duke of Kent – has always been a fast car enthusiast and a great supporter of Colin Chapman and Lotus. He is shown here during his visit to the stand at the 1982 Motor Show at the National Exhibition Centre, Birmingham, only two months before Colin's death.*

Below *Soon after the 1982 Motor Show Prince Michael thoroughly enjoyed a test drive in Nigel Mansell's Lotus 91 at Donington. Here he is being briefed by Peter Warr, Nigel and Colin.*

given ourselves three years in which to do so – 1981, 1982 and 1983. After that we planned to retire from racing and to allow private teams to run with our engines, and these would include Lotus and Ligier.

'Although we finally chose Lotus, we had made proposals to other teams. I remember taking our Chairman, Bernard Hanon, to see Williams. We made proposals to him but he turned us down. Earlier, we had almost made a deal with Tyrrell but he finally decided against going through with it.

'These talks were all part of that original plan. We felt that the British teams had excellent chassis so, as we were not too sure of ours, could we not get better results in a British chassis? The second stage of our thinking was that we needed a long-term policy, and this was the master plan of Bernard Hanon, who felt that we should first become World Champions and then afterwards take on the role of engine suppliers.

'At the time, Team Lotus were going through a very difficult and unsuccessful period, but their past reputation was sufficient to guarantee that an association with them could be a great help to Renault.

'Ligier was also asking us to supply engines for his cars, although up to the 1982 Monza race he would be tied up with Peugeot. After that, we knew he would soon be coming to us for his engines. As we wanted to sign up with two teams, not just one, we were in a hurry to conclude a deal with Lotus so as not to give Ligier the opportunity of claiming exclusive rights, which would have been against our policy. Our final meeting with Colin Chapman took place the day after the German Grand Prix at Hockenheim, in one of the suites at the Motordrom Hotel, and afterwards Colin drove me back to Frankfurt.

'Before signing the contract we also made a visit to Team Lotus and we were astonished to see the fantastic set-up at Ketteringham Hall, where the team worked in such elegant surroundings. It was the sort of place in which we would like to have operated.

'Soon after we had signed the contract, of course, Lotus won the Austrian Grand Prix with the old non-turbo Cosworth engine.'

Although Chapman was obviously looking forward to building a car with a turbocharged engine, he actually had something else up his sleeve, too. This was a concept known as 'active suspension,' which Peter Wright had been quietly developing at Ketteringham Hall. He subsequently explained to me, 'I suppose the full story goes back to 1977, when we first became involved with ground effect and when I joined Team Lotus on a full-time basis. One of the suggestions I made then was that we really needed some way of measuring the effect of changes being made by various suspension set-ups. Colin agreed that perhaps what we needed was a data system. In due course, he found a firm of consultant aeronautical engineers, based at Cranfield Aerodrome in Bedfordshire, and they built for us an aircraft type of data system which we ran on the 78. We built up a very good relationship with these people – especially when we were having our troubles with the T80 – and together we were analysing all the problems.

'It was some time in 1980 when they suddenly said, "What you need is an active suspension." What they had said was, of course, perfectly true if we were to handle ground effect properly. However, by the time they said that, we were already deeply involved with the 86 and 88 and, because it was so much simpler, we pursued the mechanical solution rather than the electronic one. Then, when the 88 twin chassis car was finally banned, we thought that, since the problems were still there, we might just as well introduce our 'Plan B', the active suspension.

'This then became a much more ambitious undertaking and yet, despite the high cost and consequent risk, much to our surprise, Colin said, unbelievably, "Let's do it." So we started by modifying a Turbo Esprit which we began working on in June 1981 and finally had it running by Christmas. There were plenty of problems but it looked good and we put Elio and Nigel in the test car at Snetterton for them to assess it, and they both came back saying that it had "definitely got something". Colin also drove it and, because the passenger had control over the system, I managed to make him spin it!'

Active suspension is one which has a 'brain'. 'When a skier hits a bump,' Peter explained, 'his legs react accordingly, but it is his brain which passes the order to his legs. Our box of electronics plays the part of the brain.'

In simple terms, the system consists of a small hydraulic suspension unit to each wheel, linked with an oil pressure system fed by a pump driven by the engine. This puts the engineer in complete command of the suspension behaviour. It is even

The Lotus 92, which appeared after Colin Chapman's death, consisted of the 91's carbon-fibre-Kevlar monocoque clad in new bodywork. It was fitted with the electronically actuated 'active-suspension', Colin's last technical breakthrough which he was never able to see in action though it will soon appear on road cars. It was during this car's first track outing that tests were interrupted by the arrival of Peter Warr with the shocking news that Colin had died from a heart attack early that morning. Picture shows Nigel Mansell in the 1983 Brazilian GP.

This photograph of Colin (one of the very last) with Fred Bushell, Andrew Ferguson and Nigel Mansell's Lotus 91 outside Ketteringham Hall was part of a special farewell gift to David Way, Head of Special Events Dept, at Players who had taken early retirement. Colin still kept his sense of fun.

possible to envisage a set-up where a car could be made to lean into a corner in much the same way as a motor cycle does!

'Eventually,' continued Peter Wright, 'after we had run the Esprit test car for about six months, we received the go-ahead to develop a Formula 1 version. When most of the money for the hardware required had been spent, in October 1982 ground effect and skirts were banned once and for all, and the new F1 regulations for 1983 demanded flat-bottomed cars. However, we decided that we should still continue with the project, as our experiences with the Esprit had been interesting and sufficiently encouraging for us to know that there would be openings for it in other fields. We first ran the Formula 1 active suspension car when Dave Scott drove it at Snetterton on 16 December 1982.

Sadly Colin Chapman was never to see the car running, but the active suspension is still being developed. Although very little is known about it, it is likely that the system will eventually appear, not only on future Lotus road cars, but also perhaps on those built by other manufacturers who will have contracted with Lotus to adopt it.

'These were very lean years,' recalled Fred Bushell, 'during which we plunged again. After American Express came in with their five-year loan, we had been able to advance despite the restrictions brought about by that particularly poor economic period, but by the autumn of 1982 we were operating at a very large trading loss. The figures for the period from August to December showed that we would have to pass the date when a repayment to American Expresss was due, causing us considerable embarrassment and putting us under 'intensive care' by our bankers. Unfortunately, the situation was made worse because American Express were themselves undergoing a dramatic change, with new UK management being appointed who had no personal relationships with us and no real inside knowledge of the situation. American Express now reviewed Lotus through eyes in New York, and relations became very strained simply because of a lack of appreciation of the problems. American Express were quite adamant that the loan repayment had to be made, so to give some temporary respite we arranged a private loan to reduce our indebtedness to them by a quarter-of-a-million pounds.

'When we were preparing a review of the business for 1980/81, although we believed that our decision to go up-market would eventually succeed, we came to the conclusion that we should not have abandoned entirely our traditional 'young executive' market, for which the Elan had been so suitable. Of course, it was the lack of demand for cars in kit form, due to the taxation changes, which really made us decide to vacate it, but now we felt that it was still the major market into which the Lotus image fitted. We decided, therefore, that we should try to market a car at a price which the young, under-30 executive could comfortably afford.

'We looked at all the engine possibilities, with the aim of working up a good relationship with a major manufacturer – as we had done years before with Ford – to supply engines and parts at the lowest basic price. We spoke to various manufacturers, including the Japanese company Toyota, one of the few with no existing connections

In 1982 Chapman succeeded in arranging a link with Toyota. It was agreed that the Japanese manufacturer would supply Lotus with engines and gearboxes for the next model line of cars, in order to attract a larger market with a lower selling price. Toyota's gearbox was also to be found on the Lotus Eclat which, in October 1982, became known as the Excel. In exchange, Lotus became consultants on roadholding and glassfibre techniques to the Japanese manufacturer. Their President Mr Toyoda is seen here (right) during a visit to Lotus.

with any other car manufacturer and who could therefore, in theory anyway, co-operate with us.

'Colin initiated the first approach and after many discussions a contract was concluded for the supply of various parts for an Elan replacement called the M90. Colin, Mike Kimberley and I flew to Tokyo to finalize the deal, which also included an arrangement whereby Lotus were to undertake some engine development work for Toyota in return. Eventually these various parts were made available to us and in the autumn of 1982 we introduced the first Lotus Excel, which was basically an Eclat using some Toyota parts, including the gearbox and rear axle. Our relationship with Toyota could not have been better but, as far as the M90 was concerned, we needed money to build it. We went to American Express again, but unsuccessfully, and although we tried several other sources, too, in truth the situation did not encourage new investors.

'We had two major financial problems. The loan from American Express had to be re-financed and, in addition, further funds had to be found to continue the development of the company. We were looking to produce a total volume of around 5,000 cars a year, as there was virtually no competition at the time and, on a hand-built basis, such a figure would simply not be practical. It was a very serious crisis and Colin knew well enough that it could even be terminal. Despite this, he did not seem to show the same concern as he had on previous occasions when the company had been having financial problems. It now seemed as though he had said to himself, "I have done all I can to keep this small car company in business, but now it doesn't really interest me any more and, in fact, if it does go down it could be a big relief"!

'We were still facing this situation when we flew to Paris together on 15 December 1982 to attend a FISA meeting. Afterwards we were due to meet Jerry Juhan, our International liaison officer, but he was held up by bad weather and did not turn up until about 8 pm. I suggested we should stay the night in Paris but Colin did not want to, so after a brief discussion with Juhan it was almost 9 pm before we left Paris. When we arrived at the airport, our pilot said that we would not be able to go direct to Hethel as it was too late, and instead we would first have to land at Stansted in order to clear Customs. Colin became very excited and annoyed over this and, once we were airborne, he ordered the pilot to fly direct to Hethel, saying, "It is diabolical in these conditions to do that. Two landings means twice as much risk." And with that he promptly fell asleep!

'Much to my surprise, I soon found that we were going to fly direct to Hethel after all, as the pilot had managed to talk his way into it with Air Traffic Control. Conditions over the English Channel were very turbulent, but once over the coast the weather did improve. Colin then woke up and appeared to be much more relaxed. With conditions in the Hethel area fairly blustery, Colin went up to the front to act as co-pilot. With quite a strong crosswind blowing the landing was somewhat rough but, having landed safely, Colin made no further comment about our having gone directly to Hethel. As always, he was charming to the Customs man who had turned out specially to clear us, and around midnight we went our separate ways.

'It was at about 5 am that Hazel Chapman phoned me to say that Colin had suffered a massive heart attack.'

Chapter 22

'In Adversity We Thrive'

In the course of their 25 years of Grand Prix racing, Colin Chapman's Formula 1 cars achieved 72 victories, 88 pole positions and 63 fastest laps, winning for him seven World Championship for Constructors' Cups and six World Championship for Drivers' titles. This is a unique record which, in recent years, can only be compared with Ferrari's.

Apart from this, he will best be remembered as the man who introduced all the major design features which have given the modern Grand Prix car its present shape. They were so effective that his rivals had to copy them in order to remain competitive. It was he who, in the 'fifties, introduced to motor racing fully adjustable suspension systems, and the chassis tuning which went with them. In the early 'sixties it was Colin Chapman who pioneered the monocoque chassis and then, in the late 'sixties, he was the first to apply wings on a Formula 1 car. Then, in the early 'seventies, he led the way towards the idea of putting most of the car's weight on to the rear wheels and, finally, in the late 'seventies, it was he who introduced ground effect to motor racing.

Not all his innovations were entirely successful – for instance, his Grand Prix turbine car. But from his fertile brain came other significant developments such as the first sports car to be made entirely with glass-reinforced plastic; his patented VARI (Vacuum Assisted Resin Injection) system; and the 'active suspension' system on which he was working at the time of his death.

Many of these developments fed back to the whole motor industry and therefore they have – or will have – an effect upon our everyday life. Indeed, it is quite amazing that he was able to come up with these discoveries time and time again, in many different spheres. All too often, most engineers have to be satisfied with just a single major discovery throughout their careers.

His sphere of activity encompassed several different fields; he was a brilliant chassis designer and yet shone just as brightly in the science of aerodynamics. He became one of the world's leading authorities on composite technology. The one aspect which held less interest for him was the engine, but despite this he still had sufficient knowledge to define the parameters for the Lotus engine. Apart from fulfilling the requirement of propelling cars from his own company, this also succeeded in helping Sunbeam to win the highly prestigious World Rally Championship in 1981.

I suppose he really treated the engine as something of an accessory to his motor

Colin was never particularly keen on vintage cars, but he nevertheless enjoyed driving the author's H6C Hispano round the Hethel test track.

cars, in complete contrast to his great rival, Enzo Ferrari, who has always been an 'engine man' at heart – perhaps typical of the Italian school. One shudders to think what might have happened had Colin, instead of creating his own cars, become the chassis engineer at Ferrari. With his chassis and Enzo Ferrari's engines the cars might have been so superior that they could possibly have destroyed motor racing!

Perhaps one of the reasons why Colin Chapman was less interested in engine design was because, particularly at the beginning of his career, he was not able to afford the investment necessary to fund the manufacture of an engine to his own design. For his racing engines he had to rely first on Coventry Climax and later on Cosworth Engineering. Indeed, during the period in which Colin was involved in Grand Prix racing, these two British engine manufacturers were the mainstay of the sport, which but for their involvement would have been limited to only one or two heavily financed teams from the large wealthy companies. (Latterly, of course, Renault were to provide turbocharged engines for the Lotus Grand Prix cars.) From this situation came the tremendous improvements to chassis and aerodynamic design because, with so many cars having more or less equal engine power, it was essential to find other ways of gaining superiority. Such circumstances especially appealed to Chapman because, while any engine was very much a long-term project, a new chassis could be designed and built much more quickly. This suited Colin's distinct lack of patience because whenever he had a new idea or a changed design on his mind, he just had to put it into practice immediately simply to find out if he was right or wrong!

Unfortunately, this side of his temperament often prompted him to give up the development of a particular concept too early, because he had already become engrossed in further new ideas. We had a clear demonstration of Colin leading himself up the garden path with the Lotus 80, while all his competitors were scoring off him with further improvements to what were basically copies of the earlier Lotus 79, on which he had given up too soon.

Of course, there are people who say that Colin Chapman did not invent a thing, and it is true that a Voisin racing car with a monocoque chassis – a wooden affair covered in light alloy – took part in the Grand Prix of Tours back in 1923. Although it is almost certain that at the time Colin designed the first Lotus monocoque chassis he had probably never heard of the Voisin, it is almost equally certain that he must have seen a BRM monocoque GP car which had been built seven years before the Lotus 25 first appeared. Neither could he have overlooked a '750 Formula special' which had been built by one enthusiast, Maurice Phillippe, later destined to become his Chief Designer. The point is that not one of these early monocoque cars proved successful because they were conceived at a time when the current technology was not yet ready for them. Chapman, however, came up with his monocoque because, at the time, the aircraft industry had just produced fuel tanks in the form of flexible bags, and he had the foresight to realize that such tanks would enable a successful monocoque racing car chassis to be built.

The 'wing car' also dates back to before the Second World War. On one occasion I remember showing Colin a photocopy of such a design dating back to the 'thirties and which had actually originated from, of all places, Algeria! The fact is that the person who thought this up was never able to have it built and, even if he had found someone capable, it would then have been far in advance of the tyre technology necessary to make it a practicality. This is not to say that Chapman did not himself sometimes introduce features which were too far advanced for the available

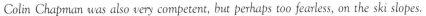

Colin Chapman was also very competent, but perhaps too fearless, on the ski slopes.

technology. For example, his first GT car, the Elite, built entirely in glass-reinforced plastic, suffered all manner of problems so that, when Lotus introduced their next car, it was built with a somewhat more conventional backbone chassis. Since then the industry has made such valuable progress in the use of composite materials (partly due, without doubt, to Colin Chapman's pioneering work with his carbon-fibre/Kevlar Formula 1 car) that Lotus are now planning their next super-car, the Etna, with an all-composite shell incorporating the same material.

During the course of Chapman's career as a car manufacturer, Lotus produced nearly 34,000 cars, which gave immense pleasure to their owners. Many of these cars are now highly sought-after collectors' 'classics', and yet both Hazel Chapman and Fred Bushell insist that the only reason Colin ever became a manufacturer was because he believed this to be the best way to make enough money to go motor racing – with him as the driver!

There is no doubt at all that his real passion was motor racing. However, until recent years it was never really a very lucrative activity, except perhaps for those relatively few drivers right at the top. Despite the injection of large amounts of sponsors' money, Team Lotus has never been a profitable company. Colin Chapman was always perfectly aware of his many achievements and considered these to be sufficient to justify his lifestyle, but for this he really had to depend upon the car company. Being assured of a living from this enabled him to devote a great deal of time and effort to the racing team.

One of the reasons for Team Lotus's lack of financial success was that most of

Left *Despite his enormous work load and the tight time schedules to which he had to keep, Colin was still very much a family man and he was often accompanied at race meetings by Hazel and daughters Sarah (standing) and Jane (sitting in the cockpit). Later, son Clive went along too.*

Right *Colin Chapman received the CBE from the Queen in 1970. Having left the family camera in their hotel, Colin had to rush back to retrieve it before this snapshot could be taken of him standing by the Victoria Memorial outside Buckingham Palace.*

Colin's numerous innovations cost small fortunes. The fact that the team's owner was also their Chief Engineer was both a great advantage and a severe handicap. It was an advantage because his talents made him for many years the best motor racing engineer, and yet it was a handicap because when he believed in something he just went ahead and did it. In most of the other teams, when their Chief Engineers thought they had found something of benefit, they first had to 'sell' their ideas to their team boss whose first question was surely, 'OK, but how much will it cost?' In Colin's case, if he had convinced himself that there was one particular way to go, then his attitude was such that the money would just have to be found. This lack of critical appraisal proved his downfall on some occasions, and it explains some of the ups and downs of Team Lotus when they became stuck up blind alleys, notably with the four-wheel drive Lotus 63 and, of course, the turbine car.

What were the qualities which enabled Colin Chapman to reach such heights? Basically, he was endowed with a tremendously clear and analytical mind, which enabled him to solve almost any problem simply by going back to first principles. 'In solving a problem,' says Hazel Chapman, 'he always came up with a way of doing so that no-one else had ever thought of; he always tackled it from a completely fresh angle. I remember him once telling me that when he was at school he was rarely very attentive, so the master often picked on him, saying, "Come on now, Chapman, you tell me how to solve this problem." Colin would promptly do so, but in a completely different way from that which the master had been explaining on the blackboard, just using pure logic. He would do anything like that. When he first evolved the new boat

Above In 1970 Colin Chapman was voted The Guardian 'Young Businessman of the Year'. Here he is receiving the trophy from Harold Wilson, Prime Minister until June of that year.

Below The JCL Marine company's boatyard at Brundall in Norfolk was overgrown and virtually derelict when Colin Chapman took it over. This was the way it looked after his extensive programme of renovation and refurbishment.

Chapman never fully appreciated the cult which he had created with the Seven, and many times he wanted to replace it with something more modern. This sketch is of one such project, produced at the time when dune buggies were very fashionable, but it was never completed and Mike Warner, who was running Lotus Racing Ltd, instead produced the Series IV Seven.

hull-moulding process, he could not see how he was going to be able to extract the hull from the mould. So he just went and sat out in the garden for hours, with his drawing pad, trying to work out a way. Of course, he finally found a solution.'

'It was fantastic how he could reduce a problem to the bare essentials,' recalls Tony Rudd.

Another attribute was his ever-present hunger for reading matter, as evidenced by his visits to shops to read all the magazines devoted to matters which interested him. Tony Rudd says that whenever he went to the United States he was always reminded by Colin to bring back any magazines he found about cars, boats, aircraft and any form of modern technology.

I once flew with him from New York to Watkins Glen, during which I mentioned some problems I was having in getting my own cabin cruiser 'up on the plane' because the engines were not sufficiently powerful. Immediately he called my attention to an article on this very subject which had been published some time earlier in the British monthly magazine *Motor Boat and Yachting*. To make sure I had understood just what he was getting at, in the garage the next day he drew out on a scrap of paper a design for a suitable wedge to be screwed to the bottom of my boat!

Colin was also very good at picking other people's brains. One day when Tony Rudd was away in Los Angeles on Lotus business, Colin phoned to ask him to pay a visit to a man living several hundred miles away. 'What shall I ask him?' said Tony. 'Never mind that,' replied Chapman, 'just find out what he is up to!' So off went Tony

Her Royal Highness the Princess Anne with Colin Chapman and Dennis Austin on the Lotus stand at the Motor Show.

Rudd, only to find out that this fellow had designed a car to which wings could be attached, thus turning it into an aeroplane! During their conversation it transpired that the 'body/fuselage' was made using papier mâché. So Tony extracted as much detail out of the man as he could and this was duly passed over to Colin. Sure enough, a few years later came the Lotus 88 with its carbon-fibre tub in which the core was paper honeycomb . . .

Colin was also endowed with an almost unbelievably good memory. He possessed what might be called a 'mental filing system', to which he could refer at any time, in much the same way as one does with today's computers. And during the course of talking with many people prior to writing this book, I found that every single one of them mentioned that one of his main qualities was his ability to motivate people. As one old friend put it, 'To make people climb a mountain when they thought they could not climb a molehill'.

'His skill at manipulating people was on a level with his engineering ability,' said Mike Kimberley. 'He was very aware of human psychology and what was needed to motivate each individual, because he was so very sensitive to human nature.'

Colin Chapman became a household name in the automobile industry, and to a large section of the general public, even those with only a fringe interest in motoring

With His Royal Highness Pince Philip, Duke of Edinburgh at the British Grand Prix in 1976.. and with His Royal Highness the Duke of Kent at Hethel.

sport. He certainly never anticipated this when he took his degree at London University, because when the time came for him to choose between civil engineering or mechanical engineering – a more suitable course for a career in the motor industry – he chose the former. The prosaic answer to that came from Hazel: 'He told me he chose civil engineering as he thought it would be easier'!

There were two significant occurrences which drew Colin towards a career with sports and racing cars. The first was that Aldershot car trial which he enjoyed so much and which gave him the desire to join in, scrap the 'special' he was in the process of converting and build a pure trials car. The second event was the speed trial and race at Silverstone in 1950 in which he did so well, despite using a very unsuitable car, mainly because of his great skill as a driver. This gave him the taste for more and drove him to build a pure circuit racing machine as his next venture. Success breeds success and soon he became involved in building more and more elaborate sports and racing cars.

Even so, the fact is that motoring and motor cars were not then paramount in his mind because he was really more interested in flying. Perhaps, had the economic position in Britain been somewhat better than it was at the time, he might well have made his career in the aircraft industry. Indeed, he used to tell Hazel that the period in

Left *A relaxed Colin Chapman climbing aboard his twin Comanche.*

Below *Colin Chapman's first Piper Navajo.*

Below right *Colin's haven in Ibiza. It was in this villa that he would prepare plans of action, and especially the famous document which led to the harnessing of ground effect.*

which he would have preferred to live was during the pioneering days of flying. He always had a longing to take to the air, and as soon as he could afford it he bought himself an aeroplane.

This first machine was a humble Miles Messenger which he acquired in October 1960 in partnership with another great flying enthusiast, Mike Costin, when they were working together in the early days of Lotus. As soon as he could afford a more modern plane he bought his first Piper Comanche, and from then on he almost always commuted to European race circuits in his own plane. He was an extremely good pilot and during the course of his life he logged several thousand hours in at least a dozen different aircraft. He eventually also acquired a helicopter, which of course he also learnt to fly himself. However busy he was, he always found time to take his pilot's instrument rating exam each year, as this was necessary to enable him to fly at night. This usually coincided with the family's summer holiday in Ibiza, where he could often be seen sunbathing with the large pilot's manual by his side!

I flew with him on many occasions and I always found it very comforting to watch him navigate with great precision and handle his aircraft with such a high level of skill.

He was also a very determined pilot and, on occasions, perhaps a trifle more than was prudent. Indeed, I can recall one such incident in 1980, when I came over to England for the British Grand Prix with David Thieme and François Mazet and we all stayed with Colin and Hazel at East Carleton Manor. On the morning of the first practice day we took off from Hethel in somewhat misty conditions, but by the time we arrived over Silverstone visibility was almost down to zero and nobody had yet

been able to land. Nevertheless, Colin decided he would attempt a landing, but as we glided down towards the runway we suddenly caught a brief glimpse of a large round balloon rushing past the plane's windows. It was the Essex advertising balloon tethered no more than a few feet above our own Team Lotus motorhome in the Silverstone paddock! Colin got the message then, so we circled and waited for the mist to lift.

Colin employed several company pilots, who looked after the aircraft, flew members of the company around on business and, of course, who did much of the flying when he was either too tired or too busy. The first of these was Mike Hamlin who stayed with Colin Chapman almost three years, longer than any of those who followed, and he can remember many instances of Colin's determination. 'On one occasion, along with Tony Rudd, Colin wanted to visit an important sponsor who at the time was holidaying in Italy,' recalls Mike. 'I had never heard of this place before and on looking it up in my pilot's flight guide, I saw that landing at the local airfield was not allowed as it was an Italian military establishment. I explained this to Colin but he was characteristically unsympathetic, saying, "I don't give a damn how you arrange it but we are going there. Consider it to be an initiative test!" Being a conscientious and law-abiding pilot, this demand caused me a major problem; how could I break the law legally?

'Eventually I decided I would drain some oil from the right-hand engine and I then poured this all over the crankcase. I filed a flight plan to an airfield ahead of the military aerodrome, and the following day we took off, ostensibly to fly there. By the time we were close to the military airfield, as intended, a large oil streak had appeared, creeping along the casing of the right-hand engine, having been sucked out through one of the ventilation slots. I then called up the airfield on the RT [radio telephone] and declared an emergency, and after several attempts we finally got a somewhat guarded answer in broken English. I explained we had a problem with an engine and would like to make an emergency landing. The controller replied, "Please wait a minute," and then, after a further short delay, gave us permission to land.

'Having landed safely we taxied over to what appeared to be the "terminal building" but which, in fact, was a small Nissen hut. I stopped the engines and soon a little man dressed in dirty shorts and a khaki vest emerged to shake hands with all three of us. He was the controller! Having then told him we needed a taxi, he rushed back into the hut, only to reappear wearing a beaten-up old cap, saying, "I am the taxi!" So we all piled into his delapidated car and he drove us into the local town. Here we failed to find the sponsor we had been hoping to see, so we decided that some lunch was necessary. Eventually, our taxi pulled up in front of a ramshackle restaurant run by a huge fat woman with a large moustache, and who the taxi driver introduced as his sister-in-law. At first she wasn't at all keen on serving us but eventually our friend persuaded her to prepare something and she later appeared with three platefuls of spaghetti. At this point Colin sat back in his chair and said, "Well Mike, what sort of mess have you got us into now?!"

'Colin was an extremely competent pilot, although he did tend to fly the plane rather as if he was in a Formula 1 car; relying on his enormous amount of skill to get him out of any difficult situations.

MIKE'S MUG

Many members of the Royal Aero Club have a close association with a rather different sort of club in Brick Street, the Steering Wheel. Devoted, as its name implies, to the sport of motor racing, many people in the aviation world whose inclinations lead them to follow that sport, have become members. (It is strategically situated halfway between 119 Piccadilly and Londonderry House.) The opening last Easter of the aerodrome at Goodwood has strengthened the bond between sporting flying and sporting motoring.

In order to promote that bond still further, the Steering Wheel have presented to the Royal Aero Club, for use as a trophy, a handsome pint tankard, known as " Mike's Mug ", which was to have been given to Mike Hawthorn, when his tragic death intervened. Mike used his Vega Gull frequently in the course of his business and the Aviation Committee has decided that the trophy shall be awarded annually " to the pilot considered to have demonstrated most convincingly by his flying the utility of light aircraft for business and executive as well as private purposes ".

This trophy will, besides being a memorial to a well-known member of the Club, enable recognition to be made of the sterling work of the many pilots who cannot, for one reason or another, compete for the popular cups and trophies of the National Air Races.

Mike's Mug. This comparatively new trophy, presented by the Steering Wheel Club to the Royal Aero Club as a memorial to Mike Hawthorn, is awarded to the pilot best demonstrating during the year the use of a private aircraft for business purposes. It has been won in 1961 by Colin Chapman, Managing Director of Lotus Cars Ltd., who has attended eighteen major motor racing events in Europe, and transacted much other business with an executive aeroplane in the course of over 200 hours' flying.

Colin Chapman was the first to be awarded 'Mike's Mug', presented annually by the Royal Aero Club from 1961 for special achievements by private pilots. These extracts from the Club's journal, the RAeC Gazette, tell the story behind the trophy. Subsequent winners of 'Mike's Mug' were, in 1962, Cyril Audrey (the RAC timekeeper who accompanied the Lotus team to Indianapolis in 1966), Jack Brabham in 1963, ex-Lotus driver Innes Ireland in 1964, when it seemed that show business personalities then took over from motor racing people. The 1965 winner was Jimmy Edwards, and Stan Stennett took it in 1966, after which either records were no longer kept, or the tankard disappeared!

'For instance, when you start up a ten-litre six-cylinder turbocharged aero engine on a winter's day, it is stone cold. The manufacturer's manual always states that the engine should be allowed to run for a couple of minutes before the pilot starts the take-off – no great penalty – in order to allow it to warm up and to get the oil circulating freely. With Colin, though, he would wind-up the engines and be airborne in twenty seconds! This would shorten engine life dramatically and we often suffered from engine problems, almost always due to beating the hell out of them when they were still cold.

'He always thought it was a tremendous challenge to land over the glow of the approach lights with practically zero-zero visibility. In his early flying days, when he had his single-engined Piper Comanche, he once took off from Elstree when he had not properly checked his fuel. He thought he had enough, but when he was half-way to his destination the engine stopped and he found the fuel gauge was registering empty – and there was thick fog below! So he just spiralled gently down into the fog, and as he caught sight of the ground he realized there was a length of concrete ahead, at which he quickly aimed the plane. As he came in to land, he noticed several dark shapes looming out of the fog, but as he was in the country he just took these to be haystacks and, at one stage, even considered using one to slow down the plane if things got really tricky. Having landed he saw a light in the distance and he walked over to what turned out to be a farmhouse. He shocked the occupants by announcing, "I have just landed on the airfield," and wondered why they refused to believe him!

'Anyway, the following morning when he came back to collect the plane, he found there was no way that he could fly it out because contractors had been digging up the runway. The 'haystacks' he had seen in the fog were actually piles of concrete debris, and the piece of runway on which he had landed was much too short for a take-off. Eventually, the mounds of rubble had to be bulldozed out of the way in order to give him sufficient clear runway to fly the plane out!

'After I had been with Colin for about six months, I remember flying with him to the Geneva Motor Show. I think it was the first time the Giugiaro mock-up of the Esprit was shown, and it received rave reviews from the press. Colin was very happy when we returned, and as we walked out across the airfield to our plane he slapped me on the shoulder, exclaiming, "Well, Mike, I must say it has taken me six months to turn you into a pilot." I just smiled back at him and replied, "Yes, Colin, and it has taken me six months to turn you into a passenger!"

'He was a hundred per cent totally endearing, sometimes quite charming and could be a very rewarding person to be with. This was mainly when he was away from the constant pressure of car manufacturing in the 'seventies. Often these pressures were enormous, and quite obviously he would then become more short-tempered than he was normally. Once he was away from these pressures he was very good fun to be with and he had a tremendous sense of humour.

'Part of the joy of having a company aircraft was that when you went to a Grand Prix you could usually get away quite quickly afterwards and be back home in time to see the edited highlights on television. One of the more interesting places is the Zeltweg circuit in Austria, where the landing strip is only about a mile-and-a-half from the track. This was in 1973 when helicopters were not so prolific as they are nowadays, and that mile-and-a-half to the circuit was rather difficult to negotiate. We therefore decided that it would be worth parking our two hired cars close to the main entrance, ready for a quick getaway. When the race ended we all climbed on to motor bikes and rode through the crowd to the main gate, where we were soon into our cars.

'However, the roads were by then jammed solid so, at Colin's instigation, we turned off the road into a cornfield – fortunately it had just been cut and so was really just stubble. We then worked our way via a very circuitous route to the airfield perimeter, only to find that there was an anti-tank ditch which had been dug all the way round the airfield. We screeched to a halt to see our airplane parked half-a-mile away on the other side of the airfield. Colin was hell-bent on taking the cars back fifty

Fast cars and planes were the joys of Colin's life. Here he proudly shows off the beautiful Giugiaro-designed Lotus Esprit on the airfield apron at Hethel, together with his new Cessna Chancellor. Note the plane's very appropriate registration letters.

yards to get a good run in an effort to leap the ditch! We almost had to physically restrain him from having a go at it, and he became quite upset at not being allowed to show his driving prowess.

'Meanwhile, of course, the cars had received the odd minor modification during their passage through hedges and down cart tracks, so we decided the best thing to do would be to leave them where they were, at the edge of the ditch, and walk across the airfield to our plane. As we were getting our luggage out of the cars we all had a laugh at the stickers displayed on the rear windows: "Avis – we collect from anywhere"! The Austrian Army attempted to arrest us, but we managed to get away in twenty minutes or so. It then fell to Peter Warr to explain to Avis three days later, when they telexed to ask where the cars were, that they weren't left at our hotel, nor were they at the track or even at the airfield, and the best he could do was to give them the approximate map reference!

'One day at Monza I went to meet Colin at the airport, where he had arrived on a regular scheduled flight. I was driving the car and when we reached a crossroads where I knew we should turn right, he called out, "Turn left here." "I'm sure we should turn right Colin," I replied. "I've been coming to Monza for twenty years and yet you are trying to teach me the way," he said, so we went left. In the end, it turned out that he was wrong and we were very late arriving at the hotel. When he was asked the reason, his immediate answer was, "Trust these pilots, they can't even navigate!"'

After some three years, Mike Hamlin got married and left Lotus. 'Basically my disagreement with Colin when I left arose only because he was not paying me,' he explained. 'The company was very short of money and, as I was self-employed, he would not sign off any of my salary payments. This went on for two months, and it was that which really killed it for me. Colin would go through these strange moods and his philosophy then was obviously, "During the times we don't need to fly, we don't need to pay the pilot." In the end I said, "Unless I get paid within 48 hours, I am finished." I wasn't paid, so I left.

'He then decided to take the most economical course, and he hired a young lad who had just qualified. He was jolly good at flying from Southampton to Basingstoke or Portsmouth, but Colin put him into a plane he had never flown before and told him to go to Spain. As always, the aircraft was heavily loaded. He read up the aircraft's flight manual the night before, and on take-off duly rotated at what should have been the right speed. Of course, nothing much happened; the nose came up but it just stayed there because he was still on the wrong side of the drag coefficient. He should have added a good ten knots to this take-off speed because of the extra weight. As it was, at the end of the runway, he ploughed straight into the top of the trees. It was lucky nobody was hurt.

'Then Colin took on another chap who wasn't even a professional pilot; he was a flying instructor with no professional licence and not even an instrument rating. This guy was so thrilled at doing a professional job without the qualification that he obviously became over-excited in the aeroplane and did things with it for which it had not been designed. One day he took up the Piper Navajo and was doing aerobatics in it when it broke up in mid air. He was killed instantly.'

Chapman's first professional pilot had been aircraft dealer Brian Kaye, who still flies to Grand Prix races regularly and who knew Colin for many years before he ever flew for him professionally. 'I sold Colin his first proper aircraft, a Piper Comanche,' he told me, 'and many other planes that followed. At first I went as his pilot, but I soon found that I just did not have the time and that was when he took on his first company pilot.

'Colin was a pilot of exceptional ability. I remember one day I was flying a helicopter to Brands Hatch. The weather was atrocious and to get there I had to follow the motorway by flying over the bridges. When I approached Brands I noticed this big shadow and then I realized that it was Colin about to land his twin Comanche and I thought, "That's quite a pilot!"'

For many years Colin remained very keen to build aircraft, but Hazel Chapman would have none of it. 'Cars are complicated enough,' she would say. But finally Colin did take the plunge by jumping on the back of the microlight boom and designing his own machine, or rather commissioning a design from Bert Rutan, the great Californian specialist, to whom he brought his knowledge of the technology of composite construction.

I saw Colin only a week or so before his untimely death. After a long interview about the new 'flat-bottomed' F1 car regulations, which had just been introduced by FISA with only three months' notice, he quickly cheered up after pulling out from behind his desk a small aluminium carrying case, in which was a scale model of his

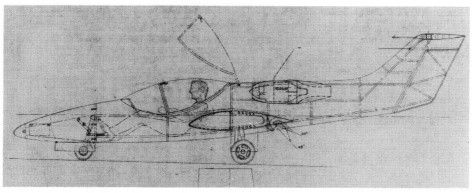

Long before he asked Bert Rutan in the United States to design a microlight, Colin had thought about building his own plane. He commissioned the design of this small twin jet – very much the type of aircraft he would have wanted to own himself! – but nothing ever came of it.

new microlight aeroplane. 'I intend to revolutionize private transport,' he said, 'by introducing a plane which will be capable of carrying two people at one hundred miles an hour, using only one gallon of fuel in an hour. This will be the cheapest way to travel.'

Once again he was endeavouring to turn existing regulations to his own advantage. To qualify and be certified as a microlight, an aircraft must have a very low wing loading. The advantage of a plane being certified as a microlight is that it dispenses with the highly expensive certification costs of more conventional aircraft, which tend to double, or even treble, their initial pure production cost. So to reach this low wing loading, and yet still have a fast and comfortable machine, he required an extremely light one, and this is where his carbon-fibre materials came to the rescue. It is a great pity that this microlight only flew after Colin's death. The project was then sold to the American firm Eippert, which subsequently stopped trading, but Lotus still work on the special engine which Colin had asked Tony Rudd to design and produce for it.

Having years earlier given up the idea of building aeroplanes, Chapman, as we have already heard, did go into boat building. 'His idea was to start a retirement business,' says Hazel, 'and also I think what used to worry him, and keep him awake when he was having difficulty in switching off, was what he was going to be able to leave behind for our son Clive. He felt terribly guilty that there was this great big factory up the road that he really did not want to leave to anyone, least of all Clive.' Clive Chapman was certainly much encouraged by Colin to take up boat racing, and he designed Clive's first boat. One day, after a rather disappointing outing, Colin took a saw, chopped a foot or so off the stern of the boat, glued back the transom, and Clive won the very next event!

Colin Chapman was an extremely competent racing driver himself and, even after he had stopped racing his own cars, he was often approached by other people wanting him to drive theirs. One memorable instance was his handling of a 3.8 litre Mk II

Above and below *Colin never saw his microlight flying either. Its design had been commissioned from Bert Rutan, the well-known American specialist in light aircraft of the 'canard' configuration, who was provided with Lotus's expertise in composite materials. It was thus made possible for this 'Chapman Microlight' to be built in the form of a proper aeroplane, albeit light enough to be classified as a microlight, so dispensing with the tremendous costs of certification. 'I am going to revolutionize individual transportation,' Colin would say. The microlight was flown for the first time in England in the Summer of 1983, from the Hethel landing strip.*

Jaguar saloon in a race at Silverstone, which many enthusiasts of the period will never forget. When I questioned Hazel as to why he had retired from race driving, it came to the surface that, in fact, he had never actually retired, and no announcement to that effect had ever been made! The pressure of business meant he was able to devote less and less time to it and, in the end, he just simply stopped racing. One thing is certain and that is nobody, least of all Hazel, asked him to stop; this was the type of decision he could only make for himself.

On the road he was what might be called a forceful driver. Walter Hayes, in a very perceptive and moving tribute he made at Colin Chapman's memorial service in Norwich cathedral, tactfully and humorously said, 'He wasn't dangerous, he was always in a hurry!'

Knowing so well the problems which a racing driver faced enabled Colin to design better cars, and it also helped him to understand more fully the psychology of the racing driver. Of the drivers he employed, Hazel recalls, 'He was envious of the life they led, which he thought was carefree, while all he had was the worries of running the business.' The relationship he had with Jimmy Clark was, of course, an ideal one. They were perfectly matched and although Jimmy was no technician, and did not necessarily know what might have to be done to a car to improve it, he was such a sensitive driver that he could describe its behaviour to Colin with such accuracy that he was able to sort out the problems promptly.

Of course, he revelled in that situation because, in motor racing, it was the 'tuning' of a car which he enjoyed the most. One thing he could not bear was a driver

Colin was always prepared to have a go at driving any fast machine. Here he is about to take a practice run in the late Tom Percival's F1 powerboat.

Above During the touring car race curtain-raiser at the 1960 British Grand Prix meeting Colin Chapman (right) and Jack Sears circulated the Silverstone circuit like this for lap after lap, almost literally banging the door handles of their 3.8 litre Mk 2 Jaguar saloons. Colin was driving a car provided by John Coombs who, fortunately, was a Jaguar dealer.

Left Walter Hayes (above) was the Editor of the now defunct Sunday Dispatch when he first met Colin. Later they met again when Hayes was promoted to head Ford's PR department. The link between Lotus and Ford then went from strength to strength with the Lotus-Cortina deal and the use of a Ford cylinder block and gearbox in the Elan. Finally, Hayes, who had been steadily climbing through the Ford hierarchy, managed to persuade them to support Keith Duckworth to the tune of £100,000 in building the phenomenally successful DFV Formula 1 engine (destined to win 155 GPs) of which Lotus enjoyed exclusive use in 1967.

instructing his mechanic on what was to be done without any reference to him. 'One day at Oulton Park,' chief mechanic Bob Dance recalls, 'Graham Hill came into the pits and asked his mechanic, Bob Sparshott, to cut off the bump stop bobbins which, of course, he did. The "Old Man" overheard this and forthwith blew his top. "This is MY car," he said, "I am the designer, you ask ME." Afterwards he called Graham and me into the transporter to make his point more clearly. You had to do things HIS way.'

Jimmy Clark's death was a dreadful blow to Colin and ended what was probably the happiest period in his life. From then on he never got along so well with his drivers because, all the time, he was looking for the same relationship he had enjoyed with Jimmy. Of course, that was impossible, because there could only ever be one Jim Clark.

Certainly Colin never got over the loss of Jimmy and I was further reminded of this only recently. As I was finishing this book I received a most moving letter, through Club Team Lotus, from a Jimmy Clark fan, David Griffiths, who recalled the time when he had once approached Colin: '. . . I had decided to get Mr Chapman to sign my autograph book and I took my opportunity at the GP meeting at Silverstone in 1979. I did not pick the best of times as the F1 Lotus was much troubled in practice and "Mr Lotus" was in a bit of an angry mood. However, I went up to him and asked him if he would sign for me. As he took the book, somewhat annoyed no doubt by being bothered by me, he went very quiet when he saw Jim's photo. He looked at it for quite a few seconds, looked up at me with what I can only describe as "moist eyes", signed the book, and handed it back without a single word . . . seeing the photo just made him seem to forget his immediate troubles for that one magical moment.'

Obviously Colin also enjoyed a good rapport with other drivers and Hazel recalls, 'He enjoyed having Emerson Fittipaldi in the team; he was also very keen on Gunnar Nilsson, who suffered such an untimely death, and he became very close to Mario Andretti, too, probably closer to him than any other driver except Jimmy. When Mario came to drive for Team Lotus Colin had known and appreciated his qualities for a long time for, apart from his tremendous guts and enthusiasm, Mario was pretty good at tuning a chassis, too. But even with Mario – who stayed five years with the team – there was still something of a generation gap.

Andrew Ferguson well remembers an occasion when Colin, returning from the circuit after the French Grand Prix in 1978, found Mario and Ronnie Peterson – who had just finished first and second – polishing off a bottle of champagne in the lobby of the Hotel Ile Rousse. He was most upset at not having been invited to share the bottle with them, and went berserk the next morning when he found that they had charged it up to his room account!

It was also a sobering thought to Colin that Elio de Angelis, whom he came to like enormously, was almost thirty years years younger than him. Perhaps it was these thoughts and feelings which made motor racing less enjoyable for him in his later years. Tucked in his motorhome, away from the chit-chat, tied up with briefing and de-briefing sessions, business appointments with sponsors, or engaged in FOCA politics, he was no longer able to enjoy the day-to-day social life which goes with Grand Prix racing. No longer was he 'one of the boys'. In fact, he was becoming so out

of touch with the everyday life of the sport that he actually employed 'informers' to keep him up to date with what was going on behind the scenes.

His mechanics respected him enormously. As Bob Dance again recalls, 'He was a bit awe-inspiring really and we all used to take notice of him. When he was coming into the workshop, everybody sprang to attention and jumped around much faster. But if you had some drama with a car, he was right in there with you, helping out and telling you what would have to be done. We knew he was never ever really beaten by a problem; he always had something up his sleeve. It was exciting work; we never knew what would happen next because he was always scheming and thinking up ways of improving his cars. When I joined Lotus everybody was afraid of the "Old Man". Tea breaks were not allowed and if he saw a sandwich or a drink flask lying around, then there would be a big drama. There would then be a report, "Watch it, the 'Old Man's' coming down!" No one was allowed to smoke, of course. These people weren't well paid either, although they worked very hard and he did appreciate that. Personally, I didn't find him difficult to get on with at all.'

The business of no tea breaks was at one time a rule which extended throughout the factory, and it created a number of problems. Colin himself was a very tidy person and he simply disliked seeing cups of tea lying around, leaving their messy stains on the benches or working surfaces. He also never smoked, and neither did he approve of others who did. He absolutely detested the sight of ashtrays full of cigarette ends. In fact, when Ketteringham Hall was restored and re-decorated for his use, he had all the window sills rebuilt at an angle of about thirty degrees to the horizontal, so that if anyone attempted to place ashtrays, ornaments or cups of tea or coffee on them, they would simply slide off onto the floor!

In the same way that he took great care of his appearance, Colin Chapman was continually fighting a weight problem. It was this that – in the Cheshunt days – earned him the nickname of 'Chunky' from those around the factory. Later, of course, this was not used so much because, through his achievements, he was inspiring much more respect. It was usually possible to judge the success of the team by the state of his waistline; if things were going well he would not find it difficult to diet, but if the team was going through a bad patch, out of frustration and worry he would eat more and the extra weight would soon become apparent.

To some Chapman seemed rather arrogant. It is true that he did not readily grant interviews to the press and, when he did, he often seemed somewhat distant. His problem was that, because he had become so well known, he found that he could not easily mingle with other people or he would become tied up permanently. With the incredible schedule he imposed upon himself, time was his most precious commodity. He therefore built up this facade deliberately so that he could then get on with all the things he had to do without unnecessary distractions.

I recently had the opportunity of talking about Colin with two of his special rivals in the Formula 1 world. The first of these was FOCA chief Bernie Ecclestone, of the Brabham team, who had this to say: 'Up until the day he died, Colin was always the

Left Colin (No 2) could always be relied upon to put up a spirited performance in any 'Celebrity Race'. Here he is performing at Brands Hatch in 1978.

Above Colin Chapman and Mario Andretti developed a strong relationship during the years in which they worked together, having a high regard for each other especially when it came to technical matters. Here Mario makes an important point during practice for the 1976 Japan GP which he won.

Below Graham Hill's parties after the British Grand Prix were famous for many years. Here Colin is fooling with his great rival of the time John Cooper.

leader when it came to technical matters. He was one of the few purists. He would always say, "Write me the regulations; give me two years' notice of any changes and I will decide whether I want to race." He would always race and always produce the goods. He was really "Mister Formula 1" – the complete guy. He knew it all, business, technical, the politics involved and the compromises which we sometimes had to make, which were against his principles but so often necessary.'

Then I asked Ken Tyrrell, who knew Colin as a competitor longer than most, for his thoughts. 'Colin,' he said, 'was usually way ahead of all the other constructors. His designs and innovations were generally those followed by other people. I suppose that when we were successful against Colin, it was probably not because we were ahead in design but, because we made our cars that much more reliable than his. Because he wanted to build cars which were as light as possible, he was often on the ragged edge, while we always tended to play safe. When Colin had drivers as good as we had in Jackie Stewart, reliability always played a large part in our successes against him.

'If it had ever been possible – and, of course, it never could have been – for Colin to have been the designer of our car and we had been responsible for the running of it, I think this could have been a very successful arrangement. We would not have allowed him to pare weight from wherever he wanted. Maybe when we went to a race meeting we would not have allowed him to experiment as much as he did. We would have said to him, "Let's concentrate on what we have here." I would imagine Colin

Rivals but friends. Colin with Frank Williams (left) and FOCA chief Bernie Ecclestone (right).

always wanted to try out new things, even when he should have been concentrating on just getting the car on to the track to do twenty laps. I can't imagine Colin ever doing, for example, a long full fuel tank test on the second day of practice. He would never get round to doing that.'

I asked Ken Tyrrell how he would best remember Colin Chapman in Formula 1 racing. 'For his tremendous competitiveness,' he replied, 'and for his absolute total rejection of any changes in the rules without there being at least two years' notice.'

Ken's best-known and most successful driver, three times World Champion Jackie Stewart, had this to say of Colin Chapman:

'My first Formula 1 drive was in a Lotus at the Rand GP at Kyalami, when I drove Jimmy Clark's car because he had slipped a disc in a snowball fight. I drove for Lotus in touring car races with the Lotus Cortina, and I also drove Elans and Formula 2 cars with the Ron Harris team. But I think Jimmy was so dominant in the Lotus team that there was really no great space for a good number two in Colin's mind. Indeed, although very talented, number two drivers like Peter Arundell and Trevor Taylor somehow became lost, and I decided it would be more appropriate for me to drive for another team.

'I think Colin Chapman was the greatest designer of racing cars in the history of motor racing. He was unparalleled; he was the most creative designer the sport has ever known; he brought a more sophisticated form to aerodynamics; he brought monocoque construction in the modern sense; ground effects in a sophisticated form; he was the leader of his time.

'I never criticized the mechanical reliability of Colin's cars, but I always felt that the Lotus was the most fragile of Grand Prix cars. I thought at one time there were rather too many mechanical failures; that I would rather drive a car that was a little more robust and would finish a race, than a car that would be faster and not finish.

'There was no question that his cars were always the fastest and they were never weak in the structure as it was intended to be used. But quite often with racing cars the plans go astray. For instance, if, say, a ball joint in one of Colin's cars, intended to work correctly in a certain direction, became out of line so that the direction of stress was changed, it might often break because there would be insufficient margin for error. I was critical at times, but that didn't detract from my appreciation of his creativity. However, I do think there were many times when he should have beefed-up his cars a little more, and then maybe they would have enjoyed more reliability.'

To those who knew him well, at heart, Colin Chapman was a very warm, generous and considerate man. The incident of the injured mechanic at Pau is very typical and there are other instances, too. For example, when Dick Scammell, his Chief Racing Mechanic, was injured in a car crash there were no problems for his family. His salary was paid while he was away in hospital, and when he returned home he found that his car had already been repaired. Then, when Peter Warr had his accident, the first to visit him after his family was Colin, carrying with him a huge parcel containing a portable colour television set, and this was in the days when a portable TV was a rarity, let alone one with colour. When he was forced to dismiss one of his drivers, he could not bear to tell the man himself, so that task always fell to the Team Manager because Colin hated having to say anything to people which would hurt them.

Many years earlier, when Lotus became a public company, Colin had given his father a Bentley saloon. After Stan Chapman's death in a road accident, he presented it to his old friend and colleague of almost thirty years, Fred Bushell, at an informal little ceremony at Ketteringham Hall in 1981.

While he put a great deal of himself into his early road cars, the Elite and the Elan, later on he gradually became somewhat disenchanted with the manufacture of cars, principally because of the tremendous amount of extra work which had become necessary due to the certification of emission control and safety rules. He was thoroughly frustrated by such legislation and its impact on the finished products. His motto was, 'Rules are for the interpretation of wise men and the obedience of fools'. He was also exasperated by the length of time it took to design and put a new car into production. Although he was able to cut this down to three years, he still felt it was much too long a time.

'At a race meeting,' says Hazel Chapman, 'you could see why he loved motor racing so much. He was there on the spot where it was all happening. He designed the cars and then they would be built in perhaps six months, or even less, and he would then become personally involved in testing them. The driver would go out on the circuit, do a few laps and then come in and tell Colin what was right or what was wrong. Colin would say, "Do this or do that," and it would be done, and his elation would know no bounds if there was then some improvement. That's what he loved so much about motor racing. He adored testing sessions where everything happened quickly and he was in control of it all.'

With the decision in 1968 that Lotus should become a public company, Colin Chapman became a very wealthy man but, with the benefit of hindsight, Hazel feels that perhaps this was not such a wise move after all. 'The pressure,' she says, 'was on

An aerial view of the Lotus factory at Hethel, about seven miles south-west of Norwich. Colin never really enjoyed running a large company and would say, 'If the staff car park is full then I know we have too many people around!'.

him all the time. You are manipulated by the Stock Exchange and there is so much going on which you know nothing about. Colin couldn't stand that side of it. He kept the maximum number of shares for himself and his family that he was allowed, because he wanted to remain the boss but, nevertheless, as far as he was concerned he had become only a puppet. We made a lot of money, but we were very green and it all came so quickly. We gave much of it to stockbrokers to invest in a portfolio of shares but they lost most of that for us, so in the end floating the company was nearly all disadvantages.'

Perhaps this is why Chapman moved his own offices, and the racing team, to Ketteringham Hall, where he could insulate himself from the factory. 'He wanted to be a one-man band again,' explained Hazel. In this superbly restored mansion surrounded by the beautiful Norfolk countryside, which he could see from the windows, he felt happier and more at peace with the world. He had the Orangery converted into a large drawing office and Team Lotus was fully established in the same building. It was an ideal arrangement; one where he could concentrate his mind on the things he enjoyed most. If he had lived, and if Lotus Cars had been forced into liquidation, as was a distinct possibility at the time of his death, it is pretty obvious that he would have stayed on at Ketteringham Hall, where he would have kept himself busy with his racing cars and his microlight aircraft.

In the earlier days, of course, he did a great deal of the design work himself, but gradually, as he found he had less and less time available, it was easier for him to employ designers and draughtsmen and pass on his instructions to them. In more recent years, he virtually gave up drawing altogether because his eyesight was beginning to deteriorate. 'When he had been at Lotus all day,' recalls Hazel, 'the problems which used to arise would drain everything from him and he even had trouble with his reading. He bought stronger and yet stronger glasses, but he still had difficulty with it. Even when I put powerful reading lamps in the lounge he still had problems.'

So Colin Chapman really ran the business through regular meetings with his executives and by directives to his engineers. A perfect example of this was a memorandum prepared for him by Tony Rudd and reproduced here. It is particularly revealing about the engineering policy he set for the company. It is also worth noting the mark against paragraph six and the word 'YES' written in his own hand:

At the policy meetings he was very much the boss and perhaps he tended to stick too much to doing things HIS way. When it sometimes turned out that this way had

Tony Rudd's 'Definitions and Philosophy of Lotus's Engineering Policy' issued in 1975. The notation against paragraph six was made by Colin Chapman at the time he approved it for distribution.

Affects	Issued By	Approved by	17.4.75
			Cancels and replaces issue dated
LOTUS CARS	A. C. RUDD	A.C.B. CHAPMAN	Page ONE

1). A Lotus

Provides its owner with prestigeous efficient transport. Prestige is given by exclusivity and racing heritage. The designer gives it efficiency by light weight, effective use of economic material and the maximum return for fuel burned in the engine and in cornering power.

2). Where a Lotus manufactured part is not essential to meet (1) use a mass produced part from the motor industry.

3). Engines and other high investment assemblies to have a basic design life of 8 - 10 years, which must include in-built capacity to accept legal and performance up-dates.

4). Lotus peculiar chassis and suspension assemblies with high cost in development - time or facilities to have a design life of 10,000 units and be concurrently used in several models.

5). Mould tool life and body process techniques to be exploited to ensure exclusivity is maintained by trend setting styling and structural changes every 4,000 units.

6). The most elegantly effective and traditionally Lotus solution is the one with the least number of parts, effectively deployed. This criteria is to be applied by section leaders and managers at every stage of the design and drawing approval procedure.

7). Only the Product Policy Committee may authorise a change in the visual standard, appearance and colour once approved.

YES

been the wrong way, he usually admitted it to the person who had been right, even though he hated having to eat humble pie.

He never liked having to do anything which did not appeal to him and his record at Lotus Cars showed that he had a somewhat grandiose disregard for matters of finance and marketing. Often a brilliant engineer makes a very poor businessman, but this was certainly not true in Colin Chapman's case. He was always quick to see opportunities, but he was not prepared to devote his time to all the financial aspects of running a large company. In this respect he was extremely lucky to have Fred Bushell's support and Fred played an important part in his own and the company's success. Whenever a particular situation became too boring for him, he would hand it over to Fred saying, 'Here you are, you sort it out, I'm going motor racing'! The situation at Lotus was never an easy one and Fred Bushell had to deal with crisis after crisis, but he always knew he could rely on Colin's flashes of brilliance to help him sort things out.

Nevertheless, the truth is that towards the end of his life Colin Chapman was not as successful as he had been in the past. With the collapse of the American market his cars were not selling in the quantities they should, and the financing of the new M90 was becoming a very serious problem. In motor racing he was terribly frustrated by his lack of success, having won only a single Grand Prix in four years. Both these factors were really complimentary to each other; the fact that he had not done well in motor racing was almost certainly due partly to him having less and less time to devote to the

The pace at which he lived and worked, and the pressures of his professional life, made Colin's hair prematurely white. In 1979, when this picture was taken at his office desk at the Hethel factory, he was only 51 years old.

A kind and thoughtful gesture by John Webb, Managing Director of Brands Hatch, was to give Colin Chapman's name to the road behind the main grandstands. Andrew Ferguson, Bob Dance and Fred Bushell (left to right) were at the official opening in 1985, with Hazel Chapman and son Clive.

design of the racing cars and the motivation of his staff. He certainly made a serious mistake in embarking on and then persevering so long with the Lotus 88. Having been the first with ground effect cars, he then expected the establishment to follow him again with the entirely new twin-chassis idea. The 88 was bound to be ruled out; if not by the regulations then by concensus, but still he stubbornly hung on to it. Of course, he was not the kind of person to give up easily but, in this case, his obstinacy was a terrible drain on his efforts which could have been used to better effect both at Team Lotus and Lotus Cars. Apart from this, there was also the enormous expense of it all.

All this began to become rather too much for him. 'I don't think he was at all happy in his last years,' recalls Hazel Chapman. 'He had trouble finding sponsors for the racing cars, the team was doing badly, his road cars were not selling and the Press were very unkind to him. I really think it was all getting him down.'

However, it would be another tragedy if one only remembered Colin Chapman as the man whose cars used to win Grand Prix races years ago. There is no doubt that he was the most creative innovator in the history of motor racing, and if he had been able to devote as much time to racing as his rivals, he would certainly have remained right at the top. Indeed, without the tremendous pressures that were heaped upon him, he might still be with us now.

Actually, Colin was convinced that he would live to be a hundred. His grandfather did not die until he was 97 and Colin would say, 'Enzo Ferrari still makes racing cars at

Colin Chapman's grave in East Carelton churchyard only a few hundred yards from his home. It bears the Lotus badge surrounded by a laurel wreath and the family motto – 'In adversity we thrive'.

eighty, so I still have thirty years to go!' His death from heart failure was a tremendous shock to everyone. He had only recently passed the annual medical examination for his pilot's licence and the doctor had said he had never seen a stronger heart.

Perhaps it is in the light of what he left behind that we can best judge Colin Chapman's impact, and certainly his heritage is enormous. Of course, racing cars will change in shape during the years to come, with changes to regulations and with the evolution of techniques and technology, but history will not forget the tremendous impact he had on motor racing during the last 25 years.

There is, though, more to it than that. The fact that Team Lotus has been able to carry on after his death, and subsequently earn further success in Grand Prix races, proves that Colin Chapman had not built the team on sand. He had put together a tremendous racing organization which, in the years to come, will certainly add more victories to the records attached to his name.

Then there remains Lotus Cars. A week after Colin's death, an agreement was reached with the American Express Company and David Wickens of British Car Auctions took over as Chairman of Lotus, with Toyota of Japan also acquiring a proportion of the equity. Then in January 1986 General Motors acquired a controlling interest in the company. There is no doubt that these people would not have made such a large investment if they were not assured that the foundations were sound. They obviously felt that they could rely on the technical team put together by Chapman to continue producing good cars to his philosophy of simple, efficient vehicles of supreme elegance and with a very high level of performance. They would also become involved in tomorrow's technology through their highly successful engineering department.

The Christmas tree was already decorated and the sun was shining when, on 22 December 1982, Colin Chapman was buried no more than a few hundred yards from his home in the small churchyard of East Carleton. At Hazel's request, the funeral service was a family affair, attended only by close friends, as she knew this was what Colin would have wanted.

Of the people who were present, most had worked with him at the factory or in Team Lotus. From the motor racing world there were some figures from the past, like Jimmy Clark's sisters and Bette Hill. There was also one of his old rivals, Ken Tyrrell with his wife Nora, and indeed motor racing was the theme on that day because Colin Chapman was, above all, a born racer.

Some hundreds of years ago, one of Colin Chapman's ancestors had raised an army in the defence of a port and, in due course, a family crest had been bestowed upon him. The motto, now engraved upon Colin's tombstone, provides a most apt description of this very remarkable man. It reads 'Crescit sub pondere Virtus' which, translated, means 'In adversity we thrive'.

Postscripts

Jane Payton (née Chapman)

My father was happiest when he was facing a challenge, whether it was the design of a new car, flying his aeroplane, talking his way out of trouble or simply playing a game of Monopoly – he wanted to win, and he usually did!

He always led the family discussions, by the end of which if he told you black was white you'd believe him. We often said he should have been a politician! He was a staunch Conservative and a tremendous admirer of Margaret Thatcher. We sat up nearly all night after one of the elections to see if Conservative got in – if they hadn't have done so I think he was quite prepared to move the whole business abroad there and then.

It has been said that he was impetuous with some of his racing car designs. He was always like that. Often, we had only just arrived somewhere and he'd want to be off somewhere else. One summer holiday we'd been at the villa in Ibiza for a few days and he suddenly said, 'Let's go to Egypt and look at the Pyramids – it's not very far from here'! So we all jumped in the aeroplane and off we went.

As well as being impetuous, daddy was also extremely generous. A friend was on her way over to see me one evening and crashed her car. He was very busy at work at the time, but I found out that the next day he had arranged for my friend to borrow a car until hers was repaired. We were often surprised when he remembered little family things during his hectic schedule. Two of my other friends were not so lucky when he reversed out of the garage at his normal 50 mph and smashed straight into their cars parked in the drive. 'They shouldn't have been in the way,' he said.

As several people have mentioned in this book, they were often swept away by his tremendous enthusiasm, and my father did have this marvellous ability to make you feel you could achieve much more than you ever thought possible. It was like this at home. When he first became interested in microlights he, of course, bought one and we all had to learn to fly it! This wasn't too bad for Sarah and Clive as they had both taken flying lessons, but I didn't really have a clue – apart from having watched daddy from the co-pilot's seat on many occasions.

We had to taxi up and down the runway doing little 'hops' – each one higher than the one before, until we were confident enough to do a circuit. I only intended to carry on practising the 'hops', but daddy was gesticulating from what seemed hundreds of feet below to go higher. I was at the top of a particularly high 'hop' when I reached the end of the grass strip and realized I would have to carry on and do a circuit or hit the trees. I decided on the circuit and realized that this was his plan all along! Half-way round (in tears with fright at this stage) I realized he hadn't told me how to get down! However, I managed to land and, sure enough, a little later I was made to do it again . . . 'So you don't lose your confidence,' daddy said!

Years earlier, when we were about nine and ten, Sarah and I were taught to drive in much the same way. It was in a Spanish Renault with a dashboard gear stick on a terraced mountainside where we were picnicing at the time! Earlier on daddy had shown us how to light a camp fire using two sticks and dried grass (a lesson from his scouting days), as a result of which we had to beat out the flames with the raffia sun mats before it spread over the entire mountainside. Visitors to the villa often wondered why we called the sunbeds the 'firebeaters'!

Daddy always liked everything neat and tidy – especially in his car and aeroplane. Any unnecessary clutter was simply dumped on the garage or hangar floor! I don't think I ever saw him 'bodge' anything. If a job was done it had to be done properly. He might have taken short cuts but the end result was always perfect. A simple thing like reading the newspaper was quite an operation – each page being smoothed completely flat and folded with a knife-pleat crease down the edge. Woe betide anyone who got to the papers first and left them in a mess!

This makes daddy sound very fastidious, which he was over many things. But I presume most perfectionists are like that! However, as a family we obviously saw a side of him that many others didn't, and although he wasn't at home as often as most fathers we always went on two family holidays a year. We used to tease him and play jokes on him and he always took it in good part, having a good sense of humour and being able to laugh at himself.

Although he didn't like to dwell on the past – one of his sayings being 'once you look back you're finished' – I do remember two stories he used to tell about the old motor racing days. Mind you, he used to exaggerate like mad! The first was when Lotus had entered two identical cars in an event and one was not ready in time for scrutineering. They wheeled the first car through and it passed. With the aid of the mechanics he then rushed it round the back, swapped the number on the side and the chassis number plate and wheeled it back to scrutineering, where they passed it as the second Lotus entry! This gave them the time they needed to finish the other car.

The second tale was when Jimmy Clark had won a Grand Prix abroad and, as well as the prize money, they had each been given two expensive watches. Obviously they didn't want to pay the import duty, so decided to smuggle them in. However, deciding it was better to declare something than nothing, Jimmy declared a bottle of drink, but when it came to daddy's turn, instead of saying '200 cigarettes', out came the words, '200 watches'! Fortunately the customs officer thought he was only joking and didn't even bother to search him.

These were the happy, successful times and obviously it wasn't always like this. Happiest at the drawing board at home or standing in the pits at a motor race, my father was not really the high-flying 'business man' that most people imagined him to be. The thought of wining and dining the right people at the right time was abhorrent to him and it was not his way of doing business.

Daddy never used to like being alone – even if he was only watching television he preferred having someone with him. He is never far from the thoughts of those he left behind, and it would be nice to think that he is now reunited with those he lost while he was still with us . . .

Sarah Chapman

Daddy had tremendous enthusiasm and energy and I think it was this, coupled with his ability to explain things in simple terms and his power of persuasion, which made up the basis of his success. He was able to persuade you to do almost anything, and when caught up with his enthusiasm you found yourself doing the most extraordinary things. I remember spending almost an entire school holiday sorting out hundreds of photographs of various boats, fitting the right interior shots to the exteriors like a giant jigsaw puzzle. But the enthusiasm and persuasion alone would not have enabled him to achieve what he did. It was the simple way in which he could explain complicated principles which I think was the most important factor in his success. This ability stemmed from his own thorough grasp of the subject, and by being able to make people understand what he was trying to achieve they were able to contribute more fully to the job in hand. He didn't often discuss business at home but liked to talk about his current design ideas. This often involved graphic descriptions of things like planet gears where, for instance, the salt and pepper would revolve with the place-mat as the principle was demonstrated!

It was his logical mind that enabled him to teach himself. Daddy was always learning and developing. Although educated at university he didn't just use that knowledge, he used the training to teach himself more. With any new subject that interested him he would get some books, read up and extract all that was useful to him and then apply the knowledge in maybe a completely different field. This is how he managed to continue developing and regularly produce new ideas. Under the tremendous pressure of motor racing you always had to come up with something new. It didn't work every time but then daddy would just think up something new yet again!

Daddy was extremely neat in the way he worked, and also very thorough. His drawing office at home doubled up as a sort of playroom for us and he would get annoyed if he went up there and found a mess in our section, as his was always very tidy. All his magazines were set out in tidy piles and his drawing pencils all lined up perfectly sharpened. His briefcase was another example of his neatness. It contained everything, a sort of round-the-world survival kit full of items in miniature: a miniature screwdriver kit, spanner set, torch, camera, first-aid, all packed with precision, and always a spare. In the case of the propelling pencils he liked, there was a spare, a spare spare and an emergency spare! His suitcase was also packed in just the same way, and he could reach into it in the dark and pick out exactly what he wanted. However, he wasn't always so tidy. We arrived at a hotel on one occasion and went straight for a swim. A shirt from daddy's suitcase was thrown on the floor. It disappeared, only to reappear later laundered and neatly folded on a chair. Daddy wanted to sit down, so the shirt reverted to the floor, disappeared and reappeared again – laundered. This happened three times in as many days and we were all highly amused, particularly daddy, as he knew the shirt was brand-new and had never been worn!

He had a great sense of humour and could often laugh at himself. One incident which occasioned this was his aim to get the smallest of items into his briefcase. He had recently purchased a miniature Minolta SLR camera and wanted a leather case for it. We went to the shop and there was a choice of two. Daddy insisted that the smaller one was sufficient and we were highly entertained watching him trying to fit in all the bits. Eventually, crying with laughter, he had to lever in the last lens with a spoon.

Daddy loved exploring and we had many adventures together. He could never stay in one place for very long, and as soon as we arrived anywhere the first job was to acquire a map. He would usually have spotted something of interest from the air on our approach and we would then set off to find it on the ground. As the kind of places which daddy liked were usually remote, it invariably turned into quite an expedition.

He liked to have people around him and was a great talker, always leading the conversations at supper parties, and other such functions. Daddy's knowledge was very broad and there wasn't much he couldn't discuss. One Christmas we were playing that game where you have to talk for one minute without stopping, about a topic which the others choose. We really thought we'd catch him out and we gave him the subject 'baking a cake'. As daddy could only just boil an egg we thought we had him, but no, somehow he managed, and even succeeded in making it quite interesting.

Flying was one of daddy's main interests, and although he loved to fly, he wasn't so keen on all the rules and regulations associated with it. That's one reason why hang-gliders and micro-lights captured his imagination. The simplicity of the concept and the freedom from formalities that was initially associated with the sport really appealed to his adventurous spirit. He liked us to be involved with his interests and, caught up by his enthusiasm, we all took our courage in both hands and learnt with varying degrees of success.

Daddy was only interested in the future and was always working on something new. This book has been about his life's work, but we as the inheritors of that work must look forward. I hope that by continuing to look to the future and approaching new ideas with some of his enthusiasm, drive and understanding, the Lotus marque will progress in the same innovative and energetic mould as that in which it was created.

Clive Chapman

How does one set about describing what life with my father was like? I could attempt an analysis and rating but I don't think that is required. Recollections of our adventures together may be more interesting and informative.

The first recorded 'classic' is the one and only time daddy was called upon to change a nappy while mummy was out. On her return, the offending article was found in the garden underneath the bathroom window! The way daddy reacted in some situations was incredible. I remember Fred Bushell telling me about an important meeting they were both involved in. Daddy, suffering from hayfever as ever, had used his handkerchief and, so as to avoid making a bulge in his suit, he picked up Fred's briefcase, put his handkerchief inside and closed it – all without a word. To daddy this was a completely logical solution to the problem. Similarly, any drinks mat which dared to stick to the water jug due to condensation on the sides was flung across the room. And yet he did not mind us teasing or laughing at such events; maybe they were all to entertain us.

If he had a short fuse to some of life's little trials he always had a lot of patience with us. The only time he came near to hitting me was one Sunday morning when we were living in our 'temporary' home in Norwich where the plumbing was somewhat antiquated. My two sisters persuaded me to spoil his hot bath by filling it with the only available water when it was still cold! He was furious and tore down a door to get at me, but when he finally did, he had calmed down completely – much to the disappointment of my sisters!

Daddy made sure that we all received the best education, although he obviously did not always have the time to see how we were getting on. He seemed to assume that we were doing all right, which was not always the case. As long as we passed the right things at the right time it was OK. If we did not we knew that we would have to do it again until we did. I think he paid more attention to my education than to the girls'. I presume he still thought that boys made better engineers; a theory that I do not hold with. Daddy never pushed me into the sciences or engineering. I just had the impression that things would be 'quieter' if I chose these as my subjects for higher study. This proved to be true, and although he could see that I was not going to set the academic world alight, he seemed satisfied enough. Having seen some of his school reports I think he felt that performance and conduct at school were not everything!

Daddy was always prepared to get excited and enthusiastic about other people's achievements as well as his own. When the Apollo missions were on TV he used to encourage us all to sit up and watch. He wanted us to appreciate the magnitude of mankind's achievements and yet he never lectured us about what he had achieved. One of his sayings was, 'Those who can do, and those who can't talk about it'.

If he despised the talkers this was nothing compared to his opinions of the arbitrators. He absolutely hated any restriction on what he could or could not do, even to the point of arguing against licences for anybody doing anything. I think this was the reason for his great interest in microlights – there was a minimum of restriction on the aircraft design and no requirement for a licence to fly the thing. This to daddy was a designer's Utopia.

Holidays were always exciting. Daddy would get the whole family together – it had to be all of us because we didn't have the chance to be a family all that often. Daddy used to say when and then mummy would be the one to get it organized. I am not sure that many people realize just how important mummy's part was in daddy's success. It was *their* success. She released him from all the everyday worries, which enabled him to concentrate entirely on his work. She provided him with a home and family whenever he needed them. I really do believe that daddy could not have got as far as he did without mummy's support.

We left for our first ski-ing holiday minus daddy (who was busy at work) but mummy was always fairly confident that he wouldn't be far behind. She had never been ski-ing before but ended up teaching us! Daddy was always great value on a ski-ing holiday. He was absolutely lethal and always crashed into other people on the slopes. This usually involved sweeping through entire lines of ski-school pupils totally out of control!

We always went to Ibiza for our Summer holiday with daddy coming out when he could between races. Whenever he was there we had to have a project to keep him busy. One year we built a raft from empty plastic chlorine containers, held within a wooden framework and using an old boat cover for a sail. Within about two weeks we were ready for the maiden voyage. I was put on it and launched into the bay with an offshore wind blowing. The plan was to follow me in the motor boat, which would not start, and so I was about a mile out to sea without a lifejacket before they got to me. I was ten years old at the time and certainly not brought up to be safety conscious!

I don't think it was this that led daddy into boat production, but it happened and, as a result, I started my powerboating career. As another project in Ibiza daddy designed a hull and estimated the performance using theories he developed after studying all the books on boats he could find. He disagreed with a lot of the classical theory and he knew he could do better. The result was that his powerboat design was, of course, half the weight of the lightest competition and it went much faster. This, naturally, led to everyone accusing us of cheating. However, we won the Junior Championship and then, with a bigger version of the junior boat, we tackled the Senior Championship. Daddy rather left me on my own at this stage and with the light weight of the hull and the increased engine size I was quite regularly flipping the boat if there was any wind blowing down the course. My solution was to put sandbags in the front of the hull, which was blasphemy as far as Daddy was concerned. He taught us all that the use of 'crutches' to get a job done was an admission of defeat. However, it was OK to put the battery in the front of the hull as we were not adding to the weight of the boat. Ultimately, I came second in the Senior Championship, having learned a great deal.

One aspect of boat-racing that I think daddy really loved was the friendly atmosphere and the lack of politics. The politics of motor racing was one aspect which I know he hated, even if he was winning the argument.

I think daddy's motor racing or business colleagues would have been surprised if they could have seen him as a family man. He taught us the value of privacy and I don't think anyone ever saw us as a real family together, which is nice. I know we all realize how lucky we were to have had the chance to share our lives with such an exceptional man.

Appendix

Lotus Type Numbers
Compiled by Andrew Ferguson, Secretary of Club Team Lotus

I	Austin Seven-based trials car with stressed skin marine plywood open body. Front axle beam split and pivoted in centre. Ford steel wheels carried wider tyres to improve traction. Successful in trials.	1948
II	Ford Ten-based trials car, also used for racing with 1,172 cc engine. Won its first race Silverstone 1950.	1949/50
III	750 Formula car – very successful and as a result came orders for replicas. Lotus Engineering founded subsequently. Car was based on a 1930 Austin Seven extensively modified, Chapman devising de-siamesed head ports to achieve phenomenal increase in power.	1951
IV	Austin Seven frame and 1,172 cc Ford engine, built for trials.	1952
V	Never built, intended to be a 100 mph, 750 Formula car.	
VI	First true production car. Space frame 'component' car with no Austin Seven ancestry. Fitted with a variety of engines including Ford Ten, MG, Ford Consul and BMW, ranging from 750 to 2,000 cc. 110 cars built.	1953-55
VII	Replacement for Mk VI as a road-going 'component' sports car. Revised several times and fitted with such engines as Ford Ten, Ford 105E and 122E, BMC A series and Coventry Climax FWA. First seen 1957 Motor Show, ran to four Series. First produced by Lotus Engineering at Hornsey, then by Lotus Components and later Lotus Racing. Series 3A had Holbay 1,600 cc crossflow engine with twin Webers. Lotus Cars also built a quantity of Series 4 VIIs after the demise of Components/Racing.	1957-1973

Production numbers:

VII Series 1	740
VII Series 2	1,324
VII Series 3	324
VII Series 4	294
	2,682

Car is still in production, and known as 'Caterham Seven'.

VIII	First aerodynamic sports-racing car, fitted with 1½ litre MG, Connaught and Climax engines. Ten built.	1954

IX	Improved version of Mk VIII designed principally for smaller-capacity engines. Ran with 1,098 cc and 1,460 cc Coventry Climax and 1,487 cc MG engines. 23 built.	1955
X	Later version of Mk VIII fitted with 1,971 cc Bristol and 1,960 cc Connaught engines. Seven built.	1955
Eleven	Space frame aerodynamic sports-racing car replacing Mk IX. Fitted with 1,098 cc and 1,460 cc Coventry Climax engines, although 1,100 cc Stanguellini, 1,457 cc twin-cam Coventry Climax, 1,484 cc Maserati and 2.5 litre Lancia Aurelia engines also tried. Employed stressed alloy skinning. Various specifications such as 'Club', 'Le Mans', 'Sports'. Around 250 built.	1956
12	First single-seater for 1957 F2. 1,475 cc twin-cam FPF Coventry Climax engine. Also used in 1958 in F1 with 2 and 2.2 litre versions of the FPF engine. Twelve cars built.	1956-57
13	Called the Eleven Series 2 for superstitious reasons.	1957-58
14	Lotus Elite, the first Lotus GT car introduced at 1957 Motor Show, but not in full-scale production until 1958. Created a sensation as it was the world's first glass-fibre monocoque GT car.	1956/58-1963
15	Sports-racing car based on the Eleven. Used twin-cam FPF Coventry Climax engines of 1,457 cc, 1,960 cc, 2,208 cc and 2,495 cc. Twin-cam 1,594 cc Ford and 3,524 cc Buick engines also used.	1958
16	F1/2 car, known as the mini-Vanwall. Fitted with FPF Coventry Climax engines of various capacities (as 15): engine first inclined at 60, later 30 degrees.	1958-59
17	Sports-racing car with 1,098 cc Coventry Climax engine to replace Mk Eleven. First cars fitted with strut-type front suspension, later replaced with double wishbones.	1959
18	First rear-engined Lotus. Initially FJ with Ford 105E or BMC A-series engine. Subsequently, F1 with 2,495 cc FPA Coventry Climax and F2 with 1,475 cc FPF. Gave Lotus their first Grand Prix victory, driven by Stirling Moss at Monaco in 1960.	1960-61
19	Rear-engined sports-racing car based on the 18. Used 1,475 cc, 1,960 cc, 1,495 cc and 2,751 cc FPF Coventry Climax engines: 2,496 cc Maserati and American V8 engines also tried.	1960-62
19B	Special version of the 19, with later suspension parts, built for Dan Gurney and fitted with Ford V8.	1962
20	FJ based on the 18 with sleeker body line. Ford 105E engine used in 997 cc and 1,098 cc forms.	1961
20B	Disc-braked version of 20, fitted with 1,498 cc Ford 109E engine.	1961
21	F1 car with 1,475 cc FPF Coventry Climax engine: Also used in Tasman Series with 2,495 cc and 2,751 cc versions of this engine.	1961

22	FJ with Ford 105E engine in 1,098 cc form. Twin-cam 1,594 cc Ford engines used for Formule Libre races.	1962
23	Rear-engined sports-racing car based on 22. Ford, Alfa Romeo and Coventry Climax engines of various capacities used. Three Series produced: Series 1 – 1,092 cc (Type 22 engine), 1,470 cc sohc, 997 cc sohc; Series 2 – 997 cc Climax twin-cam (Jimmy Clark's car had 1,498 cc twin-cam); Series 3 – 997 cc Climax twin-cam Le Mans car, 750 cc Climax twin-cam Le Mans car built for UDT.	1962
23B	1,594 cc Ford twin-cam version of 23 with modified chassis. All 23s were later produced to this chassis specification.	1963-66
24	F1 production car to take V8 Coventry Climax and BRM engines. V8 Ford and Chevrolet engines used for Formule Libre races.	1962
25	First successful monocoque Grand Prix car. V8 Coventry Climax engines used by works and V8 BRM by the Parnell team.	1962-63
25B	Modified 25 to take 2 and 2.1 litre version of BRM V8.	1964
26	Lotus Elan – successor to the production Elite which was so costly to build. Introduced 1962 Motor Show. Backbone chassis powered by Ford twin-cam 1,588 cc engine producing 105 bhp at 5,500 rpm. The first large series production car from Lotus – 12,224 were built in total.	

Series I Convertible	1,498 cc	1962
Series I Convertible	1,558 cc	1963
Series I Optional hard top	1,558 cc	1963
Series II Convertible	1,558 cc	1964-1966

(see also Type 36 and 45)

26R	Competition version of 26.	1964-66
27	Monocoque FJ car with 1,098 cc Ford 105E engine.	1963
28	Ford-Lotus Cortina saloon.	1962-66
29	Indianapolis car based on Mk 25 but with 4.2 litre Ford V8 stock-block engine.	1963
30	Large capacity sports-racing car with backbone chassis. Designed for 4,724 cc Ford V8 engine.	1965
31	F3 car based on space frame Mk 22. Later adapted for Formula Ford by the Jim Russell Racing Drivers School.	1964-67
32	Monocoque F2 car based on Mk 27, fitted with Cosworth SCA engine.	1964
32B	Built for 1965 Tasman series: 2,495 cc Coventry Climax-engined version of Mk 32.	1965
33	F1 car based on Mk 25. All works Mk 25s subsequently brought up to 33 specification.	1964-65
33T	Used in 1966 F1 with 2 litre version of Coventry Climax V8 and 2.1 litre version of BRM V8: taken to 1967 Tasman Series for Jimmy Clark.	1967

34	Indianapolis car based on Mk 29 using 4-cam Ford 4.2 litre engine. (Ran methanol in practice, gasoline in race.)	1964
35	F2/3 car based on Mk 32 fitted with Cosworth SCA and BRM engines for F2 and 1.0 Cosworth MAE and Holbay R65 for F3.	1965

36   Lotus Elan:

Series 3 fixed head coupé: similar to convertible but boot lid extended to rear, etc.	1965
(Series 2 convertible Type 26 was continued until June 1966.)	1966
Special Equipment Sports/Convertible introduced Jan 1966. Power increased by 10 to 115 bhp. Close-ratio gearbox, etc.	1966
Series 3 with electric windows introduced May	1966
Series 3 fixed head coupé Special Equipment.	July 1966
Series 4 fixed head introduced and Series 3 discontinued.	March 1968
'Sprint' version introduced February '71 with 'big valve' engine. Discontinued February 1973. (See also Types 26 and 45.)	1971-73

37	One-off Clubmen's Fomula car based on the Mk VII with IRS, fitted with 1,498 cc Ford pushrod engine.	1965
38	Indianapolis car with Ford 4-cam engine using methanol.	1965-66
39	Originally to have been 1965 F1 car to take flat-16 Coventry Climax engine, which never happened. Converted into Tasman Formula car for 1965 with 2,495 cc FPF Coventry Climax 4.	1965-66
40	Large-capacity sports-racing car based on the Mk 30 with a variety of V8 Ford engines.	1965
41	Space frame F3 car with Cosworth MAE and Holbay R66 engines.	1966-67
41B	F2 car fitted with Cosworth FVA for 1,600 cc formula.	1967
41C	Interim F3 car with later suspension.	1967-68
41X	F3 car – prototype for Type 55.	1967-68
42	1967 Indianapolis car with 4.2 litre BRM H16 engine – never raced. (Ran Snetterton test in March 1967.)	1966
42F	Two chassis built of revised 42 with four-cam Ford V8 for 1967 Indianapolis.	1967
43	F1 monocoque designed to take 3 litre BRM H16 engine.	1966
44	F2 based on Mk 35 but with Mk 41 suspension and bodywork, fitted with 1 litre Cosworth SCA engine.	1966

45   Lotus Elan:

Series 3 drop head coupé introduced. Was similar to fixed head coupé but with fixed side window frames.	June 1966
Series 3 drop head coupé 'Special Equipment' also introduced.	June 1966
Series 4 drop head coupé introduced and Series 3 discontinued.	March 1968
'Sprint' introduced Feb 1971, 'Big Valve' engine.	1971-73
Discontinued Feb 1973. (See Types 26 and 36.)	

46	The Renault-engined Europa mid-engined GT car. This was the original very basic export-only car. 1,958 built.	1967-68
47	1,594 cc Ford twin cam-engined version of 46, built for racing only. Ran in Gold Leaf colours. 55 built.	1967-68
47D	One-off project with GKN/Vandervell. Fitted with Rover V8 coupled to ZF gearbox. Used as test bed. Top speed 200 mph.	
47F	Five built for road use with Ford crossflow 1600 cc engines coupled to Renault gearbox (as per Type 51 Formula Ford Special).	
48	F2 car fitted with 1,594 cc Cosworth FVA engine. Monocoque chassis. Ran in Gold Leaf colours.	1967-68
49	Introduced as a winning F1 car at Zandvoort in 1967, fitted with the first Cosworth DFV 3 litre engine.	1967
49B	Modified 49 as used by Graham Hill to win World Championship in 1968 in Gold Leaf Team Lotus colours.	1968
49C	49B modified to take 13 inch wheels at front.	1969
49T	Tasman Formula version fitted with 2.5 litre Ford V8. Ran in Gold Leaf Team Lotus colours.	1967-68
50	Elan +2 fixed head coupé introduced at 1967 Motor Show, with 118 bhp engine, servo-assisted disc brakes and Airflow ventilation. Discontinued December 1969.	1967-69
	'Plus 2S' fixed head coupé announced October 1968 (no kit form available). In November 1968 Stromberg carburettor replaced Weber.	1968
	In Feb 1971 '+2S 130' introduced with 'big valve' engine.	1971
	In Oct 1972 five-speed gearbox car, designated '+2S 130/5'. A 'commemorative' black and gold version of car was part of the range, 118 such cars being built.	1972
	In Oct 1973 car conformed to European emission control standards. Discontinued December 1974. All told, 5,228 were built.	1973
51	Formula Ford space frame car based on Mk 31 fitted with 1.5 and 1.6 Ford engines. 165 built.	1967
51A	1968 Formula Ford car.	1968
52	Europa prototype (one-off twin-cam).	1968
53	Lotus Components sports car (never built).	–
54	Europa Series 2 introduced into UK. Was available in component form Oct 1970. Discontinued October 1971.	July 1969
55	1968 revised F3 Lotus 41X.	1968
56	1968 Indianapolis turbine.	1968
56B	Turbine F1 (ran in Gold Leaf Team Lotus colours).	1971
57	F2 de Dion car tested early 1968, but never raced (ran in Gold Leaf Team Lotus colours).	1968

58	A Type 57 converted to take Tasman 2.5 litre and modified rear end to take ZF gearbox. Tested by Graham Hill but never raced.	1968
59	1969 F2/3/B. 40 built.	1969
60	Lotus VII Series 4. First announced Nov 1969. Ford 1600 GT engine, 84 bhp at 5,800 rpm. 524 built.	1969-70
61	1969 Formula Ford. 254 built.	1969
61M	Modified version of Type 61.	1970
62	1969 sports-racing car LV240.	1969
63	1969 experimental four-wheel drive F1 (Gold Leaf Team Lotus colours).	1969
64	1969 four-wheel drive Indianapolis car.	1969
65	Federal-bodied Europa.	1970
66	Not disclosed.	–
67	Proposed 1970 Tasman car.	1970
68	Prototype Formula A.	1969
69	F2/3 car. 59 built.	1970
70	Formula A. 6 built.	1970
71	Not disclosed.	–
72	1970 F1 car, Gold Leaf Team Lotus colours, then became first black and gold car (John Player). Won 20 Grand Prix races.	1970
	Lotus 2 litre 4 cylinder 16-valve engine introduced in March. Had aluminium block and cylinder head and incorporated belt-driven twin ohc 1,973 cc engine developing 140 bhp at 6,500 rpm. It followed four years of development, 300,000 miles of testing and 3,000 hours on test bed.	1971
73	F3 car (driven Trimmer/Vermilio), later converted to F2 car for Nova 2 litre engine test.	1973
74	Team Lotus: F2 Texaco Star.	1973
	Lotus Cars: Twin Cam Europa with 1,558 cc engine Oct '71, discontinued Sept '72 when 'Special' introduced with 'big valve' engine. Five-speed gearbox standard from March 1974. Finally discontinued September 1975.	1971-75
75	Second generation Elite. The new up-market four seater production Lotus (Series 1) 2398 built. (Production ceased March 1983)	1974-80
76	Team Lotus: F1 car – John Player Special Mk I.	1975-80
	Lotus Cars: Eclat Series 1. 1,299 built. (Production ceased Sept 1982)	1975-80
	Sprint version of Eclat announced. Available only in white with 'E' cam Lotus 907 engine.	1977
77	F1 car John Player Special Mk II.	1975-76

78	F1 car – John Player Special Mk III.	1977-78
79	Team Lotus: F1 car John Player Special Mk IV – was the only car to run three prime sponsor displays, i.e. John Player (1978), Martini (1979) and Essex (1980 development car) liveries.	1978-79
	Lotus Cars also used this Type number for their Esprit (first introduced Oct 1975) Series 1. 718 built.	1976-78
	Series 2. 1,148 built.	1978-80
80	F1 car: Martini sponsorship. Ran in three events only, finished 3rd in Spanish Grand Prix (Andretti).	1979
81	Team Lotus: F1 car, Essex sponsorship. John Player Special 81 from June 1981.	1980-81
	Lotus Cars: Sunbeam project. Car won 1981 World Rally Championship.	1980-81
81(B)	First driven by Nigel Mansell, Austrian GP.	1980
82	Turbo Esprit Series I. 1,217 built.	1980
83	Series II Elite. Also received Riviera styling in limited numbers. 133 built. (Riviera production ceased Oct 1982. Elite production ceased March 1983)	1980
84	Series II Eclat (also Riviera, from October 1981). 223 built. (Riviera production ceased October 1982)	1980-82
85	Series III Esprit. 508 built. Remains in production.	1980
86	First conceived at Paul Ricard, October 1979. Was drawn by the end of that year. First 'twin-chassis' car. Completed October 1980 and ran at Jarama tests in November 1980.	1980
87	Schemed as a conventional car in the first half of 1980, with Type 88 running gear inside a Type 87 body. Had its own development/ research programme until Type 88 took precedence. Was resurrected after the Type 88 political problems and ran in both Essex and John Player Special liveries. Was initially schemed as a fully skirted car to the proposed 1980 WFMS regulations.	1980
87(B)	Interim car prior to John Player Special 91. Two cars ran in 1982 South African GP.	1982
88	An improved and lightened version of the Type 86, which caused much controversy during the 1981 racing season. Was initially schemed as a fully skirted car to the 1980 WFMS regulations, and carried Essex livery. Chassis number 1 was team's first carbon Kevlar tub. Was 'shut out' of 1981 US GP (West), Brazilian and Argentine GPs.	1981
88(B)	Entered as John Player Special 88(B) but with Courage livery for British GP 1981, where it was allowed to practise but excluded from the race.	1981
	'B' modifications were:	

(a) windscreen and gearbox oil cooler moved to outer sprung structure.

(b) panelling added to ensure the external airstream could not lick the inner sprung structure.

89	Lotus Eclat EXCEL: 2.2 litre 16-valve 2 + 2 Grand Tourer, first announced Birmingham Motor Show October 1982.	1982
90	Lotus's new small car. Project code of M.90, known as X100 from 1983.	1980
91	The 1982 F1 season car launched 17 February 1982 at Ketteringham Hall. Dubbed 'Colin's weight watcher'. Water-cooled brakes. First ran Brazilian GP – two cars Elio de Angelis and Nigel Mansell. Chassis numbers commenced 91/6, 91/7 to keep in carbon-kevlar monocoque order.	1982
92	Produced in 'active' and 'standard' versions with Cosworth power unit. 'Active' first ran Snetterton on 16 Dec 1982 (Dave Scott) and one car went to first 1983 GP (Brazil) for Mansell. Had on-board 'brain' with computer read-out in pits. Rode on hydraulic jacks instead of coil springs. Reverted to 'standard' car after its second GP in 1983 due to weight penalty.	1983
92	'Standard' car first seen at 1983 Brazilian GP as back-up for both de Angelis and Mansell. De Angelis actually drove car in the race when turbo in Renault failed on warm-up.	1983
93T	First turbo-engined JPS Formula 1 car (powered by Renault), announced London Airport Hotel 8 Feb 1983 and last car to be designed under Colin Chapman's control. First race Long Beach 1983, where it was fifth fastest in practice. Last race Canadian GP mid-way through 1983 season.	

Index